THE
Drama
OF THE
AMERICAN
POLITICAL
SYSTEM

edited by
Matthew Caverly
University of Florida

First Edition

cognella
San Diego, CA

First published in the United States of America in 2011 by Cognella, a division of University Readers, Inc.

Trademark Notice: Product or corporate names may be trademarks or registered trademarks, and are used only for identification and explanation without intent to infringe.

15 14 13 12 11   1 2 3 4 5

Printed in the United States of America

ISBN: 978-1-60927-739-0

www.cognella.com 800.200.3908

Contents

Act IV: The Semi-Periphery of National Political Organizations—The Direct Influencers of Power

Act V: The Periphery of Phantoms—The Indirect Influencers of Power—Inner Periphery: The Political Media

 Dedication

To the management, staff, and clientele of Hooters Southside and Outback Baymeadows in Jacksonville, Florida, I dedicate this work to you for providing me with good food, great drinks, and endless entertainment while I put this manuscript together.

★ Acknowledgments

I would like to extend my personal thanks to the editorial, production, and marketing staffs of Cognella Publishing's University Readers for all of their patience. I am grateful for their indefatigable assistance in recruiting, copyediting, licensing, cover production, acquisitions process, e-library, and overall guidance, as well as advice on this project from start to finish. In particular, I would like to thank Ms. Becky Smith, Ms. Jessica Knott, Ms. Erin Escobar, Mr. Kevin Hoffman, Mr. Brian Girvan, Ms. Sally Nichols, and Ms. Amy Wiltbank. Finally, I would like to thank the University of North Florida's Department of Political Science and Public Administration, in addition to the Thomas G. Carpenter Library at UNF.

The Theater of American National Politics

Editorial Preface

By Matthew M. Caverly

Welcome to *The Drama of the American National Political System*. This edited volume presents canonical as well as more modern pieces of scholarship that examine the varied contours of American national politics. My name is Matt Caverly, and I will be your narrator, guiding you through a dramatic play showcasing the actors and processes that make the American polity a unique case—as well as a living symbol for comparison with the rest of the world! The reader should be warned though: This is not a play where the audience can sit back and passively watch the show. No, this drama requires interaction between audience and players; it is a reflexive exercise, not merely a reflective one, because we, as the audience, are key players. In other words, we are a part of the show. It is to this point that I dedicate the writing of this editorial preface. The preface is organized as follows: initially, we will examine an overview of the theatrical metaphor, and then detail the organization of the readings according to their relevant "act," as listed in the Table of Contents. Finally, we will conclude with a brief summary and some closing commentary.

First, we must begin with some working definitions and related concepts. *The Drama of the American National Political System* is a theatrical metaphor, a thought experiment if you like, into the interworkings of the American national system of government and governance. It is a system in every sense of that term, conditioned by component interrelationships between the actors of government and their corresponding processes of governance. For instance, the Congress is an actor and engages in legislating, which is a process. But what is far more profound is that the Congress legislating does so in a larger system defined by inter-actor and inter-process relationships, like president-to-Congress or legislation-to-policy implementation. It is a fundamental axiom of this work that there is a uniquely American quality to these relationships, which are the result of institutional organization, constitutional fiats of power, and a corresponding body of rules and norms. Such conditions have historical antecedents and leave legacies in their wake, driving the forces of political history, and in turn, being driven by them.

Second, the theater in which the play occurs is representative of the American national polity. This is the *all* of American national politics; it is the composite of every actor, process, ethos, historical antecedent, philosophical premise, issue, event, and personality that has anything to do with the American political condition. Simply put, it is what and who we are as political beings in both state and society. However, a word of caution for the reader: just because the theater is large does not mean that it is all encompassing. More actors and processes reside *outside* the theater than within. As an example, American voting and public opinion studies over the decades have shown again and again that most people, most of the time, are disengaged from the political process. Voting in presidential elections since 1960 averages just over 50% of the eligible electorate, and in congressional elections it is even worse, with numbers ranging between 33% and 40%.[1] To be a part of the American national polity means that you must be a participant in the political community—which is how the term *polity* is employed in this text. It is drawn from the ancients, who used it as a form of an ideal *polis* or city-state that was based around commonly followed sets of individual and collective rights, as well as duties.

The theater then is the location where the plot of our drama plays out. It is an inclusive area as envisaged by the pluralists, allowing for numerous political interactions. Under the aegis of this presentation, the outcomes of such interactions reflect this ongoing democratically determined give and take.[2] A place consistent with the Jeffersonian vision of a *democratic-republic*, where power is dispersed, government is limited, and values reflect the agrarian rural nature of American society (especially in the South), at its founding with the Declaration of Independence.

At the same time, that theater can be reconceptualized as an elitist formulation reflecting the will of the few at the expense of the many.[3] The core actors are privileged, the audience is relegated to a place of observation (though potentially critical in nature), and power is primarily held by those at the center in a classically republican-oriented political condition. Rather than promoting governance by the masses as envisaged by the pluralists, this elitist theater is a place where government is by the few, for the few, and this is mandated by nothing less than the U.S. Constitution—for the Founders feared mobocracy above all else! This version of the theater is best seen as a *republican democracy*, where power is concentrated, government is strong, and values reflect the commercial urban nature of Hamiltonian America, especially in the North.

Third, we serve as the audience—students of politics—observers and evaluators of the American national political system. We have our own biases. For instance, behavioral research has indicated that most political participators interact with politics in a fundamentally partisan manner.[4] Also, we tend to acquire our political biases through a process of socialization,

---

1 Niemi, R., Weisberg, H., and Kimball, D. (2011) *Controversies in Voting Behavior*, 5th edition, Washington, DC: CQ Press.

2 Drawn from Truman, D. (1951). *The Governmental Process*, New York: Knopf.

3 Drawn from Mills, C. W. (1956). *The Power Elite*, New York: Oxford Press.

4 As depicted in Bibby and Schaffner (2008). *Politics, Parties, and Elections in America*, 6th edition, Boston: Thomson-Wasdworth, 225–231.

wherein our parents play the most important part in dictating who we become as political actors.[5] Finally, despite what is sometimes held, for most of us, once we have a partisan identification we tend to keep it.[6] However, there is a significant minority of us whose partisan flag "moves with the political winds of the times."[7] Ultimately, there is a pronounced disconnect within the audience, where an elite public that is informed, interested, efficacious, trusting, and knowledgeable about politics actively engages in the phenomenon. By doing so, these audience members become participants in the drama. This facet of society is juxtaposed against a massed public that is ignorant and disengaged, with low levels of political efficacy, trust, and knowledge. Therefore, this portion of the audience (the greater part, to be sure) remains almost completely disconnected from the drama, and only actively observes the play when political issues, events, and personalities become salient to them.[8] I hope, then, that this book will help you join the elite version of the public, relative to American politics!

Fourth, as we look across the stage, we see a unifying background—the American political culture—a set of ideas, traditions, philosophies, and cultural predilections that serve to unite us as a single national polity. Theses various factors serve as ideal points for us, places of unanimity, the things that make the United States unique in a world of nation-states. Factors such as popular sovereignty, democracy, republicanism, piety, liberty (political, social, and economic), capitalism, egalitarianism, equality of opportunity, constitutionalism, justness, limited government (however conceived), and yes, *both* liberalism and conservatism—all work together (though at times, against one another) to promote a single group of ends to which the polity dedicates itself.[9] Political conflict in the United States is channeled through the lens provided by the political culture, thus limiting it in scope, but expanding it in depth. Finally, the culture actually promotes a "within" conflict, because elements of it are mutually exclusive; for instance, at times the pursuit of capitalism works against justness, and vice versa. Or the fact that limited government in one sphere (like economics) may not exist for another (such as in social or political issues), depending on the time in American political history.[10] The larger point is that what unites us is actually more important than what divides us, something we

---

5   Campbell, A., Converse, P., Miller, W., and Stokes, D. (1960). *The American Voter*, Chicago: University of Chicago Press, 146–167.

6   Green, D., Palmquist, B., and Schickler, E. (2004). *Partisan Hearts and Minds: Political Parties and the Social Identities of Voters*. New Haven, CT: Yale University Press.

7   Mackuen, M., Erickson, R., and Stimson, J. (1989). "Macropartisanship," *American Political Science Review* 83: 1125–1142.

8   Converse, P. (1964). "The Nature of Belief Systems in Mass Publics," in Apter (ed.) *Ideology and Discontent*, New York: The Free Press.

9   Drawn from Hartz, L. (1955). *The Liberal Tradition in America: An Interpretation of American Political Thought since the Revolution*, New York: Harcourt Brace & World.

10   For the fundamentals of this debate see Rawls, J. (1971). *A Theory of Justice*, Cambridge, MA: The Belknap Press of Harvard University Press for the liberal side and Nozick, R. (1974), *Anarchy, Utopia, and the State*, New York: Basic Books for the conservative alternative.

should all remember when we engage our political friends from the other side—whichever side that may be!

Fifth, in front of the setting stands our drama's stage, the constitutional-federal structure of the American political system. This stage sets the parameters of the drama's play, because it delimits the action both in potential and in reality. The stage does this by fragmenting power; the U.S. Constitution *horizontally separates power* into theoretically coequal branches of government. Meanwhile, federalism *vertically divides power* into practically unequal levels of government. Both have been places of major conflict, dividing individuals and groups into a basic bifurcation within our society between the forces of big versus limited government.

Relative to the Constitution, the interbranch relationships have been characterized by both cooperation and conflict that has exhibited a certain periodicity. For example, in the early days of our republic, it was the Congress that stood center stage in the hearts, minds, and practice of American national politics. This institution remained dominant, only giving way to the presidency with the passing of the 19th century and the arrival of the 20th.[11] Furthermore, the relationship between the Congress and the presidency is to some extent determined by the politics of the respective policy, where the presidency tends to dominate the conduct of foreign affairs and the Congress has an edge in the domestic realm.[12] Finally, the Supreme Court is surprisingly political, both in composition and judicial conduct; however, it has tended to be deferential to the other branches, especially the presidency.[13]

Regarding federalism, the division of power from without across levels of government has led directly into a pronounced battle over interpretation, often with the judiciary as the final arbiter. The adherents of limited government have stood for states' rights, *laissez-faire* political economy, and, in general, limited government. Standing opposed to them have been those who have agitated on behalf of centralization, political-economic intervention, and a strong national government. In our political development, this dilemma became most dramatic by our great crucible—the Civil War, which forevermore decided the *ends of authority* in favor of nationalism at the expense of states' rights. However, the *means of authority* through which federalism is conducted as a policy enterprise remain very much in balance, as the two sides continue their perennial battle over issues such as taxing and spending powers. The layer cake of dual federalism may indeed have given way to the marble cake of cooperative/coercive federalism. But the extent of autonomy within both policy creation and execution between the national, state, and local levels remains largely unanswered.[14]

---

11 Sundquist, J. (1981). *The Decline and Resurgence of Congress*, Washington, DC: The Brookings Institute.

12 Wildavsky, A. (1966). *"The Two Presidencies,"* Trans-Action 4: 7–14.

13 Drawn from Pika, J., and Maltese, A. (2006). *The Politics of the Presidency*, revised 6th edition, Washington, DC: CQ Press, 257–286.

14 Drawn from Hedge, D. (1998). *Governance and the Changing American States*, Boulder, CO: Westview Press.

Sixth, and finally, we view the actors engaged in the processes of the drama itself. At the core sit those with the most relative power due to their constitutional mandate, elite composition, and historical development. The national political institutions embrace power and project it, though their reach is limited by the structures of the stage and their ultimate reliance upon the will of the people. No matter how powerful the Congress, presidency, and the Supreme Court are, they pale compared to the overarching authority granted to the American people. This is due to the concept of popular sovereignty manifested in the simple phrase of the Constitution's Preamble, "*We the People*," and in the Declaration's "*government by the consent of the governed*."

However, on a day-to-day basis, the instrument of that aforementioned sovereignty lies with the core national political institutions. Their fiats of constitutionally granted power as the legislator (the Congress), the executive (the presidency), and the judiciary (the Supreme Court) mean that they ultimately *construct, implement, and revise policy*. In the case of the proactive branches—the Congress and the presidency—these two serve as *policy makers*, or in the terms of our drama, as the star actors. And, in the case of the reactive branch—the Supreme Court—it serves as the *policy interpreter*, or in other words, the costar of the drama, playing referee to the machinations of the stars by determining (through judicial review) what is and is not appropriate "play."

Moving to the semi-periphery of the stage (so called because of its reduced level of relative power) are the political organizations—the parties, interest groups, and social movements. For the purposes of the drama, they are the *supporting cast*, guiding our stars and costar in subtle as well as marked ways. These organizations are specific political institutions, but lack constitutional grants of power. They attempt to control or influence which individuals or groups sit at the core of the national political system. What differentiates them is their ability to do just that—*parties run candidates for office*. This allows them to control the core, at least in the case of major parties like our modern Democratic and Republican parties.[15]

Notice that while all political parties have the same goal—to control government—their ability to execute this goal is dependent on the size of their support base and the amount of resources they can mobilize in their electoral/governing efforts. American parties are divided into major, third, and minor "scales," with corresponding associations relative to support size and potential for resource mobilization. Furthermore, the major parties can been seen as existing in levels, either of partisans, as in the tripartite structure of party-in-government, party-in-organization, and party-in-the-electorate; or as the parties are manifested organizationally in the classic model replicating federalism: as national, state, and local formations. In either perspective, one thing stands out: Each subdivision is largely independent of the other. This is referred to as "stratarchy" by scholars. Therefore, influence within the major parties is often based more on persuasion than coercion.[16]

This is helped by the ideological heterogeneity of America's two-party system, which works against cohesion, thus making America's major parties into what scholars call *responsive/*

---

15 Bibby and Schaffner (2008). *Politics, Parties, & Elections in America*, Chapters 2–3.
16 Ibid.

representative rather than *responsible/party government* formations. However, much recent empirical evidence suggests that there has been some polarization of the two parties—the Democrats have moved leftward on the ideological spectrum and the Republicans have correspondingly moved rightward, especially amid the party-in-government at the national level.[17]

Meanwhile, interest groups and social movements sit somewhat at the margins of the semi-periphery relative to parties, because they can only influence rather than control the core national political institutions. Furthermore, what separates an interest group from a social movement is dependent more on the means of their political action than on the ends. Interest groups are smaller, with a narrower set of activities. This allows them to be more centralized structurally, and thus more hierarchical in leadership, more homogeneous in composition and goals, as well as more steady-state in their impacts on the larger system. They do this mostly by engaging in conventional political participation like direct and indirect lobbying. Social movements are the polar opposites of this. These movements are larger with a broader scope of activity, which tends to make them structurally decentralized, more egalitarian in leadership, more heterogeneous, in both composition and goals, as well as more dynamic in system impacts. Thus, they are largely reduced to engaging in unconventional political participation such as demonstrating.[18]

Last, we move to the edges of the stage, where the actors are largely hidden in the shadows—the phantoms of the periphery are our final players. The phantoms' presence is felt more than seen, however; due to popular sovereignty, they can have overawing power. But on a day-to-day basis, these actors are the furthest removed, with the least relative power. They are the most parochial and the least national in influence and orientation. Hence, they serve as the *extras* within our dramatic metaphor. Nevertheless, they compel our attention, because it is through them that we in the audience become a part of the drama. Like the semi-periphery, there is a weighting among them. The political media sits in a privileged position in the *inner periphery* relative to the political participators and those who belong to public opinion. The latter two sit at the very edges of the stage, almost hidden by the curtains in the *outer periphery*.

The media may seem to some of you that it belongs closer to the core. We certainly *see* them more than we do, say, social movements on a day-to-day basis. However, I want to emphasize that, while the media is an institution composed of organizations, it is not *specifically political*. It is for that reason that the media engages politics in the manner that it does—overwhelmingly superficially. Most media and communications studies indicate that the media covers politics in an anecdotal rather than a systematic fashion, bringing information with interpretation over analysis, and emphasizing elections at the expense of governing. Additionally, the political media tends to promote conflict while simultaneously demoting cooperation, offering style over substance, having critical instead of complementary coverage, finding scandal, obscuring accomplishment, and generally following a strategic frame that sees politics as a game, with

---

17 Ibid.

18 Cf. Cigler, A., and Loomis, B. (2007). *Interest Group Politics*, 7th edition, Washington, DC: CQ Press.

corresponding horse-race analogies. Finally, it tends to emphasize the United States, with a concentration on domestic policy over foreign policy, it looks at national over state or local politics, and covers the presidency at the expense of the other actors in government.[19] Why is this the case?

Much effort has been placed in trying to determine a specific ideological bias in America's national media. Some trends are prescient, such as the existence of organizational leaning in media outlets like FOX NEWS or the *New York Times*, or liberal reporters and editors versus conservative publishers, as well as owners. There is also a separation between information dissemination, which is objective, and interpretation, which is anything but. And there is evidence that among the new media (e.g., talk radio and infotainment venues such as *The Glenn Beck Show* or *The Bill Maher Show*), there is an unapologetic bias. Whereas, in the old media (e.g., most traditional broadcasters and print sources), there remains a tendency to be wedded to the inverse pyramid of who, what, when, where, and how.[20]

None of the above actually answers the question "Why does the news cover politics the way it does?" According to significant research, the press does have a systematic bias, but it is not the bias you may think. Simply put, the press is a business in America: it exists to draw viewers, listeners, and readers, largely in order to sell advertising. As a result, it covers politics in the best way to maximize benefits and limit costs. In other words, the media has a *profit bias*. It covers politics superficially, because that is the way most Americans engage in politics. The media covers it confrontationally, because that is how most Americans see politics, and it emphasizes scandal, failure, negativity, and simplicity, due to the negative and relatively simplistic views most Americans hold regarding politics. The problem is that this promotes gridlock among the political elite, as well as a tendency to *not* undertake major policy initiatives or deal with pressing political problems. Additionally, it tends to promote a self-fulfilling prophecy among the political masses: If you want to be uninformed (and *mis*informed, for that matter), then the coverage will reflect that, and you become so!

On the other side though, information is actually accessible for those who want to become truly informed about politics. Thanks to raised relative education levels, the potential for a more rational, better informed public demanding better news is there. Additionally, most people in the news profession aspire to provide superior coverage, and people tend to get what they want. For instance, conservatives tend to watch FOX NEWS, because it supports their preconceived notions; liberals tend to view MSNBC or CNN, since it tends to support their own ideas and ideals about politics.[21]

As we approach the outer periphery, we encounter the political participators. These men and women engage in politics directly, mostly through voting. However, they also follow the political media, participate in social movement or interest-group activism, identify with or

---

19   Patterson, T. (1994). *Out of Order: An Incisive and Boldly Original Critique of the News Media's Domination of America's Political Process*, New York: Vintage Books.

20   Overholser, G., and Jamieson, K. H. (2005). *The Press*, New York: Oxford University Press.

21   Ibid.

against political parties, and ultimately decide who sits in the core, by engaging in the electoral process. As previously stated, most participators engage in politics in a partisan fashion, but about 9 to 12% of the electorate are true independents, accounting for the highest levels of split-ticket voting and vote defection. Somewhat paradoxically, they are also the least informed, interested, and engaged among participators. Still, this has been explained, in that most participators understand politics and recognize (for good or bad) how it works—it works *through* partisanship, not *despite* it![22]

Whether one participates in politics is determined mostly by education; of course, the higher the level of education, the more likely one is to participate. This goes hand in hand with being more likely to engage in a higher level of participation, such as donating money to a campaign or volunteering for it, rather than just voting— which is the simplest and easiest way to participate politically within our country. However, as previously stated, it is partisanship—and to a lesser extent, ideology—that tells us for whom one is likely to participate for and against in American politics.[23] Among its other important trends, participation tends to increase as you move up the ladder, both in terms of level of government and of office. For instance, presidential voter turnout is significantly higher than congressional or lesser offices, especially when comparing presidential election cycles to midterm and local elections.[24]

By definition, all political participators are also part of public opinion—but not everyone with a political attitude is a participator in American politics, national or otherwise. Public opinion has been found to be generally stable, but volatile when it comes to attitudes relative to specific things like issues, events, and personalities. The explanation for this is that the unifying influence of our background setting—the American political culture—tends to promote homogeneity on the big things such as democracy, but no such structure exists to hold a set of specifics together. As an example of this, survey research shows there are more conservative Americans than there are liberal; however, when asked to take specific policy stances, Americans tend to be a bit more liberal than conservative.[25] Some of this can be explained as simple ignorance, but not all of it. Americans are torn by the means of politics, even as they are united by the ends! In this case, the average American seems to want conservative general principles, such as a strong national defense, lower taxes, limited government, etc. But when the debate moves from generalities to specifics—like who should be taxed and how much; how and when to use the military; what programs to promote or demote within the state economy and the state-society dynamic, then a more nuanced form of reasoning takes over. General principles are then often moderated, if not completely compromised.

The 15 readings contained within this edited volume reflect the relative power lying at the heart of the American national political system. The book is organized into a series of acts (five

---

22 Conway, M. M. (2000). *Political Participation in the United States*, 3rd edition, Washington, DC: CQ Press.

23 Ibid.

24 Ibid.

25 Erickson, R., and Tedin, K. (2010). *American Public Opinion*, 8th edition, New York: Longman.

in all), showcasing each major subplot of the drama. We begin with the setting in Act I, where Daniel J. Elazar's discussion of political subcultures is located. Note how they complement, yet also deviate from, the larger American national political culture discussed in this preface. Next, we examine the stage in Act II with two readings, one by James Pfiffner, devoted to a study of the presidency of George W. Bush in constitutional contexts, and another by Kurt Lash, looking at a specific "rights debate" within federalism.

Following from there, we move to the core national political actors in Act III, and examine the Congress within a domestic policy-making context with Theodore Lowi. Then we proceed to the presidency and continue with a policy domain perspective, while stressing the foreign-affairs realm with Aaron Wildavsky's classic "Two Presidencies Thesis" and my own reimagining of that theoretical device. After that, we tackle the federal judiciary with Michael Schwartz's presentation regarding the philosophical dilemmas that plague the Supreme Court.

Leaving the core and entering Act IV's semi-periphery, we find historian Walter Dean Burnham's classic discussion of a critical realignment and what it means to our two-party system. Also in this sphere, we find economist Mancur Olson's theorization over the formation of—and most importantly the *maintenance* of—interest groups. Finally, another canonical text, this time by political scientist E. E. Schattschneider, who discusses the impact of organized interests, whether they be interest groups or social movements, on the rest of the American polity.

Proceeding to the end, we leave this act for our final Act V, where we embrace the ephemeral phantoms. To begin with, Gulati et al. discuss the news coverage in political campaigns; look for the in-depth discussion of some of the empirics cited in the preface. Next, Philip Converse and Angus Campbell present separate, seminal pieces of scholarship relative to voters in differing electoral conditions—specifically contrasting presidential elections with congressional elections. Third, John Zaller and a final piece by Converse force us to see the distribution of public opinion as a truly complex phenomenon, with implications for our daily political lives.

This brings us back to where we began: We have seen the drama unfold and we are now ready to leave the theater. But before we do leave, let us review. Remember, the theater is the polity, the audience is us, the students of politics, and the setting is the unifying set of principles called the American political culture. Furthermore, the stage structures the play by fragmenting power through the Constitution and federalism; the arrangement of the actors on that stage is according to their relative power. In that arrangement, the core national political institutions are our stars and costar; the semi-periphery of political organizations serves as our supporting cast; and the peripheral actors of the media, participators, and public opinion serve as the extras in our drama, felt more than they are seen—like phantoms. Enjoy the show!

Matthew M. Caverly
University of North Florida
Jacksonville

★
★ # Act I
★
The Setting; The American National Political
Culture—The Ends Upon Which We All
Agree

★ Political Culture and Politics in State
★ and Community
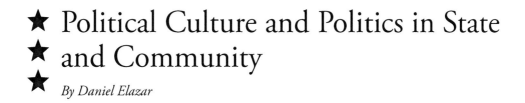

By Daniel Elazar

General Culture has its direct impact on politics from the outside, as it were. Political culture, that differentiated aspect of the overall culture which is itself a truly political phenomenon, has its direct impact from the inside. The role of cultural factors in shaping the political environment of the cities of the prairie culture, alluded to in the previous chapters, is of crucial importance in shaping the cities' politics because of its directly political character.

"Political culture" has been defined as the "particular pattern of orientation to political action" in which each political system is embedded.[1] A political culture is related to the general culture of a particular society but is by no means identical with it. As Gabriel Almond says, "because political orientation involves cognition, intellection, and adaptation to external situations, as well as the standards and values of the general culture, it is a differentiated part of the culture and has a certain autonomy." Like all culture, it is so rooted in the cumulative historical experiences of particular groups that it has become second nature to those within its embrace.

Political culture, then, is the summation of persistent patterns of underlying political attitudes and values—and characteristic response to political concerns—that is manifest in a particular political order, whose existence is generally unperceived by those who are part of that order and whose origins date back to the very beginnings of the particular people who share it. Political culture is an intrinsically political phenomenon which makes certain autonomous demands on particular political systems as well as affecting all other political demands within those systems. Political systems, in turn, are in some measure the products of the political cultures they serve and must remain in harmony with their political culture if they are to maintain themselves.

Political culture can best be understood in terms of the framework it sets for individual and group political behavior—in the political thoughts, attitudes, assumptions, and values of individuals and groups and in the range of permissible or acceptable action that flows from them. Political culture, as such, determines behavior in relatively few situations or in response to relatively few particular issues. Its influence lies in its power to set reasonable fixed limits to political behavior and provide subliminal direction for political action in particular political systems; limits and direction all the more effective because of their antiquity and subtlety whereby those limited are unaware of the limitations placed upon them.

The various aspects of political culture are made manifest through several cultural requisites or themes.[2] Political language, whether special political terms associated with particular cultures ("public servant," "good government") or the nuances of meaning inhering to common political terminology in a particular culture ("democracy", "freedom," "politics"), is of first importance in conveying and transmitting understood by all who share in a particular political culture.[3] Every political culture can be identified by its particular forms of aesthetic expression or delight ranging from the shared or recognized political symbols to accepted political styles. Standardized orientations to political life (recruitment, socialization, and appropriate behavior of political actors) and death (including the nature of and factors that bring about political death) are key aspects of political culture. Every political culture involves means for perpetuating the political system, its solidarity, and its norms, including common modes of political socialization, shared channels of political communication, and certain distinctive characteristics that animate its political institutions. Political culture plays a major role in determining the nature of people's demands for an ordered political life, the way which they organize to meet those demands, and the accepted "price of politics" in each political system. By the same token, the political culture plays a major role in defining the political needs of people in each political system—who is a person for political purposes in a particular political system; who gets what in the way of protection of life, rights, and property—and influences the way in which the system organizes to meet these needs.

A specific political culture may or may not coincide with a particular political system or civil society, since patterns of orientation to politics frequently overlap beyond the boundaries of specific political systems. Continental Europe may well have a single continent-wide political culture that crosses the national boundaries that otherwise divide it. The various national entities and, in some cases, the subnational and extranational ones as well, possess individuated subcultures of their own which give them meaningful distinctiveness without fracturing the overall universe of thought and action represented by the political culture shared across the entire continent.

The United States possesses a political culture of its own spread nationwide.[4] Each of the states of the American union possesses its own distinctive manifestation of that political culture. The manifestations—or, more properly, subcultures—operative in the American states and their component civil communities are products of the phenomena discussed in the first part of this volume—the interaction of geohistorical location, demographic streams, and patterns of the general culture, plus the influences of the national political process.

The Three Political Subcultures

Political cultural factors stand out as particularly influential in shaping the operations of the national, state, and local political systems in three ways: (1) by molding the political community's (the citizens, the politicians, and the public officials) perceptions of the nature and purposes of politics and expectations from government and the political process; (2) by influencing the recruitment of specific kinds of people to become active in government and politics—as holders of elective office, members of the bureaucracy, and active political workers; and (3) by subtly directing the actual way in which the art of government is practiced by citizens, politicians, and public officials in the light of their perceptions. Furthermore, the cultural components of individual and group behavior make themselves felt in the kind of civic behavior dictated by conscience and internalized ethical standards, in the forms of law-abidingness adhered to by citizens and officials and in the character of the positive actions of government.

The American political culture is rooted in two contrasting conceptions of the American political order, both of which can be traced back to the earliest settlement of the country. In the first, the political order is conceived as a marketplace in which the primary public relationships are products of bargaining among individuals and groups acting out of self-interest. In the second, the political order is conceived to be a commonwealth—a state in which the whole people have an undivided interest—in which the citizens cooperate in an effort to create and maintain the best government in order to implement certain shared moral principles.

The commonwealth is animated by a mystique—a vision of the proper political order yet to be attained but that is in the process of being built upon existing foundations—and maintains its strength only by maintaining the vitality of that mystique. The marketplace, on the other hand, is animated by a desire to keep the peace through a balance of interests without any necessary commitments other than the preservation of the marketplace itself. Access to the political marketplace is open to all interests that in any way acknowledge its legitimacy and are willing to abide by its rules (at least most of the time). No independent criteria are used to judge the legitimacy of those interests as a condition of participation, so any individual or group that can make its presence felt acquires the functional equivalent of citizenship. In the commonwealth, on the other hand, citizenship, or the right to legitimately participate in the government process, is a matter of very serious concern, and a priori moral criteria can legitimately be applied to determine which individuals or groups have that right.

These two conceptions have exercised an influence on government and politics throughout American history, sometimes in conflict and sometimes by complementing one another. They are so intertwined as to be practically inseparable in any particular case or situation, with marketplace notions contributing to shaping the vision of commonwealth and common wealth ideals being given a preferred position in the marketplace.

Overall, the national political culture is a synthesis of three major political subcultures that jointly inhabit the country, existing side by side in their grossest manifestations and frequently overlapping one another in their most immediate ones. All three are of nationwide proportions, having spread in the course of time from coast to coast. At the same time each subculture is strongly tied to specific sections of the country, reflecting the more or less orderly movement westward of the migrational streams discussed in Chapter Four. Considering the central characteristics that govern each and their respective centers of emphasis, the three political cultures may be called individualistic (I), moralistic (M), and traditionalistic (T).[5] Each of the three reflects its own particular syntheses of marketplace and commonwealth.

The Individualistic Political Culture

The individualistic political culture emphasizes the conception of the democratic order as a marketplace. It is rooted in the notion that government is instituted for strictly utilitarian reasons, to handle those functions demanded by the people it is created to serve. A government need not have any direct concern with questions of the "good society" except insofar as it may be used to advance some common conception of the good society formulated outside the political arena just as it serves other functions. Since the individualistic political culture emphasizes the centrality of private concerns, it places a premium on limiting community intervention—whether governmental or nongovernmental—into private activities to the minimum necessary to keep the marketplace in proper working order. In general, government action is to be restricted to those areas, primarily in the economic realm, which encourage private initiative and widespread access to the marketplace, Economic development activities—in the broadest sense—find great favor in such circumstances.[6]

The character of political participation in systems dominated by the individualistic political culture reflects this outlook. The individualistic political culture holds politics to be just another means by which individuals may improve themselves socially and economically. In this sense politics is a "business" like any other that competes for talent and offers rewards to those who take it up as a career. Those individuals who choose political careers may rise by providing the governmental services demanded of them and, in return, may expect to be adequately compensated for their efforts. Interpretations of officeholders' obligations under this arrangement vary among political systems and even among individuals within a single political system. Where the norms are high, such people are expected to provide high quality government services for the general public in the best possible manner in return for the status and economic rewards considered their due. Some who choose political careers clearly commit themselves to such norms; others believe that an officeholder's primary responsibility is to serve himself and those who have supported him directly, favoring them even at the expense of others. In some political systems, this view is also accepted by the public.

Political life within an individualistic political culture is based on a system of mutual obligations rooted in personal relationships. While in a simple society those relationships can be direct ones, societies with "I" political cultures in the United States are usually too complex to maintain face-to-face ties. So the system of mutual obligations is harnessed through political parties which serve as "business corporations" dedicated to providing the organization necessary to maintain it. Party regularity is in dispensable in the individualistic political culture because it is the means for coordinating individual enterprise in the political arena and is the one way of preventing individualism in politics from running wild. In such a system, and individual can succeed politically, not by dealing with issues in some exceptional way or by accepting some concept of good government and then striving to implement it, but by maintaining his place in the system of mutual obligations. He can do this by operating according to the norms of his particular party, to the exclusion of other political considerations. Such a political culture encourages the maintenance of a party system that is competitive, but not overly so, in the pursuit of office. Its politicians are interested in office as a means of controlling the distribution of the favors or rewards of government rather than as a means of exercising governmental power for programmatic ends, hence competition may prove less rewarding than accommodation in certain situations.

Since the individualistic political culture eschews ideological concerns in its "businesslike" conception of politics, both politicians and citizens look upon political activity as a specialized business, essentially the province of professionals, of minimum and passing (if periodical) concern to laymen, and no place for amateurs to play an active role. Furthermore, there is a strong tendency among the public to believe that politics is a dirty—if necessary—business, better left to those who are willing to soil themselves by engaging in it. In practice, then, where the individualistic political culture is dominant, there is likely to be an easy attitude toward the limits of the professionals' perquisites. Since a fair amount of corruption is expected in the normal course of things, there is relatively little popular excitement when any is found unless it is of an extraordinary character. It is as if the public is willing to pay a surcharge for services rendered, rebelling only when the surcharge becomes too heavy.

Public officials in the individualistic political culture, committed to "giving the public what it wants," are not normally willing to initiate new programs or open up new areas of government activity on their own initiative. They will do so when they perceive an overwhelming public demand for them to act, but only then, In a sense, their willingness to expand the functions of government is based on an extension of the quid pro quo "favor" system which serves as the central core of their political relationships, with new services the reward they give the public for placing them in office. The value and legitimacy of change in the individualistic political culture are directly related to its commercial concern.

The individualistic political culture is ambivalent about the place of bureaucracy in the political order. In one sense, the bureaucratic method of operating flies in the face of the favor system that is central to the individualistic political process. At the same time, the virtues of organizational efficiency appear substantial to those seeking to master the market. In the end, bureaucratic organization is introduced within the framework of the favor system; large segments of the bureaucracy may be insulated from it through the merit system, but the entire organization is pulled into the political environment at crucial points through political appointment at the upper echelons and, very frequently, the bending of the merit system to meet political demands.

The individualistic political culture is a product of the Middle States stream with its overriding commitment to commercialism and concomitant acceptance of ethic, social, and religious pluralism. It has been reinforced by the English, Continental, Eastern European, Mediterranean, and Irish streams whose products either brought that political culture with them or adapted to it as their traditional cultures broke down. Most recently, substantial segments of the Southern and Afro-American streams are adapting to it for similar reasons, as they are transplanted from their original areas of settlement. The individualistic political culture is strong or dominant in those areas where the products of the streams manifesting its characteristics are strong or dominant.

The Moralistic Political Culture

To the extent that American society is built on the principles of "commerce" in the broadest sense of the term and the marketplace provides the model for public relationships in this country, all Americans share some of the attitudes that are of first importance in the individualistic political culture. At the same time, substantial segments of the American people operate politically within the framework of two political cultures whose theoretical structures and operational consequences depart significantly from the individualistic pattern at crucial points.

The moralistic political culture emphasizes the commonwealth idea as the basis for democratic government. Politics, to the moralistic political culture, is considered one of the great activities of man in his search for the good society—a struggle for power, it is true, but also an effort to exercise power for the pursuit of justice in public affairs or the betterment of the commonwealth. Consequently, in the moralistic political culture, both the general public and the politicians conceive of politics as a public service centered on some notion of the public good and properly devoted to the advancement of the public interest. Good government, then, is measured by the degree to which it promotes the public good and in terms of the honesty, selflessness, and commitment to the public welfare of those who govern.

In the moralistic political culture, individualism is tempered by a general commitment to utilizing communal—preferably nongovernmental, but governmental if necessary—power to intervene into the sphere of "private" activities when it is considered necessary to do so for the public good or the well-being of the community, utilizing governmental resources for social regulation as well as for the promotion of economic well-being. Accordingly, issues have an important place in the moralistic style of politics, functioning to set the tone of political concern. Government is considered a positive instrument with a responsibility to promote the general welfare, thought definitions of what its positive role should be may vary considerably from era to era.[7]

Since the moralistic political culture rests on the fundamental conception that politics exists primarily as a means for coming to grips with the issues and public concerns of civil society, it also embraces the notion that politics is ideally a matter of concern for every citizen, not just those who are professionally committed to political careers. It becomes each citizen's duty to participate in the political affairs of his commonwealth.

Consequently, there is a general insistence that government service is public service, which place moral obligations upon those who participate in government that are more demanding than the moral obligations of the marketplace. There is an equally general rejection of the notion that the field of politics is a legitimate realm for private economic enrichment. Indeed, even normal advancement in income and perquisites is frequently suspect as profiting from the public weal.

Since the concept of serving the general welfare or the public interest is at the core of the political relationship, politicians are expected to adhere to it even at the expense of individual loyalties and political friendships. Consequently, party regularity is not of prime importance. The political party is considered a useful political device but is not valued for its own sake. Regular party ties can be abandoned with relative impunity for third parties, special local parties, or nonpartisan systems if such changes are believed helpful in gaining larger political goals. Men can even shift from party to party without sanctions if the change is justified by political belief. In the moralistic political culture, rejection of firm party ties is not to be viewed as a rejection of politics as such. On the contrary, because politics is considered potentially good and healthy within the context of that culture, it is possible to have highly political nonpartisan systems. Certainly nonpartisanship is not instituted to eliminate politics but to improve it by widening access to public office for those unwilling or unable to gain office through the regular party structure.[8]

In practice, where the moralistic political culture is dominant today, there is considerably more "amateur" participation in politics. There is also much less of what Americans consider corruption in government and less tolerance of those actions which are considered corrupt, so politics does not have the taint it so often bears in the "I" environment.

By virtue of its fundamental outlook, the moralistic political culture creates a greater commitment to active government intervention into the economic and social life of the community. At the same time, the strong commitment to communitarianism characteristic of that political culture tends to channel the interest in government intervention into highly localistic paths so that a willingness to encourage local government intervention to set public standards does not necessarily reflect a concomitant willingness to allow outside governments equal opportunity to intervene. Not infrequently, public officials will themselves seek to initiate new government activities in an effort to come to grips with problems as yet unperceived by a majority of the citizenry. The moralistic political culture is not committed to either change or the status quo per se, but will accept either depending upon the morally defined ends to be gained.

The moralistic political culture's major difficulty in adjusting bureaucracy to the political order is tied to the potential conflict between communitarian principles and the necessity for large-scale organization to increase bureaucratic efficiency, a problem that could affect the attitudes of "M" culture states toward federal activity of certain kinds. Otherwise, the notion of a politically neutral administrative system creates no problem within the moralistic value system and even offers many advantages. Where merit systems are instituted, they are rigidly maintained.

The moralistic political culture is a product of Puritan New England in its efforts to create the holy commonwealth and its more secularized Yankee stream. It has been strongly reinforced by the North Sea and Jewish streams, who shared the same political culture when they came to the United States. It is strong or dominant in those areas where Yankees, Scotch, Dutch, Scandinavians, Swiss, and Jews are strong or dominant.

The Traditionalistic Political Culture

The traditionalistic political culture is rooted in an ambivalent attitude toward the marketplace coupled with a paternalistic and elitist conception of the commonwealth. It reflects an older, precommercial attitude that accepts a substantially hierarchical society as part of the ordered nature of things, authorizing and expecting those at the top of the social structure to take a special and dominant role in government. Like its moralistic counterpart, the traditionalistic political culture accepts government as an actor with a positive role in the community but in a very limited sphere, mainly that of securing the continued maintenance of the existing social order. To do so, it functions to confine real political power to a relatively small and self-perpetuating group drawn from an established elite who often inherit their "right" to govern through family ties or social position. Accordingly, social and family ties are paramount in a traditionalistic political culture, even more than personal ties are important in the individualistic where, after all is said and done, a person's first responsibility is to himself. At the same time, those who do not have a definite role to play in politics are not expected to be even minimally active as citizens. In many cases, they are not even expected to vote. In return, they are guaranteed that, outside of the limited sphere of politics, family rights (usually labeled "individual rights") are paramount, not to be lightly ignored even in matters such as education and hygiene. Like the individualistic political culture, those active in politics are expected to benefit personally from their activity though not necessarily through direct pecuniary gain.

Political parties are of minimal importance in traditionalistic political cultures, since they encourage a degree of openness and competition that goes against the fundamental grain of an elite-oriented political order. Their major utility is to recruit people to fill the formal offices of government not desired by the established powerholders. Political competition in a traditionalistic political culture is usually conducted through factional alignments, an extension of the personalistic politics characteristic of the system; hence political systems within the culture tend to have loose one-party systems if they have political parties at all.

Practically speaking, a traditionalistic political culture is found only in a society that retains some of the organic characteristics of the pre-industrial social order. "Good government" in that political culture involves the maintenance and encouragement of traditional patterns and, if necessary, their adjustment to changing conditions with the least possible upset. Where the traditionalistic political culture is dominant in the United States today, political leaders play conservative and custodial rather than initiatory roles unless pressed strongly from the outside.

Whereas the individualistic and moralistic political cultures may or may not encourage the development of bureaucratic systems of organization on the grounds of "rationality" and "efficiency" in government, depending on their particular situations, traditionalistic political cultures tend to be instinctively antibureaucratic because bureaucracy by its very nature interferes with the fine web of informal interpersonal relationships that lie at the root of the political system and that have been developed by following traditional patterns over the years. Where bureaucracy is introduced, it is generally confined to ministerial functions under the aegis of the established power holders.

The traditionalistic political culture is a product of the plantation agrarianism of the Southern stream. In was supplemented by the Afro-American stream, whose products were originally absorbed into the Southern way of life as slaves. Secondary reinforcement has come from the Hispanic stream. The traditionalistic political culture is strong only where it has become the dominant political culture, in those areas settled almost exclusively by the streams which manifest its characteristics. Where those streams have moved into environments in which other political cultures have been dominant, there has been a tendency for the traditionalistic political culture to break down. In fact, as the possibilities for maintaining more than semblances of traditionalistic life have continued to decline in the United States, traditionalistic political culture has also diminished, undergoing subtle but serious changes, generally in the direction of the individualistic political culture except where strong secondary tendencies towards the moralistic political culture are present.

The Political Cultures of the Cities of the Prairie

The character and degree of complexity in the geology of specific local settlements in the United States determines whether a particular state or civil community comes closer to resembling one of the three political cultural models or combines elements of more than one within its boundaries. Three of the five states of the cities of the prairie—Illinois, Iowa, and Colorado—are so situated geohistorically that representatives of all three political subcultures have contributed to their settlement and development in significant numbers. Settlements and bands of settlements dominated by all three can be found in those states in varying conditions of cultural development and change. Accordingly, their present statewide political cultures are amalgams created out of varying degrees of conflict generated by the initial meeting of the representatives of the three and the struggle between them for the dominant position of influence within the emerging state political systems. The general outcome of the original struggle has long since been determined. It created a relationship between political culture and political system in each of the states that continues to set the limits for political behavior within them. At the same time, within the framework of the statewide political subculture, the conflict between the products of the original political cultures, substantially modified and disguised though it may be, continues to be waged. Indeed, the very conflict itself has become institutionalized as one of the "moving parts" of the state political system.

Whatever the resolution at the state level, local pockets of the other political cultures frequently entrench themselves. This is certainly true in the case of the cities of the prairie in those states. As indicated in Chapter Five, with the exception of the smaller urban centers among them, the individual civil communities are too large and complex not to also have attracted a certain diversity of populations and cultures. Accounting for both population diversity and cultural change, the political cultures of the cities of the prairie of these three states are categorized in Table 6–1.

TABLE 6.1

City	Settlement Stages			Contemporary Synthesis
Alton	Tmi	I	IT	It
Belleville	Tm	It	It	It
Champaign	Im	I	tm	Im
Davenport	IM	Im	it	IM
Decatur	im	MI	MT	Mt
E. Moline-Silvis	I			
E.St. Louis	Ti	TI	Ti	IT
Joliet	Im	I	I	Mi
Moline	M	M	I	Mi
Peoria	TMi	It	It	I
Pueblo	TMi	Im	Tim	IMt
Rockford	M	Mi	Imt	Mi
Rock Island	Itm	IM	ti	Im
Springfield	Ti	Itm	It	I
Superior	Im	MI	Mi	MI
Urbana	It	Im	Itm	Im

In Minnesota, and to a somewhat lesser extent in Wisconsin, a high degree of homogeneity in political culture has existed from the beginning. This means that the major political conflicts and cleavages have not been "culture conflicts" in their essence but have been intracultural. Consequently, the extent of the adjustment of the political system to the underlying political culture it serves has been well fixed from the beginning, at which time the relationship between political culture and political system was substantially settled more thoroughly than in the other three states. At the same time, some cultural diversity has always been present, manifesting itself particularly at the local level. The two cities of the prairie reflect both the overall statewise uniformity and local diversity.

Political Culture and the Purposes of Government

The development of these state political cultures and their impact on the cities of the prairie is discussed in the following chapters. Before turning to that discussion, however, some better delineation of the manifestations and consequences of political cultural differences is in order. The answer to the question of what are—or should be—the purposes, scope, and limits of government in the civil community is dictated in part by the external geohistorical environment. Beyond that, it is determined by the political culture. The two issues of education and planning are exemplary cases of current concern in all of the cities of the prairie that reveal the underlying political cultural differences among them.

It has been observed that, in most urban civil communities in America, there has been a shift in the orientation of government from its originally limited concern with providing some minimal level of public (read "police") services for its residents to a larger concern with participating in the management of community growth and change. This major shift in orientation at the local level is part of the change in the national climate that has taken place primarily in the twentieth century, which has seen an increased emphasis on the positive role of government in American society. While this new emphasis has affected every one of the cities of the prairie, the individualized legacy of political culture in each has contributed substantially to the manner and degree to which its residents have embraced this shift in orientation and the way in which their local governments have responded to it. The very conception of what constitutes positive government action, the perception of the legitimate scope and limits of such action, and the view of the direction such action should take reflect the underlying political culture in each civil community.

The question of the "proper" role of government in the civil community (and generally) is an old one in the cities of the prairie. Historical records show that there was a considerable division of opinion among those who settled them as to what should be the province of government and what should be left to private initiative virtually from the beginning of their respective histories. While there is no single explanation for it, this division of opinion seems to be directly related to the flow of the several streams into the cities, particularly the flow and influence of the native streams, since their products generally dominated local political decision-making bodies at least until late in the nineteenth century and set the tone for community decisions until the post-World-War-II generation.

Southern influence in the cities of the prairie has generally operated to limit the role of government. Southerners, reflecting their traditionalistic political culture, have historically displayed some willingness to use the powers and resources of government to encourage state economic development either by engaging directly in economic activities or by subsidizing favored private enterprises in a variety of ways. At the same time they have been extremely hesitant about supporting or encouraging government activity in the realm of regulation of private activities or the provision of social services. Since the high point of governmental activity of the first kind came in 1837, and the thrust of governmental expansion has since been in the latter two fields, the Southern outlook has tended to delay governmental responses to new situations in Illinois, Iowa, and Colorado to the extent that it is felt in state politics and to significantly retard it in those communities in which it has been strong. In the twentieth century, the heirs of the traditionalistic political culture seem to have modified their stance somewhat, perhaps because continued economic depression in their communities has forced them to seek both social and economic assistance from any quarter.

The Yankees, reflecting their moralistic political culture, have tended to look favorably upon government's role in promoting certain social ends, if only to insure a common public morality and a measure of equal economic opportunity. In the social realm, the Yankees have been inclined toward the promotion of public education and the regulation of the sale of liquor for similar reasons, relating to the advancement of individual and public morality. In general, government activities in the economic realm have been judged by the Yankees (and their "soul brothers" from other streams) from a moralistic perspective. That is to say, whether supporters of laissez faire or outright government ownership, "freedom of contract" or public regulation, their positions are justified on essentially moral rather than economic grounds—what they held would be best for the commonwealth.

Yankees have been found on all sides of these issues; what they have shared in common is their basic public concern. As a result, the impact of the Yankee stream in the cities of the prairie has been mixed, ranging from the advocacy of socialism to the most tenacious commitment to voluntarism and resistance to any expansion of the scope of governmental activity. This is particularly true in the twentieth century when, as the demands for change rose to new heights, the familiar patterns of the past were becoming virtually sanctified in those Yankee-descended communities where life seemed to go on as before. Ultimately, the higher visibility of the forces of change converted all but the most diehard to a perception of the need for governmental action as the most feasible means of manifesting the community's concern for its members.

The Middle States stream has built its basic conception of the proper role of government upon the individualistic political culture which it represents; hence it is a conception that begins and ends with the question of who benefits. Always pursuing "progress," roughly conceived as the expansion of commerce with the betterment of technology as its hand maiden, the pacesetters of the Middle stream have welcomed government activities aiding them in their pursuit. At the same time, those who have not benefited from that pursuit have not hesitated to look to government to aid them in redressing the political, economic, and social balance. In the nineteenth century, this situation led to a fluctuation of attitudes toward government action based on individual perceptions of what would be of benefit. In the twentieth century, it has meant a continuing shift of the majority in favor of positive government *action*—for some, especially on the national plane, where the relationship between government policy and the economy is most visible, and for others particularly on the local plane where they stood to benefit most. In any case, social (or moral) *regulation* by government has not been viewed with favor by those representatives of the individualistic political culture, since they have consistently held that such matters are the province of individual decision (unless and until they begin to openly affect the marketplace).

The nonnative streams added some subtle dimensions to the political cultures of the cities of the prairie. Most were accustomed to a greater government role in the life of the country than any native Americans were prepared to accept, though their attitudes toward positive government were not necessarily favorable. Here national as well as cultural differences were important. Scandinavians, Germans, and Dutch were generally well disposed toward direct government action to set the course of society, even when they wished to check the extent of government interests. The Continental and Eastern Europeans simply put up with government as a matter of course, while the Mediterraneans were generally antigovernment, distrusting its authority or the security it claimed to provide. Because of their centuries-long experience under slavery, the Afro-Americans looked to the governments of America with a mixture of fear of officially supported discrimination and expectation of paternalistic benefits. As these various groups became influential in the public life of the cities of the prairie, their attitudes contributed to shaping the local view of the proper role of government.

The history of public education in the cities of the prairie is and early example of the divergent approaches to the role of government influenced by differences in political culture.[9] The idea of free public education was originally brought into Illinois from the outside, a product of national influences in large measure stimulated by the federal common-school land-grant program. In the first decade of statehood, a few "enlightened" state leaders, mostly of Middle State origin, proposed that the state supplement the federal grants. The best they could get was legislation granting the localities the right to levy taxes for the support of common schools, passed in 1825. Not even the "local option" principle was sufficient to overcome Southern hostility to the idea of public education. The act remained a dead letter and was repealed a few years later. The predominantly Southern Illinoisians held that those who wanted schools for their children should pay for them themselves.

Though the General Assembly did allow local organization of the Congressional townships established by the federal land survey to manage the federal common-school grants, it was not until 1845 (at height of the Yankee in-migration) that it again allowed localities to exercise local option to levy special school taxes. Not until 1855, after the Yankees had captured a significant position in state affairs, was state legislation passed providing for even minimal state support for public elementary education. Not only was state action necessary to secure the establishment of a truly free public school system, even in a locally oriented state such as Illinois but, from the first, state action determined the mode of organization of that system. Proponents of public education wished to have the educational function handled through a system of local school governments independent of the other local authorities. The network of school districts established in 1855 was based on that principle. Though since modified many times, it remains the basis for school government in Illinois.

From 1818 to 1856, federal grants provided the only public revenues for education in Illinois other than minor allocations from general purpose local taxes. Still, some civil communities established schools, financed by tuition payments plus such public funds as were available.

The first schools in Southerner-settled Belleville were private subscription schools supported by the relatively few families that wished to educate their children. Moreover, the first of these was organized in 1815 by a Yankee missionary, one of several sent west by the Congregational churches of Massachusetts and Connecticut to help "civilize the frontier." Public education did not even become an issue until the arrival of the Germans after 1830. By the mid-1840's the German element, with its particular intellectual interests, was sufficiently strong to carry the issue. The first city school board, the School Association of Belleville, a semiprivate group, was elected in 1847, and the first semipublic school in town opened in 1848. It was supported by tuition and grants from the-school fund based on the federal land grant. Not until 1855, when the state school law was enacted, was a public school district established. The first fully free public school was organized in 1856. Belleville has since developed a reputation for maintaining a strong interest in education, based in part on the fact that its record is exceptional for its region. It was one of the first civil communities in its part of the state to promote high school (1916) and, later, junior college (1946) education at public expense, and the otherwise fiscally conservative local residents continue to support their schools with greater willingness than other governmental functions.

The other Southern-influenced communities also appear to have been dependent upon non-Southerners to initiate public education efforts. Alton, a community strongly influenced by a Yankee minority in its early years, established a semipublic school in the 1820's and the second free public school in the state (after Yankee-influenced Chicago) in 1837. As the Yankee influence declined in the face of the continued influx of Southerners and others, so did public concern with the schools. Though few settled there, Yankees appear to have been instrumental in the establishment of the state's third or fourth free public school in Springfield in 1840. The leading Middle States settlers (who formed the local majority) in that civil community perceived the advantages of basic education in promoting local progress and continued to support the public schools.

As the northern civil communities were established, free public education spread. Schools were among the first public or quasi-public institutions created in each of them, invariably under the auspices of the Yankees. Where the Yankees represented the bulk of the community, the founding of public schools preceded the establishment of any other governmental institutions. Rockford was notable in this regard, as was Moline. In both, the soon-to-come Scandinavian majority carried on the Yankee pattern.

The civil communities in the other four states did not face the problem of securing public educational facilities locally before gaining support from the state. In all four, general laws establishing free public school systems were enacted in territorial days, usually to take advantage of the available federal grants but also reflecting the values of the Yankee stream which was so strong in their initial settlement. Except in the case of Davenport, these laws preceded the organization of general purpose local government in the cities of the prairie in those states. Provision of public education, then, was considered a cardinal function of government in those civil communities from the beginning.

Lest it be assumed that culturally influenced differences in educational standards are a thing of the past among the cities of the prairie, the 1960 census figures show that the impact of the streams in the realm of education is still of some importance. Table 6–2 shows the rank order of the cities of the prairie in terms of median school years completed and percent of population that has completed high school or more. Excluding Urbana and Champaign, where the presence of the University of Illinois faculty and student body raises local educational achievement levels all out of proportion, and Rockford, whose high percentage of foreign-born means a higher number of people who had less opportunity to attend school, the Yankee-influenced Upper Midwestern civil communities stand out as having the highest level of educational achievement, while the Southern-influenced civil communities on the fringes of the greater South stand out as significantly poorer in educational achievement.

TABLE 6–2 Cities of the Prairie: Relative Educational Achievement, 1960

City	Median School Years Completed	Per-cent Completed High School or More
Urbana	12.8	66.7
Champaign	12.4	60.3
Duluth	11.5	46.5
Moline	11.4	46.4
Rock Island	11.4	45.7
Davenport	11.4	45.4
Superior	11.3	45.3
Springfield	11.1	43.3
Decatur	11.1	43.7
Rockford	11.0	43.1
Joliet	10.9	42.1
Pueblo	10.6	40.8
Peoria	10.5	40.0
Alton	10.2	38.7
Belleville	9.8	34.6
E. St. Louis	8.7	23.2

In the mid-nineteenth century, public education was the "radical" program whose acceptance and support can be used with considerable reliability as an indicator of community attitudes toward local government services. In the mid-twentieth century, the complex of activities that come under the heading "community planning" may well be considered equally suitable indicators of local conceptions of the "proper" role of local government. By the end of 1961, every one of the cities of the prairie had initiated local planning in some form. Once again, the variation in the nature and extent of community planning was substantially explained by differences in local political culture.

Eleven of the civil communities have professional planning staffs, annual planning budgets that run into five figures, and general plans either completed or in preparation. Duluth, with the oldest planning department and one of the largest professional staffs, probably has the most important planning program of any of the cities of the prairie. Not only does its planning program extend back to the 1920's, but the plans made over the years by its planners have generally been implemented under their guidance. Its planners have successfully promoted a 9,000-acre city forest reserve, a new campus for the Duluth branch of the University of Minnesota, a public port terminal, a network of public school sites, a high bridge connecting Duluth and Superior, and other projects and programs of this caliber. They have, in effect, supervised much of their civil community's public development. In Duluth, where the Scandinavians have been the dominant element almost from the first, planning is accepted as a legitimate government activity that fills an important communal need. In this respect, the Scandinavian influence so prevalent in Minnesota is almost undiluted in Duluth.

Planning is less dynamic but almost as well accepted in Davenport. The civil community's more conservative Germans, though considerably less planning-oriented than the Scandinavians, are highly predisposed to orderly development. Organized local planning was begun relatively early in Davenport, and the city had a comprehensive plan by 1945. Though the city's planning department has not accomplished any spectacular feats, it has pioneered most of the local development programs in the last half-generation.

Rockford also entered planning field early in the 1940's with a joint city-county planning operation designed to reflect the extra-municipal scope of the civil community. Despite this early interest in planning and a continued public commitment to the planning idea characteristic of a civil community with Rockford's background, little "successful" planning has been done compared to Duluth. In part, this is a result of local political conflicts. Just as the civil community's planning activities were about to enter the implementation stage, a major change in municipal regimes in 1957 cut the base of support out from under the planning staff. Since the professional planners were identified with the previous regime, they were rendered ineffective. Though some of their plans were implemented, their agency was given no substantive role in their implementation. After several years of fruitless conflict, the entire planning staff left Rockford. Despite these problems, the local planning commission has been concerned with planning as such and not just with zoning regulation, as are most of its sisters. In this it reflects something of the ambivalence toward planning present in a civil community dominated by a native stream whose leading representatives, even though theoretically committed to planning, are reluctant to accept the technocratic aspects of professionally prepared plans with their limitations on local decision-making based on moralistic considerations. In an effort to develop effective planning mechanisms without the technocratic aspects, the planning commission has attempted to assume the role of broker between influentials and interests. This effort, initiated by the politically "savvy" commissioners, was resisted by the professional planning staff and contributed considerably to the decline of their influence with the community. Since their departure, the planning commission may well have returned to the broker role conceived to be the proper one by the community leadership.

Moline has had problems between commission and staff not unlike those of Rockford, for many of the same reasons. There, too, the idea of planning as a legitimate function is apparently well entrenched despite the quality and impact of the planning program at any given time. At the same time, the conflict between its technocratic and communitarian aspects remains unresolved, a matter of conflict within the planning "establishment" itself.

Planning in the remaining civil communities rests upon the narrow edge of conflicting attitudes which are characteristic of the articulated public reaction to planning generally. On one hand, there is a national trend (financed, in part, with federal funds) toward the establishment of local planning agencies as symbolic hallmarks of the "progressive" community. This must help to explain the near-universality of organized planning institutions in civil communities of over 25,000 population. This trend has a substantive side as well in that every one of these civil communities does have apparent and visible need for planning in some form, if only for zoning and subdivision control. Every one of these communities also has at least a few influentials who are committed to planning as an idea and as a useful tool in community development and who are sincerely interested in developing local planning facilities.

One the other hand, there are substantial numbers of community influentials in all those communities who oppose planning as an infringement on private rights and a threat to established patterns from which they benefit. (The two reasons are intertwined in their overall position and cannot easily be separated.) They, in turn, can usually muster considerable popular support when planning questions are brought before the general public. In between the advocates of planning, on one hand, and its opponents, on the other, there stand the bulk of the community's influentials who are willing to support planning operations for their symbolic value and for any services they may be able to render on behalf of economic development or to promote governmental "efficiency" but who do not wish to see their particular interests touched adversely for the sake of "long-range planning" or the "planned community."

These three elements are represented in some proportion in every civil community. Clearly, the way in which the proportions are distributed provides the basis for determining the place of planning in the community. In the civil communities along the nation's middle, where the individualistic political culture predominates, the quality of the planning program depends upon the extent to which the representatives of that culture are won over to support particular planning activities and—most important—particular planners. Though timing is of the exxence in determining the chances of acceptance for particular planning activities, the personalities of the planners are even more important for their effect on the status of planning in those communities. Decatur, Pueblo, Rock Island, and Springfield have had some notable (though limited) successes in the planning realm in the past decade because of the talent of the professional planners that have served them and the ability of those planners to work with the local influentials. Champaign has utilized its planning apparatus somewhat less, perhaps less as a consequence of the planners and more as a consequence of other factors on the local political scene. Peoria has achieved little rapport between planners and influentials, and the planning program has been limited accordingly (and, for that matter, fragmented as well). In all six civil communities, the demands placed on planning are limited to the preparation of the way for further economic development or to the suggestion of means to economize in government projects.

The same factors supporting and opposing planning are present in civil communities dominated by the heirs of the South and the traditionalistic political culture, but the balance is definitely against planning as a necessary or legitimate local government activity. The differences between Alton and Joliet serve as a case in point. Civil communities of roughly the same size but located in different sections of Illinois and with visibly different demographic compositions, both have planning programs that began with the preparation of general plans in the fashion of the 1950's without having professional planners in residence. In both cities, the local planning commissions have been involved in planning projects and do not confine their activities to zoning matters only. In both, the hiring of a professional planner has been a matter of public discussion and, by 1960, a budget line for such a position existed in Joliet. In both cases, opposition from politically articulate elements prevented the hiring of any professional. One consequence of this has been to transform the planning commissions in both cities into strategic centers for the negotiation of group differences over specific projects, moving them away from the traditional function of planning commissions as providers of citizen endorsements of the planning fiats of the professionals.

In Alton, however, the general attitude is less than favorably disposed to the idea of planning, except as a means to insure the implementation of the short-range desires of the business and industrial leadership. Public attitudes toward planning were exemplified in the early 1960's by Alton's rejection of even a minimal housing code required by the federal government to comply with the standards set down by Congress to obtain urban renewal grants. The city council had only hesitatingly approved the proposed code, after the Urban Renewal Administration had lowered their requirements to the absolute minimum just to get Alton's urban renewal program under way, only to have the city's voters reject it at the polls. The fight against the code was led by the John Birch Society, whose major argument was that it restricted the individual's right to use his own property as he saw fit and that government restrictions on private use are not different from outright confiscation.

Planning is somewhat better accepted in Joliet, not as a technical activity but as a reasonable way in which to maximize return on local effort while satisfying a more broadly based group of interests and influentials. This may explain why no action was taken to hire the planner provided for in the city budget while, at the same time, the planning commission was actively involved in examining, reviewing, and modifying proposals for all the city-supported long-range improvement projects under consideration. In 1962, the planning commission was actively involved in shaping two urban renewal projects, a project for a new city hall or city-county building and a proposal for the construction of high-rise housing for the elderly on the fringes of the central business district.

Pueblo's planning efforts also reflect the marketplace orientation of the individualistic political culture but with an unusual twist. The director of the city-county planning agency, a professional planner, was himself responsible for directing the planning commission into a broker role at the strategic center of development decision-making. From the first, the Pueblo planning district was set up to embrace the entire civil community—the city proper and its unincorporated fringes—while excluding the greater part of Pueblo County, whose size and relative emptiness really remove it from the city's immediate ambit. The planning director, in an instinctive appreciation of the local political culture, turned his agency away from the development of a master plan whose utopian overtones are inevitable more appealing in a moralistic environment and put his staff to work on collecting and organizing data that would be useful to local developers of all kinds. Simultaneously, he worked to turn the planning commission itself into a broadly representative body (including members who had openly opposed its creation) with a membership that was personally influential in the civil community so that it would become a negotiating instrument rather than simply a body that ratified professional productions. He was successful in his efforts because the influentials in the community quickly perceived the utility of that kind of planning operation both as a source of good data (a substantive benefit) and as a place for important negotiations (a procedural benefit).

Belleville, the last of the cities of the prairie to enter the planning field, established a planning and zoning commission in 1961 after nearly fifteen years of false starts and aborted efforts that reflected a widespread opposition to formal planning and zoning in that civil community. There again, the conflict between planning as a symbolic "good" and a technocratic interference with individual rights lay at the roots of the delay. Even so, some steps had been taken in the direction of a planning program out of sheer necessity. By 1961, the city had pieces of a "master plan" prepared by a local engineer on a voluntary basis and a weak subdivision control ordinance. It had no zoning ordinance at all. Though the Chamber of Commerce officially encouraged the enactment of a zoning ordinance, not even the business community for whom the Chamber ostensibly spoke was eager to see one developed.

Planning in East St. Louis is a problem so different in character that it is difficult to discuss it meaningfully in this context. All such efforts initiated locally must fit into a political system in which planning is considered to be of very little value and even a detriment to its "proper" functioning. Most of the planning done in that civil community has been done through the intervention of an "outside" agency, Southern Illinois University (see Chapter Seven). The University has outflanked, as it were, the local planning institutions, which have always been so much windowdressing for a political organization dedicated to other goals.

Size seems to be an additional factor affecting the scope of planning in the three smallest of the cities of the prairie, though it has o bearing on the cultural dispositions of the civil communities concerned. In East Moline, Urbana, and Superior, local planning commissions exist primarily to handle zoning questions and to make recommendations on some to the city council. Though East Moline has a general plan (acquired in 1959 in response to a general trend in the Quad Cities area to have outside consultants prepare such plans), it is not really used. Since none of the three has professional planning staffs, their advance planning work is virtually nonexistent. Still, there exist differences in attitude toward planning among the politically articulate elements in the three communities.

Superior officially and publicly supports the planning principle in the style of Duluth. Only its poor economic position and declining population have prevented that city from developing a more extensive planning operation. As it is, the planning commission operates as a conservation agency with powers far in excess of those exercised in most communities, limiting "urban sprawl" within the city by controlling the issuance of building permits to specific areas so that the city will not be burdened with excessive costs for providing services. This device is also used to preserve the natural beauty of the area, a matter of some local concern.

East Moline publicly supports planning because it is considered the right thing to do in the Quad Cities metropolitan area. Though its political culture is far more individualistic than those of its sister cities, as their junior its city fathers feel compelled to follow their lead. "Planning" in that metropolitan area, however, is conceived of as a more moderate enterprise than in Superior—an advisory activity, as it were, even in those cities possessing planning staffs—so it has not become an onerous burden for East Moline. The city, which does not have any professionally trained people in its municipal government, can do little more than give lip service to the idea of advance planning.

In Urbana, perhaps the most homogeneously individualistic civil community of all. The planning idea was not even given lip service by the planning commission or its leading backers during the 1950's. The city's small size enabled it to remain concerned exclusively with individual zoning cases without the necessity for considering larger planning issues. This predisposition was brought out into the open late in 1962 when a leading member of the commission resigned after publicly charging that the commission was refusing to concern itself with planning. His resignation caused no significant stir in the community. Though Urbana was then acquiring parts of a general plan, it was as a result of efforts made by one of the minority aldermen on the city council rather than a serious city effort. He arranged for graduate students of planning at the University of Illinois to prepare a land-use map and secured council approval because he was able to get their services free.

While it would be inaccurate to infer the existence of a single-minded "community" attitude toward the purposes and functions of local government, or even the existence of single-minded "community" attitudes toward public support of education or planning, from the sectional location of the cities of the prairie and the distribution of the migrational streams among them, certain "general predispositions" can be seen in each community. When kept in proper perspective, those predispositions can be related to sectional and demographic patterns of political culture in the greater West.

After accounting for size differences and the idiosyncrasies present in each local situation, it is possible to discern a strong predisposition to accept a broadened view of the local government's planning function in those cities of the prairie dominated by the moralistic political culture and located in the trans-Mississippi states. In them the combination of a sectional tradition of greater government activity to cope with the conquest of the several frontiers and the settlement of communal pacesetters from the Northern streams is the crucial determinant leading to the acceptance of orthodox planning efforts as the starting point. The broadest view of the role of planning, and the planning program that has been most successful in providing community leadership, is found in Duluth where the combination of Northern streams has been most pronounced. There the utopian aspects of orthodox planning are attractive in and of themselves while the high importance of government as the major innovator innovator in the civil community has given the planners considerable authority to act on their plans. In Davenport and Pueblo, where the Northern and Middle Streams are mixed, planning as a form of negotiated development has attracted broad support. In both civil communities, less utopian planning programs have been relatively strong and quite successful in contributing to community development. Superior, closer to Duluth and the trans-Mississippi West than to the rest of Wisconsin, shares Duluth's acceptance of comprehensive planning and, indeed, implements a comprehensive plan more fully than any of its sisters.

Within the state of Illinois, where the trans-Mississippi sectional configuration is absent, the cities most influenced by the Northern streams—Rockford and Moline—have shown a general predisposition toward public planning but have had minimally successful programs, apparently because of their influentials' conflicting attitudes toward orthodox planning. In the absence of a clear tradition of visibly heavy government involvement in their previous development, accompanied by a substantial does of Yankee individualism, their willingness to accept utopian-style model-building was reduced without any proper substitute developed to take its place. Those civil communities influenced by the Middle streams and dominated by the individualistic political culture have programs whose importance has varied in relation to the planners employed and whose directions have, in any case, been limited. The key to successful planning operations in those communities has been the ability of the planners of the planners or planning commissions to get away from planning orthodoxies, adapt to a market-oriented culture by demonstrating the utility of applying planning techniques to commercial development, and then become the strategic centers of negotiation in development decision-making. Springfield and Decatur offer some notable examples of planners able to do just that while Joliet's planning commission has tried much the same route.

The civil communities most influenced by the Southern streams have been most reluctant to embark upon government-sponsored planning programs, since neither the promise of utopian improvement not the support of commercial development appeals to their traditionalistic political cultural orientation *per se*. Hence, they have created planning institutions only as a consequence of outside intervention or in response to the overwhelming pressures of necessity accompanying urbanization. The unique situations in Alton, Belleville, and East St. Louis illustrate this.

The full meaning of the foregoing differences in local political cultures can be better understood when the cities of the prairie are viewed in the context of the political cultures of their respective states.

NOTES

1. This definition and its elaboration are taken from Gabriel A. Almond, "comparative Political Systems," *The Journal of Politics,* XVII (1956), 391–409. Almond is the first political scientist to systematically attempt to define and explore the relationship of political culture to the political system. His work and the work of his colleagues have been the starting point for the theoretical aspects of my exploration of the concept, but its application has been limited because of their cross-cultural concerns as against the intracultural concerns of this study. Let it be clearly understood that this discussion of political culture and the treatment of the concept that follows is not meant to imply some kind of crude "cultural determinism." "Political culture" as a concept is difficult enough to isolate in the context of a materialistically oriented phenomenology of "science," and is that much more difficult to identify and delimit empirically. Despite this difficulty—or perhaps as a consequence of it—it remains all too easy to attribute too much to "political culture" and to overdraw the effects of political culture on political behavior. Such error invariably leads to an implication of a facile and false determinism that becomes virtually apolitical in its very nature.

2. These six themes are adapted from the works of Clyde Kluckhohn. See, particularly *Mirror for Man* (New York: McGraw-Hill, 1949). See also Charles S. Sydnor, *American Revolutionaries in the Making* (New York: Collier Books, 1962).

3. The relationship between language and culture is universally recognized as one of the utmost profundity. Kluckhohn, *op. cit.,* treats the relationship well. For a most sensitive exposition see Edward Hall, *The Silent Language* (Garden City, N.Y.: Doubleday, 1959) and *The Hidden Dimension* (Garden City, N.Y.: Doubleday, 1966). The "value-concept" as a means of expressing important ideas in other than systematically philosophical or definitional ways is effectively advanced by Max Kadushin in *Organic Thinking* (New York: The Jewish Theological Seminary of America, 1938), and *The Rabbinic Mind* (New York: The Jewish Theological Seminary, 1952). The value-concept idea is an eminently useful one in the study of language and culture, particularly in the American political setting where reliance upon implicitly understood terms is extensive.

4. Gabriel A. Almond and Sidney Verba deal with the American national political culture comparatively in *The Civic Culture* (Princeton, N.J.: Princeton University Press, 1963).

5. The names given the three political subcultures are descriptive rather than evaluative. The three subcultures are delineated here as models or ideal types and, like all models, oversimplify the complexities of reality.

6. This description and the ones following it must be considered very carefully and only after first abandoning many of the preconceptions associated with such idea-word's as *individualistic, moralistic, marketplace,* etc. In this case, for example, nineteenth-century individualistic conceptions of minimum intervention were oriented toward laissez faire with the role of government conceived to be that of a policeman with powers to act in certain limited fields. In the twentieth century, the notion of what constitutes minimum intervention has been drastically expanded to include such things as government regulation of utilities, unemployment compensation, and massive subventions to maintain a stable and growing economy—all this within the framework of the same political culture. The demands of manufacturers for high tariffs in 1860 and the demands of labor unions for workmen's compensation in 1960 may well be based on the same theoretical justification that they are aids to the maintenance of a working marketplace. Culture is not static. It must be viewed dynamically and defined so as to include cultural, change in its very nature.

7. As in the case of the "I" political culture, the change from nineteenth to twentieth century conceptions of what government's positive role should be has been great—for example, support for prohibition has given way to support for wages and hours regulation. At the same time, care must be taken to distinguish between a predisposition toward communal activism and desire for federal government activity. For example, many "M" types oppose federal aid for urban renewal without in any way opposing community responsibility for urban redevelopment. The distinction they make (implicitly at least) is between what they consider legitimate community responsibility and what they believe to be central government encroachment, or between "communalism," which they value, and "collectivism," which they abhor. Thus, on some public issues we find certain "M" types taking highly conservative positions despite their positive attitudes toward public activity generally. "M" types may also prefer government (inevitably local) intervention in the social realm as a protector of morals—as censorship or screening of books and movies—to similar government intervention in the economy.

8. In this context, it should be noted that regular party systems are sometimes abandoned in local communities dominated by the "I" political culture to institute nonpartisan electoral system in an effort to make local governments more "business like" and to take local administration "out of politics." Such antipolitical efforts are generally products of business-dominated reform movements and reflect the view that politics is necessarily "dirty" and illegitimate. In this context, see Edward C. Banfield, ed., *Urban Government* (New York: The Free Press of Glencoe, 1961), Sections III and IV.

9. See Theodore Calvin Pease, *The Story of Illinois* (Chicago: University of Chicago Press, 1949) for a brief history of public education in the state.

★
★ # Act II
★ ## The Stage; The Constitutional-Federal Structure—Horizontal and Vertical Fragmentation of Power

★ The Contemporary Presidency
★ Constraining Executive Power—George W. Bush
★ and the Constitution

By James P. Pfiffner

The modern tradition of constraining the power of political executives has deep roots in Anglo-American governmental traditions. The Magna Carta of 1215, the Habeas Corpus Act of 1679, the English Bill of Rights of 1689, the Common Law, and other documents and traditions of the British Constitution all provided precedents upon which the Framers of the U.S. Constitution drew. From the ratification of the U.S. Constitution to contemporary times, the experience and precedents of the presidency have also played an important role in laying the basis for the legitimate authority exercised by the president in the constitutional system. This article will examine several actions of President George W. Bush and argue that he has made exceptional claims to presidential authority. Four instances of President Bush's claims to presidential power will be examined: his suspension of the Geneva Conventions in 2002, his denial of the writ of habeas corpus for detainees in the war on terror, his order that the National Security Agency monitor messages to or from domestic parties in the United States without a warrant, and his use of signing statements.

The Framers of the Constitution were influenced by their English constitutional heritage with respect to individual rights and drew heavily upon British precedents. With respect to governmental structure, however, they rejected British precedent and created a separation of powers system based on a written constitution. The principles upon which they designed the Constitution included explicit limits on the powers of government and a separation of powers structure intended to prevent the accumulation of power in any one branch of government.

The system set up by the framers has worked reasonably well for more than two centuries of political experience (with the exception of the Civil War). In the nineteenth century, the Congress tended to dominate policy making, except in cases of war. In the twentieth century, however, the presidency accumulated sufficient power to play a dominating role in both

James P. Pfiffner, "The Contemporary Presidency: Constraining Executive Power: George W. Bush and the Constitution," from *Presidential Studies Quarterly*, vol. 38, no. 1, pp. 123–143. Published by Blackwell, 2008. Copyright by John Wiley & Sons, Inc. Permission to reprint granted by the rights holder.

domestic and foreign policy. One of the important constitutional confrontations between the presidency and Congress over a range of issues occurred during the "imperial" presidencies of Lyndon Johnson and Richard Nixon. In reaction to the aggrandizement of power in the presidency, Congress asserted its own constitutional authority by enacting a number of laws intended to constrain presidential power.

It is this congressional reassertion of constitutional authority in the 1670s that Vice President Dick Cheney and President George. W. Bush intended to reverse when they came to power in 2001. The administration, particularly Vice President Cheney, who had served as chief of staff to President Gerald Ford, felt that Congress overreacted to Vietnam and Watergate and hobbled presidential power in unconstitutional ways. He said,

> The feeling I had [during the Ford years], and I think it's been borne out by history, that in the aftermath, especially of Vietnam and Watergate, that the balance shifted, if you will, that, in fact, the presidency was weakened, that there were congressional efforts to rein in and to place limits on presidential authority. (Walsh 2006)

A White House aide later articulated an attitude seemingly shared by many at the top levels of the Bush administration:

> The powers of the presidency have been eroded and usurped to the breaking point. We are engaged in a new kind of war that cannot be fought by old methods. It can only be directed by a strong executive who alone is not subject to the conflicting pressures that legislators or judges face. The public understands and supports that unpleasant reality, whatever the media and intellectuals say. (Hoagland 2006)[1]

Those "conflicting pressures," of course, are *the whole point* of the separation of powers system. The atrocities of 9/11 gave President Bush the opportunity to achieve much of the expansion of executive power that he had sought since he became president. This article will take up four cases of extraordinary claims that President George W. Bush has made to executive authority under the Constitution: suspending the Geneva Conventions, denying habeas corpus appeals, National Security Agency (NSA) surveillance, and signing statements.

Suspending the Geneva Conventions and Torture

George W. Bush has been the only U.S. president to defend publicly the right of U.S. personnel to torture detainees. Probably the president did not intend for U.S. personnel to

---

1 Source: White House aide defending U.S. policies on Guantánamo Bay prisoners, secret renditions, and warrantless eavesdropping in a conversation with Jim Hoagland.

commit the egregious acts of torture that resulted in the death of many detainees. He did argue, however, that U.S. personnel needed to use aggressive techniques when interrogating prisoners captured in the war on terror. Despite declarations that "we do not torture," the aggressive interrogation procedures that were used by U.S. personnel (military, CIA, and contractors) in Guantánamo, Afghanistan, and Abu Ghraib are considered by most of the world to be torture. The Bush administration, in determining the legal basis of interrogation policy, used a narrow and technical definition of "torture" set forth in an Office of Legal Counsel memorandum of August 2002. President Bush vigorously argued that it was essential to the war on terror to continue to pursue "the program" of aggressive interrogation when he argued against the Detainee Treatment Act of 2005 and in favor of the Military Commissions Act of 2006.

Although other presidents have decided to withdraw from treaties, no other president has decided that the Geneva conventions did not apply to U.S. treatment of captives in wartime. Despite presidential leeway in interpreting treaties, the Supreme Court in the *Hamdan* decision held that the provisions of the Geneva Convention Common Article 3 invalidated the military commissions that President Bush had set up to try suspected terrorists held at Guantánamo. This decision prompted the Bush administration to convince Congress to pass the Military Commissions Act of 2006.

Despite the occurrence of torture in many U.S. wars, President Bush's *policy making* with regard to enhanced interrogation practices (or torture, depending on the definition) is unprecedented in U.S. history. In contrast to a policy that encourages or condones torture, ad hoc torture that is against the law can be punished, and the principle that torture is forbidden can be upheld. However, a policy that encourages and provides governmental sanction for coercive interrogation can easily be interpreted to justify torture, as was evident at Guantánamo and Abu Ghraib.

The Decision to Suspend the Geneva Conventions

The question of whether President Bush should declare that the Geneva Conventions did not apply to al Queda or the Taliban was the subject of a series of memoranda in early 2002. The memos culminated in a recommendation from counsel to the president, Alberto Gonzales, that the president should suspend the Geneva Conventions for members of al Qaeda. The January 25, 2002, memo recommended that the Geneva Convention III on Treatment of Prisoners of War should not apply to al Qaeda and Taliban prisoners. He reasoned that the war on terror was "a new kind of war" and that the "new paradigm renders obsolete Geneva's strict limitations on questioning of enemy prisoners."[2] Gonzales argued that exempting captured al

---

2 Memorandum for the President (January 25, 2002) from Alberto R. Gonzales, Subject: Decision RE Application of the Geneva Convention on Prisoners of War to the Conflict with al Qaeda and the Taliban. According to *Newsweek,* the memo was "actually" written by David Addington, Vice President Cheney's legal aide (Klaidman 2004). Gonzales has been criticized in the press for saying that the "new

Qaeda or Taliban prisoners from treatment according to the Geneva Convention protections would preclude the prosecution of U.S. soldiers under the War Crimes Act (1997).[3]

Secretary of State Colin Powell objected to the reasoning of the Justice Department and Gonzales. In a memo of January 26,2002, he argued that the drawbacks of deciding not to apply the Geneva conventions outweighed the advantages because "it will reverse over a century of policy ... and undermine the protections of the law of war for our troops, both in this specific conflict and in general; It has a high cost in terms of negative international reaction ... ; [and] It will undermine public support among critical allies."[4] Powell also noted that applying the convention "maintains POW status for U.S. forces ... and generally supports the U.S. objective of ensuring its forces are accorded protection under the Convention" (quoted in Greenberg and Dratel 2005, 124–25).

Despite Powell's memo, and in accord with the attorney general's and his counsel's recommendations, President Bush signed a memorandum on February 7, 2002, that stated: "Pursuant to my authority as Commander in Chief ... I ... determine that none of the provisions of Geneva apply to our conflict with al Qaeda in Afghanistan or elsewhere throughout the world because, among other reasons, al Qaeda is not a High Contracting Party to Geneva" (White House 2002). This determination denied suspected members of al Qaeda prisoner of war status and allowed the use of aggressive techniques of interrogation used by the CIA and military intelligence at Guantánamo that were later, in the fall of 2003, transferred to the prison at Abu Ghraib.

The changes in policy regarding the status of prisoners at Guantánamo upset top-level military lawyers in the Judge Advocate General Corps, including lawyers in the chairman

---

paradigm" renders the Geneva limitations "quaint." However, the context of his use of the word "quaint" is not as damning as excerpting the word makes it seem. The end of the sentence reads: "renders quaint some of its provisions requiring that captured enemy be afforded such thing as commissary privileges, scrip (i.e. advance of monthly pay), athletic uniforms, and scientific instruments." Whether this is a fair representation of the Geneva requirements is a separate issue.

3 The U.S. War Crimes Act (18 U.S.C. par. 2441 [Sup. III 1997]). Section 2441 of the War Crimes Act defines "war crimes" as a "grave breach" of the Geneva Conventions, which includes "willful killing, torture or inhuman treatment, including biological experiments, willfully causing great suffering or serious injury to body or health ... or willfully depriving a prisoner of war of the rights of fair and regular trial prescribed in this Convention."

4 Memorandum TO: Counsel to the President and Assistant to the President for National Security Affairs, FROM: Colin L. Powell (January 26, 2002), SUBJECT: Draft Decision Memorandum for the President on the Applicability of the Geneva Convention to the Conflict in Afghanistan (quoted in Greenberg and Dratel 2005, 122–25). Many of the memoranda and oral directives included statements that detainees were to be treated "humanely" despite the more aggressive interrogation techniques to which they could be subjected. The problem was that, if the detainees were in fact treated humanely, it would be more difficult to extract information from them. Thus, these statements must have been considered to be proforma, while the overall thrust of the directives was that detainees were to be subject to more aggressive interrogation techniques that were outside Geneva Convention limits.

of the Joint Chiefs of Staff's office. In 2003 a group of JAG officers went to visit the New York City Bar Association's Committee on International Human Rights. They were concerned about "a real risk of disaster," a concern that later proved to be prescient (Barry, Hirsh, and Isikoff 2004; Hersh 2004).[5]

Office of Legal Counsel Memoranda on Torture and Presidential Power

Shortly after 9/11, the Office of Legal Counsel of the Justice Department began work on legal aspects of the treatment of prisoners captured in the war on terror. Assistant Attorney General Jay S. Bybee, head of the Office of Legal Counsel, signed a memorandum written in part by John Yoo (2006, 171). The memo dealt with how U.S. personnel could avoid punishment under Title 18 of the U.S. Code (criminal law). This law, the War Crimes Act, implemented the Convention against Torture and Other Cruel, Inhuman and Degrading Treatment or Punishment for the United States (Klaidman 2004).

The Geneva Conventions require that "no physical or mental torture, not any other form of coercion, may be inflicted on prisoners of war to secure from them information of any kind whatever."[6] The Convention against Torture, as ratified by the United States, emphasizes that "no exceptional circumstances whatsoever, whether a state of war or a threat of war, internal political instability or any other public emergency, may be invoked as a justification of torture" (Bravin 2004).[7] The U.S. Torture Victims Protection Act defines torture as an "act committed

---

5 For a detailed analysis of the legal issues involved in the treatment of prisoners and the international and legal obligations of the United States regarding detainees, see Robert K. Goldman and Brian D. Tittemore, "Unprivileged Combatants and the Hostilities in Afghanistan: Their Status and Rights under International Humanitarian and Human Rights Law," American Society of International Law Task Force Paper, Washington, DC, 2002. See also Jennifer K. Elsea, "Lawfulness of Interrogation Techniques under the Geneva Conventions," Congressional Research Service Report to Congress (RL32567), Washington, DC, September 8, 2004; Jennifer K. Elsea, "U.S. Treatment of Prisoners in Iraq: Selected Legal Issues," Congressional Research Service Report for Congress (RL32395), Washington, DC, December 2, 2004; and L. C. Green, *The Contemporary Law of Armed Conflict* (New York: Manchester University Press, 1993). The skeptical attitude of many in the professional military was reflected in a 2007 op-ed piece by former Generals Charles C. Krulak (former commandant of the Marine Corps) and Joseph P. Hoar (former chief of Central Command): "As has happened with every other nation that has tried to engage in a little bit of torture—only for the toughest cases, only when nothing else works—the abuse spread like wildfire, and every captured prisoner became the key to defusing a potential ticking time bomb. Our soldiers in Iraq confront real 'ticking time bomb' situations every day, in the form of improvised explosive devices, and any degree of 'flexibility' about torture at the top drops down the chain of command like a stone—the rate exception fast becoming the rule." *Washington Post,* May 17, 2007, p. A17.
6 Article 17, paragraph 4.
7 United Nations Convention against Torture and Other Cruel, Inhuman or Degrading Treatment or Punishment (General Assembly Resolution 39/46, Annex, 39 U.N. GAOR Sup. No. 51, U.N. Doc. A.39/51, 1984). The Convention against Torture defines torture as "any act by which severe pain or

by a person acting under the color of law specifically intended to inflict severe physical or mental pain or suffering (other than pain or suffering incidental to lawful sanctions) upon another person within his custody or physical control" (18 U.S.C. Sec. 2340).

Part I of the Bybee memo interprets the above passage and construes the definition of torture narrowly; in doing so, it elevates the threshold of "severe pain" necessary to amount to torture: "We conclude that for an act to constitute torture, it must inflict pain that is ... equivalent in intensity to the pain accompanying serious physical injury, such as organ failure, impairment of bodily function, or even death" (Bybee 2002, 1, 6). This narrow definition would allow a wide range of brutal actions that do not meet the exacting requirements specified in the memo. The memo specifically excludes from torture "cruel, inhuman, or degrading treatment or punishment," some example of which are specified, such as wall standing, hooding, noise, sleep deprivation, and deprivation of food and drink. However, the memo did specify that some practices would be torture, such as severe beatings with clubs, threats of imminent death, threats of removing extremities, burning, electric shocks to genitalia, rape, or sexual assault (Bybee 2002, 15, 24, 28).[8]

In Section V, the memo argued that the president's commander-in-chief authority can overcome any law. "[T]he President enjoys complete discretion in the exercise of his Commander-in-Chief authority and in conducting operations against hostile forces" (Bybee 2002, 33). "Any effort to apply Section 2340A [of Title 18 U.S.C.] in a manner that interferes with the President's direction of such core war matters as the detention and interrogation of enemy combatants thus would be unconstitutional" (Bybee 2002, 31).

The administration used the commander-in-chief clause to argue that a presidential policy takes precedence over public law. Thus, the administration argued, the president is not bound by the law, despite the Article II, section 3 provision of the Constitution that the president "shall take care that the Laws be faithfully executed." The implication was also that the commander-in-chief

---

suffering, whether physical or mental, is intentionally inflicted on a person for such purposes as obtaining from him or a third person information or a confession."

8 According to the memo, for the law to apply, the torturer must have the "specific intent to inflict severe pain" and it must be his "precise objective" (Bybee 2002, 3). "Thus, even if the defendant knows that severe pain will result from his actions, if causing such harm is not his objective, he lacks the requisite specific intent even though the defendant did not act in good faith." Thus one could inflict pain that amounted to torture, but not be guilty of torture if the main objective was, fir instance, to extract information rather than to cause pain. This reasoning borders on sophistry. On December 30, 2004, the Bybee memo was superseded "in its entirety" by Memorandum for James B. Comey, Deputy Attorney General from Acting Assistant Attorney General Daniel Levin Re: Legal Standards Applicable under 18 U.S.C. par. 2340–2340A. The memo did not address the commander-in-chief powers of the president because it was "unnecessary" (p. 2).

clause trumps the Article I, section 8 provision that Congress has the authority to "make Rules concerning Captures on Land and Water."[9]

These memoranda, along with other policy directives by Secretary of Defense Donald Rumsfeld and others, set the conditions for torture and abuse that occurred at Guantánamo, Abu Ghraib, and Bagram Air Force Base in Afghanistan. A number of official inquiries as well as external reports documented incidents of gross abuse and torture, some resulting in the deaths of detainees (Pfiffner 2005).

The McCain Amendment

Senator John McCain (R-AZ) endured five years as a prisoner of war in Vietnam and suffered severe torture. Thus, his publicly expressed outraged at reports of torture perpetrated by U.S. soldiers and civilians at Guantánamo, Abu Ghraib, and in Afghanistan carried a large measure of legitimacy. McCain introduced an amendment to the Department of Defense Appropriations Act for 2006 to ban torture by U.S. personnel, regardless of geographic location. Section 1003 of the Detainee Treatment Act of 2005 provides that "no individual in the custody or under the physical control of the United States Government, regardless of nationality or physical location, shall be subject to cruel, inhuman, or degrading treatment or punishment."[10]

Vice President Cheney led administration efforts in Congress to defeat the bill (White 2005). Cheney first tried to get the bill dropped entirely and, when that failed, to exempt the CIA from its provisions. President Bush threatened to veto bill if it was passed. Their efforts, however, were unavailing, and the,measure was passed with veto-proof majorities in both houses, 90 to 9 in the Senate and 308 to 122 in the House. In a compromise, McCain refused to change his wording but did agree to add provisions that would allow civilian U.S. personnel to use the same type of legal defense that is accorded to uniformed military personnel.[11]

When President Bush signed the bill, however, he issued a signing statement that declared: "The executive branch shall construe Title X in Division A of the Act, relating to detainees, in a manner consistent with the constitutional authority of the President to supervise the unitary executive branch and as Commander in Chief and consistent with the constitutional

---

9 Article VI of the Constitution also provides that "all Treaties made, or which shall be made, under the authority of the United States, shall be the supreme Law of the Land."

10 The Detainee treatment Act defines cruel, inhuman, or degrading treatment as "the cruel, unusual, and inhumane treatment or punishment prohibited by the Fifth, Eighth, and Fourteenth Amendments to the Constitution, as defined in the United States Reservations, Declarations and Understandings to the United Nations Convention against Torture and Other Forms of Cruel, Inhuman or Degrading Treatment of Punishment done at New York, December 10, 1984."

11 That is, if the U.S. person undertakes interrogation practices that "were officially authorized and determined to be lawful at the time that they were conducted, it shall be a defense that such officer, employee, member of the Armed Forces, or other agent did not know that the practice were unlawful and a person of ordinary sense and understanding would not know the practices were unlawful."

limitations on the judicial power" (White House 2005). This Statement signaled that President Bush did not feel bound by the law that he had just signed.

Thus President Bush, through his Office of Legal Council, claimed that he was not bound by the Geneva Conventions, that the commander-in-chief authority invalidated any laws about prisoners, and that he was not bound by the Detainee Treatment Act. These claims attempted to place President Bush outside the checks and balances of the separation of power system and the rule of law.

Military Commissions and Habeas Corpus

The Supreme Court delivered several setbacks to President Bush's claims to executive power. In *Hamdi v. Rumsfeld* (542 U.S. 507, 2004), the Court ruled that U.S. citizens had the right to challenge their imprisonment in court. In *Rasul v. Bush* (542 U.S. 466, 2004),the Court held that noncitizens could challenge their detentions through habeas corpus petitions. And in *Hamdan v. Rumsfeld* (126 S. Ct. 2749, 2006), the Court ruled that the military commissions set up by President Bush were unlawful because they were not based on U.S. law and that they violated Common Article 3 of the Geneva Conventions.

The Supreme Court's Hamdan Decision

Despite the Bush administration's arguments that U.S. courts did not have jurisdiction over Guantánamo detainees, that the president's commander-in-chief authority was sufficient to detain people indefinitely, and that detainees were receiving sufficient due process rights, the Supreme Court ruled against the administration in the above-mentioned cases. In *Hamdi,* the Court declared that "the most elemental of liberty interests" is "the interest in being free from physical detention by one's own government ["without due process of law"]. ...history and common sense teach us that an unchecked system of detention carries the potential to become a means for oppression and abuse of others who do not present that sort of threat." Thus "[w]e reaffirm today the fundamental nature of a citizen's right to be free from involuntary confinement by his own government without due process of law."

This requirement of due process does not apply to "initial captures on the battle field," but "is due only when the determination is made to *continue* to hold those who have been seized." In making these judgments, the Court asserted that, despite administration arguments to the contrary, it had jurisdiction over executive branch imprisonments and that it was willing to enforce constitutional rights even during a time of war. In *Rasul v. Bush,* the Court (deciding on the basis of law, not on constitutional grounds) held that noncitizens also had the right to challenge their imprisonment through a habeas corpus petition.

On the issue of whether the United States is permitted to try noncitizen enemy combatants by the military commissions that the president had established, the Supreme Court in *Hamdan* ruled in the negative, overturning a Court of Appeals decision.[12] Justice John Paul Stevens, writing for the Court, concluded that the military commissions and procedures established by President Bush were not authorized by the Constitution or any U.S. law, and thus the president had to comply with existing U.S. laws, He explained that the "structures and procedures violate both the UCMJ and the four Geneva Conventions signed in 1949" (*Hamdan v. Rumsfeld* 2005, 4).The Court finally concluded: "Even assuming that Hamdan is a dangerous individual who would cause great harm or death to innocent civilians given the opportunity, the Executive nevertheless must comply with the prevailing rule of law in undertaking to try him and subject him to criminal punishment" (*Hamdan v. Rumsfeld* 2005, 7).

Perhaps the most important principle established in these Supreme Court cases was Justice Sandra Day O'Connor's statement in the majority opinion in *Hamdi*: "We have long since made clear that a state of war is not a blank check for the President when it comes to the rights of the Nation's citizens."[13]

The Military Commissions Act of 2006

In order to overcome the roadblock that the Supreme Court decisions threw in the way of administration policy, President Bush sought legislation that would authorize the creation of military commissions and spell out limits on the rights of detainees. President Bush argued that the types of harsh interrogation methods that he termed "the program" were essential to the war on terror. The administration maintained that the proposed law would allow CIA interrogators more leeway than Common Article 3 of the Geneva Conventions allowed.

President Bush argued strongly for passage of the administration's proposal, saying that it would provide "intelligence professionals with the tools they need" (Smith 2006a, 2006b; Babington and Weisman 2006). He maintained that "the professionals will not step up unless there's clarity in the law. ...I strongly recommend that this program go forward in order for us to be able to protect America" (Bush 2006).[14] The allowed interrogation techniques were

---

12 The commissions were established by military Order of November 13, 2001, "Detention, Treatment, and Trial of Certain Non-Citizens in the War against Terrorism." Available from http://www.whitehouse.gov/news/releases/2001/11/20011113-27.html.

13 In remarks after she had retired from the Supreme Court, Justice O'Connor said about the intimidation of federal judges, "We must be ever-vigilant against those who would strongarm the judiciary into adopting their preferred policies. It takes a lot of degeneration before a country falls into dictatorship, but we should avoid these ends by avoiding these beginnings." Her remarks were reported by Nina Totenberg of National Public Public Radio according to *The Raw Story* (Totenberg 2006).

14 The uniformed military, however, were not eager for the bill to pass. Major General Scott C. Black, the judge advocate general of the Army, said that "further redefinition" of the Geneva Conventions "is unnecessary and could be seen as a weakening of our treaty obligations, rather than a reinforcement of the standards of treatment" (Baker 2006).

not specified in the law, but were said to include prolonged sleep deprivation, stress positions, isolation, inducing hypothermia, excessive heat, and earsplitting noises. Members of Congress, including John McCain, also said that water-boarding[15] was not allowed by the Military Commissions Act, but their understanding was called into question when Vice President Cheney seemed to refute it (Vice President's Office 2006; Eggen 2006b; Lewis 2006).[16] On September 13, 2006, former Secretary of State Powell wrote a public letter to Senator McCain urging him to oppose the redefining of treatment allowed under Common Article 3, because "the world is beginning to doubt the moral basis of our fight against terrorism," and because "it would put our own troops at risk" (Reid 2006).

After several weeks of contentious debate between the two political parties, S3930 was passed by both houses of Congress. President Bush signed the Military Commissions Act of 2006 IPL 109–366) into law on October 17, 2006. The law gave the Bush administration most of what it wanted in dealing with detainees in ways that were prohibited by the *Hamdan* ruling. Most directly, the law authorized the president to establish military commissions to try alien detainees believed to be terrorists or unlawful enemy combatants. The vehement arguments made by President Bush that the Military Commissions Act was needed in order for the administration to continue to use "the program" of "robust" interrogation techniques constitute an admission that the administration had used them and saw them as essential to its approach to interrogation.

Importantly, the law denied alien enemy combatants access to the courts for writs of habeas corpus concerning "any aspect of the detention, transfer, treatment, trial, or conditions of confinement of an alien who is or was detained by the United States" (Section 7). Appeals that were allowed were limited to issues concerning the constitutionality of the law itself and the administration's compliance with it, but not the evidentiary basis for the detainee's imprisonment or his treatment while in custody.

---

15 Waterboarding is a technique of interrogation in which a person is bound to a flat board and his head submerged in water with a soaked cloth over his mouth (or water poured over the cloth) until the person cannot breath sufficient air and is convinced he is drowning. A Japanese office, Yukio Asano, was sentenced to fifteen years at hard labor for waterboarding an American in World War II (Pincus 2006; Shane and Liptak 2006).

16 Vice President Cheney was interviewed in the White House by a reporter who asked: "would you agree that a dunk in water [of a suspected terrorist] is a no-brainer if it can save lives?" Cheney replied: "It's a no-brainer for me… We don't torture… But the fact is, you can have a fairly robust interrogation program without torture, and we need to be able to do *that*. And thanks to the leadership of the President now, and the action of the Congress, we have that authority, and we are able to continue to [sic] Program" (emphasis added). Asked in another question about "dunking a terrorist in water," Cheney replied: "I do agree. And I think the terrorist threat, for example, with respect to our ability to interrogate high value detainees like Khalid Sheikh Mohammed, *that's* been a very important tool that we've had to be able to secure the nation" (emphasis added). The antecedent to the word "that" and "that's" in the vice president's statements is clearly "dunking a terrorist in water," indicating that the Bush administration does not consider waterboarding to be torture (Vice President's Office 2006).

The law forbids the use of testimony obtained through "torture," and it specifically outlaws the more extreme forms of torture. The interrogation methods that can be used against the accused also exclude those methods that "amount to cruel, inhuman, or degrading treatment prohibited by Section 1003 of the Detainee Treatment Act of 2005" (Section 948r). Under the administration's interpretation, the law prohibits only techniques that "shock the conscience," rather than the stricter prohibition in Common Article 3 which specifically forbids "outrages upon personal dignity, in particular humiliating and degrading treatment" (Elsea 2004, 5; Smith 2006a). The Military Commissions Act allocated significant new powers to the president. It allows the president or secretary of defense to decide unilaterally who is an enemy combatant; it allows the executive to prosecute a person using coerced testimony; and it precludes any oversight of the actions of the executive by the judiciary (Shane and Liptak 2006).[17]

Critics complained that this language did not amount to acceptance of Common Article 3 of the Geneva Conventions and would allow very harsh treatment that could amount to torture. Techniques such as stress positions, sleep deprivation, sensory deprivation, isolation, or earsplitting noises could amount to torture, said critics, depending on the intensity and duration of their use. Statements obtained with these methods could be used against a detainee if the presiding officer decides that the "interests of justice would best be served" and that "the totality of the circumstances renders the statement reliable and possessing sufficient probative value" (Section 948r).

In addition, critics of the administration argued that the new law would allow U.S. forces to capture anyone declared an "enemy combatant" anywhere in the world, including those thought to have purposefully supported hostilities against U.S. co-belligerents, and hold them indefinitely. These suspects could be held without charges being filed against them and subjected to harsh interrogation techniques with no recourse to the courts for writs of habeas corpus. Critics also questioned whether the law could constitutionally deny the writ of habeas corpus to detainees, as the law purported to do (Shane and Liptak 2006; Zernike 2006; Grieve 2006; Fletcher 2006).

At the symbolic level, the Military Commissions Act sent the message to the world that the United States would continue to use harsh interrogation techniques (including waterboarding, according to Vice President Cheney's statements) that most countries considered to be torture and in violation of Common Article 3 of the Geneva Convention. At the legal level, it purported to deny habeas corpus for most detainees and allowed harsh interrogation methods to be used. At the constitutional level, it represents a congressional ratification of executive authority to set up unilaterally military commissions, conduct trials, and sentence detainees with limited due process rights and no judicial or congressional oversight.

With the Military Commissions Act, President Bush was able to accomplish through law what he had previously asserted to be his own constitutional authority. Ratification by

---

17 It does allow appeals concerning the constitutionality of the law itself and whether the administration has complied with it.

Congress of the president's authority to deny habeas corpus appeals and due process rights to detainees, however, does not necessarily make them constitutional. It does, however, make it more difficult for the Supreme Court to constrain the president absent a change in the law by Congress. In seeking congressional sanction for his actions, President Bush did not abandon his claim that he, as president, had the constitutional authority to undertake them unilaterally.

Warrantless Electronic Surveillance by the NSA

In December 2005, the *New York Times* revealed that the Bush administration had been secretly monitoring telephone calls and e-mails between suspected foreign terrorists and people within the domestic United States. The legal right of the executive branch to conduct electronic surveillance on foreign intelligence targets is not in dispute, but the right of the government to secretly eavesdrop or wiretap suspects within the United States without a warrant is limited by the Fourth Amendment and the law.

The Foreign Intelligence Surveillance Act

During the 1970s it was revealed that the Nixon administration conducted a range of warrantless wiretaps in order to monitor their political adversaries (Senate 1976, 1978; Schwarz and Huq 2007; 31; Bazan and Elsea 2005).[18] Congress responded to these abuses by amending Title III of the Omnibus Crime Control and Safe Streets Act of 1968, which controlled electronic surveillance by the government. The act set procedures for seeking warrants for electronic surveillance and prohibited nonwarranted surveillance. Title III of the act provided an exception for certain national security surveillance undertaken under the "constitutional power of the President to take such measures as he deems necessary to protect the Nation against actual or potential attack ... [and] to obtain foreign intelligence information deemed essential to the security of the United States" (Bazan and Elsea 2005, 17).[19]

That section of Title III was repealed by the Foreign Intelligence Surveillance Act of 1978 (FISA) (Cole et al. 2006).[20] It was amended to allow for the surveillance for foreign intelligence acquisition only as long as it was carried out pursuant to FISA. The amended act specified that FISA "shall be the *exclusive means* by which electronic surveillance, as defined in section 101 of such Act, and the interception of domestic wire, oral, and electronic communications may be conducted" (emphasis added) (Bazan and Elsea 2005).[21]

FISA provides for a special court for the consideration of warrants for domestic electronic surveillance, if probable cause is shown that the suspect is likely to be an agent of a foreign

---

18 House Report no. 95–1283, Pp. 15–21, as cited in Bazan and Elsea (2005, 12–13).

19 82 Stat. 214, 18 U.S. par. 2511(3), as cited in Bazan and Elsea (2005, 17).

20 Public Law 95–511, 92 Star, 1783, as cited in Cole et al. (2006).

21 18 U.S.C. par. 2511(2)(f), Public Law 95–511, 92 Stat. 1783, as quoted in Bazan and Elsea (2005,

power. In requiring a warrant from the special FISA court, the law provides for three exceptions: (1) if the attorney general determines that the communication is among foreign powers or their agents and "there is no substantial likelihood that the surveillance will acquire the contents of any communication of which a United States person is a party"; (2) if the attorney general determines that there is insufficient time to obtain a warrant, but in such a case a FISA judge shall be notified within seventy-two hours (changed from twenty-four hours on December 28, 2001); and (3) surveillance can be conducted without a warrant for fifteen days after Congress declares war (Bazan and Elsa 2005, 25–26).

In confirming the *New York Times* report of the secret surveillance program, President Bush Said that warrantless spying on domestic persons suspected of being in contact with terrorists was "a vital tool in our war against the terrorists" and that revealing the program damaged U.S. security (Sanger 2005). "It was a shameful act for someone to disclose this very important program in a time of war. The fact that we're discussing this program is helping the enemy" (Baker and Babington 2005).

It is not as though President Bush did not have the means to undertake NSA spying within the law. He could have sought warrants by the special FISA courts set up for that very purpose. If speed was of importance, the NSA could have carried out the surveillance and come back to the FISA court within seventy-two hours for retrospective authorization, as provided for by the law. Or if the law, as written, was too narrow to allow the kind of surveillance deemed necessary (e.g., data mining or call tagging), the president could have asked Congress to change the law (which had been amended several times since 9/11). But President Bush did none of these things; instead, he secretly ordered the NSA to conduct the surveillance and, when his actions were disclosed, he asserted that he had the constitutional authority to ignore the law.

President Bush's Arguments

The administration argued that getting a FISA warrant was too cumbersome and slow and thus it had to set up a program for the NSA to conduct the warrantless surveillance in secret. The record of the FISA court, however, does not seem to indicate that the administration had trouble obtaining warrants. From the time that the court was created in 1978 to the end of 2005, it issued 18,748 warrants and refused only 5 (Baker and Babington 2005). This is about as close to a rubber stamp as one could wish for. As for the problem of speed, if the need was immediate, the NSA could act immediately and come back to the court for authorization within seventy-two hours.

The administration also argued that it had consulted with Congress about the program, because it had informed the leadership and the chair and ranking members of the Senate and House intelligence committees. President Bush said, "Not only has it been reviewed by Justice Department officials, it's been reviewed by members of the United States Congress" (Lichtblau 2006). This argument was challenged, however, by Senator Jay Rockefeller, one of the few members who had been briefed on July 17, 2003. The members of Congress were sworn to secrecy and told that they could not inform their colleagues or staffers about the program. After the briefing, Rockefeller expressed his concern by handwriting a letter to Vice President Cheney and copying the note and putting a sealed copy in his safe as evidence that he had expressed his concern. He had no alternative route to raise concerns about what he saw as potentially illegal actions by the administration. He wrote to the vice president, "Clearly, the activities we discussed raise profound oversight issues" (Babington and Linzer 2005).

The administration also argued that the congressional Authorization to Use Military Force (AUMF) passed in a joint resolution after the September 11, 2001, attacks gave the president power by declaring that the president could

> use all necessary and appropriate force against those nations, organizations, or persons he determined planned, authorized, committed, or aided the terrorist attacks that occurred on September 11, 2001, or harbored such organizations or persons, in order to prevent any future acts of international terrorism against the United States by such nations, organizations or persons. (Brimmett 2006)[22]

The act, however, made no mention of foreign or domestic surveillance in its wording. The argument of the administration that the AUMF overcomes the FISA law would entail the implication that Congress intended to repeal the section of the law that declared FISA to be "the exclusive means by which electronic surveillance … may be conducted."

When Congress was considering the authorization for the president to use force, the administration tried to insert in the language of the resolution a provision that would have allowed the "necessary and appropriate force" could be applied "in the United States" as well as against the "nations, organizations, or persons" who were involved in the 9/11 attacks. This language was rejected by the Senate, undermining the argument that the AUMF intended to repeal FISA (Daschle 2005). In addition, because Congress explicitly provided for warrantless wiretaps for fifteen days subsequent to a declaration of war, how could a resolution on the use of force, which carries less legal or constitutional weight than a declaration of war, authorize wiretaps with no limitation?[23]

---

22 Authorization for Use of Military Force, Public Law 107–40, 115 Stat. 224 (2001), passed the House and Senate on September 14, 2001, and signed by the president on September 18, 2001.

23 The NSA surveillance revelations also raised the issue of whether President Bush was truthful in reassuring questioners about government surveillance and civil liberties. In remarks in Buffalo, New York on April 20, 2004, President Bush said: "Now, by the way, any time you hear the United States government talking about wiretap, it requires—a wiretap requires a court order. Nothing has changed, by the way. When we're talking about chasing down terrorists, we're talking about getting a court order before we do so. It's important for our fellow citizens to understand, when you think Patriot Act, constitutional guarantees are in place when it comes to doing what is necessary to protect our homeland, because we value the Constitution" (Bush 2004).

Attorney General Alberto Gonzales, in explaining why the administration did not seek to amend FISA to allow for the warrantless wiretaps, replied that he was advised that such an amendment was unlikely to pass Congress (Eggen 2006a). It is contradictory, however, to argue that Congress likely would not grant the needed authority for warrantless wiretaps if it were asked and that at the same time, Congress had approved presidential authority for warrantless wiretaps in passing the AUME (Cole et al. 2006). It was also disclosed that Justice Department lawyers drafted legislative changes to the USA Patriot At that would have provided a legal defense for government officials who wiretapped with "lawful authorization" from the president. There would be no need for such legislation if the president clearly had inherent authority to authorize such wiretaps.[24]

In addition to Senator Rockefeller's concerns, members of the Bush administration Justice Department also had serious reservations. When the White House sought approval of continued use of the program in 2004, Acting Attorney General James B. Comey (John Ashcroft's deputy) refused to grant his approval. As a result, Andrew Card, the Chief of staff, and White House Counsel Gonzales made a special trip to the hospital to try to get Attorney General John Ashcroft (who was in the hospital recovering from major surgery) to approve the program. With a dramatic statement from his bed, Ashcroft, with Comey present, refused to overrule his deputy (Lichtblau and Risen 2006; Lichtblau 2006; Klaidman, Taylor, and Thomas 2006). Comey was then called to the White House and informed that the program would continue. Only the threat of resignations by Ashcroft, Comey, and several other high-level Justice Department officials convinced President Bush to heed the concerns of the lawyers. Only after President Bush convinced them that their concerns had been met did they agree to the continuation of the program. What happened at the White House meeting has not been disclosed.

The question here is not whether there is a serious threat from terrorism or whether the government ought to be able to wiretap U.S. citizens without a warrant. It may or may not be good policy to allow the government to conduct such surveillance, but the constitutional process for making such decisions entails the legislative process and judicial interpretation of the law. President Bush claimed that, despite the laws enacted by Congress and duly signed by the president, he had inherent authority to ignore the law and set up a secret surveillance program that could act without warrants. The question is one of constitutional presidential authority versus the constitutional rights and duties of the other two branches. The Constitution does not give the president the authority to ignore the law. The wisdom of surveillance policy is a separate issue.

David Addington, Vice President Cheney's chief of staff and counsel, expressed his attitude toward the FISA court when he said: "We're one bomb away from getting rid of that obnoxious court" (Goldsmith 2007, 181). Jeffrey Goldsmith, director of the Office of Legal Counsel, who was involved with policy making regarding the Terrorist Surveillance Program,

---

24 Justice Department spokespersons said that the drafts were not intended to affect NSA spying and that the proposals were not presented to the attorney general or the White House (Eggen 2006a).

said, "After 9/11 they [Cheney and Addington] and other top officials in the administration dealt with FISA they way they dealt with other laws they didn't like: they blew through them in secret abased on flimsy legal opinions that they guarded closely so no one could question the legal basis for the operations" (Goldsmith 2007, 181). Goldsmith pointed out that even the NSA's lawyers were not allowed to examine the legal documents that justified the Terrorist Surveillance Program (Goldsmith 2007, 182).

Signing Statements

Article I, section 1 of the Constitution begins: "All legislative Powers herein granted shall be vested in a Congress of the United States, which shall consist of a Senate and House of Representatives." Article II of the Constitution provides that "the executive Power shall be vested in a President of the United States of America" and that "the President shall be Commander in Chief of the Army and Navy of the United States." Despite the Article II provision that the president "shall take Care that the Laws be faithfully executed," signing statements have been used to argue that Article II provisions trump Article I of the Constitution.

The idea of presidential signing statements begins with the reasonable presumption that each coordinate branch of government should have a role in interpreting the Constitution and its own constitutional powers. As James Madison said in Federalist no. 49, "The several departments being perfectly co-ordinate by the terms of their common commission, none of them, it is evident, can pretend to an exclusive or superior right of settling the boundaries between their respective powers." Thus, within the checks and balances of the Constitution, no single branch has the final say as to what the Constitution says or what public policy shall be. Each branch has a role in interpreting the Constitution, but each is subject to checks and balances from the other two branches.

Presidents since James Monroe have occasionally issued statements upon the signing of bills into law, although it was unusual for the first 150 years of the Republic. Most of these signing statements were rhetorical and meant to show presidential support for the legislation or occasionally to record publicly presidential reservations about the law. Rhetorical signing statements began to increase with the Truman administration. The more important use of signing statements, however, has been to register questions about the constitutionality of the law in question. The use of signing statements for this purpose began to be taken seriously during the Ford and Carter presidencies, but took a significant jump during the Reagan presidency, during which they were used in a strategic manner to signify presidential disapproval of parts of a law that he was signing (Kelley 2002).

The Reagan administration took a step toward changing the status of signing statements in 1986 when it arranged with West Publishing Company to publish signing statements in the Legislative History section of *The United States Congressional Code and Administrative News,* which provides information about the background for the development of a law that might be relevant to its future interpretation by courts. Attorney General Edwin Meese explained that the purpose of the administration's action was so that the president's thinking when signing a bill into law "will accompany the legislative history from Congress so that all can be available to the court for future construction of what that statute really means" (Garber and Wimmer 1987).

Such a purpose seems reasonable, because it merely calls to the attention of the courts the president's perspective on the law. This benign interpretation of signing statements, however, was undercut by Meeese's later statement of the intent of signing statements in 2001, in which he said that, in addition to expressing the president's view of a law, it would indicate "those provisions of the law that might not be enforced" (Kelley 2002). There is a big difference, however, between expressing an opinion on the meaning of a law and refusing to enforce the provisions of a law of which a president disapproves. Presidents Carter, Reagan, G. H. W. Bush, and Clinton occasionally used signing statements to indicate that they had reservations about the laws they were signing and might not enforce.

President George W. Bush, however, has used signing statements to an unprecedented extent. He issued more than 1,000 constitutional challenges to provisions in 150 laws in his first six years in office (Kelley 2007; American Bar Association 2006). He also used signing statements to assert the unilateral and unreviewable right of the executive to choose which provisions of laws to enforce and which to ignore. For instance, he has used them to indicate that he does not feel bound by all of the provisions of laws regarding: reporting to Congress pursuant to the Patriot Act, the torture of prisoners, whistleblower protections for the Department of Energy, the number of U.S. troops in Colombia, the use of illegally gathered intelligence, and the publication of educational date gathered by the Department of Education (Savage 2006, 2007, 228–49).

One problem with signing statements of this sort is that they can accomplish what the Framers decided not to give the president: an absolute veto. The constitutional process calls for bills to be passed by Congress and presented to the president for his signature or veto. However, a signing statement, in effect, allows the president to sign the bill and later to decide whether he does not want to comply with part of the law. It also allows the president to achieve, in effect, an item veto, which the Supreme Court has declared unconstitutional. In the passage of legislation, members of Congress often vote for a bill because of assurances that certain provisions have meaning. However, if the executive can unilaterally decide not to enforce whatever portion of laws it believes infringe on its constitutional power, the votes of a majority of the members of Congress are effectively nullified.

The belief that he could selectively enforce the law pursuant to his signing statements may be part of the reason that President Bush did not issue any vetoes for the first five and a half years of his administration, a record unmatched since Thomas Jefferson. An example (discussed above) of the potentially unchecked nature of signing statements occurred when President Bush strongly opposed and threatened to veto the Detainee Treatment Act, sponsored by Senator McCain, forbidding torture. It was passed by both houses of Congress by veto-proof majorities. President Bush signed the law in a ceremony at the White House with John McCain present, symbolizing the administration's intent not to use torture in order to obtain information from prisoners.

In his accompanying signing statement, however, President Bush indicated that he did not feel bound by the law and that he would enforce the law "in a manner consistent with the constitutional authority of the President" (White House 2005). Thus, the president reserved for himself the right to ignore the law when he deemed it to conflict with his commander-in-chief power, but he avoided the constitutional process of having to subject his veto to a possible override by Congress. Because the administration had previously asserted that Congress could not limit the way in which the executive treated prisoners, the implication was that it would not consider itself bound by the provisions of the law. The administration also seemed to claim in the signing statement that it could avoid judicial review.

The implications of these sweeping claims to presidential authority are profound and undermine the very meaning of the rule of law. Despite the Constitution's granting of lawmaking power to the Congress, the Bush administration maintained that executive authority and the commander-in-chief clause can overcome virtually any law that constrains the executive. President Bush was thus claiming unilateral control of the laws. If the executive claims that it is not subject to the law as it is written but can pick and choose which provisions to enforce, it is essentially claiming the unitary power to say what the law is. The take care clause of Article II can thus be effectively nullified.

Even though some limited circumstances may occur in which the president is not bound by a law, expanding that limited, legitimate practice to more than a thousand threats to not execute the law constitutes an arrogation of power by the president.[25] The Constitution does not give the president the option to decide *not* to faithfully execute the law. If there is a dispute about the interpretation of a law, the interaction of the three branches in the constitutional process is the appropriate way to settle the issue. The politics of passage, the choice to veto or not, and the right to challenge laws in court all are legitimate ways to deal with differences in interpretation. But the assertion by the executive that it alone has the authority to interpret the law and that it will enforce the law at its own discretion threatens the constitutional balance set up by the Constitution

Thinking Constitutionally

Even if one posits that President Bush has not and would not abuse his executive power, his claim to be able to ignore the law, if allowed to stand, would constitute a dangerous precedent that future presidents might use to abuse their power. Joel Aberbach points out that "in the end, this is not a partisan issue, for someday the Democrats will have unified control, and even that somewhat-less-disciplined party might countenance a government of the type Bush and Cheney have apparently structured" (Aberbach 2007). Madison argues in Federalist no. 10, "Enlightened statesmen will not always be at the helm." Thinking constitutionally means looking ahead and realizing that future executives will likely claim the same authority as their

25 For instance, if a law contains a one-house legislative veto provision or a clearly unconstitutional infringement on the president's appointment power.

predecessors. Claims to executive power ratchet up; they do not swing like a pendulum unless the other two branches protect their own constitutional authorities.

The rule of law is fundamental to a free society and to democracy, because neither can exist without it. As Thomas Paine argued in *Common Sense,* "In America THE LAW IS KING. For as in absolute governments the King is law" (emphasis in original). Madison put it this way in Federalist no. 47: "The accumulation of all powers, legislative, executive, and judiciary, in the same hands, whether of one, a few, or many, and whether hereditary, self-appointed, or elective, may justly be pronounced the very definition of tyranny." In each of the following cases of claims to constitutional authority, President Bush was asserting that he alone could exercise the authority of each of the three branches:

1. Geneva Conventions and torture: President Bush acted as *lawmaker* in suspending the treaty, which according to Article VI of the Constitution is "the supreme Law of the Land," *executive* in carrying out the policy by interrogation prisoners with harsh interrogation practices, and *judge* by keeping the proceedings secret and asserting that any appeal could only by to him and that the courts had no jurisdiction to hear appeals.
2. Military tribunals: President Bush acted as *lawmaker* in creating the commissions himself, not in accord with enacted laws, *executive* in detaining suspects in prisons, and *judge* in conducting the trials, imposing sentences, and serving as the final appeal.
3. Denying habeas corpus to detainees: President Bush acted as *lawmaker* in suspending habeas corpus, which authority the Constitution gives to Congress, *executive* in imprisoning detainees and not allowing them to appeal for writs of habeas corpus and denying them the aid of counsel (until forced to by the Supreme Court), and *judge* in asserting that executive branch determinations of detainee status were final and that appeals could only be within the executive branch.
4. NSA warrantless wiretapping: President Bush acted as *lawmaker* by determining that he could ignore the regularly enacted law and impose his own rules in order to conduct surveillance in the United States, *executive* in ordering the NSA to carry out his policies, and *judge* by arguing that it was his inherent right as president to do ti in secret and avoid obtaining warrants from the FISA court.
5. Signing statements: President Bush was *undermining* the separation of powers and the rule of law itself by claiming the authority to ignore those parts of the law that he claimed impinged on his own prerogatives and refusing to accept the legitimacy of either Congress or the courts to limit his authority.

The president should have enough power to accomplish reasonable policy goals, but not enough to override the other two braches unilaterally, acting merely on the basis of his own judgment. In these case of extraordinary claims to executive authority, President Bush was claiming that the checks and balances in the Constitution were not binding on him. The U.S. Constitution created a system in which the concentration of power in one branch could be countered by actions of the other two branches. Congress and the courts still may act to undo some of President Bush's extraordinary assertions of executive authority, but his claims have severely challenged the balance of constitutional authority. The principles of constitutionalism and the rule of law underpin the foundations of the U.S. policy. Insofar as President Bush, in cases such as these, refused to acknowledge the constitutional limits on his executive authority, he undermined both of these fundamental principles.

References

Aberbach, Joel. 2007. Supplying the defects of better motives? In The George W. Bush legacy, edited by Colin Campbell, Bert A. Rockman, and Andrew Rudalevige, 112–34. Washington, DC: CQ Press.

American Bar Association. 2006. Task Force on Presidential Signing Statements and the Separation of Powers Doctrine. July 2006. Available from http://www.abanet.org/op/signingstatements/aba_final_signing_statements_recommendation-report_7-24-06.pdf.

Babington, Charles, and Dafna Linzer. 2005. Senator sounded alarm in '03. *Washington Post,* December 20, p. A10.

Babington, Charles, and Jonathan Weisman. 2006. Senate approves detainee bill backed by Bush. *Washington Post,* September 29, p. 1.

Baker, Peter. 2006. GOP infighting on detainees intensifies. *Washington Post,* September 16, p. A01.

Baker, Peter, and Charles Babington. 2005. Bush addresses uproar over spying. *Washington Post,* December 20, p. A01.

Barry, John, Michael Hirsh, and Michael Isikoff. 2004. The roots of torture. *Newsweek,* May 24, Pp. 28–34.

Bazan, Elizabeth B., and Jennifer K. Elsea. 2005. Presidential authority to conduct warrantless electronic surveillance to gather foreign intelligence information. January 5. Washington, DC: Congressional Research Sevice.

Bravin, Jess. 2004. Pentagon report set framework for use of torture. *Wall Street Journal,* June 7.

Brimmett, Richard F. 2006. Authorization for use of military force in response to the 9/11 attacks (P.L. 107–40): Legislative history (RS22357). January 4. Washington, DC: Congressional Research Service.

Bush, George. 2004. President Bush: Information sharing, Patriot Act vital to homeland security. The White House, April 20. Available from http://www.whitehouse.gov/news/releases/2004/04/print/20040420-2.html.

———. 2006. Press conference of the president, September 15. Available from http://www.white-house.gov/news/releases/2006/09/20060915-2.html.

Bybee, Jay S. 2002. Memorandum for Alberto R. Gonzales, counsel to the president re: Standards of conduct for interrogation under 18 U.S.C. Sec. 2340-2340A, August 1, Pp. 1–33. Reprinted in Greenberg and Dratel (2005, 172–217).

Cole, David, Curtis Bradley, Walter Dellinger, Ronald Dworkin, Richard Epstein, Philip B. Heymann et al. 2006. On NSA spying: A letter to Congress. *New York Review of Books,* February 9, p. 42.

Daschle, Tom. 2005. Power we didn't grant. *Washington Post,* December 23, p. A21.

Eggen, Dan. 2006a. 2003 draft legislation covered eavesdropping. *Washington Post,* January 28, p. A02.

———. 2006b. Cheney's remarks fuel torture debate. *Washington Post,* October 27, p. A09.

Elsea, Jennifer K. 2004. Lawfulness of interrogation techniques under the Geneva Conventions. Congressional Research Service Report to Congress (RL32567), September 8. Washington, DC: Congressional Research Sevice.

Fletcher, Michael A. 2006. Bush signs terrorism measure. *Washington Post,* October 18, p. A4.

Garber, Marc N., and Kurt A. Wimmer. 1987. Presidential signing statements as interpretations of legislative intent: An executive aggrandizement of power. *Harvard Journal on Legislation* 24: 367.

Goldsmith, Jack. 2007. *The terror presidency.* New York: Norton.

Greenberg, Karen J., and Joshua L. Dratel, eds. 2005. *The torture papers: The road to Abu Ghraib.* New York: Cambridge University Press.

Grieve, Tim. 2006. The president's power to imprison people foreve. Salon, September 26. Available form http://www.salon.com/politics/war_room/2006/09/26/tyrannical_power/indes.html.

Hamdan v. Rumsfeld, Secretary of Defense et al. Slip Opinion. 2005. Available from http://www.supremecourtus.gov/opinions/05pdf/05-184.pdf.

Hersh, Seymour M. 2004. The gray zone. *New Yorker,* May 24, p. 42.

Hoagland, Jim. 2006. Two leaders' power failures. *Washington Post,* March 9, p. A19.

Kelley, Christopher S. 2005. "Faithfully executing" and "taking care"—The unitary executive and the presidential signing statement. Paper presented at the American Political Science Association annual convention, August 28, Boston.

———. 2007. http://www.users.muohio.edu/kelleycs. Retrieved June 7, 2007.

Klaidman, Daniel. 2004. Homesick for Texas. *Newsweek,* July 12, p. 32.

Klaidman, Daniel, Stuart Taylor, Jr., and Evan Thomas. 2006. Palace revolt. *Newsweek,* February 6, p. 39.

Lewis, Neil A. 2006. Furor over Cheney remark on tactics for terror suspects. *New York Times,* October 28, p. A8.

Lichtblau, Eric. 2006. Bush defends spy program and denies misleading public. *New York Times,* January 2, p. 11.

Lichtblau, Eric, and James Risen. 2006. Justice deputy resisted parts of spy program. *New York Times,* January 1, p. 1.

Pfiffner, James P. 2005. Torture and public policy. *Public Integrity* 7(4): 313–30.

Pincus, Walter. 2006. Waterboarding historically controversial. *Washington Post,* October 5, P. A17.

Reid, Tim. 2006. Republicans defy Bush on tougher CIA interrogation. Times Online, September 15. Available form http://www.timesonline.co.uk/tol/news/world/us_and_americas/article639839.ece.

Sanger, David E. 2005. In address, Bush says he ordered domestic spying. *New York Times,* December 18, p. A01.

Savage, Charlie. 2006. Bush challenges hundreds of laws. Boston Globe, April 30. Available from http://www.boston.com/news/nation/articles/2006/04/30/bush_challenges_hundreds_of_laws/.

———. 2007. *Takeover.* New York: Little Brown.

Schwarz, Frederick A. O., and Aziz Z. Huq. 2007. *Unchecked and unbalanced.* New York: The New Press.

Senate. 1976. Final report of the Select Committee to Study Governmental Operations with Respect to Intelligence Activities. Report no. 94–755. *Intelligence activities and the rights of Americans,* Book II, 94th Cong., 2d sess., April 24, 169.

———. 1978. Report no. 95-511, Title I, 92 Stat. 1796. Codified as amended at 50 U.S.C. par. 1801 et seq. October 25. Available from http://uscode.house.gov/download/pls/50C36.txt.

Shane. Scott, and Adam Liptak. 2006. Shifting power to a president. *New York Times,* September 30, p. 1.

Smith, R. Jeffrey. 2006a. Behind the debate, CIA techniques of extreme discomfort. *Washington Post,* September 16, p. A3.

———. 2006b. Detainee measure to have fewer restrictions. *Washington Post,* September 26, p. 1.

Totenberg, Nina. 2006. Retired Supreme Court justice hits attacks on courts and warns of dictatorship. *The Raw Story,* March 10. Available from http://rawstory.com/news/2006/Retired_Supreme_Court_Justice_hits_attacks_0310.html.

Vice President's Office. 2006. Interview of the vice president by Scott Hennen, WDAY at Radio Day at the White House, October 24. Available from http://www.whitehouse.gov/news/releases/2006/10/print/20061024-7.html.

Walsh, Kenneth T. 2006. The Cheney factor. *U.S. News & World Report,* January 23, p. 48.

White, Josh. 2005. President relents, backs torture ban. *Washington Post,* December 16, p. 1.

White House. 2002. Memorandum re: Humane treatment of al Qaeda and Taliban detainees, signed by President Bush, February 7. Available from http://usinfo.state.gov/xatchives/display.html?p=washfile-english&y=2004&m=June&x=20040623203050cpataruk0.1224024&t=live feeds/wf-latest.html.

———. 20050 President's statement on signing of H.R. 2863, the "Department of Defense, Emergency Supplemental Appropriations to Address Hurricanes in the Gulf of Mexico, and Pandemic Influenza Act, 2006." December 30. Available from http://www.whitehouse.gov/news/releases/2005/12/20051230-8.html.

Yoo, John. 2006. Senate approves broad new rules to try detainees. *New York Times,* September 29, P. 1.

James P. Pfiffner is a university professor in the School of Public Policy at George Mason university. He has written or edited ten books on the presidency and American national government, including The Strategic Presidency, The Modern Presidency, *and* The Character Factor.

AUTHOR'S NOTE: I am grateful to James Dunkerley, dean of the Institute for the Study of the Americas, and Nicholas Mann, dean of the School of Advanced Study at the University of London for their hospitality during my six-month visit with them in 2007 as S. T. Lee Professorial Fellow. Other colleagues in the United States and the United Kingdom gave me helpful comments and advice as this article was being prepared, and I would like to thank Joel Aberbach, sharrar Ali, Niels Bjerre-Poulson, Mary Boardman, Nigel Bowles, Lara M. Brown, Brian Cook, Philip Davies, John Dumbrell, George Edwards, Lou Fisher, Hugh Heclo, Jon Herbert, Mathew Holden, Don Kash, Nancy Kassop, Jeremy Mayer, Iwan Morgan, Dick Pious, Paul Quirk, Jon Roper, Richard Rose, Herman Schwartz, Bob Spitzer, and Jeffrey Weinberg.

On Federalism, Freedom, and the Founders View of Retained Rights

A Reply to Randy Barnett

By Kurt T. Lash

I want to thank Randy Barnett for commenting on my article, *A Textual-Historical Theory of the Ninth Amendment*. Professor Barnett's essays on the Ninth Amendment in the 1990s triggered the modern debate over the original meaning of the Ninth, and his recent book, *Restoring the Lost Constitution*, synthesizes his earlier work and presents a sophisticated theory of constitutional rights.[1] I welcome his thoughts and I completely understand his critical stance regarding my work; if my conclusions are correct they significantly undermine some of Barnett's key assertions about the original meaning and modern application of the Ninth Amendment. In his current essay, I believe that Barnett has identified some conceptual issues that could benefit from some additional clarification. His "individualist" reading of the Ninth and Tenth Amendments, however, is at odds with the common understanding of popular sovereignty at the time of the Founding and is contradicted by key pieces of historical evidence. Most of all, Barnett's failure to address Madison's actual testimony about the federalist meaning of the Ninth and Tenth Amendments critically undermines his effort to put a libertarian spin on an expressly federalist historical record.

Professor Barnett' response[2] and this Reply present only a snapshot of the large historical debate between Barnett and myself regarding the original meaning of the Ninth Amendment. A more detailed look at the original sources which constitute the subject of this debate can be found in two articles I originally published in the *Texas Law Review* and in a forthcoming article in the *Iowa Law Review, The Inescapable Federalism of the Ninth Amendment*.[3] The *Iowa* piece contains an extensive analysis of the historical documents and issues which informed the drafting, ratification, and application of the Ninth Amendment and provides a point-by-point

---

1 *See* Randy E. Barnett, Restoring the Lost Constitution: The Presumption of Liberty (2004).

2 *See* Randy E. Barnett, *Kurt Lash's Majoritarian Difficulty*, 60 Stan. L. Rev. 937 (2008).

3 *See* Kurt T. Lash, *The Inescapable Federalism of the Ninth Amendment*, 93 IOWA L. Rev. (forthcoming 2008), available at http://papers.ssrn.com/abstract=953010.

comparison of Barnett's reading of the evidence with my own. In this brief Reply to Barnett's response essay, I want to clear up some terminological matters and focus on a few of his key historical claims.

1. Terminology

A. Federalism and Majoritarianism

I begin with some issues of terminology. In his current essay, Barnett characterizes my approach to the Ninth Amendment as "majoritarian" (hence the title of his essay). In prior work, however, Barnett described my approach to the Ninth as federalist.[4] I think this latter term best captures my approach to the Ninth since it highlights one of the key differences between Barnett and myself in our reading of the historical record. For example, I *agree* with Barnett that the Ninth protects individual rights from federal abridgment. Where we differ involves the effect of the Ninth Amendment on the states. Barnett believes the retained rights of the Ninth are individual in nature and this limited set of rights is applied against the states by way of the Fourteenth Amendment's Privilege or Immunities Clause. I, on the other hand, view the Ninth as protecting both individual and collective rights against federal abridgment.[5] Although some individual rights originally left to state control were applied against the states through the adoption of the Fourteenth Amendment, many (indeed, most) remain under the collective control of the people in the states, free from undue federal interference (including interference from federal courts) even after the adoption of the Fourteenth. Aspects of the original federalist protections of the Ninth thus remain in effect.

B. Individual v. Non-Individual Rights

Once of the issues which may give rise to some confusion regards how Professor Barnett and I define individual rights. As I use the term, individual rights are those which can be exercised by an individual alone. For example, a single individual may engage in the right to free speech by openly criticizing the government. Collective and majoritarian rights, on the other hand, can only be exercised by a defined group of individuals, for example the people in convention

---

4 *See* Randy E. Barnett, The Ninth Amendment: It Means What It Says, 85 Tex. L. Rev. 1, 19(2006).

5 Professor Barnett finds it significant that I employ terms that are not (or are rarely) found in the original sources, such as "majoritarian" and "collective." Of course neither can one find Barnett's preferred term "individual natural rights" in any original source discussing the Ninth Amendment. The reason Barnett and I use these terms is in order to communicate our best reading of the original meaning of the Ninth Amendment in terms familiar to modern constitutionalists.

exercising their collective right to alter or abolish their form of government.[6] The theory of popular sovereignty maintains that no one person can (legitimately) exercise this power alone, but only as a participant in a collective act. The same is true for any action that requires the assent of a majority. One can, of course, conceive of collective and majoritarian rights as "individual rights" in the sense that each member of the defined group has a right to participate in the group action (a "share" of the collective right, if you will). But this does not make the collective or majoritarian right "individualist" unless one is willing to destroy the distinction between individual and non-individual rights. The Founders certainly did not.[7]

C. Collective and Majoritarian Rights

Professor Barnett believes that I have not properly distinguished between collective and majoritarian rights. Perhaps some clarification is in order, but Barnett is wrong to think the terms are completely independent. Collective rights *are* majoritarian rights. When meeting in their collective sovereign capacity (for example, in convention), a majority of "the people" have the right to determine their fundamental law.[8] Rights and powers which the people leave to the ordinary political process are *also* controlled through majoritarian procedures (both in voting for representatives and in representative voting). Thus, although I agree with Barnett that a retained sovereign right is not the same thing as a right held by a governing majority, the majority of the collective people nevertheless have the right to determine which of their retained rights shall or shall not be delegated to a governing majority. Although Barnett may disagree with this on account of his libertarian theory of constitutional legitimacy, the Founders embraced a theory of government that Barnett affirmatively *rejects:* popular sovereignty.[9]

---

6 A single government act may violate *both* an individual and a collective right, such as occurred when congress passed the Alien and Sedition Act. According to Madison, this Act violated both the individual right to free speech and the collective right of the states protected by the Tenth Amendment. *See* Kurt T. Lash, *A Textual-Historical Theory of the Ninth Amendment,* 60 Stan. L. Rev. 895, 911 (2008).

7 At the time of the Founding, distinguishing between persons and "the People" was of critical importance. *See* Christian G. Fritz, American Sovereigns: The People and America's Constitutional Tradition Before the Civil War 9.-100 (2008) (discussing early struggles over how to define the difference between the acts of mere individuals (and individual factions) and the true sovereign acts of "the people" in conventions).

8 For example, a number of states ratified the original Constitution by majority vote, despite the existence of state constitutional provisions seemingly requiring a supermajority vote. *See* Akhil Reed Amar, *Philadelphia Revisited: Amending the Constitution Outside Article V,* 55 U. Chi. L. Rev. 1043, 1049 (1988).

9 *Compare* Barnett, *supra* note 1, at 11–14 (rejecting popular sovereignly as a normative theory of constitutional legitimacy), *with* Gordon S. Wood, The Creation of the American Republic: 1776–1787 344–89 (1998) (describing the Founders' embrace of popular sovereignty). Although Barnett quixotically attempts to make sovereignty an individual right, outside of a monarchy, and individual cannot exercise sovereign power. This is what distinguishes individual from nonindividual rights.

It is possible that part of what Barnett is driving at is the distinction between the ordinary majorities of the political process and the "higher law" majorities of the people acting in their collective sovereign capacity (such as during a constitutional convention). If so, Barnett is right to distinguish between the two kinds of majorities, but the distinction makes no difference to my overall thesis: the Ninth Amendment leaves certain matters under the control of the sovereign people in the states who may then either place the matter beyond the reach of ordinary political majorities (by enshrining a right in their state constitution) or leave the matter within the hands of the state legislature and the ordinary political process.[10] In other words, the point of my articles on the Ninth Amendment is not o celebrate majoritarianism as such, but to recapture the Ninth Amendment's federalist focus on the people's retained right to decide certain matters on a state level.

In past essays I have contrasted my federalist model with what I refer to as Barnett's libertarian model—a characterization to which he has not previously objected. Here, Barnett seems to think I use the term disparagingly,[11] preferring instead to call his approach "individualist" or an "individual rights" model of the Ninth Amendment. I cannot agree with Barnett's attempt to claim the rhetorical high ground as providing the "pro-individual rights" reading of the Ninth Amendment. Barnett's approach to the Ninth Amendment is no more protective of individual rights than mine (a point he seems to recognize, however grudgingly).[12] Both of us believe that the Ninth Amendment protected individual rights against federal action and *did not* protect individual rights against state action. Barnett, however, insists that the Ninth protected *only* individual rights and that this same set of rights is protected against state action by the Fourteenth Amendment. It is because his approach links the Ninth and Fourteenth Amendments and envisions a "presumption of liberty" against *any* government action that I label his approach libertarian.[13]

By embracing the term "federalist," I bear the burden of overcoming the pejorative associations of the term with the dark historical legacy of "states' rights" rhetoric. Today, it is common to view state majorities, and not the national government, as the more likely offender

---

10 Barnett embraces a libertarian theory of rights which constrains the power of the people in the states to pass certain laws, even in the absence of any specific constitutional restriction. *See generally* Barnett, *supra* note 1. Whatever the merits of Barnett's normative theory of liberty, at the time of the Founding, the people of the states *did* exercise control over individual liberty on a variety of subjects that we today would consider violations of fundamental rights, from the establishment of religion to the prohibition of speech defaming Jesus Christ. *See* Kurt T. Lash *Power and the Subject of Religion,* 59 Ohio St. L.J. 1069 (1998).

11 *See* Barnett, supra note 2, at 965.

12 Barnett has never refuted my claim that my federalist reading of the Ninth also protects individual rights. *See id.* His argument is that I am wrong to read the Ninth as *also* protecting collective majoritarian rights.

13 Although I refute Barnett's claims about a libertarian Ninth Amendment, I take no position on the theoretical workability of libertarian constitutionalism.

of individual freedoms. At the time of the Founding, however, the primary concern of those whose votes were critical to ratification was the potentially tyrannical federal government. This middle group generally considered preserving the sovereign prerogatives of the people in the states to be the best way of preserving individual rights. As Samuel Adams (an eventual supporter of the Constitution) wrote to Richard Henry Lee:

> I mean my friend, to let you know how deeply I am impressed with a sense of the Importance of Amendments; that the good People may clearly see the distinction, for there is a distinction, between the *federal* Powers vested in Congress, and the *sovereign* Authority belonging to the several States, which is the Palladium of the private, and personal rights of the Citizens.[14]

Men like Adams, who ratified the Constitution on the condition of an added Bill of Rights, did so because they believed that prohibiting any unduly latitudinous construction of federal power would protect state autonomy and thereby preserve individual liberty. If the idea of preserving individual liberty through the mechanism of state-protective amendments seems counterintuitive, one need only recall the controversy over the nationally enacted Alien and Sedition Acts. These statues are stark reminders of how broad assertions of federal power can threaten individual liberty. Madison himself insisted that the Acts violated both individual freedom and the reserved powers of the people in the several states.[15]

D. Democracy v. Majoritariansim

Having labeled my approach "majoritarian," Professor Barnett proceeds to try and show how the key players in the Founding were *antimajoritarian*. In his attempt to establish the antimajoritarian nature of the Philadelphia Convention, for example, Barnett quotes concerns about "democracy" and equates these with concerns about majoritarianism.[16] The Founders concerns about "democracy," however, referred to the failure of wisdom and virtue in the state legislatures, not the fundamental concept of majority rule.[17] Many of the Founders (and all of the ones quoted by Barnett in this section) believed that the ruling class should be made up of a natural aristocracy, men of education and property who understood the long term needs of the community. The radically egalitarian nature of the Revolution, however, opened the doors to a much broader class of political representatives which, in the minds of many Founders, diluted both the

---

14 Letter from Samuel Adams to Richard Henry Lee (Aug. 24, 1789), *in* Creating the Bill of Rights: The Documentary Record from the First Federal Congress, 286 (Helen E. Veit et al. eds., 1991).

15 *See* James Madison, Virginia Resolutions Against the Alien and Sedition Acts, Dec. 21, 1798, *in* Writings 589 (Jack N. Rakove ed., 1999); *see also* Madison, Report on the Alien and Sedition Acts (1800), *in* Writing, supra, at 608 [hereinafter Madison, Report on the Alien and Sedition Acts].

16 *See* Barnett, *supra* note 2, at 943

17 *See* Wood, *supra* note 9, at 474–75.

virtue and economic wisdom necessary for a properly functioning legislature.[18] The men who met in Philadelphia were members of the aristocracy who had suffered through the consequences of this "leveling" of democratic rule.[19] Madison shared the Founders' general concerns about "leveled democracy," and thus stressed the republican benefits of majoritarian elections held in an extended republic.[20] This process would both protect minorities (a group which included creditors) and help ensure that federal legislation would reflect the long term *collective* interests of the community thus avoiding many of the "democratic" problems plaguing the states. In short, concerns about "democracy" were not so much antimajoritarian as they were pro-republican, a very different matter.[21]

State legislation, however, remained a problem which Madison unsuccessfully attempted to address through a proposed amendment which would have protected the individual right to religious and expressive freedom in the states.[22] Madison's failed amendment illustrates his commitment to individual rights, a fact that leads Barnett to insist that Madison must have drafted a Bill which also protected individual rights. I, of course, agree: Madison *did* draft a Bill protecting individual rights. What is at issue is whether these were the *only* rights protected by the Bill. Barnett's purely individualist reading of the Ninth and Tenth Amendments leads him to take a purely individualist view of the concept of "the people." Analyzing this claim requires us to back up a bit and consider the nature of popular sovereignty at the time of the Founding.

E. Popular Sovereignty and the Federal Constitution

American popular sovereignty has its roots in England where "the people" came to be associated with the people's representative in Parliament. The emphasis here was not on individual citizens, but on a collective governmental body meeting in its official capacity. As Edmund Morgan put it, "[m]ere people, however many in number, were not *the* people."[23] Instead, Parliament was viewed as the embodiment of the *people themselves*.[24] The concept of popular sovereignty found

---

18 *See* id.

19 Barnett insists that I explain how my view of the Ninth differs from the Republican Guarantee Clause. One obvious difference is that the Ninth limits federal power whereas the Guarantee Clause stands as a *grant* of federal authority to intervene in cases of local insurrection, a problem often attributed to an unduly "democratic" spirit. *See generally* Fritz, *supra* note 7, at 80–116 (discussion how fear of popular insurrection influenced the Framers).

20 *See* The Federalist No. 10, at 82–84 (James Madison) (Clinton Rossiter ed., 1961).

21 As Madison put it in *Federalist No. 10*, *"To secure the public good and private rights against the danger of such a faction, and at the same time to preserve the spirit and form of popular government is then the great object to which our inquiries are directed." Id.* At 80 (emphasis added).

22 *See* I Documentary History of the First Federal Congress of the United States of America: March 4, 1789–March 3, 1791, at 158 (Linda Grant De Pauw et al. eds., 1972).

23 Edmund S. Morgan, Inventing the People: The Rise of Popular Sovereignty in England and America 60 (1988).

24 *See* Bruce Ackerman, We The People: Foundations 9 (1991) (discussing how under the English Parliamentary system, the government has the full sovereign authority to act in the name of "We the

its way to the English colonies where it evolved in the period between the Revolution and the adoption of the Constitution, with the critical development being a distinction between the government and the sovereign people. As chronicled by Gordon Wood, the idea evolved that the people collectively held ultimate law making authority which they exercised when meeting in special extra-governmental conventions.[25] As Chris Fritz has recently noted, although "the people" at the time of the Founding excluded numerous groups, the concept remained nevertheless collective.[26] No doubt, each member of the accepted polity held a "share" of the "people's sovereignty," but this is what makes the right collective as opposed to individual.

Prior to the adoption of the Constitution, "the people" existed as independent sovereigns in the "free and independent" states. When the people met in their state conventions to consider the proposed Constitution, one of the major issues became whether they would remain an independent sovereign people after ratifying the Constitution. The issue of potential "consolidation" kept many moderates on the fence in regard to the proposed Constitution. Federalists who supported the Constitution thus were at pains to assure these doubters that ratifying the Constitution would not affect a "consolidation" of the states into one unified and undifferentiated mass.[27] As Alexander Hamilton wrote in *Federalist No. 32*, "State governments would clearly retain all the rights of sovereignty which they before had, and which were not by [the Constitution] *exclusively* delegated to the United States."[28] Madison similarly insisted that the proposed Constitution was "neither a national nor a federal Constitution, but a composition of both," which "leaves to the several States a residuary and inviolable sovereignty over all [non-delegated] objects."[29] It was because the doubters were not altogether convinced by these promises that supporters of the Constitution ultimately were forced to produce a Bill of Rights ensuring limits on the power of the federal government. In short, had the Ninth and Tenth Amendments declared a unified national people, not only would they have been rejected by the states, this would have imperiled the Federalist effort to ratify and preserve the Federal Constitutions.[30]

Although Barnett is right to view James Madison as suspicious of state majorities, in 1791 Madison's primary concern was passing a Bill that would answer concerns raised in the state conventions which, if unanswered, might ultimately lead to a second national convention. This required drafting a Bill of Rights that reflected the concerns of moderates in the state conventions who were far more comfortable with local government than with extensive powers

---

People")

25 *See* Wood, *supra* note 9, at 319–43.

26 *See* Fritz, *supra* note 7, at 5.

27 *See* Wood, *supra* note 9, at 524–32 (discussing Federalist assurances that the proposed Constitution would not result in the consolidation of the states into a single national mass).

28 Federalist no. 32, at 198 (Alexander Hamilton) (Clinton Rossiter ed., 1961).

29 Federalist No. 39, at 246, 245 (James Madison) (Clinton Rossiter ed., 1961).

30 Leonard W. Levy, Origins of the Bill of Rights 39 (1999) (discussing Madison's belief that adding a Bill of Rights would help head off a second constitutional convention).

of the proposed and untried national government. The result was a series of amendments which managed to simultaneously protect individuals against federal action while preserving the retained sovereign rights and powers of the people in the states.[31] As United States Supreme Court Justice Samuel Chase wrote only a few years after the adoption of the Bill of Rights:

> All power, jurisdiction, and rights of sovereignty, not granted by the people by that instrument, or relinquished, are still retained by them in their several States, and in their respective State Legislatures, according to their forms of government.[32]

Having clarified some of the critical terms in this debate, before moving to the history it is worth pausing a moment to clarify Professor Barnett's and my claims about the Ninth Amendment. I claim that the Founders understood the "other rights" of the Ninth Amendment to include all manner of retained rights, individual and otherwise.[33] The Ninth established a rule of strict construction which reserved ultimate authority over all these rights to the collective Sovereign people in the several states. Professor Barnett insists, on the other hand, that the "other rights" of the Ninth include *only* individual rights. Indeed, Barnett insists that *every* time "the people" is used in the Bill of Rights it refers to individual people and not the people as a collective.[34] In light of the history surrounding the Bill of Rights in general, and the Ninth Amendment in particular, Barnett has chosen a burden too heavy to carry.

II. History

A. The Ninth Amendment as Madison's "Sui Generis" Contribution to the Bill of Rights

Professor Barnet insists that Madison drafted an Amendment which reflected the Federalists' worries about how a Bill of Rights might be read as an exclusive list of limitations on federal power, and that none of the proposals emanating from the state conventions addressed this particular concern.[35] A quick look at the state proposals contradicts his assertion. Consider, for example, Virginia's 17th proposed amendment:

---

31 *See* Fritz, supra note 7, at 205–06 ("Madison—like many other Americans—viewed the people as a collective sovereign—made up of the people of the several states.").

32 Campbell v. Morris, 3 H. & McH. 535, 554–55 (Md. 1797).

33 It is important to bear in mind that rights at the time of the Founding included all of these categories. *See* Richard A. Primus, the American Language of Rights 124 (1999) ("Rights [at the time of the Founding] were predicated sometimes of individuals, sometimes of government institution, sometimes of "the people" as a collective, sometimes of abstractions like colonies or countries.").

34 *See* Barnett, supra note 2, at 946.

35 *Id*. At 108.

That those clauses which declare that Congress shall not exercise certain powers be not interpreted in any manner whatsoever to extend the powers of Congress. But that they may be construed either as making exceptions to the specified powers where this shall be the case, or otherwise as inserted merely for greater caution.[36]

This is a straightforward attempt to avoid reading a list of enumerated rights as implying otherwise unlimited federal power. This is the very concern that Barnett claims the state proposals did not address.[37] Other states proposed similar amendments.[38] Although these proposals use the language of denied powers rather than "enumerated rights," the meaning was the same to the Founders. As Madison wrote the same year he drafted the Ninth Amendment, limiting federal power amounted to the "same thing" as securing a right.[39] Madison's original version of the Ninth echoed the same concern raised by Virginia and other states:

The exceptions here or elsewhere in the constitution, made in favor of particular rights, shall not be so construed as to diminish the just importance of other rights retained by the people; or as to enlarge the powers delegated by the constitution; but either as actual limitations of such powers, or as inserted merely for greater caution.[40]

---

36 Amendments Proposed by the Virginia Convention (June 27, 1788), *in* The Complete Bill of Rights: The Drafts, Debates, Sources, and Origins 675 (Neil H. Cogan ed., 1997) [hereinafter Complete Bill of Rights]. North Carolina submitted the same proposal as Virginia. James Madison was a member of the committee that drafted the Virginia proposal, and he expressly noted the role the Virginia proposals played in his propose draft of the Bill of Rights. *See* Letter from James Madison to George Washington (Nov. 20, 1789), *in* 2 The Bill of Rights: A Documentary History 1185 (Bernard Schwartz ed., 1971).

37 Oddly, Barnett associates Virginia's seventeenth proposed amendment with Article II of the Articles of Confederation. *See* Barnett, *supra* note 2, at 961 n. 116 (Article II of the Articles of confederation "tracks Virginia's 17th proposed amendment"). This is not correct. Article II states, "Each state retains its sovereignty, freedom and independence, and every power, jurisdiction and right which is not by this Confederation expressly delegated to the United States in Congress assembled." Art. II, Articles of Confederation (1781). This is clearly echoed in Virginia's first proposed amendment which stated "[1] that each State in the Union shall respectively retain every power, jurisdiction and right which is not by this Constitution delegated to the Congress of the United States or to the departments of the Federal Government." Amendments Proposed by the Virginia Convention (June 27, 1788), in Complete Bill of Rights, supra note 36, at 675. Bothe Article II and Virginia's first proposed amendment are obvious precursors to the Tenth Amendment.

38 *See* Lash, *supra* note 3, at notes 49–54 and accompanying text.

39 *See* Letter from James Madison to George Washington (Dec. 5, 1789), *in* 5 Documentary History of the Constitution of the United States of America, 1786–1870, at 221–22 (1905) [hereinafter Documentary History of the Constitution].

40 James Madison, Speech in Congress Proposing Constitutional Amendments, June 8, 1789, *in* Writings, *supra* note 15, at 437, 443.

Madison's draft has a fairly obvious relation to Virginia's "17th proposal" (which Madison *also* helped draft).Although the ultimate deletion of the "enlarged powers" language raised concerns in Virginia, Madison insisted that the final version of the Ninth continued to reflect the same concerns raised by Virginia's 17th proposal. At the time, Madison explained all of this in a letter to George Washington.[41] Although Barnett and others have attempted to characterize this letter as meaning something other than its plain language, recently uncovered evidence involving the debate in the Virginia Assembly strongly supports the view that Madison meant what he wrote.

B. The Virginia Debates

Ignoring what Madison actually *said* about the final language of the Ninth Amendment,[42] Barnett embraces a reading of the Ninth that Madison expressly *rejected*—the exaggerated claims of the Anti-Federalist majority in the Virginia Senate. This is puzzling for a number of reasons, not the least if which is the fact that, if their reading of the proposed Bill of Rights reflected any kind of widespread understanding, the Ninth (and probably the entire Bill) would have been rejected.[43] This was, after all, the Anti-Federalists' goal.[44] In other works, I have emphasized the importance of the dispute over the Ninth Amendment in the Virginia Assembly.[45] Not becayse I think the Anti-Federalists had the correct understanding of the Ninth, but because the Virginia debate in its entirety sheds important light on letters Madison

---

41 *See* Letter from James Madison to George Washington (Dec. 5, 1789), *in* 5 Documentary History of the Constitution, *supra* 39, at 221–22.

42 I am referring to Madison's remarks both in his letter to Washington, *supra* note 40, and in his speech against the proposed Bank of the United States. *See* James Madison, Speech in Congress Opposing the National Bank, Feb. 2, 1791, *in* Writings, *supra* note 15, 480, 480–90.

43 The Senate majority's claims about the Tenth Amendment, for example, were an obvious effort to make the Tenth as objectionable as possible by claiming that it referred to the consolidated people of the United States, rather the people in the several states. The Tenth Amendment would never have been ratified under such a reading given the widespread fears (and Federalist denials) that the proposed Constitution would consolidate the states into a single undifferentiated national people. For an historical study of the true, and rather surprising, purpose behind the addition of "or to the people" to the Tenth Amendment, see Kurt T. Lash, *The Original Meaning of an omission: The Tenth Amendment, Popular Sovereignty and "Expressly" Delegated Power,* 83 Notre Dame L. Rev. (forthcoming May 2008).

44 *See* Levy, *supra* note 30, at 42 (discussing how the Anti-Federalists in Virginia wished to "sabotage the Bill of Rights").

45 Barnett gently chides me for seeming to have abandoned claims made in earlier pieces regarding the significance of the Virginia debates regarding the Ninth Amendment. *See* Barnett, *supra* note 2, at 953 n. 71. Once again, this essay focuses on the text of the Ninth Amendment and discusses history only as it supports the apparent meaning of the text. For an in depth study of Virginia Debates and their significance in terms of the original meaning of the Ninth Amendments, see Lash, *supra* note 3, at notes 10.-33 and accompanying text.

and others wrote in response to that debate. Again, interested readers can find my full analysis of the Virginia Debates in another article.[46] For now, it is enough to say that Barnett's reliance on the unsuccessful politically driven views of the Virginia Anti-Federalists is a rather curious choice for representing the true original meaning of the Ninth and Tenth Amendments.[47] I'll stick with Madison.

Madison did not limit his federalist description of the Ninth Amendment to his private letters but publicly announced this understanding in a major speech that he delivered while the Bill of Rights remained pending in the states.[48] I have discussed Madison's speech opposing the Bank of the United States in detail elsewhere[49] but readers should be aware that not only does this speech contain a detailed account of the origins and meaning of the Ninth and Tenth Amendments, it stands as the most detailed discussion of any of the first ten amendments while the Bill remained pending before the states.

In his speech, Madison explained that advocates of the proposed Constitution had assured doubters in the state conventions that delegated federal power would be narrowly construed.[50] The state conventions had appended declarations along with their notice of ratification reflecting their reliance on the rule of strict construction.[51] According to Madison, the Bill of Rights had been added to make this rule an express part of the Constitution with the Ninth Amendment preventing a "latitude of interpretation" and the Tenth Amendment "excluding every source of power not within the constitution itself."[52] Finally, Madison insisted that the proper application of these amendments would protect the reserved powers of the state governments.[53] Madison thus presented the Ninth and Tenth Amendments as federalist guardians of the collective powers and rights of the people in the state. No account of the original meaning of the Ninth Amendment is complete (to put it mildly) without addressing Madison" Bank speech, but it is nowhere to be found in Barnett's essay.

---

46 *See* Lash, *supra* note 3.

47 If one accepts the Senate Report as an accurate representation of the public meaning of the proposed amendments, then presumably one accepts the Senate's claim that the Free Exercise Clause "does not prohibit the rights of conscience from being violated or infringed," and the Establishment Clause allows Congress to "levy taxes, to any amount, for the support of religion or its preachers; and any particular denomination of Christians might be so favored and supported by the general government. …" *See* Saturday, December 12, 1789, Journal of the Senate of the Commonwealth of Virginia 60, 62 (Richmond 1828).

48 *See* Madison, *supra* note 42, at 480–490.

49 *See* Lash, *supra* note 3 (manuscript at 38 & n.134).

50 *See* Madison, *supra* note 42, at 489.

51 *Id.*

52 *Id.*

53 *Id.* At 490.

C. St. George Tucker

"[The federal Constitution] is a compact freely, voluntarily, and solemnly entered into by the several states, and ratified by the people thereof, respectively. ..."

—St. George Tucker[54]

Historians familiar with Tucker's work and its place in early constitutional theory know that Tucker presented a sophisticated and influential federalist reading of the Constitution as a compact between the people of the individual states. A strong advocate of the retained sovereignty of the people in the states, Tucker believed that the original Articles of Confederation remained operative even after the adoption of the federal Constitution unless expressly overruled. This meant that Tucker believed states continued to retain all powers, jurisdictions and rights not expressly delegated to the United States, including the "right of withdrawing itself from the confederacy without the consent of the rest."[55] Not surprisingly, Tucker's states' rights view of the Constitution came under heavy fire in Joseph Story's *nationalist* 1833 Commentaries on the Constitution.[56]

Barnett insists that Tucker embraced an individual rights reading of the Ninth Amendment. If by this Barnett means that Tucker believed the rights protected by the Ninth included individual rights, I would agree. Barnett, however, insists that Tucker had a purely individualist reading of the people in both the Ninth and Tenth Amendments. This simply is not true. For example, Tucker's first reference to the Ninth and Tenth Amendment presents them as protecting collective rights, in particular the collective right of the people to alter or abolish an abusive government.[57] Even in those place where Tucker speaks of the people's retained personal indi-

---

54 St. George Tucker, *View of the Constitution of the United States, in* 1 Blackstone's Commentaries app. 140, app. 155 (photo. Reprint 1969) (St. George Tucker ed., William Birch Young & Abraham Small 1803).

55 St.George Tucker, *Of the Several Forms of Government, in* 1 Blackstone's Commentaries, *supra* note 54, at app. 7 & app. 75.

56 See, e.g., 1 Joseph Story, Commentaries on the Constitution of the United States 393–407 (Melville M. Bigelow ed., William S. Hein & Co. 5th ed.1994) (1833). For a discussion of Story's treatment of Tucker's constitutional theories, see Kurt T. Lash, *"Tucker's Rule": St. George Tucker and the Limited Construction of Federal Power,* 47 Wm. & Mary L. Rev. 1343, 1382 (2006).

57 According to Tucker:

It must be owned that Mr. Locke, and other theoretical writers, have held, that "there remains still inherent in the people a supreme power to remove or alter the legislative when they find the legislative act contrary to the trust reposed in them: for, when such trust is abused, it is thereby forfeited, and devolves to those who gave it."

2 Blackstone's Commentaries, *supra* note 54, at 161. In the footnote accompanying this text, Tucker states "[t]his principle is expressly recognized in our Government" and cites the Ninth and Tenth Amendments (which Tucker refers to as "Amendments to the C.U.S. Art. 11, 12"). *Id.* At n.25.

vidual rights, he clearly follow the federalist model I present in my article regarding the dual nature of retained individual rights. According to Tucker, the reason *why* federal power must be strictly construed when impinging upon personal rights is because the individual remains under a prior obligation to the collective people of his particular state.[58]

The entire thrust of Tucker's work was to construct a federalist theory of state autonomy. This is certainly how his treatise was received at the time. For example one of Tucker's contemporaries, Judge John Overton, a member of the second North Carolina Ratifying Convention that ratified the Ninth Amendment cites the exact same passage Professor Barnett reads as establishing an "individualist" account of the Ninth. Unlike Barnett, however, Overton reads Tucker as presenting a federalist reading of the Ninth and Tenth Amendments.[59] So did later commentators like Joseph Story. In the end, whatever else one makes of Tucker, one cannot understand his work as conflicting in any way with his fundamental theory of the retained sovereignty of the people in the several states. Doing so contradicts a mountain of historical scholarship, the understanding of his contemporaries, and the testimony of Tucker himself.

D. The Tenth Amendment

One of the more surprising aspects of Barnett's essay is his attempt to characterize the people as a solely "individualist" expression throughout the Bill of Rights. I do not dispute that the term could be used in conjunction with individual as well as collective rights, but Barnett insists that "when the Bill of Rights uses the term 'the people' it consistently refers to individuals and not political collectives or electoral majorities, and all the enumerated rights it protects belong to individuals and not collectives or majorities."[60] Rather startlingly, Barnett insists that "the people" is used only in an "individualist" and not a collective sense in both the Ninth *and* Tenth Amendments. His only evidence in support of this rather unprecedented claim about the Tenth is the Report of the Virginia Senate and the fact that "people" is used in reference to individual rights elsewhere in the Bill of Rights and in statements made by the majority in *Chisholm v. Georgia.*[61]

---

58 Tucker, *supra* note 54, at app. 151 ("[A]s a social compact it ought likewise to receive the same strict construction, wherever the right of personal liberty, of personal security, or of private property may become the subject of dispute; because every person whose liberty or property was thereby rendered subject to the new government, was antecedently a member of a civil society to whose regulations he had submitted himself, and under whose authority and protection he still remains, in all cases not expressly submitted to the new government.").

59 *See* Kurt T. Lash, *A Textual-Historical Theory of the Ninth Amendment,* 60 Stan. L. Rev. 896. 918–19 (2008). Barnett rests his reading of Tucker on the same passage cited in support of federalist reading by Judge Overton. See Barnett, *supra* note 2, at 960.

60 Barnett, *supra* note 2, at 926.

61 *Id.* At 953–54.

To begin with, I disagree with his reading of the Virginia Senate and the *Chisholm* majority. These were not attempts to establish an individualist reading of "the people." Instead, both examples involve attempts to establish a *national* reading of "the People" (though for very different reasons). Nevertheless, I do not deny that rights of the people were understood to include individual as well as collective rights. All such rights, however, were retained under the sovereign control of the collective people in the states. Thus, when Congress passed the Sedition Act, Madison maintained that it had violated the individual right to free speech, and trespassed on a matter reserved to the collective people in the states under the Tenth Amendment.[62] Tucker also referred to powers reserved to the people under the Tenth Amendment as including individual rights—but only those prohibited to both the federal and state governments by the federal *and state* constitutions. Reserving powers to the people, and not their state governments, in other words, required a collective act of the sovereign people in the states.[63]

On the other hand, Barnett is right to point out that Tucker read both the Ninth and Tenth Amendments as calling for a strict construction of federal power, and that this differs from statements I've made in the past that only the Ninth, and not the Tenth, represented a rule of construction.[64] As far as Tucker's reading of the Tenth as a rule of construction is concerned, it is clear that he was deeply influenced by James Madison's 1800 *Report on the Virginia Resolutions,* a report that focused on Tenth Amendment objections to the Alien and Sedition Acts.[65] However, Tucker was not alone in reading the Tenth as calling for a narrow construction of federal power.[66] Thus, I concede that although the primary semantic meaning of the Tenth simply declares the principle of reserved non-delegated power, the text was often read as implying a rule of strict construction. Barnett may believe that conceding this secondary (implied) meaning of the Tenth somehow undermines my claims about the Ninth. I think not. As my research of the Founding has progressed, I have become more and more convinced that these amendments were generally understood as working in combination. This

---

62 *See* Madison, supra note 15, at 610.

63 Tucker cites, in this regard, the rights protected from federal or state action in Article I, Sections 9 and 10. *See* I Blackstone's Commentaries, *supra* note 54, at app. 308–09. These restrictions on state power, of course, did not go into effect until after being ratified by the people in their separate state conventions. As Chris Fritz has recently put it, these state ratifying conventions simultaneously ratified the federal constitution and amended their own state constitution to the degree necessary to accommodate the federal text. *See* Fritz, *supra* note 7, 140.

64 *See,* e.g., Lash, *The Lost Original Meaning of the Ninth Amendment,* 83 Tex. L. Rev. 331, 336 (2004) (the Tenth "does not prevent expansive interpretations of enumerated federal powers" (emphasis omitted)).

65 *See* Madison, Report on the Alien and Sedition Acts, *supra* note 15, at 608; Kurt T. Lash, *James Madison's Celebrated Report of 1800: The Transformation of the Tenth Amendment,* 74 Geo. Wash. L. Rev. 165, 182–83 & n. 141 (2006). In my upcoming Iowa piece, *The Inescapable Federalism of the Ninth Amendment, supra* note 3, I explain *why* Madison focused on the Tenth Amendment, and not the Ninth, in his criticism of the Alien and Sedition Acts. *See id.* at nn. 229–49 and accompanying text.

66 *See generally* Lash, *supra* note 43.

explains the remarkably consistent pattern of their joint citation in support of the retained sovereignty of the people in the several states.[67] Nevertheless, I remain convinced that Madison presented the *best* original semantic understanding of the amendments in his speech, where he presented the Ninth as controlling a latitude of construction and the Tenth as limiting the federal government to delegated powers.

E. The Relevance of the Eleventh Amendment

Finally, I strongly agree with Barnett's view that the debates which led to the adoption of the Eleventh Amendment are relevant to our understanding the original meaning of the Ninth. I have felt this way for some time (actually, it was research into the Eleventh amendment that ultimately led me to the Ninth). A deep investigation of the original meaning of the Eleventh Amendment is beyond the scope of this (already long) reply. There are a few intriguing clues, however, that suggest the issue is well worth exploring.

To begin with, notice the text of the Eleventh Amendment:

> The Judicial power of the United States shall not be construed to extend to any suit in law or equity, commenced or prosecuted against one of the United States by Citizens of another State, or by Citizens or Subjects of any Foreign State.[68]

Why add the seemingly superfluous phrase "shall not be construed" instead of simply stating that "the judicial power of the United States shall not extend"? The phrase would not be superfluous, of course, if it was meant to signal that the Chisholm majority had wrongly construed the judicial power of the United States. An original version of the Eleventh, in fact, did not include the "construed" language—it was rejected. We also know that those who led the movement to add the amendment understood that they had three choices: accept the Court's decision (and prepare to be sued); reject the Court's reasoning and add an amendment clarifying the original understanding; or accept the Court's reasoning as correct, but nevertheless add an amendment because the results now seemed inexpedient.[69] The second view, that the Court had misconstrued the Constitution, was repeated throughout the states that called for a response to *Chisholm*.[70] Again, the text also appears to coincide with the second

---

67 Full a comprehensive account of the post-adoption jurisprudence of the Ninth and Tenth Amendments, see Kurt T. Lash, *The Lost Jurisprudence of the Ninth Amendment*, 83 Tex. L. Rev. 597 (2005).

68 U.S. Const. amend. XII.

69 See John Hancock's Address to the Massachusetts General Court (Sept. 18, 1793), *reprinted in* 5 Documentary History of the Supreme Court of the United States, 1789-1800, 417 (Maeva Marcus ed., 1994) [hereinafter Documentary History of the Supreme Court].

70 For just a few of many examples, see Brutus, Indep. Chron. (Boston, Mass.), July 18, 1793, reprinted in Documentary History of the Supreme Court, *supra* note 69, at 392 ("If you acquiesce in the

choice. Finally, had the amendment been drafted as an exception from otherwise preexisting power, this would have called into play the rule of construction where an exception to a rule strengthens the otherwise applicable rule. This is John Manning's view of the Eleventh, a view Barnett expressly shares.[71] This approach reads the Eleventh as expressing the very opposite rule of the Ninth: the enumeration of one immunity *shall be construed* to deny other immunities. But the Eleventh appears to be drafted in precisely the opposite manner: the language "shall not be construed" suggests that, instead of declaring an exception to a pre-existing power, the amendment clarifies the proper application of a pre-existing rule. The Manning-Barnett approach thus seems to conflict with both the text and the views of those who called for the amendment.

But these are just textual and historical clues. They suggest that an investigation of the historical Eleventh Amendment may reveal a far deeper connection between the Ninth, Tenth and Eleventh Amendments than has yet been appreciated. While I cannot hope to sufficiently explore those connections here, I'll close this section with the statement of a theorist whose views Professor Barnett respects: St. George Tucker. Here is Tucker's statement on the Eleventh Amendment:

> If it be asked, what would be the consequence in case the federal government should exercise powers not warranted by the constitution, the answer seems to be, that where the act of usurpation may immediately affect an individual, the remedy is to be sought by recourse to that judiciary, to which the cognizance of the case properly belongs, Where it may affect a state, the state legislature, whose rights will be invaded by every such act, will be ready to mark the innovation and sound the alarm to the people [citing the Federalist Papers]: and thereby either effect a

---

construction given to the Federal Constitution, relative to the judiciary powers thereby vested in the Federal Government, (which two of the Associate Judges have decided in favor of their own jurisdiction) you will seal your own *extinction*, as a legislative body."); Governor John Hancock, Address to the Massachusetts General Court (Sept. 18, 1793), in Documentary History of the Supreme Court, *supra* note 69, at 416 ("I cannot conceive that the People of this Commonwealth, when they, by their representatives in Convention, adopted the Constitution of a General Government, expected that each State should be held liable to answer on *compulsory civil process*, to every individual resident in another State or in a foreign Kingdom. Three Judges of the United States of America, having solemnly given it as their opinion, that the several States are thus liable, the question has thus become highly important to the people."); *Proceedings of the Georgia House of Representatives*, Augusta Chron., Dec. 14, 1792, reprinted in Documentary History of the Supreme Court, *supra* note 69, at 161–62 ("Be it resolved by the Senate and House of Representatives of the state of Georgia … that they do not consider the 2d section of the 3d article of the federal constitution to extend to the granting power to the supreme court of the United States, or to any other court having jurisdiction under their authority, or which they may at any period hereafter under the constitution, as it now stands, constitute.").

71 *See* Randy E. Barnett, *The People or the State?*; Chisholm v. Georgia *and Popular Sovereignty*, 93 Va. L. Rev. 1729, 1743–48 (2007).

change in the federal representation, or procure in the mode prescribed by the constitution, further "declaratory and restrictive clauses", by way of amendment thereto. An instance of which may be cited in the conduct of the Massachusetts legislature: who, as soon as that state was sued in the federal court, by an individual, immediately proposed, and procured an amendment to the constitution, declaring that the judicial power of the United States shall not be construed to extend to any suit brought by an individual against a state.[72]

Tucker cites *Chisholm* as an "act of usurpation" or the "exercise [of] powers not warranted by the constitution." The proper remedy for usurpations affecting the state involve the state legislatures "sound[ing] the alarm *to the people*", who can then either use the majoritarian process to remove offending representatives or exercise their sovereign right to seek "declaratory and restrictive" amendments. Tucker's example of the people's response to a recent "act of usurpation" was the addition of the Eleventh Amendment.

Tucker (and the states that called for an amendment) believed that the *Chisholm* majority erroneously construed the Constitution. But what exactly was the perceived error? The text of Article III, after all, authorized federal courts to hear suits "between a state and citizens of another state." The only way the Chisholm majority could have erred would be if they should have strictly construed this clause to refer only to those suits where a state is a party plaintiff, not a defendant, thus preserving the immunity of the state from suits brought by private individuals. The need to strictly construe the delegated powers of Article III was the basis of Justice Iredell's dissent in *Chisholm*.[73] The Eleventh Amendment, in other words, may have been a response to a perceived failure to apply the very rule of construction meant to be established by the Ninth and Tenth Amendments.

Conclusion

If I am right about the original understanding of the Ninth and Tenth amendments, why then did the Confederate States feel compelled to add the words "of the several states" to their version of these clauses?[74] After all, according to my theory, this was already the original understanding of

---

72 Tucker, *supra* note 54, at app. 153.

73 Chisholm v. Georgia, 2 U.S. 419, 449–50 (1793) (Iredell, J., dissenting) ("I think every word in the Constitution may have its full effect without involving this consequence, and that nothing but express words, or an insurmountable implication (neither of which I consider, can be found in this case) would authorize the deduction of so high a power.").

74 See Confederate Const. art. VI, § 5 (March 11, 1861) ("The enumeration, in the Constitution, of certain rights shall not be construed to deny or disparage others retained by the people of the several states."); *id.* § 6 ("The powers not delegated to the Confederate States by the Constitution, nor prohibited by it to the States, are reserved to the States, respectively, or to the people thereof.").

the clauses. Professor Barnett's analysis has already hinted at an answer to this question. Although the reasoning of the *Chisholm* majority was rebuked by the adoption of the Eleventh Amendment, the same strongly nationalist reading of federal power was restored by John Marshall, first in dicta, in *Fletcher v. Peck*,[75] and later as a matter of law in cases like *McCulloch v. Maryland*[76] and *Gibbons v. Ogden*.[77] The latter two of these cases triggered vociferous objection,[78] with James Madison in particular objecting to Marshall's suggestion in *McCulloch* that the people existed only in a national capacity and had no independent sovereign existence in the several states.[79] Madison feared that unduly nationalist opinions like Marshall's threatened the delicate balance between the federal government and the states. We know, of course, that the center did not hold and the nation ultimately divided over competing notions of national power and state sovereignty. Accordingly, when the Confederate States drafted their own constitution, they restored language which reflected what they (and Madison) believed had been the original understanding retained powers and rights. For his part, Madison rejected the secessionist ideas of Calhoun and the Nullifiers. But the likewise rejected the wholly nationalist ideas of men like Alexander Hamilton and John Marshall. Indeed, in many ways the story of the Ninth Amendment is the story of "Madison's Middle" and his vision of a nation neither wholly national nor wholly federal.

---

75 10 U.S. (6 Cranch) 87, 139 (1810) ("The constitution as passed, gave the courts of the United States jurisdiction in suits brought against individuals states. …This feature is no longer found in the constitution; but it aids in the construction of those clauses with which it was originally associated.").

76 17 U.S. 316, 404–405 (1819) ("The government of the Union, then (whatever may be the influence of this fact on the case), is, emphatically and truly, a government of the people. In form, and in substance, it emanates from them. Its powers are granted by them, and are to be exercised directly on them, and for their benefit.").

77 22 U.S. (9 Wheat.) 1, 71, 75 (1824) ("This instrument contains an enumeration of powers expressly granted by the people to their government. It has been said, that these powers ought to be construed strictly. But why ought they to be so construed? Is there one sentence in the constitution which gives countenance to this rule?… [The commerce power], like all others vested in Congress, is completed in itself, may be exercised to its utmost extent, and acknowledges no limitations, other than are prescribed in the constitution.").

78 *See* G. Edward White, *The Marshall Court and Cultural Change*, 1815–35, at 1, 541–80(1988).

79 *See* James Madison, Detached Memoranda, 1819?, in Writings, *supra* note 15, at 745, 755–56 (criticizing Marshall's "expounding the power of Congs—as if no other Sovereignty existed in the states supplemental to the enumerated power of Congs").

Act III

The Core; The American National Political
Institutions—The Centers of Policymaking
Power Congress

★ Four Systems of Policy, Politics, and
★ Choice

★

★ *By Theodore J. Lowi*

The politics vocabulary is not rich in distinctions among governmental functions and policies. Even the great Cushman seems to have been satisfied with a distinction between regulation and nonregulation, based upon an even simpler dichotomy between coercion and noncoercion.[1] Perhaps this poverty of language is due to the widespread liberal attitude that since government itself is not a problem, the best approach is simply to point out and describe the unit or activity of concern. Part of the problem also lies in the fact that prevailing fashions in political science have put heaviest stress on the politics rather than the government side of the field. In many dimensions of politics there are well-developed vocabularies, indication indeed where the major theoretical interests have been. Students of politics do occasionally turn to policy and government, but the tendency has been to do so only because the interesting conflict are around issues, and many issues involve basic policies. But the issue of policy was not the part of these issues that came in for serious analysis.

Regulation is obviously only one of several ways governments seek to control society and individual conduct. There are rather specific purposes that are best pursued through regulatory techniques, and the reading of any account of regulatory administration suggests that there is a distinct set of moral and political-process consequences associated with this kind of governmental commitment. But this implies that there might be other government commitments to serve other ends involving other moralities and other processes. If this is the case, then no one type is meaningful except in comparison to other types.

There is more to the urge for classification than the desire for complexity. Finding different manifestations or types of a given phenomenon is the beginning of orderly control and prediction. Taxonomy before ontogeny *or* phylogeny. Moreover, to find the *basis* for classification reveals the hidden meaning and significance of the phenomenon, suggestion what the important hypotheses ought to be concerned with.

This is precisely what a policy taxonomy might do for the study of politics. To break through the weak and designative vocabulary of public law is perhaps to bring public policy—government—into a proper, analyzable, relationship with those dimension of political science that

Theodore Lowi, "Four Systems of Politics, Policy, and Choice," from *Public Administration Review*, vol. 32, no. 4; July/August 1972, pp. 298–310. Published by Blackwell, 1972. Copyright by John Wiley & Sons, Inc. Permission to reprint granted by the rights holder.

are already well developed. In hard and practical terms, a good taxonomy of policies might ennoble this underdeveloped part of the field by converting these important phenomena into "variables," which make them more esthetic to the scientist in political science.

One such attempt to formulate a politically relevant policy taxonomy has been made, and, although still in the process of development, it is possible to report upon it here, in fact, using this as part of the process of developing the scheme. The purpose here will be to bring the board, theoretical policy considerations concretely to bear upon some real political situations to see if each enrichens the other. It should soon be amply clear why one can say little new about the politics of regulation without introducing the general policy context within which regulation is only one small, albeit important, part.

Since reference can readily be made to the earlier publication, only scant attention will be paid here to the rationale and the details of the scheme.[2] The perspective of the entire approach is the very opposite of the typical perspective in political science, for it begins with the assumption that policies determine politics. But the assumption is without value unless the taxonomy of policies captures features of real government that are politically significant; and the most significant political fact about government is that government coerces. Different ways of coercing provide a set of parameters, a context, within which politics takes place.

Table I is an attempt to identify and derive logically the types of coercion available to governments.[3] According to the vertical dimension, coercion can be remote or immediate; in a governmental context is can be remote if sanctions are absent, or if they are indirect—as for example a program based on a service of subsidy where the coercive element is displaced onto the general revenue system.

While the vertical dimension is usually easy to locate in the statute, the horizontal dimension offers a few more difficulties. Nonetheless it is clear that some policies do not come into operation until there is a question about someone's behavior. For example, there is a general rule covering all fraudulent advertising, but it is applicable only to the conduct of individual advertisers. In strong contrast, some policies do not need to wait for a particular behavior, but rather do not touch behavior directly at all. Instead they work through the environment of conduct. For example, a minor change in the Federal Reserve discount rate can have a major impact on my propensity to invest, yet no official need know of my existence.

Beyond the examples provided in each cell, there does not seem to be need for providing elaborate definitions here. The essential aspect of each type is provided or strongly implied in the cross-tabulation of each of the properties along the margins. This is the beauty of finding a basis of distinction work with.

There are various ways to work from the scheme toward its normative and empirical implications. Some of the process variables are indicated around the margins of the paradigm. Cross-tabulations among these common-sense relationships produces many complex hypotheses that are systematically related to each other and to a common and known analytic posture. For example, it is not hard to document historically that the overwhelming proportion of policies produced by the federal government during the 19th century were distributive; it is also not hard to place alongside that the other well-documented fact, that

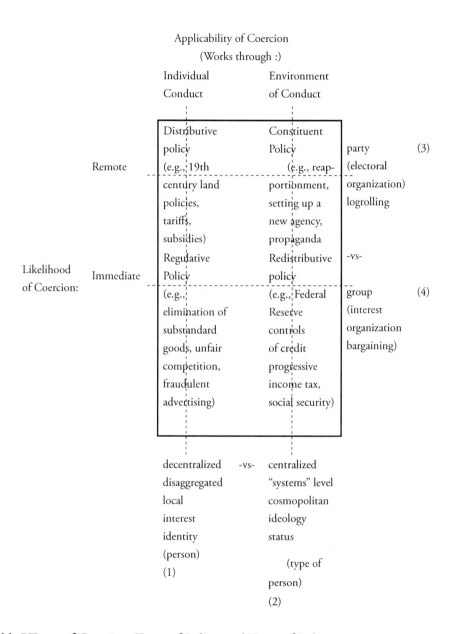

Table I Types of Coercion, Types of Policy, and Types of Politics

the period produced a strong partisan politics, then became dominated y localized, logrolling, nonideological parties. The paradigm puts the two sets of facts into an intimate interrelation. The two separate sets of facts can be pulled together systematically in detail and yet in relation to other sets of facts by mixing marginal characteristics (1) and (3) in a context established for them on Table I. Oblique turns in politics can be anticipated systematically by moving to another cell and mixing the marginal characteristic accordingly, as for example combining items (1) and (4) for an initial look at what tends to develop around regulatory policies. And so on.

Of all the ways of testing the hypotheses drawn from this scheme, perhaps the most effective, as well as the most useful one to begin with, is that of looking through the eyes of the top-most officials at the political system and how and to what extent the system shifts obliquely as their view of it shifts from on policy prism to another. The way to do this is with actual accounts; one of the virtues of the policy scheme is that it converts ordinary case studies from chronicles and teaching instruments into data. Yet the cases themselves require some preparation for this somewhat novel usage; and this can be provided by a brief and superficial review of variations in the lives of a few Presidents, as these were seen, or could have been seen, by them.

From Cleveland to FDR: What Makes Presidential Politics?

The "Republican Era" of 1869–1901 is generally thought of as a period of congressional dominance and presidential passivity. To Woodrow Wilson, the period was not merely congressional government; congressional government meant committee government. And in his overview of that era, Leonard White observed that the presidency was at "low ebb" and that despite hard fought battles between the two branches, the theory and practice of government was congressional supremacy. This went virtually unchallenged, according to White, Binkley, and others, from Grant through McKinley.[4] To students of that period it was for good reason that Woodrow Wilson could write *Congressional Government* and Bryce could ask Why Great Men Are Not Chosen President. The only thing Presidents were strong about was their faith in the separation of powers, which meant steadfast passivity in the policy-making process.[5]

Even Grover Cleveland, despite his standing as one of the stronger Presidents, was unquestionably passive in his relations with Congress. According to Woodrow Wilson, Cleveland "thought it not part of his proper function to press his preference in any other way than by recommendation in a message and upon acceptance of Congress… "[6] It was simply an established fact about Presidents and had been true of all Presidents during and before the Republican Era, virtually from Jefferson to Buchanan, when, except for brief moments, Congress dominated.

This kind of dominance, especially by the committees, has been experienced whenever distributive policies have prevailed, and it so happened that such was the case for most of the 19th century, when the federal government turned out little but land disposal programs, shipping subsidies, tariffs, internal improvements, and the like. The federal level of politics was stable, and could have been governed by congressional committee and party logrolling precisely because policies dealing with slavery, public health, property, and so on were left to the states—which were duly radicalized.[7]

Out of this stable situation, politically speaking, grew the practice, then the theory, of presidential obligation that prevailed until the Wilson Administration. Yet there were exceptional moments, and these underscore the influence that policy has upon politics. For, whenever politics took an exceptional turn, there seems to have been an exceptional policy issue at the bottom of it. Interesting cases, actually anticipating the New Deal, can be found in the Cleveland and the Harrison Administrations.[8]

President Cleveland seems to have allowed himself a single important exception to the accepted presidential posture of his day. On the one issue of repeal of the Silver Purchase Act he exerted strong leadership, legislative leadership in particular. In his efforts to secure the repeal "he gave one of his few instances of leadership," even though he had to compromise with "his theory of separated powers to do it." He was "humiliated by the necessity of purchasing the support of a Democratic member of the finance committee of the upper house …," but he did it all the same, as part of a pattern of leadership not to be seen on a regular basis again for many years to come. Thus, when later an important tariff was being framed, "he played no effective part."[9]

Actually Harrison, though a much weaker man, headed a more vigorous Administration. Central leadership was of course not characteristic of it. Harrison more than shared Cleveland's view; to him, the President should be guided by his party in Congress. Nevertheless, his Administration is associated with many important political changes, all in the direction of greater vigor, greater political centrality and responsibility. It was during his Administration that Congress began the most far-reaching reforms in its history. In brief, the House gave itself a new constitution by adopting at long last an organized and codified set of rules. These were "Reed's Rules," named after their author, Speaker Thomas B. Reed, and they were concerned in particular with controlling individual congressmen, reducing dilatory tactics, and confining deliberation to relevant and efficient channels. All of this in turn amounted to an assertion of central leadership and of the parliamentary Congress over the tightly entrenched committees and individual, power-seeking congressmen.

After Harrison, Presidents would, at least more frequently, see a real Congress and deal directly with legislative problems. Presidents would thereafter also see more and more nationally organized interest groups, for the late 19th century witnessed the most phenomenal growth of such organizations oriented to political influence and capable of sustaining pressure. It began somewhat earlier at the state level with commodity associations, but it spread to labor and business, the most effective eventually being the trade associations, almost all of whose foundings date during or after the mid-1890's. The number and strength of these interest groups provided political alternatives to the parties in policy formulation, and by 1900 parties in Congress went into a decline in their capacity to discipline members, a decline from which they have never fully recovered.

All of this is associated in turn with the rise of new kinds of public policy, new at least at the national level. These are regulatory and redistributive policies. As earlier observed, state governments had from the beginning of the Republic regularly enacted regulatory laws—for example, in the fields of property, quarantine and public health, crime, construction, banking, marriage and the family, trade occupations, etc. On rarer occasions states also attempted to redistribute wealth. Surely state politics had a radical reputation because of the policies they were obliged to make. These kinds of policies kept state politics perpetually on the edge of organized turmoil.

When this type of policy entered national government in large enough numbers, the politics would surely follow soon thereafter. And the policies would change the politics regardless of the character of the men or the party that inhabited the presidency organized the Congress.

The Roosevelt Era

All of these tendencies came to a head in the 1930's, because Roosevelt was responsible for expanding national government on all fronts through all kinds of policies. The politics of the New Deal cannot be understood except by indentifying and appreciating the multiple patterns of policy and of politics. Multiple patterns can be found before, but in the 1930's and thereafter, passage of large numbers of all four types of policies was so regular and frequent that these patterns began to institutionalize themselves into clear and distinct systems of politics.

Lack of full appreciation of these multiple patterns of policy and politics had led to many and conflicting interpretations of Roosevelt. For example, Leuchtenberg could argue that the New Deal was a "broker State," yet that this "clashed with the fact that he was agent, both willingly and unwillingly, of forces of reform that business found unacceptable."[10] On top of this, many have argued that he was the savior of capitalism while others argued he was the chief enemy. He was to some a social democrat, to others a corporativist, to others simply a savvy and scheming politician.

These conflicting characterizations and interpretations become more interesting when all of them are taken as accurate and correct. Each simply applies to a special set of conditions; and each loses value when over-generalized to the whole man rather than to aspects of his behavior. Each interpretation comes out of one set of policy issues; the observer must have had that set in mind as he tried to describe, vainly, the entire man and the whole New Deal.

For example, Binkley, like most students of the period, stressed Roosevelt's unqualified and unprecedented leadership during the 100 days, and goes on to explain it as an emergency phenomenon. Yet, almost immediately, he saw that Roosevelt faced a "crucial test" over the economy bill (a constituent policy providing for severe reductions in the salaries of government personnel and the compensation of veterans). Only the most strenuous party discipline kept dissident Democrats in line.[11] Thus, here the pattern was not presidential power but national party power which tends, if at all, to re-emerge whenever constituent issues emerge. This could have been predicted, with some degree of confidence, by knowing only the formal provisions of the bill.

Roosevelt was indeed a strong President, but his strength was conditioned and shaped by its environment, and the most determinative part of that environment was the policy environment. Roosevelt responded to more pressures than any national leader ever had. And in translating those pressures into special and meaningful political forces that were shaped by the type of policy the demand became. It is in this sense that the Roosevelt Revolution is the key to American politics even into the 1970's. Granted, it was a bit of a revolution in terms of the scale of its expansion, and in terms of the extent to which it turned round the Constitution. But the precise meaning of the revolution will be found in the multiplicity rather than the scale of policy actions. This multiplicity of policies differentiated politics.

Thus, the impression of Roosevelt the strong, Roosevelt the opinion leader, the social democrat, is gained primarily from the unprecedentedly large number of redistributive programs he formulated and sent up to Congress. On these, during and after the 100 days, he overwhelmed the opposition with the support of the masses and the force of rhetoric heavily laden with class fear and antagonism. Congress operated like a meek Parliament before a mighty Crown. During the first two months alone these programs included: suspension of the convertibility of dollars into gold, suspension of gold export, the Emergency Banking Act loosening Federal Reserve authorization on loans to member banks, broad authority to issue unsecured greenbacks up to $3 billion under the Thomas Amendment to the AAA, temporary desposit insurance, and authority to purchase up to $2 billion in gold or foreign exchange— the first step toward devaluation. These were all presidential in that they were created there, were approved quickly by a cooperative Congress, and amounted to large and explicit grants of power back to the President.

But on other matters Roosevelt looked more like the classic politician, playing the role of broker, the cajoler, the man in the center more by placement than power. Indeed, his broker role included an unprecedented willingness to alienate a large share of national sovereignty in order to get enough consensus for formulation and passage of legislation. And this is why Roosevelt looks, through the prism of regulatory issues, like a 1930's European corporate syndicalist. Only a brief look at such programs as AAA (parity provisions), the Securities Act, the Glass Steagall Banking Bill, and NIRA will reveal the distinctly different political process around the President—and this was going on exactly at the same time the President was also the social democratic leader. In these regulatory matters he was willing to share power and to co-opt business support because neither his presidency nor anyone else's has had sufficient independent power to pass important regulatory programs without paying a big price to build a coalition for the purpose. Access to public opinion and use of lofty rhetroic are resources that simply do no spend well in the regulatory area.

Thus, to this vastly popular and unilaterally powerful President (as he could easily have seen himself through the prism of redistributive policies), it must have been something of a comedown to look out at the world through the prism of securities and banking and labor regulatory legislation. Every account of these policies in 1933 and 1934 stresses the pronouncedly congressional factor. Despite the fact that the Securities Act of 1933 and the Securities and Exchange Act of 1934 were drafted by Landis, Cohen, and Corcoran in the White House (or Cambridge), both acts were gone over carefully and were very creatively rewritten in congress.[12] House treatment of the Public Utility Holding Company Act of 1935 was "one of the most comprehensive and complete... ever given... any bill."[13] House and Senate versions were different from one another, and both were different from the White House. The final draft, worked out in conference committee, was quite different from all of these. And to any observer, President, or casual reader of the accounts, this looks like congressional, not presidential, power.

Or, take the Wagner Act, well after the opening blast of the New Deal. It was of congressional origin and was dominated by congressional forces. President Roosevelt held out for a few changes in particularly objectionable parts, but he was dragged along more as an unhappy supplicant than as a leader of nation, government, and party.[14]

But Roosevelt does not constitute a sufficient case. The real question here is whether this differentiated pattern, set during the 1930's, became institutionalized into separate and predictable systems of policy and politics. Rather than concentrate only on the 1930's, it would be better to span the entire period since those formative days. Strong *and* weak Presidents have been in the office since then, and the test will be whether, regardless of that, they face the same kinds of politics when the policy conditions are the same. If this is true, it would mean that strong Presidents may increase the amount of political action or the level of intensity, but they are less likely to alter the pattern of politics except insofar as they pursue one type of policy overwhelmingly more than the three others.

The Record Since Roosevelt: Stabilized Variation

The "Summary of Case Studies" (Table II) presents a pattern of stabilized variation. Once we began regularly to get a goodly number of policies of all four types, we also began to witness four quite different types of politics. Were it not for the possibility of overstating the argument, one could say that each is a distinct subsystem.

The summary is comprised of 17 published case studies. Many are book-length, all are very detailed, and each was written by a reputable scholar. Our task was essentially to "interview" each author by addressing certain questions to his case study. The questions are presented in shorthand across the top of the summary. For example, it was important to learn what each author had to say about the typical participant in his story (column 1)—if indeed the author was struck by anything worth reporting on that subject. As is clear, almost all authors did stress some characteristic of the participants that could be coded, as indicated by the adjectives running down column (1). To take one case, Bailey and Samuel were impressed by the quality of "every man for himself," in the formulation of the Rivers and Harbors Act of 1950.[15] For another that has been covered in enormous detail, the politics of the traditional tariff has by all observers been considered highly individualized.[16]

Each author, through his case, was also asked if he had anything special to report on how the actors seemed to related to each other (column 2). Did they mainly engage in mutual back scratching? Or, does the author report that he found careful strategy over long periods along broad, ideological lines? Or was there careful plotting and coalition building but along sector or other more special line of cleavage? Ideological ties and long and stable lines of cleavage were reported by McConnell in his accounts of Farm Security and Farmers Home Administrations, as did Munger and Fenno in the fight over aid to education. In contrast, all of the authors of the middle six grouping of cases reported unstable cleavages (coalitions) based on sector and trade lines. It was this type of case, of which there were so many in the 1940's and '50's, that provided the empirical basis for the formalizing of the pluralist interpretation of American politics.[17]

The President is most likely to perceive for himself the patterns reported on columns (5) through (8) of the summary. Her the authors were asked what they had to report about the relative importance of lobbying, congressional committees, the floor, and the White House, respectively, to the final outcome of the program. No author undertakes to write a policy-making case study unless he intends to have something significant to say about the relative importance of these "loci of power."

The first thing one is struck by in the returns from these 17 cases is their sheer variation. Yet, if we could really generalize about national politics, would there not be a great deal of similarity in these adjectives?

The second thing one is struck by is the pattern of variation. Other readers might use different adjectives, but that is not likely to change the pattern much, since the adjectives used here were either used in the original or were careful translations of longer accounts. Even if something is lost by converting a paragraph or section into a single, summary word, the repetition and regular variation of these word across 17 important cases cannot be taken lightly.[18]

What the Roosevelt watchers report as exceptions to the general rule of Roosevelt mastery, therefore, turn out on closer examination to be not exceptions at all, but the rule under certain conditions that can be known in advance and understood in theoretically and jurisprudentially interesting terms. In all four of the distributive cases—the top group on the summary—the authors report that the President was either out of the picture altogether or was in it as a very weak and striving supplicant. Often the only way the President has been able to get into this act has been to try to convert the legislation into something else besides pork barrel—as Roosevelt succeeded in doing once and no more on TVA, and as Kennedy succeeded once in doing with his emergency public works proposal, which he tied to fiscal planning and general redistribution. But usually the committees succeed in severing these redistributive features from distributive bills.

A variety of words describe Presidents in the six cases of regulatory legislation, but one thing runs dramatically through all of them: whether the President is strongly involved (as in AAA legislation on parity), or is stalemated due to squabbles within his own branch and party (as was true in the case of Taft-Hartley), Congress dominates the regulatory process. And this is the parliamentary Congress—the floor, not the committees. Sometimes the President has presented full-blown draft legislation, and sometimes the relevant committee will draft the original version. But in either event, according to the authors of the six regulatory cases, there is likely to be a lot of rewriting on the floor, through the amending process, and through conference

Table III is a statistical confirmation of the results in the summary. It is a count of the actual amending actions involved in the 13 post-1948 bills on the summary, plus all bills in the 87th Congress, First Session, that received roll call votes in both houses. We used eight

Table II Variations In The Policy Process Summary Of Case Studies I: Actors And Their Roles

Case	Attribute							
	(1) Primary Units	(2) Relationships Among	(3) Stability Among	(4) Bu.-Prof. Factor	(5) Lobby Role	(6) Committee Role	(7) Floor Role	(8) Executive role
Distributive								
Rivers—Harbors '50	single	logrolling	highest	some	very high	determinative	counsensual	supplicative
Airports Aid '58–'59	single	logrolling	very high	low	high	determinative	counsensual	supplicative
ARA	single	logrolling	highest	low	high	creative	counsensual	supplicative
Tariff, '50's	single	logrolling	highest	low	low	crative	counsensual	supplicative
Regulative								
FDA, '38	tr. assn.	bargaining	high	high	low	creative	very creative	supplicative
Rent Control '50	tr. assn.	bargaining	low	low	low	creative	creative	supplicative
Robinson-Patman	tr. assn.	bargaining	low	low	very high	creative	creative	passive
AAA '38	tr. assn.	bargaining	low	low	very high	creative	not asc.	Coordinative
Taft-Hartley	tr. assn.	bargaining	low	low	very high	creative	passive (stalemated)	
Landrum-Griffin	tr. assn.	bargaining	moderate*	low	high	conduit	very creative	coordinative & supplicative
Redistributive								
Farm Security Administration	(Bu. Only)	ideol.	high	highest	very high	none	none	legislative

Farmers Home Administration	(Bu. Only)	ideol.	very high	highest	high	lobbyist	not ascertained	legislative
Social Security '35	Peaks	ideol.	very high	highest	moderate	conduit	consensual	legislative
Federal Aid to Education	Peaks	ideol.	very high	high**	high	lobbyist	contentious	inactive*
Employment Act '46	Peaks	ideol.	very high	high**	moderate	very low	very creative	legislative
Excess Profits	***	ideol.	very high	high**	moderate	lobbyist	contentious	supplicative
Internal Revenue '54 (exemption and rates)	Peaks	ideol.	high	highest	moderate	low–creative**	contentious	legislative

* Pro's high, anti's low.

** Professionalism very high; agency personnel involvement as lobbyists or draftsmen not high.

*** No mention is made of any group or associations. The "business community" is termed "unanimous" and "concerted" but not managed.

Legend

Lobby role: *Very high* if prominent and creative in legislature, executive, and grass roots; *high* if prominent and creative at any point; moderate if only prominent; and *low* if no evidence of anything.

Committee role: *conduit, lobbyist, creative, determinative*, in that rough order of importance.

Floor role: *consensual, contentious* (if a lot of debate but little alteration of the bill), *creative* (if evidence of alteration).

Executive role: *passive, coordinative, supplicative, legislative* in that order.

* Failed of passage. As a general rule, if executive activity is low on a redistributive activity, the bill is probable doomed. This is not true of the other two types.

** Point Committee on Internal Revenue Taxation very creative—especially its staff; but it is not a legislative committee. The Ways and Means Committee and Finance Committee were much less creative, much more ratifiers of accords reached between JCIRT and Treasury lawyers.

Table III Evidence Of Floor Creativity: Amendments

Three example of straight amendment counts:

	(1) Average Number of Amendments Offered Per Bill	(2) Per Cent of These Passed	(3) Per Cent of Significant Amendments Passed Over Sponsor	Weighted Means, a Summary of All 8 Levels of Amending Action: House	Sente
Distributive Bills (N=22)	5.8	41.8%	0	.05	.16
Redistributive Bills (N=25)	9.1	62.4%	24%	.15	.45
Regulative Bills (N=15)	12.8	48.9%	67%	.46	.50

types of amending activity, and we ranked them according to degree of difficulty: (1) number of amendments offered; (2) per cent passed; (3) number of important amendments offered; (4) per cent of those that passed; (5) number of amendments offered over objections of the sponsor; (6) per cent of those that passed; (7) number of important amendments offered over objections of sponsor; (8) per cent of these that passed. The average amending activity, using each of the eight types, were tallied, and the results of three of these are presented in the table. We then attached weights from 1 to 8 to these categories to reflect roughly the degree of difficulty a member would have in getting each type of amendment adopted, and the "weighted mean" for each chamber is presented in the last column.

First, we can see that floor activity jumps up dramatically from distributive to redistributive bills. Since other evidence (see the summary) indicates presidential dominance over redistributive legislation, this finding suggests that on redistributive bills we get something like an acting out of the intent of the framers: direct communication between Exective and Legislative Branches. But the evidence in Table III is really classic for regulative bills. The goose egg for significant creativity in distributive legislation tends to dramatize the fact that on 67 per cent of all regulative bills at least two significant amendments were added during floor debate in the House despite the objections of the sponsor, who is usually the committee chairman. Indeed, that is a lot of rewriting, a lot of creativity, especially in the era of the "rise of the presidency" when Congress' reputation for creativity has declined.

The "weighted mean" adds considerable confirmation.[19] Obviously the overall level of floor action was much higher in the Senate, where smaller size and permissive rules prevail. But within the Senate amounts of floor action, i.e., the evidence of floor creativity, varied from policy type to policy type, in a predictable way.

In House and Senate the dramatic jump upward was from distributive to regulative. This is much more significant in the House because of the many rules significant in the House because of the many rules that discourage access to the floor under any circumstances. But even in the Senate, the reputation for floor creativity would hardly exist if we went back to the period when federal legislation was all distributive.

Finally, in the Senate, as in the House, there is a significant jump from distributive to redistributive in evidence of floor creativity. This finding will bear further examination. Since history and the cases have revealed the special role of the Exective on redistributive matters, and since we now see also the considerable creativity of Congress as well, we might be led to reformulate our notions of policy and institutions, and how they relate to each other. It is quite conceivable that political scientists can develop criteria for policy choice in terms of predicted and desired impacts on the political system, just as economists, biologist, and the like attempt to predict and guide policies according to their societal impacts.

Implications for Prediction and Choice

Neither these data nor data of any other sort would support a drastically diminished interpretation of presidential power. His freedom to commit us to war, his command of secret information and diplomacy, his power to use executive agreements are all too impressive. But these impressive powers have overshadowed real variations even in that area defined, quite erroneously, as "foreign policy."[20] One need only note the amount of revision of factual and normative interpretation about presidential power since the Vietnam failures to realize the variability that was probably masked in the political science of national power during the 1950's and '60's.

All of this is to say that presidential power, and all other political phenomena must be put in proportion and perspective. Whether we are concerned about the issue of presidential power or the issue of adopting a regulatory approach to a social problem, and whether we are concerned with the objective business of prediction or the normative business of choosing a particular outcome, perspective must reside in at least two considerations: (1) prediction or choice must begin by recognizing the possibility of more than one pattern, and by pattern we must mean whole models rather than incremental differences in specific behavior patterns; and (2) if predictions can be made at this massive, institutional level, then they can, and inevitably will, become a major criterion for policy choice—i,e., really good theory is unavoidably normative.

(1) If this essay has shown anything, it is that almost any generalization about national politics is inapplicable to as many as two-thirds of the cases of policy formulation. If we reverse the generalization by adding a "not," the new generalization would also tend to be inapplicable to about two-thirds of the known cases. The policy framework provides a basis for stating the conditions under which a given proposition is applicable, rather than merely helping improve the batting average from .333 to .335, or something of the sort. The policy framework locates the smaller universe where the batting average might be .677 or higher, and additionally it

puts each of the generalizations into a theoretically orderly relation to all others. In turn, this produces new insights but, more important, it builds the propositions toward whole models rather than merely stringing out specific x-y statements.

One example alluded to earlier, where whole models of government and politics are seen to be involved, has to do with the conventional wisdom that American politics is all subsumed under a "presidential system," with exception. The cases and statistics here suggest first that several models have been masked over by the notion of a single system with multiple centers of power. One of the worst consequences of this assumption is its central construct, the "rise of presidential power, the decline of legislative power." *Sub rosa* it is then recognized that presidential power is not unilateral, nor is it even remotely equivalent to executive power; but those ambiguities are left theoretically unsettled. When one allows for multiple models rather than multiple power centers in a single model, many tendencies that must be left as ambiguities or anomalies can be brought explcitly to the center and handled rather easily. At least two such models involve a very strong Congress, and in one or perhaps both of these, presidential and congressional power are consonant, not zero-sum.

This bears further pursuit. Evidence of floor creativity is stronger for strong Presidents, such as Kennedy and Johnson, than for weak Presidents, such as Eisenhower, or Truman during his first three years in office. And floor creativity, as Table III shows, is high for redistributive bills, when the presidential role is most pronounced, for strong as well as for weak Presidents. What this really means is that the levels of political responsibility in the two branches ten to be consonant, and that they exist together in counterpoise to the administrative or bureaucratic levels of both branches. When the President is weak it is his bureaucracies and the congressional committees—the levels of low political responsibility—that tend to dominate the process; when the President is strong it is because he controls the bureaucratic levels.

(2) If the policy scheme developed in this essay, or some superior one to come along, can predict when a President will be strong and weak, as well as when other gross institutional patterns will prevail, then it is no step at all to a policy science for political scientists. This kind of wisdom provides criteria for choosing among policies, criteria that do not require the imposition of private goals upon legislators or the people. To illustrate, if two policies have about an equal chance of failure or success in the achievement of some social purpose the legislature has agreed upon, then that one should be preferred that has the most desirable impact on the political system. It should be the expertise of the political scientist to specify these kinds of consequences, and a policy framework would be necessary to do this. This is science, yet it reaches to the very foundations of democratic politics and the public interest. Let us pursue both, the second first.[21]

For a public interest to be involved at all, at least one of two properties must be present: The policy should be large enough in scope to affect a large number of people in a consistent way. This could be true of constituent polices, where a basic structural change in the system tends to create a class even where it does not directly define one, as for example in electoral reforms.

Or, the policy must, regardless of its scope, express a clear rule of law. A rule of law identifies the citizen in each person, the public part of each of us. The making of a real law (as contrasted with a policy-without-law) is an act of setting a public morality upon some action or status hitherto considered private.[22]

Distributive policy, in this context, clearly comes closest to being a complete privatization of the public. Much of it is intended to be *sub rosa,* and usually succeeds, given the capacity of these policies for continual fission according to the number of individuals making claims. To take but one contrasting example, regulatory politics that embody even vague rules of law cannot be fully privatized. The directly coercive element introduces public concerns of increasingly general applicability.[23] The overriding point is that these policy considerations, within the arena's framework, provide a systematic and plausible basis for defining good and bad legislation—without holding one moral code absolutely above another.

We can also judge public policy as good or bad in still another sense, a sense that leads toward fundamental questions about the relationship between public policy and democracy. If we want an open and public politics, we are limited to certain kinds of policies—regardless of whether the manifest goals of these policies are fulfilled. Again we would try to avoid distributive policies, because nothing open and democratic can come of them. But more nuance can be added. There can be moments in history, or changes of fashion, where the presidency is thought to be too powerful—perhaps we live in such a period today. In such a situation, Keynesian fiscal policies should be resisted, and regulatory policies should be preferred, for the latter tend to bring things to Congress and tend to invigorate interest group action. If anxiety about unlimited presidential power in international affairs continues to grow, regulatory provisions could even be tied to treaties or executive agreements. To trace this out is to illustrate rather dramatically the possibilities of looking at politics through policies: The best way, in other words, to open up the presidency and to expose the relations he is developing with another country is to put into policy terms some reciprocal commitments that require internal controls in both countries. For example, a provision requiring exchange of stock between two or more corporations, or their countries, in order to deal with air or water pollution would destabilize the politics of both countries, at least enough to gain entrée into what is going on. Requirements for inspection of financial institutions dealing in our foreign aid would do about the same thing.

Finally, if we wished to introduce strong national parties into our system, we might try to pursue more goals through constituent policies—like effective public propaganda in the birth control field, or dealing with monopolies by changing the rules protecting their limited liability rather than by adding regulations affecting their conduct.

The point is that if we can discover empirically the policy conditions underlying our political patterns, we have a basis for better public policies as well as better political science. Should we regulate? If there is the slightest contribution to political theory or policy science in this article, it would be in having established a basis for actually answering that question.

Sources for Table II

Rivers and Harbors Act of 1950. Stephen K. Bailey and Howard Samuel, *Congress at Work* (New York: Holt, 1952).

Airports Aid, 1958–59. Randall P. Ripley, "Congress Champions Aid to Airports." In F.N. Cleaveland, *Congress and Urban Problems* (Washington, D.C.: The Brookings Institution, 1968).

Area Redevelopment Act. John Bibby and Roger Davidson *on Capitol Hill* (New York: Holt, Rinehart and Winston, 1967).

Tariff. Raymond Bauer, *et al., American Business and Public Policy* (New York: Atherton, 1963).

Food, Drug and Cosmetic Act. David Cavers, "The Food, Drug and Cosmetic Act of 1938: Its Legislative History and its Substantive Provisions," *Law and Contemporary Problems* (Winter 1939).

Rent Control, 1950. Bailey and Samuel, *op cit.*

Robinson-Patman. Joseph C. Palamountain, *The Politics of Distribution* (Cambridge: Harvard University Press, 1955).

Agricultural Adjustment Act. Charles Hardin, *The Politics of Agriculture* (New York: The Free Press, 1952); and Gilbert Fite, *George Peek and the Fight for Farm Parity* (Norman: University of Oklahoma Press, 1954).

Taft-Hartley. Bailey and Samuel, *op. cit.*

Landrum-Griffin. Alan McAdams, *Power Politics in Labor Legislation* (New York: Columbia University Press, 1964).

Farm Security and Farmers Home Administrations. Grant McConnell, *The Decline of Agrarian Democracy* (Berkeley: University of Califorina Press, 1953).

Social Security. Paul H. Douglas, *Social Security in the* U.S. (New York: Whittlesey House, 1936); and Edwin E. Witte, *The Development of the Social Security Act* (Madison: University of Wisconsin Press, 1962).

Aid to Education. Frank Munger and Richard Fenno, *National Politics in Federal Aid to Education* (Syracuse: Syracuse University Press, 1962).

Employment Act of 1946. Stephen K. Bailey, *Congress Makes a Law* (New York: Columbia University Press, 1950).

Excess Profits. Bailey and Samuel, *op.cit.*

Internal Revenue. Stanley S. Surrey, "The Congress and the Tax Lobbyist: How Special Tax Provisions Get Enacted," *Harvard Law Review* (1957). Pp. 1145 ff.

Notes

1. Robert Cushman, President's Committee on Administrative Management, Report with Special Studies (Washington, D.C., U.S. Government Printing Office, 1937); and Cushman, *The Independent Regulatory Commissions* (London: Oxford University Press, 1941). P. 3.

2. Theodore Lowi, "American Business and Public Policy, Case Studies and Political Theory," *World Politics* (July 1964); and Lowi, "Decision Making vs. Policy Making: Toward an Antidote for Technocracy," *Public Administration Review* (May/June 1970).

3. To visualize the analysis best, the reader should substitute "statute" for "policy." This gives up a great deal of information about policies in the real world, but clarity is gained by having a clear and common unit to classify. Moreover, even from this partial and formalized operational definition of policy, there is a great deal of predictive and ethical value in the classification scheme.

4. Leonard White, *The Republican Era* (New York: The Free Press, 1958); and W. Binkley, President and congress (New York: The Free Press, 1958); and W. Binkley, *President and Congress* (New York: Vintage Ed., 1962), Pp. 215 ff.

5. See especially Binkley, *op. cit.,* Pp. 217–218.

6. Quoted in ibid., p. 217. The essence of Wilson's treatment will be found in *Congressional Government* (New York: Meridian Edition, n.d.), Pp. 58–81.

7. This goes a long way toward explaining the Huntington paradox, the spectacle of a highly dynamic economy developing in the context of a stable, "undeveloping" policy. See Samuel P. Huntington, "Political Modernization: America vs. Europe," *World Politics* (April 1966), Pp. 378–414.

8. Earlier instances, such as the Fugitive Slave Act of 1850, are dealt with in another article.

9. Binkley, *op. cit.,* Pp. 225, 217, 227.

10. Leuchtenberg, Franklin D. Roosevelt and the New Deal, 1932–1940 (1963), Pp. 87–94, esp. 90.

11. Binkley, *op.cit.,* Pp. 296–298.

12. Landis' own account has been republished in *Lowi, Legislative Politics USA* (Boston: Little, Brown, 1965), Pp. 143 ff.; see also Chamberlain, *The President, Congress and Legislation* (New York: Columbia University Press, 1946), Pp. 58 ff.

13. *Ibid.,* p. 72.

14. Leuchtenberg, *op. cit.,* Pp. 150 ff; and compare James McG. Burns, *The Lion and the Fox* (New York: Harcourt, 1956): "Quite unwittingly the new President acted as midwife in the rebirth of labor action" (p-215). "Neither Roosevelt nor Miss Perkins had much to do with this provision (Sec. 7A, NRA). Framed mainly by congressmen and labor leaders, it was simply part of a bargain under which labor joined the NRA's great 'concert of interest'" (pp. 215–216). "… Roosevelt failed to see the potentialities of an enlarged labor movement… " (p. 216). The Wagner Act: "was the most radical legislation passed during the New Deal… yet … he threw his weight behind the measure only at the last moment, when it was due to pass anyway" (p. 219). These are not the portrait of a lion *or* a fox, but only of a man running hard to keep up with history.

15. Bailey and Samuel, cited on the bibliography accompanying the summary.

16. Schattschneider, and also Bauer, *et al.,* cited in the bibliography.

17. See David B. Truman. *The Governmental Process* (New York: Knopf, 1951), especially his notes on sources in chapters XI-XV, dealing with policy formulation; see also Earl Latham, *The Group Theory of Politics* (Ithaca: Cornell University Press, 1952) whose opening theoretical chapter generalized on a pattern developed in the rest of his book, a case study of the federal attempt to

regulate basing points practices in the cement industry and elsewhere. This case is very frequently cited in Truman.

18. Eighteen additional cases have been given the same treatment, but they are not yet ready for the same presentation. The pattern is about the same, although a few surprise exceptions bear checking out or explaining.

19. Each category of amending activity was dichotomized, so that the action on each bill and for each type of amendment could be scored 0 or 1—then multiplied by the difficulty weights, as described above. For example, if two or more significant amendments were added to a bill despite the objections of the sponsor, that was scored 1 and multiplied by 8. (If fewer than two such amendments passed, it was then scored 0 and did not increase the score.) These scores were then cumulated for all bills in each policy category, and the average shown on the table was the result of dividing by each of the N's.

20. Some of these variations can be captured in the fourth category, constituent or system maintenance policy. These are not dealt with in this essay because of many considerations too complicating for this first effort at reanalyzing cases. However, I have dealt with some of these patterns elsewhere, and have argued at length that the so-called foreign policy area actually breaks down into the four types captured in the paradigm. The break comes when one asks about the kinds of disciplines governments place upon their own populations in order to carry out foreign influence. For example, setting up a Marshall Plan is not the same kind of policy as actions revising our relations with Red China. Foreign policy is no more of a single piece than agriculture policy or any other conventional, subject-matter designation. And, as shown with the different types of agriculture policy, the politics of each type of foreign policy will vary accordingly. See my chapter in James Rosenau (ed.). *The Domestic Sources of Foreign Policy* (New York: The Free Press, 1967).

21. A more elaborate argument, with many more illustrations, will be found in my companion paper, "Population Policies and the Political System," mimeo., 1971.

22. Cf. Hannah Arendt, The Human Condition, Chapter II and Pp. 193–199, especially her treatment of the Greek concept of law making as akin to architecture in that laws define a space entirely restricted to citizens.

23. Obiviously a distinction is being made here when a continuum is involved. There are degree of vagueness, degrees to which a rule of law is present. However, any rule, no matter how vague, begins to transform distributive into regulatory patterns. For example, adding a vague and very mild anti-discrimination provision to an education subsidy statute can turn established distributive patterns literally inside out. On the other hand, it should be added that very broad delegations of regulatory authority to an agency can lead in the long run to a decline into and all too stable and private politics. Thus, the rule of law criterion is a good one that is often not provided in quantity sufficient to produce the predicted results. Cf. my *The End of Liberalism*, (New York: Norton, 1969); esp. chapters V and X.

The Two Presidencies

By Aaron Wildavsky

The United States has one president, but it has two presidencies; one presidency is for domestic affairs, and the other is concerned with defense and foreign policy. Since World War II, presidents have had much greater success in controlling the nation's defense and foreign policies than in dominating its domestic policies. Even Lyndon Johnson has seen his early record of victories in domestic legislation diminish as his concern with foreign affairs grows.

What powers does the president have to control defense and foreign policies and so completely overwhelm those who might wish to thwart him?

The president's normal problem with domestic policy is to get congressional support for the programs he prefers. In foreign affairs, in contrast, he can almost always get support for policies that he believes will protect the nation—but his problem is to find a viable policy.

Whoever they are, whether they begin by caring about foreign policy like Eisenhower and Kennedy or about domestic policies like Truman and Johnson, presidents soon discover they have more policy preferences in domestic matters than in foreign policy. The Republican and Democratic parties possess a traditional roster of policies, which can easily be adopted by a new president—for example, he can be either for or against Medicare and aid to education. Since existing domestic policy usually changes in only small steps, presidents find it relatively simple to make minor adjustments. However, although any president knows he supports foreign aid and NATO, the world outside changes much more rapidly than the nation inside—presidents and their parties have no prior policies on Argentina and the Congo.

The world has become a highly intractable place with a whirl of forces we cannot or do not know how to alter.

The Record of Presidential Control

It takes great crises, such as Roosevelt's hundred days in the midst of the depression, or the extraordinary majorities that Barry Goldwater's candidacy willed to Lyndon Johnson, for presidents to succeed in controlling domestic policy: From the end of the 1930s to the present (what may roughly be called the modern era), presidents have often been frustrated in their domestic programs. From 1938, when conservatives regrouped their forces, to the time of his death, Franklin Roosevelt did not get a single piece of significant domestic legislation passed. Truman lost out on most of his intense domestic preferences, except perhaps for housing. Since Eisenhower did not ask for much domestic legislation, he did not meet consistent defeat, yet he failed in his general policy of curtailing governmental commitments. Kennedy, of course, faced great difficulties with domestic legislation.

In the realm of foreign policy there has not been a single major issue on which presidents, when they were serious and determined, have failed. The list of their victories is impressive: entry into the United Nations, the Marshall Plan, NATO, the Truman Doctrine, the decisions to stay out of Indochina in 1954 and to intervene in Vietnam in the 1960s, aid to Poland and Yugoslavia, the test-ban treaty, and many more. Serious setbacks to the president in controlling foreign policy are extraordinary and unusual.

Table 2.1, compiled from the Congressional Quarterly Service tabulation of presidential initiative and congressional response from 1948 through 1964, shows that presidents have significantly better records in foreign and defense matters than in domestic policies. When refugees and immigration—which Congress considers primarily a domestic concern—are removed from the general foreign policy area, it is clear that presidents prevail about 70 percent of the time in defense and foreign policy, compared with 40 percent in the domestic sphere.

Table 2.1 Congressional Action of Presidential Proposals from 1948–1964

Policy Area	Congressional Action		
	Percent Pass	**Percent Fail**	**Number of Proposals**
Domestic policy (natural resources, labor, agriculture, taxes, etc.)	40.2	59.8	2,499
Defense policy (defense, disarmament, manpower, misc.)	73.3	26.7	90
Foreign policy	58.5	41.5	655
Immigration, refugees	13.2	86.0	129
Treaties, general foreign relations, State Department, foreign aid	70.8	29.2	445

Source: Congressional Quarterly Service, Congress *and the Nation,* 1945–1964 (Washington, 1965).

World Events and Presidential Resources

Power in politics is control over governmental decisions. How does the president manage his control of foreign and defense policy? The answer does not reside in the greater constitutional power in foreign affairs that presidents have possessed since the founding of the Republic. The answer lies in the changes that have taken place since 1945.

The number of nations with which the United States has diplomatic relations has increased from 53 in 1939 to 113 in 1966. But sheer numbers do not tell enough; the world has also become a much more dangerous place. However remote it may seem at times, our government must always be aware of the possibility of nuclear war.

Yet the mere existence of great powers with effective thermonuclear weapons would not, in and of itself, vastly increase our rate of interaction with most other nations. We see events in Assam or Burundi as important because they are also part of a larger worldwide contest, called the cold war, in which great powers are rivals for the control or support of other nations. Moreover, the reaction against the blatant isolationism of the 1930s has led to a concern with foreign policy that is worldwide in scope. We are interested in what happens everywhere because we see these events as connected with larger interests involving, at the worst, the possibility of ultimate destruction.

Given the overriding fact that the world is dangerous and that small causes are perceived to have potentially great effects in an unstable world, it follows that Presidents must be interested in relatively "small" matters. So they give Azerbaijan or Lebanon or Vietnam huge amounts of their time. Arthur Schlesinger, Jr., wrote of Kennedy that "in the first two months of his administration he probably spent more time on Laos than on anything else." Few failures in domestic policy, presidents soon realize, could have as disastrous consequences as any one of dozens of mistakes in the international arena.

The result is that foreign policy concerns tend to drive out domestic policy. Except for occasional questions of domestic prosperity and for civil rights, foreign affairs have consistently higher priority for presidents. Once, when trying to talk to President Kennedy about natural resources, Secretary of the Interior Stewart Udall remarked, "He's imprisoned by Berlin?

The importance of foreign affairs to presidents is intensified by the increasing speed of events in the international arena. The event and its consequences follow closely on top of one another. The blunder at the Bay of Pigs is swiftly followed by the near catastrophe of the Cuban missile crisis. Presidents can no longer count on passing along their most difficult problems to their successors. They must expect to face the consequences of their actions—or failure to act—while still in office.

Domestic policy making is usually based on experimental adjustments to an existing situation, Only a few decisions, such as those involving large dams, irretrievably commit future generations. Decisions in foreign affairs, however, are often perceived to be irreversible. This is expressed, for example, in the fear of escalation or the various "spiral" or "domino" theories of international conflict.

If decisions are perceived to be both important and irreversible, there is every reason for presidents to devote a great deal of resources to them. Presidents have to be oriented toward the future in the use of their resources. They serve a fixed term in office, and they cannot automatically count on support from the populace, Congress, or the administrative apparatus. They have to be careful, therefore, to husband their resources for pressing future needs. But because the consequences of events in foreign affairs are potentially more grave, faster to manifest themselves, and less easily reversible than in domestic affairs, presidents are more willing to use up their resources.

The Power to Act

Their formal powers to commit resources in foreign affairs and defense are vast. Particularly important is their power as commander-in-chief to move troops. Faced with situations like the invasion of South Korea or the emplacement of missiles in Cuba, fast action is required. Presidents possess both the formal power to act and the knowledge that elites and the general public expect them to act. Once they have committed American forces, it is difficult for Congress or anyone else to alter the course of events. The Dominican venture is a recent case in point.

Presidential discretion in foreign affairs also makes it difficult {though not impossible) for Congress to restrict their actions. Presidents can use executive agreements instead of treaties, enter into tacit agreements instead of written ones, and otherwise help create *de facto* situations not easily reversed. Presidents also have far greater ability than anyone else to obtain information on developments abroad through the Departments of State and Defense. The need for secrecy in some aspects of foreign and defense policy further restricts the ability of others to compete with presidents. These things are all well known. What is not so generally appreciated is the growing presidential ability to *use* information to achieve goals.

In the past presidents were amateurs in military strategy. They could not even get much useful advice outside of the military. As late as the 1930s the number of people outside the military establishment who were professionally engaged in the study of defense policy could be numbered on the fingers. Today there are hundreds of such men. The rise of the defense intellectuals has given the president of the United States enhanced ability to control defense policy. He is no longer dependent on the military for advice. He can choose among defense intellectuals from the research corporations and the academies for alternative sources of advice. He can install these men in his own office. He can play them off against each other or use them to extend spheres of coordination.

Even with these advisers, however, presidents and secretaries of defense might still be too bewildered by the complexity of nuclear situations to take action—unless they had an understanding of the doctrine and concepts of deterrence. But knowledge; of doctrine about deterrence has been widely diffused; it can be picked up by any intelligent person who will read books or listen to enough hours of conversation. Whether or not the doctrine is good is a separate question; the point is that civilians can feel they understand what is going on in defense policy. Perhaps the most extraordinary feature of presidential action during the Cuban missile crisis was the degree to which the Commander-in-Chief of the Armed Forces insisted on controlling even the smallest moves. From the positioning of ships to the methods of boarding, to the precise words and actions to be taken by individual soldiers and sailors, the president and his civilian advisers were in control.

Although presidents have rivals for power in foreign affairs, the rivals do not usually succeed. Presidents prevail not only because they may have superior resources but because their potential opponents are weak, divided, or believe that they should not control foreign policy. Let us consider the potential rivals—the general citizenry, special interest groups, the Congress, the military, the so-called military-industrial complex, and the State Department.

Competitors for Control of Policy

The Public

The general public is much more dependent on presidents in foreign affairs than in domestic matters. While many people know about the impact of social security and Medicare, few know about politics in Malawi. So it is not surprising that people expect the president to act in foreign affairs and reward him with their confidence. Gallup Polls consistently show that presidential popularity rises after he takes action in a crisis—whether the action is disastrous as in the Bay of Pigs or successful as in the Cuban missile crisis. Decisive action, such as the bombing of oil fields near Haiphong, resulted in a sharp (though temporary) increase in Johnson's popularity.

The Vietnam situation illustrates another problem of public opinion in foreign affairs: it is extremely difficult to get operational policy directions from the general public. It took a long time before any sizable public interest in the subject developed. Nothing short of the large scale involvement of American troops under fire probably could have brought about the current high level of concern. Yet this relatively well developed popular opinion is difficult to interpret. While a majority appear to support President Johnson's policy, it appears that they could easily be persuaded to withdraw from Vietnam if the administration changed its line. Although a sizable majority would support various initiatives to end the war, they would seemingly be appalled if this action led to Communist encroachments elsewhere in Southeast Asia. (See "The President, the Polls, and Vietnam" by Seymour Martin Lipset, *Transaction*, Sept/Oct 1966.)

Although Presidents lead opinion in foreign affairs, they know they will be held accountable for the consequences of their actions. President Johnson has maintained a large commitment in Vietnam. His popularity shoots up now and again in the midst of some imposing action. But the fact that a body of citizens do not like the war comes back to damage his overall popularity. We will support your initiatives, the people seem to say, but we will reserve the right to punish you (or your party) if we do not like the results.

Special Interest Groups

Opinions are easier to gauge in domestic affairs because, for one thing, there is a stable structure of interest groups that covers virtually all matters of concern. The farm, labor, business, conservation, veteran, civil rights, and other interest groups provide cues when a proposed policy affects them. Thus people who identify with these groups may adopt their views. But in foreign policy matters the interest group structure is weak, unstable, and thin rather than dense. In many matters affecting Africa and Asia, for example, it is hard to think of well-known interest groups. While ephemeral groups arise from time to time to support or protest particular policies, they usually disappear when the immediate problem is resolved. In contrast, longer lasting elite groups like the' Foreign Policy Association and Council on Foreign Reflations are composed of people of diverse views; refusal to take strong positions on controversial matters is a condition of their continued viability.

The strongest interest groups are probably the ethnic associations whose members have strong ties with a homeland, as in Poland or Cuba, so they are rarely activated simultaneously on any specific issue. They are most effective when most narrowly and intensely focused—as in the fierce pressure from Jews to recognize the state of Israel. But their relatively small numbers limits their significance to presidents in the vastly more important general foreign policy picture—as continued aid to the Arab countries shows. Moreover, some ethnic groups may conflict on significant issues such as American acceptance of the Oder-Neisse line separating Poland from what is now East Germany.

The Congress

Congressmen also exercise power in foreign affairs. Yet they are ordinarily not serious competitors with the president because they follow a self-denying ordinance. They do not think it is their job to determine the nation's defense policies. Lewis A. Dexter's extensive interviews with members of the Senate Armed Services Committee, who might be expected to want a voice in defense policy, reveal that they do not desire for men like themselves to run the nation's defense establishment. Aside from a few specific conflicts among the armed services which allow both the possibility and desirability of direct intervention, the Armed Services Committee constitutes a sort of real estate committee dealing with the regional economic consequences of die location of military facilities.

The congressional appropriations power is potentially a significant resource, but circumstances since the end of World War II have tended to reduce its effectiveness. The appropriations committees and Congress itself might make their will felt by refusing to allot funds unless basic policies were altered. But this has not happened. While Congress makes its traditional small cuts in the military budget, presidents have mostly found themselves warding off congressional attempts to increase specific items still further.

Most of the time, the administration's refusal to spend has not been seriously challenged. However, there have been occasions when individual legislators or committees have been influential. Senator Henry Jackson in his campaign (with the aid of colleagues on the Joint Committee on Atomic Energy) was able to gain acceptance for the Polaris weapons system and Senator Arthur H. Vandenberg played a part in determining the shape of the Marshall Plan and so on. The few congressmen who are expert in defense policy act, as Samuel P. Huntington says, largely as lobbyists with the executive branch. It is apparently more fruitful for these congressional experts to use their resources in order to get a hearing from the executive than to work on other congressmen.

When an issue involves the actual use or threat of violence, it takes a great deal to convince congressmen not to follow the president's lead. James Robinson's tabulation of foreign and defense policy issues from the late 1930s to \961 (table 2.2) shows dominant influence by Congress in only one case out of seven—the 1954 decision not to intervene with armed force in Indochina. In that instance President Eisenhower deliberately sounded out congressional opinion and, finding it negative, decided not to intervene—against the advice of Admiral Radford, chairman of the Joint Chiefs of Staff.

This attempt to abandon responsibility did not succeed, as the years of American involvement demonstrate.

The Military

The outstanding feature of the military's participation in making defense policy is their amazing weakness. Whether the policy decisions involve the size of the armed forces, the choice of weapons systems, the total defense budget, or its division into components, the military have not prevailed. Let us take budgetary decisions as representative of the key choices to be made in defense policy. Since the end of World War II die military has not been able to achieve significant (billion dollar) increases in appropriations by their own efforts. Under Truman and Eisenhower defense budgets were determined by what Huntington calls the remainder method: the two presidents estimated revenues, decided what they could spend on domestic matters, and the remainder was assigned to defense. The usual controversy was between some military and congressional groups supporting much larger expenditures while the president and his executive allies refused. A typical case, involving the desire of the Air Force to increase the number of groups of planes is described by Huntington in *The Common Defense*:

> The FY [fiscal year] 1949 budget provided forty-eight groups. After the Czech coup, the Administration yielded and backed an Air Force of fifty-five groups in its spring rearmament program. Congress added additional funds to aid Air Force expansion to seventy groups. The Administration refused to utilize them, however, and in the gathering economy wave of the summer and fall of 1948, the Air Force goal was cut back again to forty-eight groups. In 1949 the House of Representatives

picked up the challenge and appropriated funds for fifty-eight groups. The president impounded the money. In June, 1950, the Air Force had forty-eight groups.

The great increases in the defense budget were due far more to Stalin and modern technology than to the military. The Korean War resulted in an increase from 12 to 44 billions and much of the rest followed Sputnik and the huge costs of missile programs. Thus modern technology and international conflict put an end to the one major effort to subordinate foreign affairs to domestic policies through the budget.

It could be argued that the president merely ratifies the decisions made by the military and their allies. If the military and/or Congress were united and insistent on defense policy, it would certainly be difficult for presidents to resist these forces. But it is precisely the disunity of die military that has characterized the entire postwar period. Indeed, the military have not been united on any major matter of defense policy. The apparent unity of the Joint Chiefs of Staff tufas out to be illusory. The vast majority of their recommendations appear to be unanimous and are accepted by the secretary of defense and the president. But this facade of unity can only be achieved by methods that vitiate the impact of the recommendations. Genuine disagreements are hidden by vague language that commits no one to anything. Mutually contradictory plans are strung together so everyone appears to get something, but nothing is decided. Since it is impossible to agree on really important matters, all sorts of trivia are brought in to make a record of agreement. While it may be true, as Admiral Denfield, a former chief of naval operations, said, that "On nine-tenths of the matters that come before them the Joint Chiefs of Staff reach agreement themselves "the vastly more important truth is that "normally the *only* disputes are on strategic concepts, the size and composition of forces, and budget matters"

Military Industrial

But what about the fabled military-industrial complex? If the military alone is divided and weak, perhaps the giant industrial firms that are so dependent on defense contracts play a large part in making policy.

First, there is an important distinction between the questions "Who will get a given contract?" and "What will our defense policy be?" It is apparent that different answers may be given to these quite different questions. There are literally tens of thousands of defense contractors. They may compete vigorously for business. In the course of this competition, they may wine and dine military officers, use retired generals, seek intervention by their congressmen, place ads in trade journals, and even contribute to political campaigns. The famous TFX controversy—should General Dynamics or Boeing get the expensive contract?—is a larger than life example of the pressures brought to bear in search of lucrative contracts.

But neither the TFX case nor the usual vigorous competition for contracts is involved with the making of substantive defense policy. Vital questions like the size of the defense budget, the choice of strategic programs, massive retaliation vs. a counter-[insurgency] strategy, and

Table 2.2 Congressional Involvement in Foreign and Defense Policy Decisions

Issue	Congressional Involvement (High, Low, None)	Initiator (Congress or Executive)	Predominant Influence (Congress or Executive)	Legislation or Resolution (Yes or No)	Violence at Stake (Yes or No)	Decision Time (Long or Short)
Neutrality Legislation, the 1930's	High	Exec	Cong	Yes	No	Long
Lend-Lease, 1941	High	Exec	Exec	Yes	Yes	Long
Aid to Russia, 1941	Low	Exec	Exec	No	No	Long
Repeal of Chinese Exclusion, 1943	High	Cong	Cong	Yes	No	Long
Fulbright Resolution, 1943	High	Cong	Cong	Yes	No	Long
Building the Atomic Bomb, 1944	Low	Exec	Exec	Yes	Yes	Long
Foreign Services Act of 1946	High	Exec	Exec	Yes	No	Long
Truman Doctrine, 1947	High	Exec	Exec	Yes	No	Long
The Marshall Plan, 1947–48	High	Exec	Exec	Yes	No	Long
Berlin Airlift, 1948	None	Exec	Exec	No	Yes	Long
Vandenberg Resolution, 1948	High	Exec	Cong	Yes	No	Long
North Atlantic Treaty, 1947–49	High	Exec	Exec	Yes	No	Long
Korean Decision, 1950	None	Exec	Exec	No	Yes	Short
Japanese Peace Treaty, 1952	High	Exec	Exec	Yes	No	Long
Bohlen Nomination, 1953	High	Exec	Exec	Yes	No	Long
Indo-China, 1954	High	Exec	Cong	No	Yes	Short
Formosan Resolution, 1955	High	Exec	Exec	Yes	Yes	Long
International Finance Corporation, 1956	Low	Exec	Exec	Yes	No	Long
Foreign Aid, 1957	High	Exec	Exec	Yes	No	Long
Reciprocal Trade Agreements, 1958	High	Exec	Exec	Yes	No	Long
Monroney Resolution, 1958	High	Cong	Cong	Yes	No	Long
Cuban Decision, 1961	Low	Exec	Exec	No	Yes	Long

Source: James A. Robinson, Congress and Foreign Policy-Making (Homewood, IL: Irwin, 1962)

the like were far beyond the policy aims of any company. Industrial firms, then, do not control such decisions, nor is there much evidence that they actually try. No doubt a precipitous and drastic rush to disarmament would meet with opposition from industrial firms among other interests. However, there has never been a time when any significant element in the government considered a disarmament policy to be feasible.

It may appear that industrial firms had no special reason to concern themselves with the government's stance on defense because they agree with the national consensus on resisting communism, maintaining a large defense establishment, and rejecting isolationism. However, this hypothesis about the climate of opinion explains everything and nothing. For every policy that is adopted or rejected can be explained away on the grounds that the cold war climate of opinion dictated what happened. Did die United States fail to intervene with armed force in Vietnam in 1954? That must be because the climate of opinion Was against it. Did the United States send troops to Vietnam in the 1960s? That must be because the cold war climate demanded it If the United States builds more missiles, negotiates a test-ban treaty, intervenes in the Dominican Republic, fails to intervene in a dozen other situations, all these actions fit the hypothesis by definition. The argument is reminiscent of those who defined the Soviet Union as permanently hostile and therefore interpreted increases of Soviet troops as menacing and decreases of troop strength as equally sinister.

If the growth of the military establishment is not directly equated with increasing military control of defense policy, the extraordinary weakness of the professional soldier still requires explanation. Huntington has written about how major military leaders were seduced in the Truman and Eisenhower years into believing that they should bow to the judgment of civilians that the economy could not stand much larger military expenditures. Once the size of the military pie was accepted as a fixed constraint, the military services were compelled to put their major energies into quarreling with one another over who should get the larger share. Given the natural rivalries of the military and their traditional acceptance of civilian rule, the president and his advisers—who could claim responsibility for the broader picture of reconciling defense and domestic policies—had the upper hand. There are, however, additional explanations to be considered.

The dominant role of the congressional appropriations committee is to be guardian of the treasury. This is manifested in the pride of its members in cutting the president's budget. Thus it was difficult to get this crucial committee to recommend even a few hundred million increase in defense; it was practically impossible to get them to consider the several billion jump that might really have made a difference. A related budgetary matter concerned the planning, programming, and budgeting system introduced by Secretary of Defense McNamara. For if the defense budget contained major categories that crisscrossed the services, only the secretary of defense could put it together. Whatever the other debatable consequences of program budgeting, its major consequence was to grant power to the secretary and his civilian advisers.

The subordination of the military through program budgeting is just one symptom of a more general weakness of the military. In the past decade the military has suffered a lack of intellectual skills appropriate to the nuclear age. For no one has (and no one wants) direct experience with nuclear war. So the usual military talk about being the only people to have combat experience is not very impressive. Instead, the imaginative creation of possible future wars—in order to avoid them—requires people with a high capacity for abstract thought combined with the ability to manipulate symbols using quantitative methods. West Point has not produced many such men.

The State Department

Modern presidents expect the State Department to carry out their policies. John F. Kennedy felt that State was "in *some* particular sense 'his' department." If a secretary of state forgets this, as was apparently the case with James Byrnes under Truman, a president may find another man. But the State Department, especially the Foreign Service, is also a highly professional organization with a life and momentum of its own. If a president does not push hard, he may find his preferences somehow dissipated in time. Arthur Schlesinger fills his book on Kennedy with laments about the bureaucratic inertia and recalcitrance of the State Department.

Yet Schlesinger's own account suggests that State could not ordinarily resist the president. At one point, he writes of "the president, himself, increasingly the day-to-day director of American foreign policy" On the next page, we learn that "Kennedy dealt personally with almost every aspect of policy around the globe. He knew more about certain areas than the senior officials at State and probably called as many issues to their attention as they did to his." The president insisted on his way in Laos. He pushed through his policy on the Congo against strong opposition with the State Department. Had Kennedy wanted to get a great deal more initiative out of the State Department, as Schlesinger insists, he could have replaced the secretary of state, a man who did not command special support in the Democratic party or in Congress. It may be that Kennedy wanted too strongly to run his own foreign policy. Dean Rusk may have known far better than Schlesinger that the one thing Kennedy did not want was a man who might rival him in the field of foreign affairs.

Schlesinger comes closest to the truth when he writes that "the White House could always win any battle it chose over the [Foreign] Service; but the prestige and proficiency *of* the Service limited the number of battles any White House would find it profitable to fight." When the president knew what he wanted, he got it. When he was doubtful and perplexed, he sought good advice and frequently did not get that. But there is no evidence that the people on his staff came up with better ideas. The real problem may have 00 been a lack of good ideas anywhere. Kennedy undoubtedly encouraged his CO staff to prod the State Department. But the president was sufficiently cautious not to push so hard that he got his way when he was not certain what that way should be. In this context Kennedy appears to have played his staff off against elements in the State Department.

The growth of a special White House staff to help presidents in foreign affairs expresses their need for assistance, their refusal to rely completely on the regular executive agencies, and their ability to find competent men. The deployment of this staff must remain a presidential prerogative, however, if its members are to serve presidents and not their opponents. Whenever critics do not like existing foreign and defense policies, they are likely to complain that the White House staff is screening out divergent views from the president's attention. Naturally, the critics recommend introducing many more different viewpoints. If the critics could maneuver the president into counting hands all day ("on the one hand and on the other*), they would make it impossible for him to act. Such a viewpoint is also congenial to those who believe that action rather than inaction is the greatest present danger in foreign policy. But presidents resolutely refuse to become prisoners of their advisers by using them as other people would like. Presidents remain in control of their staff as well as of major foreign policy decisions.

How Complete Is the Control?

Some analysts say that the success of presidents in controlling foreign policy decisions is largely illusory. It is achieved, they say, by anticipating the reactions of others, and eliminating proposals that would run into severe opposition. There is some truth in this objection. In politics, where transactions are based on a high degree of mutual interdependence, what others may do has to be taken into account But basing presidential success in foreign and defense policy on anticipated reactions suggests a static situation which does not exist. For if presidents propose only those policies that would get support in Congress, and Congress opposes them only when it knows that it can muster overwhelming strength, there would never be any conflict. Indeed, there might never be any action.

How can "anticipated reaction" explain the conflict over policies like the Marshall Plan and the test-ban treaty in which severe opposition was overcome only by strenuous efforts? Furthermore, why doesn't "anticipated reaction" work in domestic affairs? One would have to argue that for some reason presidential perception of what would be successful is consistently confused on domestic issues and most always accurate on major foreign policy issues. But the role of "anticipated reactions" should be greater in the more familiar domestic situations, which provide a backlog of experience for forecasting, than in foreign policy with many novel situations such as the Suez crisis or the Rhodesian affair.

Are there significant historical examples which might refute the thesis of presidential control of foreign policy? Foreign aid may be a case in point. For many years, presidents have struggled to get foreign aid appropriations because of hostility from public and congressional opinion. Yet several billion dollars a year are appropriated regularly despite the evident unpopularity of the program. In the aid programs to Communist countries like Poland and Yugoslavia, the Congress attaches all sorts of restrictions to the aid, but presidents find ways of getting around them.

What about the example of recognition of Communist China? The sentiment of the country always has been against recognizing Red China or admitting it to the United Nations, But have presidents wanted to recognize Red China and been hamstrung by opposition?

The answer, I suggest, is a qualified "no." By the time recognition of Red China might have become a serious issue for the Truman administration, the war in Korea effectively precluded its consideration. There is no evidence that President Eisenhower or Secretary Dulles ever thought it wise to recognize Red China or help admit her to the United Nations. The Kennedy administration viewed the matter as not of major importance and, considering the opposition, moved cautiously in suggesting change. Then came the war in Vietnam. If the advantages for foreign policy had been perceived to be much higher, then Kennedy or Johnson might have proposed changing American policy toward recognition of Red China.

One possible exception, in the case of Red China, however, does not seem sufficient to invalidate the general thesis that presidents do considerably better in getting their way in foreign and defense policy than in domestic policies.

The World Influence

The forces impelling presidents to be concerned with the widest range of foreign and defense policies also affect the ways in which they calculate their power stakes. As Kennedy used to say, "Domestic policy … can only defeat us; foreign policy can kill us "

It no longer makes sense for presidents to "play politics" with foreign and defense policies. In the past, presidents might have thought that they could gain by prolonged delay or by not acting at all. The problem might disappear or be passed on to their successors. Presidents must now expect to pay the high costs themselves if the world situation deteriorates. The advantages of pursuing a policy that is viable in the world, that will not blow up on CO presidents or their fellow citizens, far outweigh any temporary political disadvantages accrued in supporting an initially unpopular policy. Compared with domestic affairs, presidents engaged in world politics are immensely more concerned with meeting problems on their own terms. Who supports and opposes a policy, though a matter of considerable interest, does not assume the crucial importance that it does in domestic affairs. The best policy presidents can find is also the best politics.

The fact that there are numerous foreign and defense policy situations competing for a president's attention means that it is worthwhile to organize political activity in order to affect his agenda. For if a president pays more attention to certain problems he may develop different preferences; he may seek and receive different advice; his new calculations may lead him to devote greater resources to seeking a solution. Interested congressmen may exert influence not by directly determining a presidential decision, but indirectly by making it costly for a president to avoid reconsidering the basis for his action. For example, citizen groups, such as those concerned with a change in China policy, may have an impact simply by keeping their proposals on the public agenda. A president may be compelled to reconsider a problem even though he could not overtly be forced to alter the prevailing policy.

In foreign affairs we may be approaching the stage where knowledge is power. There is a tremendous receptivity to good ideas in Washington. Most anyone who can present a convincing rationale for dealing with a hard world finds a ready audience. The best way to convince presidents to follow a desired policy is to show that it might work. A man like McNamara thrives because he performs; he comes up with answers he can defend. It is, to be sure, extremely difficult to devise good policies or to predict their consequences accurately. Nor is it easy to convince others that a given policy Is superior to other alternatives. But it is the way to influence with presidents. For if they are convinced that the current policy is best, the likelihood of gaining sufficient force to compel a change is quite small. The man who can build better foreign policies will find presidents beating a path to his door.

★ The Multiple Presidencies
★ Across the Issue Areas of American Foreign Policy in
★ Presidential-Congressional Relations
By Matthew Caverly

"Journeys, great and small, always begin at the beginning!"

—Mark Twain

Introduction

In this chapter, we will examine the broad contours of the *multiple presidencies thesis's* findings by looking longitudinally across the 50 plus year history of the Post War Era (1953–2004). In that effort, I will follow the basic structure laid out in the previous chapters for report and analysis of the relevant findings including an introduction, followed by setting the historical contexts in political and economic terms for extant presidential-congressional foreign policy relations and then a dissection of the findings regarding the longitudinal models. Lastly, I will engage in a discussion of those base findings emanating out of the time series and regression analyses within the politico-economic historical contexts that they find themselves in. This chapter will close with a summary of the finer points of the study's findings and serve as a stepping stone into the cross-sectional analyses to come.

First of all, the historical context is more than just an anecdotal narrative of the presidential-congressional foreign affairs relationship. It is in fact a "setting event," which serves as the springboard for the quantitative modeling that follows it. Variables do not exist as phenomena unto themselves, rather they are themselves both products of and inhabitants within a certain context (or, in theory anyway multiple contexts). It is vitally important to remember that these variables are only indicative of their mutual and co-dependent interaction with the unit level actors (the president and Congress) within the specified timeframe of the study itself. The history is important because it provides for the appropriate selection of indicators and conditions their temporal impacts. With that in mind, I will concentrate on developing a narrative of the role played by the issue areas of foreign policy across political time.

The findings result from two general types of models, both of which are leveled at the structural impacts on presidential-congressional relations as measured by the dependent variable—the annual presidential success rate (in either foreign policy or the various issue areas of foreign policy—national security, domestic security, diplomacy, trade, foreign aid and immigration). One model type is a time series formation which tracks relations as either single entities (autocorrelations) or as groups (cross-correlations) across a given time frame by accounting for the role of time in a quantitative fashion (McClary and Hay 1975). I employ both in order to check for stasis and dynamism within as well as across the dependent variables.

Another model that I utilize is a simple multivariate regression of the role that the various issue area success scores (the secondary dependent variables) play in relation to overall presidential foreign policy success (the primary dependent variable).[1] This is important because it answers a basic contention of the multiple presidencies thesis that foreign policy is in actuality a polyglot of only loosely related issue areas. Other secondary support measures are also employed but I will discuss those within the text of the section itself. Finally, additional longitudinal regression models employing some of the secondary dependent variables are specified and run in order to look at basic patterns of relationships that were hypothesized in Chapter 2. These models look at certain historical and economic conditions operating at the macro-level whereby they exert a phenomenon-specific relationship influencing the structural settings of presidency-centered v. congress-centered conditions. In this effort, I also test for the influence of "periods of presidential-congressional foreign policy history" (War Power 1953–1972, Confrontation Politics 1973–1989, Imperial Presidency Politicized 1990–2000 and the Extra-Systemic Dilemma 2001–2004?). These last models serve as the starting off point for the cross-sectional analyses contained in the rest of this work.

Finally, the discussion section matches the empirics with the theory, by pulling together the elements of the historical context section with those of the empirical findings section. The history sets the context, while the models analyze it and then in this section, the two are brought together by the theoretical premises of the multiple presidencies thesis. Essentially, the two previous sections are re-discussed but under the framework of an analogy provided by the theory which not only suggests the utility of the theory but also brings what would otherwise be somewhat disparate analyses into a coherent systematized framework. Lastly, we take a final review of the chapter as a whole before moving on to the further articulations promised for in the cross-sectional portion of this study.

---

1 See relevant portions of the methods chapter (3) for a deeper discussion of these contrasting dependent variables.

Issue Areas Across Political Time

Throughout the "path of time" followed in this analysis, one overarching initial conclusion can be made regarding the role of the issue areas of foreign policy, that being—they matter and they do so in a systematic fashion. Having said that, how they matter, when they matter and their potential for mattering in the future is subject to a great deal of within and across case variance. The reason for this is simple; time itself has had a political impact on the executive-legislative relationship in foreign policy.

Our study begins in the year 1953, which was originally selected by me for methodological reasons since that is when the editorial staff at *Congressional Quarterly* began to systematically record presidential position voting within the Congress. It has proved to have a strong analytical prowess as well. In this year, we as a country saw the end of the first major point when the Cold War "got hot." The Korean War (1950–1953) was certainly not the first place of American-Soviet conflict but in the short decade after the end of the Second World War (the Post-War Era) it was the most intense by any measure of magnitude. Unlike the preceding Cold War conflicts of the late 1940's over Greece, Turkey and Germany; Korea was a major power war. This type of war not only reaches the magnitude measures of intensity and duration associated with designating major from minor wars (Singer and Small 1983).[2] It also has the characteristic of involving one or more major powers (states in the Westphalian system), in this case not only the US but also Britain and to a much reduced extent France (due to their protracted involvement in the Indochina War 1946–1954) (Cashman 1993). Furthermore, Communist China certainly qualified as a "quasi-major power" at least militarily and after the Yalu River intervention in late fall 1950 they took the place of the North Koreans as the central antagonists faced by the United Nations (UN).[3]

The Korean War arguably had almost as great an impact on the domestic populace of the United States as World War II, being the fact that, Truman utilized the war to engage in a partial mobilization of men and materiel (Milkis and Nelson 2003). This "partial" mobilization included a permanent extension of the draft, reserve and guard duration call-ups, increases in income and corporate taxes, rationing of industrial and consumer goods as well as perhaps most pervasively placing war economy controls over strategic resources like steel, coal and oil (Milkis and Nelson 2003). In fact, it was because of this mobilization activity that the United States economy suffered a severe retraction beginning in the summer of 1953 as the Armistice took effect and the country moved to a major de-mobilization of its war economy and conventional armed forces (Milkis and Nelson 2003). The corresponding "Korean War

---

2 These measure are usually indexes developed based around casualties, size of forces, duration of deployment, size and number of battles and material costs as well as the geographic scope of what must be seen as a type of "militarized dispute" (Singer and Small 1983, Vasques 1994, Cashman 1993, Singer 1999).

3 While it is now known that the Soviets were directly involved militarily in the Korean and Vietnam Wars, such combat involvement was mostly constrained to air power and air defense in limited quantities.

Recession," while not as pervasive in its impacts regarding the recessionary macroeconomic readjustments following each of the two World Wars (1919–1921 and 1946), this recession was deep enough and entrenched enough that it caused the Democratic Party to lose the Congress and was instrumental in Stevenson's defeat in the 1952 elections (Milkis and Neslon 2003 and Department of Commerce 2006, archive report).

While this was the first time in twenty years that the Republican Party had gained control of the White House as they did with Eisenhower's inauguration in 1953, just before between 1947 and 1948 the 80th Congress had been a Republican one. Therefore in the early days of the mid-1950s, notions of the entrenchment of the New Deal realignment were certainly not as powerful as they are now seen in retrospect to have been (from Mayhew 2002). A new "Red Scare" driven by the activities of Joseph McCarthy (R-WI) coupled with Eisenhower's "New Look" foreign policy with its emphasis on deterrence through "Mutually Assured Destruction" made the Cold War into an ever present and ominous everyday fear for the common man and woman in America (Snow and Brown 1999). In contrast to David Halberstam's (2000) picture of 1950s America as a lost age of innocence and opportunity, the 1950s from a foreign policy perspective were a series of crises some seen, some inferred.

The question of military intervention into the Indochina War at the Battle of Dien Bien Phu in 1954 split the Eisenhower "war cabinet" between Hawks calling for some form of military "solution" led by Vice-president Nixon and Doves cautioning against such an endeavor as led by a ground war weary Pentagon (Greenstein 1993). Eisenhower defected from direct intervention but set the US on a course for increased military, political and economic involvement in what would soon be the countries of North and South Vietnam (Ellsberg 1971). Real, though minor military intervention in Lebanon in 1958 as well as the diplomatic efforts during the Suez Canal Crisis of 1956 would foreshadow future American military adventures in years to come. Additionally, shows of force in the South China Sea and the Black Sea by the US Navy against communist counterparts were flashpoints that bordered on the deadly during this time.

Despite recessions in 1953–54 and 1958, the American economy grew at unprecedented rates during the 1950's as it enjoyed the fruits of its Post-War position as the clear global economic hegemon. The other great powers were still rebuilding after the destruction of the Second World War including America's rivals in the Sino-Soviet bloc. The US economy accounted for about ½ of the world's GNP during this period, it had ½ the world's gold reserves, the US dollar was the de facto world currency upon which all others were pegged and the US enjoyed wide trade and international finance balances (Kegley and Wittkopf 2001; Department of Commerce 2006, archive reports). Finally, the United States had the highest industrial capacity and was the number one provider of global goods and services for all economic sectors (Papp, Johnson and Endicott 2006, Department of Commerce 2006, archive reports) Perhaps due to this as well as its free world leadership position, the US was the number one provider of foreign aid to both the First (though reconstructing) and Third Worlds (US AID 2006, archive reports and Snow and Brown 1999). As the fifties came to a close, the US looked ahead with promise as well as consternation to the decades to come—they would be both delighted and dejected by what they found.

The 1960's saw a return to Democratic control over the White House after regaining the Congress six years previously in 1954. Along with the arrival of Camelot, came an influx of liberal Northern Democrats in the 1958 mid-term elections, calling for the completion of Roosevelt's policy promises which included a more idealist-centered foreign affairs (from Davidson 1996 in Thurber 1996 and Papp, Johnson and Endicott 2006). The Kennedy doctrine's "flexible response" in combination with a more open diplomacy in the wake of the Bay of Pigs fiasco of 1961 and the hairbreadth nuclear showdown brought on by the Cuban Missile Crisis in 1962 saw the start of diplomatic accomodationism between the American and Soviet empires (Sorensen 1965 and Alison 1971). However, the dagger of Southeast Asia would plunge into the heart of such diplomatic accomplishments as the Open Air Test Treaty of 1963. At the time of the Kennedy assassination, a new optimism had developed regarding US foreign affairs but that optimism would be surely tested in the second half of the decade in the place called Vietnam.

The Vietnam War (1965–1973) amounted to a modern crucible at least as regards US foreign policy making. As the public opinion polls supporting "Johnson's War" declined, especially in the wake of the Tet Offensive in 1968—the Congress founds its voice in the vaunted realm of national security politics. First, a within party debate broke out between the Old Guard Democrats who would ultimately support Vice-president Hubert Humphrey's campaign for the White House in 1968 and the Young Turks rallying around such figures as Eugene McCarthy and Robert Kennedy. In the Congress, a politics of deference continued but extensions of Johnson's leadership outside of national security began to be questioned, especially in areas as diverse as immigration, foreign aid, trade and even Cold War diplomacy with the USSR itself (CQ Almanacs 1967–1968, various legislative histories and Sundquist 1981). After Tet not even national security was left to the purview of the president.

The return of divided government with the election of Republican Richard Nixon in 1968 exacerbated the conflict between the presidency and the Congress into an all out war of central v. adjacent decision makers in both foreign policy and domestic policy (from Fisher 2000, Aldrich and Rohde 2005 as well as Papp, Johnson and Endicott 2006). Specifically, regarding foreign policy this battle would lead to the resurgence of congressional authority both real and imagined in a fashion not seen since the revolt against Wilson's foreign policy Idealism in the 1920's ratification fight over the Treaty of Versailles.[4] The 1970s saw the immediate aftereffects of this protracted struggle with the War Powers Act of 1973 passed over Nixon's veto, the mid-1970s era congressional investigations of the CIA's covert activities both at home and abroad over the previous thirty years, the Jackson-Vanick Amendments regarding Jewish emigration

---

4 Idealism as a philosophy of foreign policy stresses cooperation through open diplomacy, international institutional development and nation-state adherence to the precepts and conditions of international law (Papp, Johnson and Endicott 2005).

from the USSR and the subsequent de-funding of the Vietnam War through the foreign aid appropriations process (Sundquist 1981).

The 1980s, which is sometimes viewed as a restoration of presidential power resulting from the prominence of the Reagan presidency, was in fact, a time of extended partisan conflict between the Republican president and the Democratic House of Representatives.[5] After the 1986 mid-term elections, a fully Democratic Congress offered routine foreign policy alternatives to Reagan's efforts in South Africa, military policy, defense budgets and perhaps most notably Central America. Complicating all of this was that by the 1970s, US relative decline was pervasive and being felt by the domestic polity.

Dollar overhang, a condition where more US currency was "in float" in international markets than the US Mint could account for was in place as early as 1960 (Kegley and Wittkopf 2001). The pervasiveness of this problem led to the Nixonian scheme of dollar devaluation which ended formalized liquidity of international financial and currency markets (Kegley and Wittkopf 2001). Additionally, trade surpluses had turned into trade deficits by the mid 1960s, routine budget surpluses had become routine budget deficits after 1969. Then there was the emergent problem of First World competition from Japan and the European Community which placed the US industrial and agricultural sectors in tight economic straits as some worried that the American Eagle was being displaced by the Japanese economic Samurai (Kennedy 1986). Free trading presidents of both parties faced off against ever increasing numbers of protectionists in the Congress again of both parties (Lindsay 1994).

In the debate over the North American Free trade Agreement (NAFTA), the World Trade Organization (WTO) and the Free Trade Area of the Americas (FTAA) free trading regimes this familiar pattern of a protectionist Congress v. a free trading president continued well into the 1990s. However, the most prolific structural change to the international system was political not economic as the Soviet Empire collapsed into the dustbin of world history in late 1991. The end of the Cold War provided the opportunities of a "peace dividend" due to the decline of systemic conflict but this promise was left unfulfilled as the realities of a world without super power boundaries set in (Snow and Brown 1999, Papp, Johnson and Endicott 2006). War in the Persian Gulf followed by conflicts and potential conflicts brought on by the new security's ethno-political strife and the old security's concerns regarding the maintenance of a "national strategic interest" (from Mathews 1989 and Mearsheimer 2001). The Balkans, Somalia, the Sudan, Rawanda, Haiti, Liberia, Senegal, Russian descent, Chinese ascent and of course Iraq would test both the first Bush's "new world order" and Clinton's "selective engagement" foreign policy doctrines. However, that would only be the beginning of the real importance of a globalized world with its attendant forces on integration juxtaposed against the forces of fragmentation. These countervailing forces have led to creation of a political world that is unipolar only in military concerns, multipolar economically and most troubling

---

5 See Milkis and Nelson (2003) for this alternative viewpoint regarding the "Restoration Presidency" of Ronald Reagan.

for foreign policy decision makers and analysts polyglot socio-culturally (Papp, Johnson and Endicott 2006).

The foreign policy polity that we now occupy is one where diffusion and confluence go hand in hand on any array of issue areas from national security all the way to immigration. The aftermath of the twin towers attack on September the 11th 2001, have led us to re-evaluate the role of presidency-centered v. Congress-centered conditions regarding where the power in foreign policy lies, if it should lie there and why this is so. Recently, we have seen the securitization of immigration as a part of the "War on Terror" with prolonged employment of troops both regular and guard. Port and border security has brought trade into the security realm and an entirely new Cabinet Department devoted to domestic security has since been established. But, this has not necessarily led to a re-presidentialization of foreign policy as recent research has shown that the Congress has been heavily involved in the creation and implementation of these foreign policy efforts (Wolfsenberger in Dodd and Oppenheimer 2005). Nevertheless, W. Bush's "Bull Horn Moment" cannot be underestimated as to its initial and even long term impact as envisioned in the real Wars in Afghanistan and Iraq accomplished with overwhelming support/acquiescence by the Congress, including the opposition party. Finally, the Patriot Act and other domestic surveillance initiatives by the current administration have allowed for the development or at least the potential development of a domestic intelligence capability not seen since the height of the Soviet Union's Committee on State Security (KGB). And, again the Congress largely acquiesced to this "securitized" power into the domestic sphere. The ebb and flow of executive-legislative relations in foreign policy construction and implementation continues but it has been subject to some patterns and it is to these patterns that we now turn.

Empirical Findings

One of the central hypotheses that emanates out of the prescriptions of the multiple presidencies thesis is that the issue areas of foreign policy can be shown to manifest themselves in divergent patterns. The initial descriptive findings of the longitudinal analysis certainly support that contention. As Figures 4-1 and 4-2 suggest, the multiple issue areas of foreign policy whether as discrete or mixed entities appear in a robust fashion.[6] Taking a closer look at these two figures, we can see some significant differences in the distribution of the issue areas. First of all, the discrete issue areas: national security, domestic security, diplomacy, trade, foreign aid and immigration which are at the core of the theory's expectations regarding their presence as roll call phenomena are more prevalent in their presence within the data set than the mixed versions (which are composites of core categories). Second, among these core categories there are a "big three," composed of national security (31% of all votes), trade (23% of all votes) and foreign aid (20% of all votes). Third, national security is the category with the largest percentage of votes which is something that is consistent with hypothesized notions for the existence

---

6 All figures and tables relevant to this chapter are found in sequential order after the summary section.

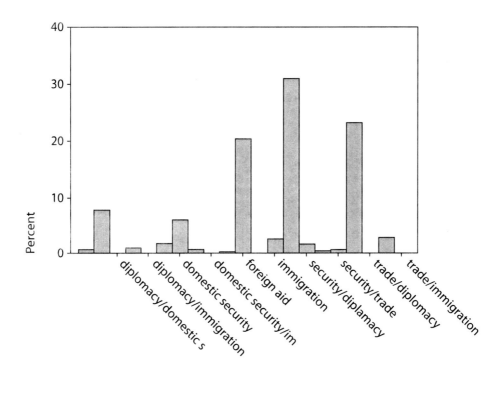

Figure 4-1 Issue Areas of Foreign Policy Bar Chart Across Political Time (1953–2004)

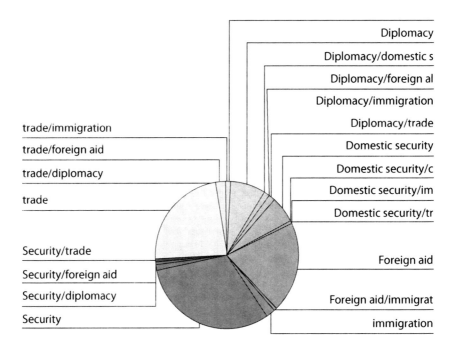

Figure 4-2 Issue Areas of Foreign Policy Pie Chart Across Political Time (1953–2004)

Supporting Table for Figures 4-1 & 4-2
Issue Area of Foreign Policy

		Frequency	Percent	Valid Percent	Cumulative Percent
Valid	Deleted Cases	29	.9	.9	.9
	diplomacy	257	7.7	7.7	8.6
	diplomacy/domestic security	1	.0	.0	8.6
	diplomacy/foreign aid	34	1.0	1.0	9.6
	diplomacy/immigration	1	.0	.0	9.6
	diplomacy/trade	57	1.7	1.7	11.3
	domestic security	196	5.9	5.9	17.2
	domestic security/diplomacy	18	.5	.5	17.7
	domestic security/immigration	1	.0	.0	17.8
	domestic security/trade	4	.1	.1	17.9
	foreign aid	679	20.3	20.3	38.2
	foreign aid/immigration	1	.0	.0	38.2
	immigration	82	2.5	2.5	40.7
	security	1036	31.0	31.0	71.7
	security/diplomacy	50	1.5	1.5	73.1
	security/foreign aid	14	.4	.4	73.6
	security/trade	19	.6	.6	74.1
	trade	768	23.0	23.0	97.1
	trade/diplomacy	1	.0	.0	97.1
	trade/foreign aid	89	2.7	2.7	99.8
	trade/immigration	7	.2	.2	100.0
	Total	3344	100.0	100.0	

of an "opportunity structure" for presidential empowerment within this area of foreign policy.[7] Lastly, the lack of a sustained systematic presence regarding most of the issue areas, including the mixed issue areas rejects hypothesized conditions regarding the steady dispersion of foreign policy into a multiplicity of issue areas. I believe that the "core strength" exerted by national security, trade and foreign aid as points of ongoing confluence for issue development between the executive and legislative branches accounts for this finding but future research needs to be done in this area.

---

7 See Chapter 2's extended discussion of the importance of opportunity structures' role within the multiple presidencies thesis.

A related finding is the lack of a systematic role for the domestic security (5.9% of all votes) and diplomacy (7.7% of all votes) categories. As high politics arena categories, one would expect that they would be more prevalent within the data than they actually are. However, it is conceivable that the domestic security issue area has been largely over-shadowed by position taking in the national security category so much to the point that domestic security and to a lesser extent diplomacy is in effect a sub-category. If this is true, then the hypothesized relation between presidential position taking and success more generally is even more a function of the inherent opportunity structure that security represents for presidential power in foreign affairs.

Table 4-1 Across Political Time (1953–2004): Annual Presidential National Security v. Trade Policy Success

	t	df	Sig. (2-tailed)	Mean Difference	95% Confidence Interval of the Difference	
					Lower	Upper
annual presidential success score in national security policy	266.943	3142	.000	.746402	.740919	.751884
annual presidential success score in trade policy	196.990	3343	.000	.713475	.706374	.720576

Table 4-2 Across Political Time (1953–2004): Annual Presidential National Security v. Foreign Aid Policy Success

	t	df	Sig. (2-tailed)	Mean Difference	95% Confidence Interval of the Difference	
					Lower	Upper
annual presidential success score in national security policy	266.943	3142	.000	.746402	.740919	.751884
annual presidential success score in foreign aid policy	217.138	3197	.000	.723677	.717143	.730212

Moving on to more analytical findings, we discern differential patterns as to the longitudinal success rates of presidents regarding the core issue areas. I concentrated on these at the expense of the mixed formulations because of their stronger appearance, analytical role within the theory and easier methodological interpretability. I will save discussion of the mixed issue areas for the cross-sectional chapters where they become most manifest (chapters 6-8). As Tables 4-1 and 4-2 indicate, there are statistically significant differences in the mean percentage success rates for presidents across the three main issue areas—national security (74% success), trade (71% success) and foreign aid (72% success). This not only supports hypothesized contentions, it also follows the expected patterns of success with presidents routinely doing better in the high politics arena than in the low politics one, however this is offset by the lack of sustained presence of three of the issue areas across time—domestic security, diplomacy and immigration. It also follows expected patterns with national security as the single most successful issue area for presidential foreign policy position vote "wins" (74% overall). Additionally, as the table points out the mean success rate for presidents is greater on national security than on trade and foreign aid. A means test confirms a statistically significant difference in success between the issue areas (p=.05). It is a debatable question as to the substantive significance of such an empirical claim, therefore deeper analytical inquiry is necessitated.

Standard deviations and standard mean errors are quite small, which is indicative of the fact that I am employing *population* rather than *sample* statistics. As an implication, it is entirely possible that much of the variation or lack thereof noted in the two presidencies literature is a result of its overwhelming reliance on samples and even sub-samples as opposed to the population data which is available, just painstaking to get at (see Bond and Fleisher 1988, Malbin and Brookshire 2000 and Conley 1997 for some relatively recent "sampling" endeavors). One major analytic finding out of this table is that despite hypothesized claims there is no marked difference in the "degree" of presidential success relative to the non-security issue areas (see Tables 4-1 and 4-2). We would expect a variation in the success rate regarding comparisons between national security success-trade and national security success-foreign aid. However, these expectations were not born out; in fact there is no discernible difference in the success rates in trade (71%) v. foreign aid (72%) (Again, see Tables 4-1 and 4-2). There are two possible explanations, one is methodological and the other theoretical.

Methodologically, it is conceivable that the sheer number of "data points" is overwhelming any inherent differences that "lie below the surface" due to the reliance on population data. A future research project may differentiate these votes out along "types" based on the relative value of the vote itself (majority procedural, majority final, supermajority procedural and supermajority final). I do this in the cross-sectional chapters, but looking at it longitudinally is certainly something to examine at a later date. Theoretically, if we are keeping in mind the notion that what is presidency-centered serves as the base ordering principle for the study overall, then the further we "move" away from security (e.g. the low politics arenas) the less subject issue areas are to the ordering principle itself and hence "within low politics arena" variance may not be able to be discerned with this type of research program. Not only is this a point for further study unto itself, it also provides an empirical referent which in large measure supports the basic thesis regarding the role of issue areas and opportunity structures in the president's foreign policy success rate (see Chapter 2). So far, the study is supported by basic descriptive and minor analytic empirics but what happens when those empirics are examined in a more robustly systematic manner?

Time series analysis examines data longitudinally with the specific contribution that it accounts mathematically for the "impact of time" itself on the phenomenon of interest (from McCleary and Hay 1975). Its principal limitation is its tendency to develop systematic error over time which is referred to by time series analysts as "serial autocorrelation of the disturbance term" (McCleary and Hay 1975, introduction). While this problem is particularly endemic to ordinary least squares (OLS) models, the relatively limited nature of this study's application of such analyses should serve to limit the negative impacts at least generally. Looking at a base univariate ARIMA model tracking the foreign policy success and core issue area success scores across time we can gain at least a modest systematic perspective on the executive-legislative foreign affairs relationship. The models specified take on the following characteristics:

Model 1 FPn~(1,0,0)

Where $\theta > 0$

Model 2 NSn~(1,0,0)

Where $\theta 1 > 0$

Model 3 DSn~(1,0,0)

Where $\theta 2 > 0$

Model 4 Dn~(1,0,0)

Where $\theta 3 > 0$

Model 5 Tn~(1,0,0)

Where $\theta 4 > 0$

Model 6 FAn~(1,0,0)

Where $\theta 5 > 0$

Model 7 IMMn~(1,0,0)

Where θ5>0

Lags for all models= 50, where each lag is an annualized measure beginning with 2004 as the base year of interest and closing with the year 1953 (the origination point).

What the above is referring to is the statistical distribution of each of the time series models as to their specific type and character of the observations being tracked across time. For instance, model 1 is specified as *FPn~(1,0,0) where* θ*>1*. What this is referencing is that the time series model for the dependent variable presidential foreign policy success is distributed (represented by the tilda symbol ~) as a population (represented by the capital letters *FP*) of all presidential position votes on foreign policy between 1953 and 2004 (represented by the letter *n*). Furthermore, the numbers contained within the parentheses *(1,0,0)* indicate the type of time series model being employed as a first-order autoregressive model. In this case, the dependent variable is regressed against itself at descending intervals beginning at the base year of 2004 and working back in time (the notions of t and t-minus) to the origination point for the study in 1953. Finally, the concept of θ is the Greek letter theta and is a statistical convention for any number or integer. But, in this analysis the numbers employed as primary and secondary dependent variables (the respective 1953–2004 annual presidential success rates in foreign, national security, domestic security, diplomacy, trade, foreign aid and immigration policies) are always greater than zero.

The models are of the type first-order autoregressive and measure the alteration in the various core success rates across time. One limitation of this type of autoregressive integrated moving average (ARIMA) modeling is that it has limited forecasting abilities because it only accounts for within rather than across case variance over time (McCleary and Hay 1975, introduction). However, as Figure 4-1 indicates the models "map out" in an expected fashion with some interesting twists which previous non-time series analysis neglected. This type of time series model is best thought of as a "regression on itself," whereby the current observation (presidential success in some issue area of foreign policy in 2004) is seen as the "outcome" of previous annualized presidential success rates back in de-sequential order to the year 1953 (McCleary and Hay 1975, chapter 2). Finally, since seasonality is not of concern due to the annualized nature of the data, simple first differencing is all that is necessary to re-impose stationarity on the series' of concern by accounting for natural drift in the respective trend lines (from McCleary and Hay 1975, chapter 2).

First of all, model stationarity is met in the first 20 lags within foreign policy as well as national security, trade and foreign aid success rates. **Stationarity** is a time series concept that roughly approximates a model fitness test like the *F-test* in regression analysis. It is referring to the lack of natural *drift* or seasonal presence of *trend* within the data. This means that the model can be said to be actually *explaining* an outcome as opposed to one appearing by mere chance. In other words, the sooner a time series attains stationarity the stronger the model is as an explanatory device. This is an indicator of the systemic presence that the "big three" have as indicators of foreign policy interaction between the president and the Congress. On the other side of the coin, diplomacy does not attain stationarity until the thirty-seventh lag, well over halfway into the distribution of the data and most importantly, domestic security as well as

Figure 4-3

Model 1

Across Political Time (1953–2004): Annual Presidential Foreign Policy Success Time Series Autocorrelation Analysis

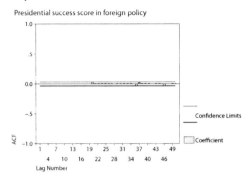

Note: see Appendix Table iv-1 for readout of this and the following six models.

Model 2

Across Political Time (1953–2004): Annual Presidential National Security Success Time Series Autocorrelation Analysis

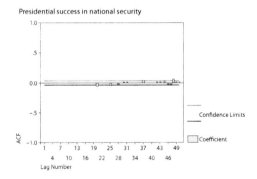

Model 3

Across Political Time (1953–2004): Annual Presidential Domestic Security Success Time Series Autocorrelation Analysis

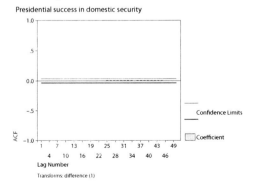

Model 4
Across Political Time (1953–2004): Annual Presidential Diplomatic Policy Success Time Series Autocorrelation Analysis

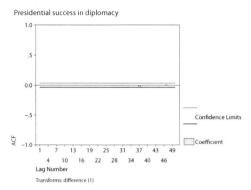

Model 5
Across Political Time (1953–2004): Annual Presidential Trade Policy Success Time Series Autocorrelation Analysis

Model 6
Across Political Time (1953–2004): Annual Presidential Foreign Aid Policy Success Time Series Autocorrelation Analysis

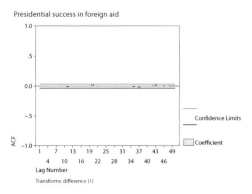

Model 7

Across Political Time (1953–2004): Annual Presidential Immigration Policy Success Time Series Autocorrelation Analysis

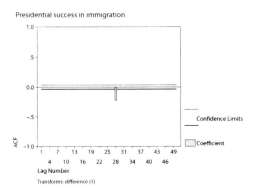

immigration *never* attains stationarity (Figure 4-3). Two immediate conclusions can be drawn from these empirics. First, security abroad is a place of presidential power not security within. Second, the dominant presence of the "big three" (national security, trade and foreign aid) are once again limiting the potential for the "lesser three" (domestic security, diplomacy and immigration) as places of presidential-congressional interaction.

Following the issue of stationarity, we see the pattern repeat itself when analyzing the modified Q statistics (the Box-Ljung statistic). The modified Q statistic measures each autocorrelation for its probability of difference from zero and the presence of a "white noise" phenomenon amidst the stochastic and trend process terms (together they amount to the measure of endogenous variance in a time series) (Box and Ljung 1978). As Table 4-3 indicates, measurable autocorrelations are present in all of the models except immigration and somewhat surprisingly domestic security. However, a second look at the domestic security category does indicate a high probability for rejecting the null hypothesis that all inferred autocorrelations will be 0 and just the opposite conclusion is reached by interpreting the probabilities emanating out of the immigration modified Q statistics (see Appendix Table iv-1).

Additionally, Figure 4-3 indicates that there are two general trends prevalent among the "big three" (national security, trade and foreign aid) regarding the movement of the respective success rates across time. The first major trend is that national security tends to be relatively steady state and since foreign policy success is high (also revealed in this figure) then that means that variation in the overall success rate is more associated with non-security oriented issue areas. This confirms a major hypothesis of the multiple presidencies thesis and even identifies those issue areas responsible for the before mentioned variance (Figure 4-3). It is in the "low politics arena" of trade and foreign aid where such variations in the series' trends are observed. For instance, while the trend line for national security success has only a single major break in it after stationarity, trade has four (Figure 4-3). And, in both trade and foreign aid, the success rates are subject to a high rate of increase in the size of the Q statistic relative to national security which follows a

Figure 4-4

Model A

Across Political Time (1953–2004): Annual Presidential Foreign and National Security Policy Success Time Series Cross-Correlation Analysis

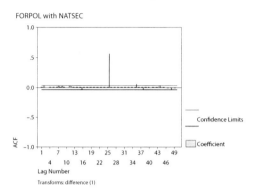

Note: see Appendix Table iv-2 for readouts of this and the other cross-correlation analyses (Models A, B and C—only shown in the appendix).

Model B

Across Political Time (1953–2004): Annual Presidential Foreign and Trade Policy Success Time Series Cross-Correlation Analysis

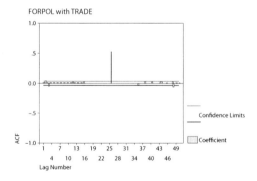

more incremental pattern that is easier to explain through the increase in T—the total number of observations (in Appendix Table iv-1) (from Box and Ljung 1978). The foreign policy success rate series has two major breaks and since these are at distal places in the time series itself, this indicates that the foreign policy success rate today is not as correlated with that of the past. What explains this? From our analysis so far, change in trade and foreign aid seems more likely candidates than national security but let us take a closer look with some cross-correlations.

The cross-correlations look at *between* case differences across time and project inferences regarding the overall relationships between the elements of the series themselves (McCleary and Hay 1975, chapter 5). As Figure 4-4 shows, foreign policy success is a *function of* national security success (model A), ceteris paribus due to its high correlation coefficient function (CCF) of .564. However, as the figure also shows a case can be made for trade given its equally high CCF of .525 (model B). Foreign aid places in third with a CCF of .24 but from a time series perspective we cannot discern the *exact determinant mechanism* for presidential foreign aid success (see Appendix Table iv-2). We can only eliminate foreign aid and all other issue areas by implication as contenders. So, the question remains—is it national security or is it trade? Simple multiple regression models applied longitudinally can shed some light on this question.

For this portion of the analysis, I specify two models, the first is a multivariate ordinary least squares regression (OLS) employing foreign policy success as the dependent variable and both national security success as well as trade success as the explanatory factors with a disturbance term for error. All of the three variables are the full cross-time annualized position vote success scores with no attention paid to political time differences—those will be dealt with in coming chapters. Therefore the first model takes the form:

Foreign Policy = National Security + Trade + E

Where all variables are population indicators

Table 4-3 Across Political Time (1953–2004): Annual Presidential Foreign Policy Success Regression Analysis of Central Core Issue Area Success (National Security and Trade)

Foreign Policy=National Security + Trade + E

	Un-standardized Coefficients		Sig.
	B	Std. Error	
(Constant)	.155	.007	.000
annual presidential success score in national security policy	.420	.009	.000
annual presidential success score in trade policy	.364	.006	.000

R Square	Adjusted R Square	Std. Error of the Estimate	Durbin-Watson
.702	.702	.072	.026

Predictors: (Constant), Annual Presidential Success Score in Trade Policy, Annual Presidential Success Score in National Security Policy

Dependent Variable: Annual Presidential Success Score in Foreign Policy N=3335

The second model is posited in order to test two of the fundamental hypotheses coming from the multiple presidencies thesis. That issue area success is indicative of the degree of "presidentialization/securitization v. congressionalization/domestication of the specific votes themselves within the foreign policy domain. With that in mind, this model takes two forms with the first as:

Model 2-A1:

National Security=Securitization + Domestication + e

Table 4-4 Across Political Time (1953–2004): Annual Presidential Foreign Policy Success Regression Analysis of All Issue Area Policy Success (National Security, Domestic Security, Diplomacy, Trade, Foreign Aid and Immigration)

| | Un-standardized Coefficients | | Sig. |
	B	Std. Error	
(Constant)	.126	.011	.000
annual presidential success score in trade policy	.314	.008	.000
annual presidential success score in foreign aid policy	.044	.008	.000
annual presidential success score in immigration policy	.020	.005	.000
annual presidential success score in national security policy	.222	.011	.000
annual presidential success score in domestic security policy	.196	.007	.000
annual presidential success score in diplomatic policy	.068	.005	.000

R Square	Adjusted Square	RStd. Error of theDurbin-Estimate	Watson
.808	.807	.046	.036

Predictors: (Constant), Annual Presidential Success Score in Immigration Policy, Annual Presidential Success Score in Diplomatic Policy, Annual Presidential Success Score in National Security Policy, Annual Presidential Success Score in Trade Policy, Annual Presidential Success Score in Domestic Security Policy, Annual Presidential Success Score in Foreign Aid Policy
Dependent Variable: Annual Presidential Success Score in Foreign Policy

Where securitization and domestication are dummy variables coded as a result of the content analysis of the relevant vote summaries.

Model 2-A2:

Trade =Securitization + Domestication + e

Model 2-B

Foreign Policy=Securitization + Domestication + e

Where this serves as the baseline model for comparison relative to notions of presidency-centered v. Congress centered conditions.

As Table 4-3 tells the findings are within the expected range for the predictions of the theory. According to the results of the first model, while both explanatory variables correlate positively and robustly (p-value=0) with foreign policy success, the un-standardized correlation coefficient is significantly higher for national security *beta=.42* than for trade *beta=.364*. When the model is re-specified to include all issue areas the results are even more emblematic of a multiple presidencies interpretation of executive-legislative relations in foreign policy. As Table 4-4 indicates, while trade has the highest correlation value, the two security oriented issue areas together trump it by a significant amount (.31 for trade, .22 for national security and .19 for domestic security). Also, in general trade is the only substantively significant factor amongst the "low politics arena," although it is true and also supportive of the larger theory that all issue areas of foreign policy enjoy a "statistically" significant relationship (alpha set at .05) with the dependent variable (Table 3-4).

The second model(s)' shows a clear role for securitization in the success rate of president's in foreign policy along predicted directions. As a presidency-centered condition, securitization has a significant relationship with national security and foreign policy success, however the correlations are relatively weak (Table 4-5). Even more troubling, as Table 4-5 reveals the relationship is negative suggesting that as the presence of securitization among foreign policy votes increases there is a corresponding *decrease* in the success rate whether foreign or national security in orientation. Why is this so? Perhaps, it is because of the longitudinal aspect of the data itself since actual variance within is not captured by this particular model. Therefore, we will leave this topic for now and re-address it in the cross-sectional models where a more specified approach is possible. Additionally, when securitization is utilized in the trade version of the success model and subject to a backwards elimination technique for model specification, it is maintained in the re-specified model (Table 4-5). As a side note, this also occurs when the formulation is run with foreign aid success as the secondary dependent variable in place of the trade success rate (Appendix Table iv-2).

When taking the view of Congress-centered conditionality, similarly supportive yet *qualified* results are also found. Domestication of votes serves the same role in influencing the foreign

Table 4-5 Models of the Impacts of Securitization and Domestication of Foreign Policy Votes on Various Annual Presidential Success Rates

Model 1

Across Political Time (1953–2004): Annual Presidential Foreign Policy Success Regression Analysis of Securitization and Domestication of Foreign Policy Votes

Foreign Policy=Securitization + Domestication + E

	Un-standardized Coefficients		Sig.
	B	Std. Error	
(Constant)	.753	.004	.000
Securitization of Vote	-.030	.006	.000
Domestication of Vote	-.034	.005	.000
R Square	Adjusted R Square	Std. Error of the Estimate	Durbin-Watson
.013	.013	.131	.034

Predictors: (Constant), Domestication of Vote, Securitization of Vote
Dependent Variable: Annual Presidential Success Score in Foreign Policy

Models 2a & 2b

Across Political Time (1953=2004): Annual Presidential National Security Policy Success Regression Analysis of Securitization and Domestication of Foreign Policy Votes

Model 2a: National Security=Securitization + Domestication + E
Model 2b: National Security=Securitization + E

Models		Un-standardized Coefficients		Sig.
		B	Std. Error	
2a	(Constant)	.759	.005	.000
	Securitization of Vote	-.023	.007	.001
	Domestication of Vote	-.008	.007	.250
2b	(Constant)	.754	.003	.000
	Securitization of Vote	-.019	.006	.002

R Square	Adjusted R Square	Std. Error of the Estimate	Durbin-Watson
.004	.003	.155	.035

Predictors: (Constant), Domestication of Vote, Securitization of Vote
Dependent Variable: annual presidential success score in national security policy

Model 2c

Across Political Time (1953–2004): Annual Presidential Trade Policy Success Regression Analysis of Securitization and Domestication of Foreign Policy Votes

Trade=Securitization + Domestication + E

Model		Un-standardized Coefficients		Sig.
		B	Std. Error	
2c	(Constant)	.760	.006	.000
	Securitization of Vote	-.047	.009	.000
	Domestication of Vote	-.076	.009	.000

R Square	Adjusted R Square	Std. Error of the Estimate	Durbin-Watson
.024	.023	.206	.052

Predictors: (Constant), Domestication of Vote, Securitization of Vote
Dependent Variable: Annual Presidential Success Score in Trade Policy

Table 4-6 Across Political Time (1953–2004): Annual Presidential Foreign Policy Success Regression Analysis of Executive-Legislative Orders of Political Time in Foreign Affairs

	Un-standardized Coefficients		Sig.
	B	Std. Error	
(Constant)	.700	.016	.000
War Power Order 1953–1972	.134	.016	.000
Confrontation Politics Order 1973–1989	.005	.016	.777
Imperial Presidency Politicized 1990–2000	-.125	.016	.000
Extra-Systemic Dilemma 2001–2004	.143	.018	.000

R Square	Adjusted R Square	Std. Error of the Estimate	Durbin-Watson
.479	.478	.095	.030

Predictors: (Constant), Extra-Systemic Dilemma 2001–2004, Imperial Presidency Politicized 1990–2000, War Power Order 1953–1972, Confrontation Politics 1973–1989
Dependent Variable: Annual Presidential Success Score in Foreign Policy

policy success rate and non-security issue area success rates (measured with trade success as a proxy) for the Congress as the securitization phenomenon dies for the presidency (Table 4-5). Whereas securitization does not "drop" out of the model for trade (and foreign aid as well), it is domestication that "drops" out of the national security model but remains as a strong and negative indicator of trade (and foreign aid) success (Table 4-5). What this really means is that domestication is inherent to the low politics arena (with trade as the proxy *beta*=-.07) and likewise, securitization holds a similar position in both politics' arena (with national security as the proxy *beta*=-.019). Lastly, as you can see in Table 4-5, a negative relationship between domestication and trade success is found. Unlike the results for securitzation's impact, these findings are in comportment with the precepts of the multiple presidencies. It is to be expected that as an issue is subject to successful domestication (read congressionalization) then the president will have a more difficult time getting his way on the vote in question due to the nature of the Congress' opportunity structure in domestic (read more intermestic) types of foreign policies.

The last set of longitudinal empirics deals with the role played by the concept of "political time" as an explanatory (potential or real) of presidential success rates in foreign policy and its component issue areas. The model uses our standard dependent variable of annual presidential success in foreign policy and regress the impacts of the four periods of political time. Therefore, the model is specified as follows:

Foreign Policy=War Power Order + Confrontation Politics Order + Imperial Presidency Politicized Order + Extra Systemic Dilemma Order + E

Where each order is operationalized by a dummy variable.

The results as seen in Table 4-6, portray the start of a complex story that the rest of this work attempts to clarify. Three of the four periods have a statistically significant relationship with foreign policy success. This is a fascinating finding and difficult to interpret but as an initial observation the one period that lacks significance, the Confrontation Politics Order 1973–1989, is the one most associated within the literature as congressional resurgence in foreign policy. If anything the association ought to be negative but it is simply non-existent. Or, is it? Think about this. A large amount of scholarship on roll call analysis has found that during the 1970s and 1980s there was something of a "roll call boom." The Congress as part of its reform efforts began to record more and more votes, especially on procedural mechanisms which themselves increased during this time (Shull and Shaw 1999, Rohde 1991, Page and Jordan 1992, Lindsay and Steger 1993). Therefore, it is possible that the votes during this time are "flooding the data set," essentially "polluting the observations" leading to counterintuitive inferences in a population based model that is longitudinal in its composition (from Enders 2004, chapter 5).

Another interesting finding is that despite only being four years in length, the last period—the Extra-Systemic Dilemma has a significant relationship with position vote success in foreign policy. While this does support the expectations of the theory, the reader should take this finding with some caution as our current president is well known for *not* taking positions on roll call votes (Leloup and Shull 2003). Therefore, this period may have the same problem as the previous one discussed but only from the opposite direction. Too few position votes, just like too many may also cause this period of time to not be directly comparable with ones around it (see Shull and Shaw (1999) for an extended discussion on the "comparability" of presidential position voting across different periods of time).

A final finding that comports well with expectations of the multiple presidencies thesis but may seem counterintuitive relates to the Imperial Presidency Politicized (1990–2000). As Table 4-6 suggests, there is a negative significant relationship between this period of time and the success rate in foreign policy. While some may feel this is not in keeping with the theory, I can assure them that it is. Here is why. What was once freely given for extended periods of time is now quickly taken away (see the difficulties our current president is having relative to the Iraq War). Furthermore, the highly politicized nature of the executive-legislative divide that has been particularly pervasive since the late Reagan administration has worked in general against presidents and for the Congress. This is because divided government is best seen as a Congress-centered condition and unified as a presidency-centered. However, W. Bush's year and a half of split control government between May of 2001 and December of 2002 might represent something of an aberration from the norm. Of course, much of that time saw an unusually high level of of bi-partisanship in the wake of 9/11. But, even during this time the Congress was already returning to its partisan roots as the 2002 mid-term campaign season came under way (CQ Almanac 2002, "election report").

Finally, we need to examine the role of other historical and economic indicators exerting a macro-level impact on the extant executive-legislative foreign policy relationship. The first such model tests the historical conditionality regarding the size and scope of the US military establishment's role in determining national security success. This model is specified in the following manner:

National Security=War + Armed Forces + Defense Budget + E

What this model's findings portray, as shown in Table 4-7, is a mixed bag, as to the applicability of the theory across time. For instance, while the base hypothesis of the military establishment as measured by the size of the armed forces and the percentage of the budget allocated to it is upheld. Only size of the armed forces is in the expected direction wherein, as the size of the armed forces increases there is a corresponding increase in the national security success rate. And, the budget measure is actually in a reverse relationship regarding expected outcomes where as the percentage increases, there is a corresponding systematic declination in the president's rate of success in national security votes. What might be most interesting is the fact that the war dummy variable has a negative relationship with national security. However, in this case it could be that the limited amount of actual war during the timeframe of the analysis might be limiting the inferential capacities of this measure. I should also like to point out that while the relationship is negative and passes statistical significance (p=.05) it is quite weak (*beta*=-.07) so how reliable the interpretation is certainly open to question.

Table 4-7 Macro-Level Historical-Economic Conditions as Determinants of Presidential Core Issue Area Success
Model 1
Across Political Time (1953–2004): Annual Presidential National Security Success Regression Analysis of Macro-Historical Determinants
National Security=War/Peace + Armed Forces + Defense Budget + E

	Un-standardized Coefficients		Sig.
	B	Std. Error	
(Constant)	.386	.013	.000
war	-.072	.006	.000
Annual Size of US Armed Forces in millions	.239	.012	.000
Defense Outlays as a % Annual Federal Budget	-.518	.060	.000

R Square	Adjusted R Square	Std. Error of the Estimate	Durbin-Watson
.223	.222	.132	.032

Predictors: (Constant), Defense Outlays as a % Annual Federal Budget, war, Annual Size of US Armed Forces in millions
Dependent Variable: Annual Presidential Success Score in National Security Policy

Model 2
Across Political Time (1953–2004): Annual Presidential Trade Policy Success Regression Analysis of Macro-Economic Determinants
Trade=Budgetary Conditions + GDP + Business Cycle + International Finance/Trade + E

	Un-standardized Coefficients		Sig.
	B	Std. Error	
(Constant)	.766	.008	.000
Annual Trade and International Finance Balance in Billions	-3.286E-05	.000	.000
Annual Real GDP as measured by current dollars in trillions	-.015	.001	.000
Business Cycle Conditions	.074	.008	.000

Budgetary Conditions in Billions of current dollars	.001	.000	.000

R Square	Adjusted R Square	Std. Error of the Estimate	Durbin-Watson
.252	.251	.180	.030

Predictors: (Constant), Budgetary Conditions in Billions of current dollars, Business Cycle Conditions, Annual Trade and International Finance Balance in Billions, Annual Real GDP as measured by current dollars in trillions

Dependent Variable: Annual Presidential Success Score in Trade Policy

Model 3
Across Political Time (1953–2004): Annual Presidential Foreign Aid Policy Success Regression Analysis of Macro-Economic Determinants

Foreign Aid= Budgetary Conditions + GDP + Business Cycle + International Finance/Trade + E

	Un-standardized Coefficients		Sig.
	B	Std. Error	
(Constant)	.778	.007	.000
Annual Trade and International Finance Balance in Billions	1.179	.000	.622
Annual Real GDP as measured by current dollars in trillions	-.031	.001	.000
Business Cycle Conditions	.047	.007	.000
Budgetary Conditions in Billions of current dollars	2.844	.000	.444

R Square	Adjusted R Square	Std. Error of the Estimate	Durbin-Watson
.177	.176	.173	.036

Predictors: (Constant), Budgetary Conditions in Billions of current dollars, Business Cycle Conditions, Annual Trade and International Finance Balance in Billions, Annual Real GDP as measured by current dollars in trillions

Dependent Variable: Annual Presidential Success Score in Foreign Aid Policy

Cross-sectional study with this variable should lead to a truer assessment of this variable's impact (see Chapter 5).

The next two models within Table 4-7 examine the impacts of macro-level economic indicators and presidential success in trade and foreign aid respectively. Accordingly, each model is specified as such:

Model 2

Trade=Budgetary Conditions + GDP + Business Cycle + International Finance/Trade + E
And

Model 3

Foreign Aid= Budgetary Conditions + GDP + Business Cycle + International Finance/ Trade + E

The second model, which correlates the economic indicators with trade success across time, finds statistically significant relationships across the board. These results support the broad hypothesis regarding macro-level impacts on issue area success rates. The signs are in the expected directions with one exception. Regarding the general condition of the economy, when it is healthy (read non-recessionary), when the budget deficit is low or even in surplus conditions and when the level of economic interdependence is low (as measured by trade/ finance surpluses (or at least only modest deficits), then presidents have more success in trade votes. But when the opposite is true, such success is in decline due to the emergence of congressional conditionality over presidential conditionality within the variables (Table 4-7, Model 2). The deviating factor is economic growth (in this case measured as Real GDP), these results suggests that as real gross domestic product (GDP) grows success in trade declines. This is a bit counterintuitive, however, it can be explained on methodological grounds as a "proxy" or "indirect" variable which cannot adequately capture the "real" relationship with trade success as the more direct observations in the other variables do.

Model 3 offers up an interesting set of findings by replicating the previous model's independent variables and looking at their relationship with foreign policy success. Only Real GDP and business cycle conditions have demonstrable impacts on presidential success in foreign aid across time. Additionally, the correlations are modest among both variables and only the business cycle behaves in expected ways (*beta*=.04). Of course, remember that Real GDP (*beta*=-.031) had a similar "deviating" impact on trade success and due to a smaller proportion of foreign policy votes related to foreign aid; this deviation impact would be even more decisive (Table 4-7, Model 3). Now, let us return to the "movie" of executive-legislative foreign policy relations and bring it all together.

The Multiple Presidencies Across the Issue Areas of Foreign Policy

So how do we relate the events of the contextual narrative with the systematic findings of the longitudinal study? The answer is the multiple presidencies thesis. The story of executive-legislative relations in foreign policy during the Post-War Era is a long and extremely complex one, however, if viewed from the perspective of multiple sets of presidential-congressional relations across the component issue areas of foreign affairs it is not nearly as complex as first thought. The reason for this is that security serves somewhat as an anchor to the ship of state steered by the president and crewed by the Congress. As this analogy goes, when the ship hits troubled waters in the sea of foreign policy, then the president-captain is in charge like in the time of the War Power Order 1953–1972 with its heightened Cold War tensions that led immediately out of one hot war in Korea and into another in Vietnam. Meanwhile, as détente became the diplomacy of the day, Vietnamization and the Nixon Doctrine became focal points for future Cold War strategy the waters of the foreign policy sea calmed down but the crew got antsy.[8] The captain(s) (in the form of Nixon himself and later at least in an electoral fashion Ford and Carter) were displaced in mutinies by a recalcitrant Congress. Finally, a moderated status quo develops wherein the president-captain and the Congress-crew develop a tandem institutional relationship where storms rise (like wars in the Middle East) with a congressional rally-round-the president phenomenon. However, as quickly as the crisis comes it begins to fade and the calm waters bring about congressional-crew discontent with the president-captain's day-to-day voyaging in the foreign policy sea. Keep this rough analogy in mind, as we move into the cross-sectional chapters and take snapshots of the executive-legislative foreign policy relationship. The album that will ultimately result will provide a companion to the movie of presidential-congressional longitudinal foreign relations that was offered in this chapter.

Summary

This chapter has discussed the longitudinal analysis and findings relative to the multiple presidencies across the issue areas (national security, domestic security, diplomacy, trade, foreign aid and immigration) of foreign policy. In this effort, I have started with an opening historical narrative regarding the broad contours of executive-legislative relations in this domain of policy making. Next, we examined the findings related to such foreign affairs relations by employing time series, mean percent differencing and simple multiple regressions. While not all of the

---

8 Vietnamization refers to a strategic policy initiated by the Nixon administration in 1969 to gradually drawdown American forces in the Vietnam War and ultimately lead to a "peace with honor" as America would retreat from active participation in Southeast Asian conflict. The strategy was built around a combination of aggressive diplomacy with the enemy and the simultaneous movement toward turning over first combat and ultimately logistical operations against the North Vietnamese Army and the Viet Cong to the South Vietnamese government.

findings support the thesis, most of them do and they do so in both general as well as specific ways. Essentially, foreign policy success is a function of the component issue area success rates, especially those in the high politics arena (national security, domestic security and diplomacy). Within that, national security has the most privileged position and hence impact on positively influencing presidential success as hypothesized by the notion of presidency-centered conditions. However, it was found that the negative impact of securitization on foreign and national security success is a major impediment for the theory's general application. Clearly, more research needs to be done in order to explain this discordant finding or at least account for its presence within the established framework of the multiple presidencies.

Likewise, the low politics arena (trade, foreign aid and immigration) are least associated with presidential success as they are Congress-centered conditions. This is especially true of foreign aid and immigration but trade is also quite limited in its systematic impact as well. Finally, the big three of national security, trade and foreign aid seem to be the driving forces within the foreign policy domain, something vitally important to realize for this and other studies employing an "issue areas analysis."

Then, we examined the quantitative indicators for periodicity regressed against the dependent variable and found significant if not always intuitive relationships. Coming out of these findings, we saw how the multiple presidencies thesis, as a theory of presidential-congressional foreign policy relations can be shown to provide a strong heuristic for bringing together the qualitative narrative with the quantitative indicators themselves through analogous reasoning. And, now let the War Power Cometh!

★ Our Fractured Supreme Court
★
★ By Michael W. Schwartz

Shortly after taking office, Chief Justice John Roberts embarked on a campaign within the Court and, unusually, in the press, to revive the tradition of unanimity in Supreme Court decisions. He has spoken of his concern that the Supreme Court is losing its legitimacy in the public's mind because of the frequency of dissenting opinions, arguing that this diminishes the respect and acceptance its decisions receive, and that the Court's public standing is enhanced if its decisions are unanimous, or nearly so. For example, in a lengthy interview with legal journalist Jeffery Rosen published last year in the Atlantic, he suggested that "the Court is… ripe for a… refocus on functioning as an institution, because if it doesn't it's going to lose its credibility and legitimacy as an institution." The chief justice harked back to the early days of the Supreme Court under the leadership of John Marshall who, among other things, led the Court to adopt as consistently as possible the practice of speaking with a single voice. Not infrequently, the voice was that of Marshall himself, but the point is that the Court decided cases unanimously, without dissents and concurrences.

The chief justice's campaign is conservative in the strict sense: There can be no dispute that fractionated decisions used to be a rarity and have become commonplace on the Court. Until the early 1940s, there were fewer than ten dissenting opinions for every 100 issued by the Court; after 1941, that figure increased sevenfold, and has remained at that level or higher ever since. The justices' work product increasingly consists more of composing dissents and concurrences than of writing opinions for the Court: until 1941, 80 to 90 percent of all opinions were opinions for the Court; now the number is less than 50 percent. More than a third of its 68 rulings in 2006–07 were decided by a 5–4 margin—and others by less lopsided, but still nonunanimous, votes—with separate opinions proliferating like mushrooms after a summer rain.

At the extreme, this proliferation of opinions makes a joke of the Court's core function, "to say what the law is," in Chief Justice Marshall's phrase. Better than any statistics is the following verbatim excerpt from the Supreme Court's reports, published some years ago by the *New Yorker,* without comment, under the heading "The Jurisprudential Life":

Michael Schwartz, "Our Fractured Supreme Court," from *Policy Review,* vol. 1, no. 147, pp. 3–16.

> Blackmun, J., announced the Judgment of the Court and delivered the opinion of the Court with respect to Parts III-A, IV, and V, in which Brennan, Marshall, Stevens, and O'Connor, JJ., joined, and opinion with respect to Parts I and II, in which O'Connor and Stevens, JJ., joined, and opinion with respect to Part III-B, in which Stevens, J., joined, and an opinion with respect to Part VI. O'Connor, J., filed an opinion concurring in part and concurring in the judgment, in Part II of which Brennan and Stevens, JJ., joined. Brennan, J., filed an opinion concurring in part and dissenting in par, in which Marshall and Stevens, JJ., joined. Stevens, J., filed an opinion concurring in part and dissenting in part, in which Brennan and Marshall, JJ., joined Kennedy, J., filed an opinion concurring in the judgment in part and dissenting in part, in which Rehnquist, C. J., and White and Scalia, JJ., joined.

This was how the modern Court "decided" a case involving important issues relating to when a Christmas crèche could be displayed on public property.

In calling for consensus on the Court, Chief Justice Roberts has on his side the overwhelming majority of the people who have served as justices during its history. Indeed, so much was consensus the norm prior to the 1940s that there was a flavor of ethical breach associated with dissent. For example, Canon 19 of the 1924 Canons of Judicial Ethics directed the members of "courts of last resort" to "use effort and self-restraint to promote solidarity of conclusion and the consequent influence of judicial decision." The historical record as revealed in internal Supreme Court documents leaves no doubt that the common practice was for justices who had expressed disagreement with the majority's view in the Court's conferences to refrain from doing so publicly. Justices who accepted this norm of consensus and adhered to it include men remembered today in part for their dissents, such as Louis D. Brandeis and Oliver Wendell Holmes. Thus Holmes, known to history as the "Great Dissenter," actually viewed the practice with distaste, feeling it "useless and undesirable as a rule, to express dissent." Nor did he like to be praised for his dissents: "I rather shudder at being held up as the dissenting judge and more or less contrasted to the Court," Holmes wrote in a letter to Felix Frankfurter.

> In European legal systems, particularly those influenced by French practice, dissent is vanishingly rare.

Foreign practice also supports the chief justice's concern about published dissent. In the legal systems of continental Europe, particularly those influenced by French judicial practice, dissent is nonexistent or vanishingly rare and considered "a violation of the oath of judicial office." Although the American toleration for judicial dissent is often said to be a carryover from the practice of the British law lords in having each member of a panel read an individual decision, when Chief Justice Marshall enforced public unanimity, he was in fact following the existing practice of the highest English court available for cases from the colonies. Moreover, the House of Lords' jurisdiction does not extend to declaring acts of Parliament unconstitutional.

Thus the lords' practice cannot result in the spectacle of a divided judicial ruling setting aside the wishes of popularly elected legislators and executive officers, as increasingly happens here.

It isn't just precedent and foreign practice that support judicial consensus, however. There are good reasons why the Supreme Court, for most of its history, and the courts of other nations have disfavored dissenting opinions. There is, first and foremost, the fundamental value of achieving respect of the Court's—i.e., the majority's—decision. The principal professional obligation of justices who may have disagreed on the issue in conference, but were outvoted, is to assure that the majority's decision is obeyed and accorded public respect. It is hard to see any practical effect of a dissent other than diminishing the respect accorded to the majority's decision. At least where constitutional decisions are involved, a Supreme Court decision is final in a way that no other public act in the American political system can be said to be: It is forever beyond any possibility of majoritarian change or any change at all, barring a constitutional amendment or a change of judicial heart. How can the dissenting justice justify withholding form so momentous a public action any possible quantum of support his or her status as a member of the Court may lend to it? How can the dissenting justice excuse his or her failure to accord the decision the same degree of respect and acceptance that everyone else in the country is obliged to give it?

Beyond the question of how many votes a particular decision receives, divided rulings are always accompanied by numerous opinions. This circumstance is wildly at odds with the basic purpose of a Supreme Court decision: not only to settle the immediate dispute between the immediate parties, but also to enable the rest of us—or at least our lawyers—to understand what the law is concerning related or similar issues. Indeed, Chief Justice William Howard Taft, the architect of the modern Supreme Court, in explaining why he sought a broad discretion for the Court to decide which cases it would hear and rule on, said—in testimony before Congress in 1922—that the Court's "function is for the purpose of expounding and stabilizing principles of law for the benefit of the people of the country," and—in an address to New York lawyers in that same year—"to help the public at large to a knowledge of their rights and duties and to make the law clearer." Obviously, the proliferation of dissents—and, as well, "concurring" opinions which, while joining the majority's conclusion, dissent from its reasoning—have precisely the opposite effect. Indeed, it not infrequently happens—as in the crèche case made sport of by the *New Yorker*—that there is no opinion for the Court, not even one for which the bare minimum of five votes can be obtained.

> The Court's members spend nearly as much time preparing nondecisive opinions as they do actually deciding cases.

Moreover, the justices' dedication of important amounts of their time to producing dissents and concurrences may be part of the reason why, over the last several decades, the number of cases the Court has heard and decided has fallen far below historic norms. As recently as 30 years ago, the Court decided 176 cases, while last term it decided just 68—this while by all conceivable measures the number of cases involving questions of federal law that were litigated in the state and federal courts multiplied enormously. It may seem almost too obvious to mention, but it would certainly come as a surprise to the drafters of the Constitution to learn that the Court's members spend nearly as much time preparing nondecisive opinions as they do actually deciding cases

The Supreme Court's immersion in separate opinion-writing stands in stark contrast to the practice of the federal Courts of Appeals, where "dissensus" is far rarer—even though a dissenting opinion at the Court of Appeals level can be justified by the possibility of further review of the case. Indeed, the chief justice's campaign for reviving the tradition of Supreme Court unanimity seems to derive in part from his own experience as a member of the Court of Appeals for the District of Columbia Circuit, "whose judges," as legal journalist Benjamin Wittes has written in the New Republic. "span the range of American politics yet manage unanimity on a far wider array of cases—including very difficult cases—than do the justices."

Last but by no means least, a Court that often divides sharply in deciding controversial issues invites the kind of nomination/confirmation controversies that have become such an unsavory staple of contemporary political life. When every vote counts, and the Court's power may come to reside as a practical matter in the mind of a single "swing justice"—until recently, Justice Sandra Day O'Connor; now, Justice Anthony Kennedy—it is hard to blame people for approaching each judicial selection with the fervor and partisanship of an ordinary political election. Although Chief Justice Roberts has not made this point, his preference for unanimity or near-unanimity may well rest in part on a belief that these recurrent political melodramas have a cumulative effect that is seriously subversive of public respect for the federal courts.

The Case for Dissent

Yet the reaction to the chief justice's unusual public campaign in favor of unanimity has itself been far from unanimous. Edward Lazarus, a frequent commentator on the Court and author of *Closed Chambers* (Times Books, 1998), challenges head-on the chief justice's idea that unanimity is a good thing. On this view, "split decisions and passionate dissents are sometimes better [than unanimity]." As Lazarus suggests, today's dissent may be tomorrow's majority opinion, pointing, as defenders of dissents inevitably do, to the first Justice John Marshall Harlan's famous dissent from the Court's endorsement of racial segregation in *Plessy v. Ferguson.* Yet, even that talismanic dissent has never commanded a Court: *Brown v. Board of Education* was decided on different grounds, and Justice Harlan's assertion that "our Constitution is colorblind" has been rejected by the Court's toleration of race-conscious policies throughout American life.

There is merit to Lazarus's point that "dispensing justice well simply isn't a numbers game." But it is really a stretch to try to defend the casual recourse to dissent among today's justices by invoking Justice Harlan's *cri de coeur* protesting a decision that, s he saw it—correctly—simply gutted a core national commitment established by the blood of hundreds of thousands of soldiers in a civil war. Indeed, even though Justice Harlan has come to be known, like Holmes, as "the Great Dissenter," he, no less than Holmes and Brandeis, routinely suppressed his personal views once they had failed to persuade the other justices, and joined decisions he had not supported in conference. In fact, Brandeis withheld fully written opinions in the interest of not compromising the Court's decisiveness.

Yet Lazarus is far from alone in questioning the importance of consensus. Many justices of the Court—men far apart from one another on the ideological bandwidth—have been enthusiasts for judicial dissent. Thus the liberal William O. Douglas told the Court in a memorandum quoted in David O'Brien's standard text on the Court, *Storm Center* (W.W. Norton, 1986), that he "defend[s] the right of nay justice to file anything he wants," and Douglas wrote in one of his books, *America Challenged,* that "the right to dissent is the only thing that makes life tolerable for a judge of an appellate court... the affairs of government could not be conducted by democratic standards without it." In another Court memorandum quoted by O'Brien, Douglas's conservative contemporary, Justice Felix Frankfurter, dismissed unanimity as an "appealing abstraction" that should be rejected on the basis that it "smother[ed] differences" that "ought to be expressed." Justice Antonin Scalia, in a 1994 address reprinted in the *Journal of Supreme Court History,* argued that the practice of issuing concurring and dissenting opinions constitutes an integral part of the Court's proper functioning: "the Court ... is not just the central organ of legal *judgment;* it is the center stage for significant legal debate."

There is a certain romance associated with the practice of dissent. Is this what the Founders had in mind?

Indeed, the chief justice's campaign to restore the tradition of Supreme Court consensus challenges what appears to be a widely-held belief that the practice of individual expression of views by the justices is desirable. Justice Scalia's comment aptly evokes this view: The Court's role is not simply to decide cases; it is to reflect varying views on questions of great national moment. The opinions issued by its members are valuable *not* solely as justifications of a particular decision but as documents produced by state actors attempting to shine the light of reason and logic upon controversial public issues that otherwise are matters of political maneuvering and speechmaking.

There is even a certain romance associated with the practice of Supreme Court dissent. In a grandiloquent formulation, Chief Justice Hughes—who was nearly as successful as his predecessor, William Howard Taft, in discouraging published dissent—remarked that "[a] dissent in a court of last resort is an appeal to the brooding spirit of the law, to the intelligence of a future day... " Years ago, the liberal journalist Alan Barth published an encomium to the practice of dissent, titled *Prophets With Honor* (Vintage Books, 1975), describing the practice as a "form of prophecy in the Biblical sense of the term." More recently, and on the other end of the jurisprudential spectrum, Regnery Publishing issued *Scalia Dissents* (2004), to broadcast the "writings" of the "Supreme Court's wittiest, most outspoken Justice." Whether this is what the Founders had in mind when their Constitution declared that there shall be "one supreme Court" may be doubted.

The modern proliferation of separate opinions is also an aspect of the broader change in American political life that has seen the politicization of the judicial process sharply increase: As Benjamin Wittes succinctly puts it, "For both sides in the war over the courts, [jurisprudential modesty] is a virtue to be embraced by the other." This view of the world is perhaps best captured by an anecdote law Professor Mark Tushnet recounts in his book *A Court Divided* (W.W. Norton, 2005) about Justice William Brennan, the spark-plug of the Warren Court: "Each year Brennan asked his law clerks to name the most important rule in constitutional law. Brennan gave them the answer after they stumbled around, naming one great case after another. 'This,' he said, holding up one hand with his fingers spread, 'is the most important rule in constitutional law.' Brennan knew that it took five votes to do anything, and, he may have thought, with five votes you can do anything."

Revolution in the Court

Chief justice Roberts' unusual public campaign for judicial unanimity involves much more than a nostalgic yearning for the halcyon days of John Marshall. The real question his argument raises is this: Why should we have a Supreme Court decision at all if the Court can't make up its institutional mind? What positive good is served by having a "decision" whose binding force is subverted by members of the Court itself?

The Court's evolution into a body that feels no obligation to make up its collective mind before laying down the law has occurred without any real debate. No one decided to abandon the norm of consensus in favor of a norm of self-expression. Indeed, students of the Court cannot agree about what happened in the early 1940s, when the era of free-wheeling dissent began. Some put it down to the leadership deficiencies of Chief Justice Harlan Fiske Stone, whose tenure began in 1941, whose background did not include prior service on a Court of Appeals, and whose professional life as a law professor and law school dean—so some say—inclined him to value free, individual expression more than institutional solidarity. Stone, like his contemporary Douglas and his successors Frankfurter and Scalia (both also legal academics), highly valued dissent, and in sharpest contrast to Chief Justice Taft did not think it appropriate to try to dissuade members of the Court from dissenting. Others point to the fact that the Court Stone presided over—a Supreme Court of Roosevelt loyalists—was composed largely of men with no prior judicial experience, strong views on public policy issues, and professional backgrounds that put a high premium on self-expression.

Stone's appointment as chief coincided with a sharp rise in dissents. But it remains something of a mystery whey the Court's promiscuous resort to dissent has persisted, and indeed increased, long after Stone and his Court passed from the stage. It has been argued, with some force, that each succeeding generation of justices was socialized into Court whose values did not include consensus, and whose routine practice included frequent dissents and concurrences. But there have been deliberate efforts since Stone—including, notably, President Truman's selection of Stone's immediate successor, Fred Vinson—to renew the tradition of Supreme

Court consensus, and they have conspicuously failed. Some observers have laid the blame at the door of the justices' law clerks—each justice now has four—and, indeed, David O'Brien's *Storm Center* reports the case of a justice publishing a concurrence for no other reason than that "it would break [his] law clerk's heart" to suppress an opinion the clerk had worked so hard on. Yet it is hard to believe that the apprentices have so much sway over the sorcerers. The persistence of dissent remains something of a mystery.

> The Court that has become so hospitable to judicial self-expression is radically different from the institution Marshall led.

But one thing is clear: The Court that has become so hospitable to judicial self-expression is in crucial respects radically different from the institution John Marshall led. The current chief justice's appeal to the example of the Marshall era fails to take account of enormous institutional changes in the Court since that time.

By far the most important, although little appreciated by nonlawyers, is the change in the Court's functioning—perhaps it is not too much to say in its essential character r—that was authorized by Congress in 1925 at the insistent urging of then-Chief Justice Taft. In all the years prior to 1925, the Supreme Court had functioned as an appellate court to review lower court decisions, state and federal, rejecting claims of federal rights, Indeed, until 1891, it was the only federal appellate court for most such claims. It was obliged to hear nearly all claims that federal rights had been denied, whether by the lower federal courts or the state supreme courts.

But is 1925, for the first time, Congress gave the Supreme Court the power not only to decide cases, but also to decide which cases it would decide. Specifically, after lengthy and ardent lobbying by Chief Justice Taft, Congress enacted the justly named "Judges' Bill," which had been drafted by members of the Court and which gave the Court, for the first time in its history, the ability to decide which claims of federal right it would hear and which it would refuse to hear. Taft not only saw to the drafting of the bill, he also orchestrated congressional testimony to support it, procured backing from the American Bar Association for the proposed new law, and even wrote a portion of President Coolidge's state of the union address urging Congress to enact it.

Taft's revolution in Supreme Court practice was accomplished by Congress's adoption of a statute eliminating virtually all of the Court's obligatory appellate jurisdiction. Where once the jurisdictional statutes applicable to the Court since the eighteenth century would have obligated it to reconsider a federal claim rejected by a lower court, now Congress empowered the Court to decide whether to grant or withhold, in its absolute discretion, an opportunity for Supreme Court review of a lower court decision. The device chosen bore the name "writ of certiorari," for whose issuance a disappointed litigant had to file a "petition." It would have been more direct to shay that appeals simply became a matter of Supreme Court grace. While vestiges of obligatory jurisdiction lingered after 1925, in successive enactments Congress has eliminated *all* of the Court's mandatory appellate jurisdiction. What's more, by exercise of its own rule-making power and by other means, the Supreme Court itself largely rendered discretionary the small piece of its appellate jurisdiction that by statute was obligatory.

In granting the Court this discretionary certiorari power, Congress imposed no statutory limitations on how the Court might exercise it, neither in 1925 nor statutory limitations on how the Court might exercise it, neither in 1925 nor thereafter. In effect, Congress has made a wholesale delegation to the Court itself of Congress's constitutional authority under Article III to define the Court's jurisdiction. As every law student learns, while Article III defines and grants to the courts the "judicial power" of the United States, it gives to Congress the power to limit the appellate jurisdiction of the Supreme Court, by granting it authority to provide "Exceptions" form, and "Regulations" of, the full constitutional power. The Judges' Bill was, in substance, the enactment of a truly gigantic black hole of an "Exception"—excepting from the Court's appellate jurisdiction any and all cases the Court chose not to hear—and an entirely contentless "Regulation"—leaving it to the Court itself to define its own jurisdiction and in later legislation on the same subject, Congress has done nothing more than repeal statutes that imposed mandatory jurisdiction on the Corut.

> In successive enactments Congress has eliminated all of the Court's mandatory appellate jurisdiction.

This momentous change in the nature of the Supreme Court's functioning was adopted without any serious debate in congress or within the legal profession. As Frankfurter (then a professor at Harvard Law School) concluded in his classic study of Supreme Court jurisdiction, *The Business of the Supreme Court,* in enacting the 1925 Judges' Bill, Congress "deferred to the prestige of the Supreme Court and its Chief Justice, whose energetic espousal largely helped to realize the Court's proposal." Energetic, and somewhat disingenuous. Much of Taft's presentation to Congress (in his own words and through surrogates) concentrated on the supposed unmanageability of the Court's appellate docket under the old jurisdictional dispensation. Yet it is clear that Taft's driving motivation was to redefine the role of the Court in American life. As Taft expressed his view of the Supreme Court in 1922—a view, in effect, endorsed by Congress when it passed the Judges' Bill—"The real work the Supreme Court has to do is for the public at large, as distinguished from the particular litigants before it." Professor Robert Post of the Yale Law School, in a deeply-researched study of Taft and his Court published in the Minnesota Law Review, quotes a contemporary article expressing the same view this way: "the specific rights of particular parties are no longer the essence of the controversies before the Supreme Court. ... [O]ne might well say that the Supreme Court is abandoning its character as a court of last resort, and is assuming the function of a ministry of justice."

Lest this seem to treat rather high-handedly the rights of individual litigants, it should be remembered that at the end of the nineteenth century Congress created the federal courts of appeals, to which disappointed litigants had access as a matter of right. Taft's point was that one trial and one appeal were "all the hearings a litigant should have." The business of the Supreme Court was no longer to assure all litigants of a hearing. "The business of the Supreme

Court," he stated, "should be to consider and decide for the benefit of the public and or the benefit of uniformity of decision."

> The Court grants of denies "cert" without full briefs, without oral argument, and without a written explanation.

But what has happened in the four score years since Congress enacted the Judges' Bill cannot remotely be described as achieving "the benefit of uniformity of decision." On the contrary, the increasing division on the Court has coincided with the establishment and legitimization, over and above the Court's constitutionally granted "judicial power" to decided cases, of another kind of power—the power to define its own legal agenda, free of any obligation to hear any given case. Moreover, it is free to exercise this power without being subject to any of the usual limitations on how courts act. Thus, when the Court grants or denies a petition for certiorari, it does so without receiving full briefs, without hearing oral argument, and without issuing a written explanation of its action.

Nor does the Court consider certiorari petitions according to any meaningful standard. There is a rule listing the criteria that guide that consideration, but they are so vague and open-ended as to amount to no real rule at all. H.W. Perry's Deciding to decide (Harvard University, 1992) quotes an (unnamed) justice as follow; "You know, they say that the British acquired the empire in a fit of absentmindedness, and speaking for myself, I sometimes think that is the way we create our agenda." Perry's book and the writings of other social scientists who discuss how the Court has exercised the certiorari power Taft won for it read a little like the work of ancient augurers, attempting to divine from judicial notebooks and off-the-record interviews what drives the Court's certiorari decisions. So far as the entrails reveal what goes on behind the velvet curtain, it appears that (a) the justices by and large make their certiorari decisions independently, and not as a Court, and (b) the justices act on the basis of their own subjective sense of what issues are "important" and how the Court should use its judicial power. The question of whether the Court can reach an institutional view on the issue presented by a petition does not seem to arise at all.

Which brings us back to Chief Justice Roberts's campaign for consensus. He has presented his effort to reestablish Supreme Court consensus as an attempt to persuade individual justices to subordinate their individuality to the best interests of the institution. The underlying assumption seems to be that the question of whether the Court decides cases institutionally or as the sum of nine distinct voices is a matter for the members of the Court themselves to decide.

But this assumption is deeply problematic. It is pointless to leave the reinstitution of consensus to the very men and women who have jettisoned it, and who benefit from the regime of self-expression. At a recent conference at Pepperdine University School of Law (October 19, 2007), Jeffrey Rosen reported that Justice Scalia "snarled sweetly 'Good luck,'" when asked about the chief justice's campaign for unanimity; and said that other reacted as negatively, if less sarcastically, (A tape of the conference may be viewed at http://howappealing. law.com/112807.html#030139 [accessed January 21, 2008].)

Indeed, the results of the most recent term make clear beyond doubt that the achievement of unanimity is out of the Court's reach even with a chief justice as explicitly and publicly committed to it as is Justice Roberts. The ink was hardly dry on a June 12, 2007 *New York Sun* editorial congratulating the Court on deciding a number of case unanimously and expressing satisfaction that "the nine justices often see their duties to the law in similar ways," when a virtual torrent of divided decisions—decisions by a 5–4 Court—came cascading down the steps of the marble palace. The Court last term decided nearly three times as many cases by a 5–4 vote than it had just the year before (24 vs. nine).

The Case for Consensus

No, if the chief justice's goal of restoring the norm of Supreme Court unanimity is to be achieved, change will have to be imposed from the outside, which means by Congress. As is evident from the history sketched briefly above, at the time congress gave the Supreme Court its certiorari discretion, it was taken for granted that the Court was governed by an internal norm of consensus. Of the more than 1, 500 full opinions rendered by the Court under Taft's leadership, 84 percent were unanimous. He could hardly have anticipated that 70 years after the Court was empowered to confine itself to clarifying the law the corresponding figure would be, as it was for 1993–95, a mere 27 percent. As detailed in Robert Post's able study of the Taft Court, Taft himself was a great foe of dissenting opinions, being of the view that "it is more important to stand by the Court and give its judgment weight rather than merely to record my individual dissent." Post quotes him stating that "most dissents elaborated are a form of egoism"; "[t]hey don't do any good, and only weaken the prestige of the Court," adding that Taft went so far as to lobby President Harding against appointing a prominent state court judge to the Supreme Court on the basis that the candidate "evidently thinks it is more important that he should ventilate his individual views than that the Court should be consistent."

And, having particularly in mind the conception of the Court that Taft sought to realize by procuring enactment of the Judges' Bill, it is instructive to consider his observation that "It is much more important what the Court thinks than what any one [justice] thinks." Taft's conception of the Court's "main purpose [as being] to lay down important principles of law... and to make the law clearer" can hardly be squared with the now endemic practice of the justices in failing to arrive at a consensus as to "what the Court thinks" while devoting extensive resources to telling readers of its decisions "what any on [justice] thinks."

> "It is much more important what the Court thinks than what any one [justice] thinks," said Chief Justice Taft.

In short, Chief Justice Roberts's campaign for consensus should prompt reflection not on how the magic of John Marshall and his day can be recaptured, but on whether the modern Court has wisely and properly used the discretion it was granted under successive congressional enactments, starting in 1925, to set its own agenda. And, if the conclusion is reached that it has not acted wisely—that it has not used the power Congress granted it for the purposes Chief Justice Taft envisioned of "mak[ing] the law clearer" and assuring "uniformity of decision"—a more effective remedy than the chief justice's appeals to his colleagues may well exist: namely, amending the certiorari statute to require the Court to grant review only of cases it concludes it can decide unanimously or nearly so. Congress would be exercising its explicit constitutional authority to regulate the Court's jurisdiction so that it would be directed to do just what Chief Justice Taft contemplated when the Judges Act was passed. It would be using its power to make exceptions to that jurisdiction for cases that are, for one reason or another, not susceptible of being decided on a clear and uniform basis.

Such an amendment of the certiorari statute would likely also lead to an extensive reform of the Court's rules detailing the process by which it decides whether to "grant cert." But more deliberation and transparency in this important phase of the Court's work—its decision to place a given issue on the nation's legal/political agenda—would seem to be an unalloyed good thing.

It may be objected that the Court cannot be sure at the cert-granting stage of a case whether it will be able to decide the case unanimously. But that is no good reason for not considering the issue at all. Nor does the grant of certiorari require that the Court go ahead and decide the case. There already exists a practice at the Court of dismissing petitions after briefing and even after argument if it is determined that for some reason the case should not have been accepted for review. This procedure is known, in a rare instance of judicial self-criticism, as dismissing a petition as "improvidently granted" (acronymically, "digging a case"). While it is now resorted to infrequently, it is readily available should the Court decide not to act at all.

This raises the question whether no decision is better than a divided decision. If the Court's power were limited to hearing cases on whose decisions its members could agree, it is conceivable that many cases it now hears would go unheard—but not inevitable. Once a new congressional mandate had taken hold, it is reasonable to expect that the Court's members would accept as their core responsibility the decision of cases on terms to which all of them could agree. More extensive discussion among the justices than now occurs would become common, as would a more flexible—and probably narrower—approach to articulation constitutional norms. The Court would tend to become a more deliberative body than it now is, reflecting the variety of views people hold on controversial issues, while adding what has increasingly been lacking—the articulation of a resolution that all "sides" can tolerate. Sitting justices who could not accept this regime could, of course, resign—the modern practice of justices holding onto their seats decade after decade has itself recently come in for sharp criticism, including calls for the imposition of judicial term limits.

> A congressional mandate of unanimity might go a long way toward depoliticizing the Supreme Court.

It also is reasonable to expect that judicial centrism would characterize future designees for seats on the Court. Men and women committed to—and temperamentally capable of—achieving consensus on difficult issues would be sought out and nominated. We might well witness and end to the spectacle of presidential campaigns turning significantly on which "side" would be able to lock in control of the Court for a generation. Gone would be the peculiar senatorial hearings which seek to expose, without discussing them, how nominees would deal with future judicial issues. It is hard to believe they would be mourned.

What about a world in which the Court's members simply denied review rather than accepting the mandate that they decide cases unanimously? What would the effects of that be? The simplest answer is that there would be more variety in the way the same questions were decided in different parts of the country: To the extent that state Supreme Court decisions went unreviewed by the justices, they would be final within the state's borders; and to the extent that the decisions of federal Courts of Appeals were denied cert—assuming Congress were to retain that arcane and obscure terminology—their decisions would be final within the boundaries of their judicial circuits.

This hardly seems cause for alarm. Even now, it is common for the Court to deny review in cases where the petitioner claims there is a "circuit conflict" among the federal Courts of Appeals or even that a state court has failed to follow federal law. Indeed, Justice John Paul Stevens and other present members of the Court have actually argued that such intercourt conflict is desirable, permitting what they call "percolation" of difficult issues within the lower levels of the country's judiciary. In addition, careful research by Arthur Hellman of the University of Pittsburgh Law School strongly suggests that the problem of intercircuit conflict is much less extensive or long-lasting than some have claimed. And, of course, to the extent that the Supreme Court's members perceive that such conflict is intolerable, the new jurisdictional statue would not forbid them from intervening—it would only require them to act on a basis that commands unanimous concurrence. Even those, like Alan Barth, who have praised dissents, concede that dissenting opinions do not "always, or even very often, embody great wisdom." Against the first Justice Harlan's dissent in *Plessy*—which, as noted, proposed a "color-blindness" standard that the modern Court has refused to endorse—must be set the vastly greater number of instances in which, as Barth put it in *Prophets With Honor*, "a dissent expresses no more than an aberrant view arising out an individual justice's prejudices."

In the larger perspective, a statute requiring Supreme Court unanimity could well have an inhibiting effect on certain kinds of constitutional litigation, as proponents of aggressive judicial action on subjects of political controversy internalized the notion that they could not achieve a national result that was not broadly acceptable to an ideologically divers Supreme Court. Justice Brennan's "five-finger exercise" would become a relic. A congressional mandate of unanimity might go a long way toward depoliticizing the Supreme Court and the American judicial process more generally.

The fact that the Judges' Bill of 1925 was enacted with barely a ripple of dissent, as were the later statutes excusing the Court from any jurisdictional obligations, probably reflects a perception that issues of judicial jurisdiction are technical and of no general public interest. As this article has tried to suggest, nothing could be further from the truth. It would be unfortunate indeed if the circumstance that the issues raised by Chief Justice Roberts's campaign for Supreme Court consensus involve matters of legal procedure failed to win them the public attention they deserve. The great nineteenth-century legal historian Sir Henry Maine famously observed that the substantive law that governs our everyday lives has the look of having been "gradually secreted in the interstices of procedure." A similar thought may well apply to the constitutional law that the Supreme Court has been handing down in its modern era.

Act IV
The Semi-Periphery of National Political Organizations—The Direct Influencers of Power

★ Toward a Definition of Critical
★ Realignment
★

By Walter Dean Burnham

For many decades it has been generally recognized that American electoral politics is not quite "all of a piece" despite its apparent diverse uniformity. Some elections have more important long-range consequences for the political system as a whole than others, and seem to "decide" substantive issues in a more clear-cut way. There has long been agreement among historians that the elections of those of 1800, 1828, 1860, 1896, and 1932, for example, were fundamental turning points in the course of American electoral politics.

Since the appearance in 1955 of V. O. Key's seminal article, "A Theory of Critical Elections," political scientists have moved to give this concept quantitative depth and meaning. In his article, Key isolated New England data in order to demonstrate the differential impact of a compressing sectionalism in the 1890's and of a class-ethnic polarity which emerged in the 1928–36 period.[1] Duncan MacRae Jr. James A. Meldrum, in 1960, employed the sophistications of factor analysis applied to residuals to isolate realigning cycles from short-term deviation in Illinois, a discriminant technique that, surprisingly, has been little used in subsequent articles on American voting behavior. They concluded that it is usually more appropriate to conceptualize critical realignments as involving a closely spaced but massive series of adjustments in the mass base than as single events.[2]

In the same year the authors of *The American Voter* developed a typology of elections which included realigning elections—although, of course, on the basis of historical evidence rather than on grounds then observable in survey-research data.[3] Also writing in 1960, E. E. Schattschneider—employing little data but fertile insight—addressed our attention to the utility of viewing the structure of politics brought into being by realignments as systems of

---

1 V. O. Key, Jr., "A Theory of Critical Elections," 17 *Journal of Politics,* Pp. 3–18 (1955).

2 Duncan MacRae, Jr., and James A. Meldrum, "Critical Elections in Illinois: 1888–1958," *54 American Political Science Review,* Pp. 669–83 (1960).

3 Angus Campbell *et al., The American Voter* (New York: Wiley & Sons, 1960), Pp. 531–38.

action; in the aftermath of realignment, not only voting behavior but institutional roles and policy outputs undergo substantial modification.[4]

Work done by a number of scholars during the 1960's has fleshed out our empirical knowledge of some of the processes associated with critical realignment. For example, evidence has been brought forward that the adjustments of the 1890's were accompanied and followed by significant transformations in the rules of the game and in the behavioral properties of the American electorate. It has also been suggested that each era between realignments can be described as having its own "party system," even if the formal names of the major parties which form most of its organizational base happen to remain unchanged. A Schattschneiderian analysis has very recently been applied to California for the 1890–1910 period and found to work quite well.[5]

At the same time, there has been rather little effort directed to the task of exploring these phenomena in terms of their implications for effective analysis of American politics across time and space. While Key entitled his seminal article "A *Theory* of Critical Elections," and while both he and Schattschneider clearly regarded realignments of fundamental analytical importance, one is impressed with how little theorizing has been forthcoming in this area. One reason for this paucity may well be an annoying incompleteness in certain key ranges of data analysis; this often leaves us in controversy not only as to the implications of the facts of change, but even as to the structure of those facts themselves.[6]

It now seems time to attempt at least an interim assessment of the structure, function, and implications of critical realignments for the American political process. Such an effort is motivated in particular by the author's view that critical realignments are of fundamental importance not only to the system of political action called "the American political process" but also to the clarifications of some aspects of its operation. It seems particularly important in a period of obvious political upheaval not only to identify these phenomena and place them in time, but to integrate them into a larger (if still very modest) theory of movement in American politics.

Such a theory must inevitably emphasize the elements of stress and abrupt transformation in our political life at the expense of the consensual, gradualist perspectives which have until recently dominated the scholar's vision of American political processes and behavior. For the realignment phenomenon focuses our attention on "the dark side of the moon." It reminds us that politics as usual in the United States is not politics as always; that there are discrete types of voting behavior and quite different levels of voter response to political stimuli, depending

---

4 E. E. Schattschneider, *The Semisovereign People* (New York: Holt, Rinehart & Winston, 1960), especially Pp. 78–96.

5 Michael Rogin, "California Populaism and the 'System of 1896,'" 22 *Western Political Quarterly*, Pp. 179–96 (1969).

6 Such seems more than implicit, for instances, in the arguments made recently by H. D. Price; see his contribution to Oliver Garceau (ed.), *Political Research and Political Theory* (Cambridge: Harvard University Press, 1968), especially Pp. 115–20.

on what those stimuli are and at what point in time they occur; and that American political institutions and leadership, once defined (or redefined) in a "normal phases" of our politics, seem to become part of the very conditions that threaten to overthrow them.

The work of survey research over the past generation has heavily confirmed what earlier students and practitioners of politics in the United States noted: once a stable pattern of voting behavior and of generalized leadership recruitment has been established, it tends to continue over time with only short-term deviations. As is well known, for example, party identification in the 1952–64 period showed only the most glacial movement, in sharp contrast to the actual partisan outcomes of elections. When differentials in turnout among population groups are taken into account, it is possible to derive both a "normal vote" and a normal majority part— about 52 to 53 per cent Democratic for the country as a whole in recent years.[7] Short-term deviations occur, of course, and have been showing a marked tendency to increase since the 1940's. But the dominant structure of party-oriented voting, which comes out more clearly in the aggregate totals for Congress than in presidential elections, has remained highly fixed until very recently. Thus recent presidential and congressional elections present the national profile shown in Table 1.1.

Stable phases in the alignment cycle are not identical, of course, with complete uniformity of behavior. Not only are deviating elections such as 1952 or 1956 possible, but also secular trends within regions or discrete groupings of voters and even fairly major but localized read-justments—for example, the emergence and flourishing of presidential Republicanism in the South during the Eisenhower era. Such movements can be of considerable long-term political significance in their own right. For example, between the 193's and the mid-1960's there was a trend toward secular realignment in favor of the Democrats in much of the Northeast, and in favor of the Republicans in border and Midwestern states such as Kentucky and Ullionis.[8] Indeed, one of the aspects of the contemporary political scene which we shall examine at some length is the increasing instability of major sectors of the mass electorate.[9] Since this trend in no small way acts as a limiting condition on nationwide realignment in the current era, it is of the greatest importance for the analysis of contemporary electoral politics in this country.

---

7 See Philip E. Converse, "The Concept of a Normal Vote," in Angus Campbell *et al., Elections and the Political Order* (New York: Wiley & Sons, 1968), Pp. 9–39.

8 John H. Fenton, *Midwest Politics* (New York: Holt, Rinehart & Winston, 1966), Pp. 214–18; and, by the same author, *Politics in the Border States* (New Orleans: Hauser, 1957), Pp. 114–17.

9 American party alignments since World War II have shown very high lability compared with those of most other Western polities. See Richard Rose and Derek Urwin, "Persistence and Change in Western Party Systems Since 1945," (Cologne: Conference on Comparative Social Science, 26–31 may 1969, mimeo), especially Table 7B following p. 17. The only set of parties which show a larger standard deviation of vote change over this period are the Gaullist and MRP parties in France, and the reason in that case is obvious. Standard deviations of magnitudes comparable with those for the two American parties are also found for the two major Canadian parties (not surprisingly) and for the German CDU/CSU. No other major parties in the nineteen countries studied reveal standard deviations which are nearly so large.

Table 1.1 National Presidential and Congressional Election, 1944–1968

	Presidential	Congressional
% Democratic of total vote	49.0	52.1
Variance	45.65	8.05
Standard Deviation	6.76	2.84
% Republican of total vote	47.9	46.6
Variance	43.91	6.31
Standard Deviation	6.63	2.51
% Democratic of two-party vote	50.6	52.8
Variance	39.30	7.14
Standard Deviation	6.27	2.67

It is enough to say for the present that any working definition of the concept "critical realignment" must, practically speaking eliminate both deviating election situations—even landslides such as Theodore Roosevelt's in 1904 or Warren Harding's in 1920—and gradual secular realignments. It must also emphasize that while there are large historical, territorial, and stratification differences in the stability of "stable phases," they reveal comparatively far more of a component of political inertia at the mass base than do realigning eras.

In its "ideal-typical" form, the critical realignment differs from stable alignments eras, secular realignments, and deviating elections in the following basic ways.

1. The critical realignment is characteristically associated with short-lived but very intense disruptions of traditional patterns of voting behavior. Majority parties become minorities; politics which was once competitive become noncompetitive or, alternatively, hitherto one-part areas now become arenas of intense partisan competition; and large blocks of the active electorate—minorities, to be sure, but perhaps involving as much as a fifth to a third of the voters—shift their partisan allegiance.

2. Critical elections are characterized by abnormally high intensity as well.
   a. This intensity typically spills over into the party nominating and platform-writing machinery during the upheaval and results in major shifts in convention behavior from the integrative "norm" as well as in transformations in the internal loci of power in the major party most heavily affected by the pressures of realignment. Ordinarily accepted "rules of the game" are flouted; the party's processes, instead of performing their usual integrative functions, themselves contribute to polarization.
   b. The rise in intensity is associated with a considerable increase in ideological polarizations, at first within one or more of the major parties and then between

them. Issue distances between the parties are markedly increased, and elections tend to involve highy salient issue-clusters, often with strongly emotional and symbolic overtones, far more than is customary in American electoral politics. One curious property of established leadership as it drifts into the stress of realignment seems to be a tendency to become more rigid and dogmatic, which itself contributes greatly to the explosive "bursting stress" of realignment. Federalist leadership just before 1801 stands in marked contrast to the Jeffersonian afterward, for example, The same may be said (perhaps less certainly) of the inherited inner-circle political style of a John Quincy Adams as the antideferential democratic revolution got under way; of the inflexible leadership of a James Buchanan in 1857–61, which effectively foreclosed a middle-of-the-road northern Democratic alternative to the Republicans; of the rigid defense of the status quo waged by Grover Cleveland and Herbert Hoover in our two greatest depressions; and of Lyndon Johnson's unhappy second administration.[10]

c. The rise in intensity is also normally to be found in abnormally heavy voter participation for the time. This significant increase in political mobilization is not always or uniformly present, to be sure. It is particularly true of realigning cycles with a strong sectional thrust that the areas which are propelled most strongly to one partly or the other tend to be those in which turnout does not increase much, or even declines. Similarly, while increases in participation during the 1928–36 period were very heavy in most of the country, they were slight or nonexistent in the South, because the restrictive structure of local politics which had been created at the turn of the century was not disturbed until long after World War II. Moreover, the net effect of the New Deal realignment was to make the South even more lopsidedly Democratic than it had been before, With such exceptions, however, there has still been a general tendency toward markedly increased participation during realigning eras.

3. Historically speaking, at least, national critical realignments have not occurred at random. Instead, there has been a remarkably uniform periodicity in their appearance. A variety of measures can be employed to examine this periodic phenomenon. Sudden shifts in the relationship between percentages for a given political party in one election and the next can be easily detected through autocorrelation and may present strong evidence of realignment.[11] Another technique, analogous to discriminant-function or change-in-universe-state analysis, will be discussed later. Here it is sufficient to assert that this periodicity has had an objective existence, that it is one of the most striking historically conditioned facts associated with the evolution of American electoral politics, and that it is of very great analytical importance.

---

10 Certainly this generational collision was of very great prominence in the 1968 Democratic convention at Chicago. For an excellent delegate's-eye view of this, see Aaron Wildavsky, "The Meaning of 'Youth' in the Struggle for Control of the Democratic Party" (mimeo).

11 Gerald Pomper, "Classification of Presidential Elections," 29 *Journal of Politics,* Pp. 535–66 (1967); and Walter Dean Burnham, "American Voting Behavior and the 1964 Election," 12 *Midwest Journal of Political Science,* Pp. 1–40 (1968).

4. It has been argued, with much truth, that American political parties are essentially constituent parties.[12] That is to say, the political-party subsystem is sited in a socioeconomic system of very great heterogeneity and diversity. For a variety of reasons (to be discussed in greater detail later) this party system has tended to be preoccupied with performing the functions of integration and "automatic" aggregation of highly diverse and often antagonistic subgroupings in the population to the near exclusion of concern for development of "modern" mass organization in the European sense. It is neither structured nor widely perceived as a cohesive policy link between voters and officials. The conditions in which our political parties operate, and their normal operating styles and limitations, have produced not a little anguish among an older generation of political scientists who grew to professional maturity during the New Deal and who rightly saw the structure and functioning of our major political parties as a major obstacle to the realization of democratic accountability.[13] It has been well said that "electorally, American parties represent outcomes *in general*: parties seldom shape or represent outcomes *in particular.*"[14]

Critical realignments emerge directly from the dynamics of this constituent-function supremacy in American politics in ways and with implications which will be analyzed subsequently. Here we will only note that since they involve constitutional readjustments in the broadest sense of the term, they are intimately associated with and followed by transformations in large clusters of policy. This produces correspondingly profound alternations in policy and influences the grand institutional structures of American government. In other words, realignments are themselves constituent acts: they arise from emergent tensions in society which, not adequately controlled by the organization or outputs of party politics as usual, escalate to a flash point; they are issue-oriented phenomena, centrally associated with these tensions and more or less leading to resolution adjustments; they result in significant transformations in the general shape of policy; and they have relatively profound aftereffects on the roles played by institutional elites.[15] They are involved with redefinitions of the universe of voters, political parties, and the broad boundaries of the politically possible.

To recapitulate, then, eras of critical realignment are marked by short, sharp reorganizations of the mass coalitional bases of the major parties which occur at periodic intervals on

---

12 Theodore J. Lowi, "Party, Policy, and Constitution" in William N. Chambers and Walter Dean Burnham (eds.), *The American Party Systems* (New York: Oxford University Press, 1967), Pp. 238–76.

13 The locus *classicus* here is, of course, the report of the APSA's Committee on Political Parties, *Toward a More Responsible Two-Party System* (1950).

14 Lowi, op. cit., p. 263.

15 The most obviously plausible example of synchronization of institutional-role and policy-output change with critical realignment is the Supreme Court of the United States. The literature is voluminous if frequently inferential, and the subject merits a more explicit relational treatment than it has received. For an excellent account of elite attitudes under the pressure of the crisis of the 1890's and the enormous impetus this gave to judicial creativity in this period, see Arnold M. Paul, *Conservative Crisis and the Rule of Law* (Ithaca, N.Y.: Cornell University Press, 1960).

the national level; are often preceded by major third-party revolts which reveal the incapacity of "politics as usual" to integrate, much less aggregate, emergent political demand; are closely associated with abnormal stress in the socioeconomic system; are marked by ideological polarizations and issue-distances between the major parties which are exceptionally large by normal standards; and have durable consequences as constituent acts which determine the outer boundaries of policy in general, though not necessarily of policies in detail.

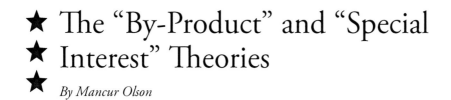

★ The "By-Product" and "Special
★ Interest" Theories

By Mancur Olson

A. The "By-Product" Theory of Large Pressure Groups

If the individuals in a large group have no incentive to organize a lobby to obtain a collective benefit, how can the fact that some large groups are organized be explained? Though many groups with common interests, like the consumers, the white-collar workers, and the migrant agricultural workers, are not organized,[1] other large groups, like the union laborers, the farmers, and the doctors have at least some degree of organization. The fact that there are many groups which, despite their needs, are not organized would seem to contradict the "group theory" of the analytical pluralists; but on the other hand the fact that other large groups have been organized would seem to contradict the theory of "latent groups" offered in this study.

But the large economic groups that are organized do have one common characteristic which distinguishes them from those large economic groups that are not, and which at the same time tends to support the theory of latent groups offered in this work. This common characteristic will, however, require an elaboration or addition to the theory of groups developed in this study.

The common characteristic which distinguishes all of the large economic groups with significant lobbying organizations is that these groups are also organized for some other purpose. The large and powerful economic lobbies are in fact the by-products of organizations that obtain their strength and support because they perform some function in addition to lobbying for collective goods.

---

1 "When lists of these organizations are examined, the fact that strikes the student most forcibly is that *the system is very small.* The range of organized, identifiable, known groups is amazingly narrow; there is nothing remotely universal about it." E. E. Schattschneider, *The Semi-Sovereign People* (New York: Holt, Rinehart & Winston, 1960), p. 30.

The lobbies of the large economic groups are the by-products of organizations that have the capacity to "mobilize" a latent group with "selective incentives." The only organizations that have the "selective incentives" available are those that (1) have the authority and capacity to be coercive, or (2) have a source of positive inducements that they can offer the individuals in a latent group.

A purely political organization—an organization that has no function apart from its lobbying function—obviously cannot legally coerce individuals into becoming members. A political party, or any purely political organization, with a captive or compulsory membership would be quite unusual in a democratic political system. But if for some nonpolitical reason, if because of some other function it performs, an organization has a justification for having a compulsory membership, or if through this other function it has obtained the power needed to make membership in it compulsory, that organization may then be able to get the resources needed to support a lobby. The lobby is then a by-product of whatever function this organization performs that enables it to have a captive membership.

An organization that did nothing except lobby to obtain a collective good for some large group would not have a source of rewards or positive selective incentives it could offer potential members. Only an organization that also sold private or noncollective products, or provided social or recreational benefits to individual members, would have a source of these positive inducements.[2] Only such an organization could make a joint offering or "tied sale" of a collective and a noncollective good that could stimulate a rational individual in a large group to bear part of the cost of obtaining a collective good.[3] There are for this reason many organizations that

---

2 An economic organization in a perfectly competitive market in equilibrium, which had no special competitive advantage that could bring it a large amount of "rent," would-have no "profits" or other spare resources it could use as selective incentives for a lobby. Nonetheless there are many organizations that do have spare returns they can use for selective incentives. First, markets with some degree of monopoly power are far more common than perfectly competitive markets. Second, there are sometimes important complementaries between the economic and political activities of an organization. The political branch of the organization can win lower taxes or other favorable government policies for the economic branch, and the good name won by the political branch may also help the economic branch. For somewhat similar reasons, a social organization may also be a source of a surplus that can be used for selective incentives.

An organization that is not only political, but economic or social as well, and has a surplus that provides selective incentives, may be able to retain its membership and political power, in certain cases, even if its leadership manages to use some of the political or economic power of the organization for objectives other than those desired by the membership, since the members of the organization will have an incentive to continue belonging even if they disagree with the organization's policy. This may help explain why many lobbying organizations take positions that must be uncongenial to their membership, and why organizations with leaders who corruptly advance their own interests at the expense of the organization continue to survive.

3 The worth of the noncollective or private benefit would have to exceed its cost by an amount greater than the dues to the lobbying branch of the organization, or the joint offering would not be sufficient

have both lobbying functions and economic functions, or lobbying functions and social functions, or even all three of these types of functions at once.[4] Therefore, in addition to the large group lobbies that depend on coercion, there are those that are associated with organizations that provide noncollective or private benefits which can be offered to any potential supporter who will bear his share of the cost of the lobbying for the collective good.

The by-product theory of pressure groups need apply only to the large or latent group. It *need not* apply to the privileged or intermediate groups, because these smaller groups can often provide a lobby, or any other collective benefit, without *any selective* incentives, as Chapter I showed. It applies to latent groups because the individual in a latent group has no incentive voluntarily to sacrifice his time or money to help an organization obtain a collective good; he alone cannot be decisive in determining whether or not this collective good will be obtained, but if it is obtained because of the efforts of others he will inevitably be able to enjoy it in any case. Thus he would support the organization with a lobby working for collective goods only if (1) he is coerced into paying dues to the lobbying organization, or (2) he has to support this group in order to obtain some other noncollective benefit. Only if one or both of these conditions hold will the potential political power of a latent group be mobilized.

This chapter will attempt to show how the largest economic pressure groups in the United States are in fact explained by the byproduct theory. It will argue that the main types of large economic lobbies—the labor unions, the farm organizations, and the professional organizations—obtain their support-mainly because they perform some function besides lobbying. It will argue that labor unions are a dominant political force because they also deal with employers, who can be forced to employ only union members; that farm organizations obtain their members mainly through farm cooperatives and government agencies; and that professional associations rely in part on subtle forms of coercion and in part on the provision of noncollective services to get their membership. Finally, it will argue that the many organizations representing industries with small numbers of firms are explained by a theory of "special interests," which rests on the special capacity for organized action in small groups.

B. Labor Lobbies

The labor union is probably the most important single tpye of pressure-group organization and accordingly deserves first place in any discussion of large lobbying organizations. Though

---

to attract members to the organization. Note that on page 51, note 72, selective incentives were defined to be values larger in absolute magnitude than an individual's share of the costs of the collective good.

4 An organization that lobbied by lobbying also for noncollective "political" goods, like individual exceptions to (or advantageous interpretations of) a general rule of law, or for patronage for particular individuals, etc. The point is not that the organization must necessarily also be economic or social as well as political (though that is usually the case); it is rather that, if organization does not have the capacity to coerce potential members, it must offer some noncollective, i.e., selective, benefit to potential members.

the opponents of the labor unions are exaggerating when they claim that the Democratic candidates in industrial states are merely puppets of labor leaders, it is quite clear that the Democrats in these states are normally very friendly to labor, and that the Republicans usually treat the labor unions as the major source of enemy strength. The membership of the AFL-CIO is *several times larger* than the membership of any other lobbying organization. The labor unions have, moreover, an impressive organizational network to match their numbers: there are about 60,000 to 70,000 union locals in this country.[5] Labor leaders have claimed that they could influence about 25 million voters.[6] Their purely political expenditures are measured in the millions.[7] In 1958 some candidates may have been elected as a result of the large labor vote brought put by "right-to-work" proposals on the ballot in some industrial states. In Michigan the Democratic party came out of the doldrums as labor organization grew.[8] There were about 200 unionists who were either delegates or alternate delegates to the 1952 pemocratic national convention.[9] The late Sumner Slichter argued that "the American economy is a laboristic economy, or at least is rapidly becoming one." By this he meant "that employees are the most influential group in the community and that the economy is run in their interest more than in the interest of any other economic group."[10] Professor Slichter may have been mistaken, but if so only because many business, professional, and agricultural organizations unite in intense opposition to what they regard as the excessive claims of labor.

Just as there can be little doubt that labor unions are a significant political force, neither can there be much question that this political force is a by-product of the purely industrial activities that unions regard as their major function. As Chapter III pointed out, it was only when labor unions began to concentrate on collective bargaining with employers and abandoned the mainly political orientation of the earlier American unions, that they came to have any stability or power. It was only when the labor unions started to deal with the employers, who alone had the power to *force* the workers to join the union, that they began to prosper. It is, moreover, hard to see how the labor unions could have obtained and maintained the "union shop" in a democratic country like the United States if they had been *solely* political organizations. Labor unions came to play an important part in the political struggle only long after they had forsaken political action as a major goal. It is worth noting that the Wagner Act, which made organizing a union with compulsory membership much easier, and which led to the greatest increase in union membership, was passed *before* labor unions came to play a really important role in politics. The experience of Great Britain also shows that a democratic nation is often happy to overlook compulsory membership in organizations that engage in collective bargaining, but hesitant to make membership in a political organization in any degree automatic. Although,

5 V. O. Key, *Politics, Parties, and Pressure Groups,* 4th ed. (New York: Crowell, 1958), p. 62.

6 Dayton David McKean, *Party and Pressure Politics* (Boston: Houghton Mifflin, 1949), p. 464.

7 For example, *ibid.,* Pp. 47.5–476.

8 Key, p. 73.

9 *Ibid.*

10 Sumner H.Slichter, *The American Economy* (New York: Alfred A. Knopf, 1950), p. 7.

as Chapter III explained, it has long been taken for granted in Britain that unionists will often not work with nonunion men, there has been a great deal of bitter controversy over whether union men should "contract in" or "contract out" of a contribution to the Labour party. (The vast majority of the members of that party, incidentally, are a by-product of the trade unions' activities; all except a small minority belong through the trade unions.)[11] If, then, it is true that a democratic nation would not normally want to make membership in a purely political union compulsory, and that compulsion is essential to a stable labor movement of any size, then it follows that the political power of unions is a by-product of their nonpolitical activities.

C. Professional Lobbies

Many of those who criticize organized labor because of the coercion entailed in labor unions are themselves members of professional organizations that depend upon compulsion as much as unions do. Many organizations representing prosperous and prestigious professions like the law and medicine have also reached for the forbidden fruits of compulsory membership. There is in fact a pervasive tendency towards compulsion in professional associations generally. "The trend," writes Frances Delancey, "is toward the .professional guild."[12] This is what many other scholars have also observed. "A characteristic of the politics of the professional association," according to V. O. Key, "is their tendency to seek the reality, if not invariably the form, of a guild system."[13] J. A. C. Grant argues that the guild "has returned. Its purposes are the same as in the Middle Ages."[14] The guild form of organization is often adopted not only by the ancient and learned professions, but also by undertakers, barbers, "beauticians," "cosmeticians," plumbers, opticians, and other groups interested in professional status.[15] This adoption of the guild form of organization is evidence for the by-product theory of large pressure groups, for compulsory membership has always been, Grant points out, "the first rule" of the guild system.[16]

The self-regulating guild with compulsory membership has reached its furthest degree of development in many state bar associations. Many state legislatures have been induced to

---

11 B. C. Roberts, *Trade Union Government and Administration in Great Britain* (Cambridge, Mass.: Harvard. University Press, 1956), Pp. 369–380 and 551–553; G. D. H. Cole, *A Short History of the British Wording Class Movement, 1789–1947,* new ed. (London: George Allen & Unwin, 1948), Pp. 296–299, 310–315, 423–424; Charles Mowat, *Britain Between the Wars* (Chicago: University of£ Chicago Press, 1955), Pp. 336–337; and Martin Harrison, *Trade Unions and the Labour Party Since 1945* (London: Ruskin House, George Allen & Unwin, 1960), *passim.*

12 Frances Priscilla DeLancey, *The Licensing of Professions in West Virginia* (Chicago: Foundation Press, 1938), p. 140.

13 Key, p. 136.

14 J. A. C. Grant, "The Gild Returns to America," *Journal of Politics,* IV (August 1942), 316.

15 Grant, "The Gild Returns to America, II," *ibid.,* IV (November 1942), 463–476.

16 Grant's first installment (August 1942), 304.

require *by law* that *every* practicing lawyer must be a member of the state bar association.[17] These bar associations have closed shops enforced by government, and thus should be the envy of every labor union.

The modern professional associations or guilds are moreover coming to resemble "miniature governments."[18] They have "all the types of power normally exercised by government."[19] State governments often give the professional groups authority to govern themselves (and to a degree their clients) and to discipline any members of the profession that do not maintain the "ethical" standards the profession finds it expedient or appropriate to maintain. It follows that, even when membership in these associations is not a legal requirement, the individual in professional practice knows that he has an interest in maintaining-membership in good standing with the professional association.

The advantages of maintaining membership and good relationships with a professional association may be illustrated by the fact that it was not found expedient to release the name of a doctor who had written to a congressional committee to argue that "the central organization of the AMA in Chicago has no idea what the average physician wants his patients to have."[20] Oliver Garceau, author of the classic work on the American Medical Association, has argued that the recalcitrant doctor in trouble with organized medicine may face "a genuine economic threat."[21] When the American Medical Association blocked the Denver city council's program, for Denver General Hospital in 1945, a Denver councilman, according to *Time* magazine, was driven to exclaim: "Nobody can touch the American Medical Association ... Talk about the closed shop of£ the AFL and the CIO—they are a bunch of pikers."[22]

The role of coercion, even in its subtler forms, in the American Medical Association is, however, probably less important as a source of£ membership than the noncollective benefits the organization provides its membership. According to Garceau, there is "one formal service of the society with which the doctor can scarcely dispense. Malpractice defense has become a prime requisite to private practice."[23] One doctor who hact founded a cooperative hospital, and lost his membership in his medical society, discovered that not only had he lost his chance to have other doctors testify in his behalf during malpractice suits, but that he had lost his

---

17 M, Louise Rutherford, *The Influence of the American Bar Association on Public Opinion and Legislation* (Philadelphia, 1937), Pp. 32–34; McKean, p. 568.

18 Grant (August 1942), 324.

19 *Ibid.*

20 U.S. Congress, House Committee on Interstate and Foreign Commerce, 83d Cong., 2d Sess., *Health Inquiry,* Part 7 (1954), p. 2230, quoted in Key, p. 139.

21 Oliver Garceau, *The Political Life of the American Medical Association* (Cambridge, Mass.; Harvard University Press, 1941), Pp. 95, 103.

22 *Time* (Feb. 19, 1945), p. 53, quoted in McKean, p. 564.

23 Garceau, p. 103.

insurance as well.[24] The many technical publications of the American Medical Association, and the state and local medical societies, also give the doctor a considerable incentive to affiliate with organized medicine. The American Medical Association publishes not only its celebrated *Journal,* but also many other technical periodicals on various medical specialties. Since the nineteenth century the *Journal* alone has provided a "tangible attraction for doctors."[25] The importance of this attraction is perhaps indicated by a survey conducted in Michigan, which showed that 89 per cent of the doctors received the *Journal of the American Medical Association,* and 70 per cent read a state society journal, but *less than 30 per cent* read any *other* type of medical literature.[26] The *Journal* has been, moreover, the "prime money maker of the organization."[27] Much of the organization's revenue, according to Garceau, comes from drug companies' advertisements—advertisements which Garceau believes helped companies obtain the AMA seal of approval for their products.[28] The conventions of the American Medical Association and

---

24 *Ibid,,* p. 104. Those who are not members of thier local medical societies can, now at least, usually get malpractice insurance, though they must apparently pay higher rates. One student of the economics of medicine, Reuben Kessel, describes the situation in this way:

"County medical societies play a crucial role in protecting their members against malpractice suits. Physicians charged with malpractice are tried by their associates in the private judicial system of organized medicine, If found innocent, then local society members are available for duty as expert witnesses in the defense of those charged with malpractice. Needless to say, comparable services by society members for plaintiffs in such actions are not equally available. By virtue of this monopoly over the services of expert witnesses and the tacit coalition of the members of a society in the defense of those charged with malpractice, the successful prosecution of£ malpractice suits against society members is extremely difficult.

"On the other hand, for doctors who are *persona-non-grata* with respect to organized medicine, the shoe is on the other foot. Expert witnesses from the ranks of organized medicine are abundantly available for plaintiffs but not for defendants. Therefore the position of the plaintiff in a suit against a non-society member is of an order of magnitude stronger than it is for a suit against a society member. Consequently it should come as no surprise that the costs off malpractice insurance for non-society members is substantially higher than it is for society members. Apparently some non-society members have experienced difficulty in obtaining malpractice insurance at any price."

Kessell also argues that the nonmember of the county medical society may have difficulty getting on a hospital staff. "This control over hospitals by the AMA has been used to induce hospitals to abide by the Mundt Resolution. This resolution advises hospitals that are certified for intern training that their staff ought to be composed solely of members of local medical societies. As a result of this AMA control over hospitals, membership in local medical societies is a matter of enormous importance to practicing physicians. Lack of membership implies inability to become a member of a hospital staff." Reuben Kessell, "Price Discrimination in Medicine," *Journal of Law and Economics,* I (October 1958), 2–53, esp. 30–31 and 44–45.

25 Garceau, p. 15.

26 *Ibid.,* p. 99.

27 *Ibid.,* p. 16

28 *Ibid.,* p. 89.

many of its constituent organizations also provide technical information needed by doctors, and thus give the member a "direct return in education"[29] for .the investment in dues, just as the medical journals do.

In short, by providing a helpful defense against malpractice suits, by publishing medical journals needed by its membership, and by making its conventions educational as well as political, the American Medical Association has offered its members and potential members a number of selective or noncollective benefits. It has offered its members benefits which, in contrast with the political achievements of the organization, can be withheld from nonmembers, and which accordingly provide an incentive for joining the organization.

The American Medical Association, then, obtains its membership partly because of subtle forms of coercion, and partly because it provides noncollective benefits. It would have neither the coercive power to exercise, nor the noncollective benefits to sell, if it were solely a lobbying organization. It follows that the impressive political power of the American Medical Association and the local groups that compose it is a by-product of the nonpolitical activities of organized medicine.

It is interesting to ask why no organization of college professors has acquired anything like the political power of the American Medical Association. Probably the most important factor is that, in the academic profession, the learned societies are independent of the political association.[30] If the American Association of University Professors could usurp the functions of the learned societies, it could rival the AMA. If subscriptions to the scholarly journals, and attendance at the conventions of the learned societies, were restricted to members of the AAUP, professors would probably be as well organized and as powerful as doctors. If the AAUP published as many technical journals as the American Medical Association, almost every faculty member would have an incentive to join, and the AAUP membership would presumably rise above its present level,[31] and dues and participation could perhaps also increase.

---

29 *Ibid.,* p. 66.

30 "One important structural difference exists between the AAUP and the AMA. The AMA performs two kinds of functions for its members. In addition to serving physicians in the capacity of a craft union, i.e., protecting and advancing their economic interest, it provides the services of an outstanding scientific organization. For example, it publishes scientific journals, standardizes drugs, protects the public from harmful medicines, and provides a forum for scientific papers. The AAUP, on the other hand, has but one dimension: it is a craft union for college teachers. For scientific services its members look to the professional organizations serving their subject fields." Melvin Lurie, "Professors, Physicians, and Unionism," *AAUP Bulletin,* XLVIU (September 1962), 274.

31 As of January 1, 1965, die AAUP had 66,645 members. *AAUP Bulletin, LI* (March 1965), 54.

D. The "Special Interest" Theory and Business Lobbies

The segment of society that has the largest number of lobbies working on its behalf is the business community. The *Lobby Index,*[32] an index of organizations and individuals filing reports under the Lobbying Act of 1946 and 1949, reveals that (when Indian tribes are excluded), 825 out of a total of 1,247 organizations represented business.[33] Similarly,, a glance at the table of contents of the *Encyclopedia of Associations* shows that the "Trade, Business, and Commercial Organizations" and the "Chambers of Commerce" together take up more than ten times as many pages as the "Social Welfare Organizations," for example.[34] Most of the books on the subject agree on this point. "The business character of£ the pressure system," according to Schattschneider, "is shown by almost every list available."[35] This high degree of organization among businessmen, Schattschneider thinks, is particularly important in view of the fact that most other groups are so poorly organized; "only a chemical trace" of the nation's Negroes are members of the National Association for the Advancement of Colored People; "only one sixteen hundredths of 1 per cent of the consumers" have joined the National Consumers' League; "only 6 per cent of American automobile drivers" are members of the American Automobile Association, and only "about 15 per cent of the veterans" belong to the American Legion.[36] Another scholarly observer believes that "of the many organized groups maintaining offices in the capital, there are no interests more fully, more comprehensively, and more efficiently represented than those of American industry."[37] Burns and Peltason say in their text that "businessmen's 'unions' are the most varied and numerous of all."[38] V. O. Key points out that "almost every line of industrial and commerical activity has its association."[39] Key also expresses surprise at the extent of the power of organized business in American democracy:

32 U.S. Congress, House, Select Committee on Lobbying Activities, *Lobby Index, 1946–49,* Report No. 3197, 81st Cong., 2d Sess., 1950, H.R. 298.

33 Schattschneider, *Semi-Sovereign People* (note 1, above), p. 30.

34 *Encyclopedia of Associations,* 3rd ed. (Detroit: Gale Research Co.), I, 3. See also U.S. Department of Commerce, *Directory of Trade Associations* (Washington, 1956), p. iii; in addition see W. J. Donald, *Trade Associations* (New York: McGraw-Hill, 1933); Benjamin S. Kirsh, *Trade Associations in Law and Business* (New York: Central Book Co., 1938); Clarence E. Bonnett, *Employers' Associations in the United States* (New York: Macmillan, 1922) and *History of Employers' Associations in the United States* (New York: Vantage Press, 1956); and Trade Association Division, Chamber of Commerce of the United States, "Association Activities" (Washington, 1955), mimeo.

35 Schattschneider, *Semi-Sovereign People,* p. 31.

36 *Ibid.,* p. 35–36.

37 E. Pendleton Herring's comment in *Group Representation before Congress* (Washington: Brookings Institution, 1929), p. 78, which is quoted approvingly by McKean, Pp. -485–486.

38 James MacGregor Burns and Jack Walter Peltason, Government by the people, 4th ed (Englewood Cliffs N.J: Prentice-Hall, 1960), p.293.

39 Key, p. 96.

"The power wielded by business in American politics may puzzle the person of democratic predilections: a comparatively small minority exercises enormous power."[40]

The number and power of the lobbying organizations representing American business is indeed surprising in a democracy operating according to the majority rule. The power that the various segments of the business community wield in this democratic system, despite the smallness of their numbers, has not been adequately explained. There have been many rather vague, and even mystical, generalizations about the power of the business and propertied interests, but these generalizations normally do not *explain why* business groups have the influence that they have in democracies; they merely assert that they always have such an influence, as though it were self-evident that this should be so. "In the absence of military force," said Charles A. Beard, paraphrasing Daniel Webster, "political power naturally and necessarily goes into the hands which hold the property."[41] But why? Why is it "natural" and "necessary," in democracies based on the rule of the majority, that the political power should fall into the hands of those who hold the property? Bold statements of this kind may tell us something about the ideological bias of the writer, but they do not help us understand reality.

The high degree of organization of business interests, and the power of these business interests, must be due in large part to the fact that the business community is divided into a series of (generally oligopolistic) "industries" each of which contains only a fairly small number of firms. Because the number of firms in each industry is often no more than would comprise a "privileged" group, and seldom more than would comprise an "intermediate" group, it follows that these industries will normally be small enough to organize voluntarily to provide themselves with an active lobby—with the political power that "naturally and necessarily" flows to those that control the business and property of the country. Whereas almost every occupational group involves thousands of workers, and whereas almost any subdivision of agriculture also in-volves thousands of people, the business interests of the country normally are congregated in oligopoly-sized groups or industries. It follows that the laboring, professional, and agricultural interests of the country make up large, latent groups that can organize and act effectively only when their latent power is crystallized by some organization which can provide political power as a by-product; and by contrast the business interests generally can voluntarily and directly organize and act to further their common interersts without any such adventitious assistance. The multitude of workers, consumers, white-collar workers, farmers, and so on are organized only in special circumstances, but business interests are organized as a general rule.[42]

---

40 *Ibid.,* p. 83

41 Charles A. Beard, *The Economic Basis of Politics* (New York: Alfred A. Knopf, 1945), p. 103; see also McKean, p. 482.

42 The advantage in having a small number of large units in a group can be illustrated very simply by considering the extreme case of the very large firm with a political interest unique to itself. Such a firm is a "group of one," and analogous to the monopoly or monopsony in the marketplace. When a large firm is interested in legislation or administrative regulations of unique importance to itself, there is little doubt that it will act in its interest. It is in an even more favorable position than the firms in the privileged

The political advantages of the small groups of large units—the business interests—may account for some of the concern about "special interests." As Chapter V pointed out, there may be a sense in which the narrow "special interests" of the small group tend to triumph over the (often unorganized and inactive) interests of "the people." Sometimes the contrast drawn between the "special interests" and the "people" is nothing more than a convenient rhetorical device for politicians and journalists. At other times, however, practical observers may be sensing the fact that the organized and active interest of small groups tend to triumph over the unorganized and unprotected interests of larger groups. Often a relatively small group or industry will win a tariff, or a tax loophole, at the expense of millions of consumers or taxpayers in spite of the ostensible rule of the majority. This is what the distinction between privileged and intermediate groups, on the one hand, and large, latent groups, on the other, would lead one to expect.

The main type of organization representing the business interests is the trade association, and it is not difficult to show how small and "special" the interests the trade associations represent are. Professor Schattschneider points out how few members most trade associations have:

Of 421 trade associations in the metal products industry listed in *National Associations of the United States,* 153 have a membership of less than 20. The median membership was somewhere between 24 and 50. Approximately the same scale of memberships is to be found in the lumber, furniture and paper industries where 37.3 per cent of the associations listed had a membership of less than 20 and the median membership was in the 25 to 50 range.

The statistics in these cases are representative of nearly all other classifications of industry.[43]

"Pressure politics," Schattschneider concludes, "is essentially the politics of small groups."[44] V. O. Key points out that the effective or supporting membership of these trade associations is often much smaller than would be expected; "in almost half of them," he says, "nearly 50 per cent of the cost is borne by a handful of members."[45] The trade associations are therefore normally rather small, and this smallness must be the principal reason that so many of them exist. Many of the trade associations, however, are able to derive still further strength because they provide some noncollective services for their members in addition to lobbying. They provide noncollective or nonpublic benefits the same way that many nonbusiness organizations do, and thus they have not only the advantage of being composed of rather small numbers of rather substantial or well-to-do business members, but in addition all the opportunities that

---

group. In the case of the single large firm, the ordinary rules of the market tend to apply. Markets evolve. Washington is said to be host to numerous lawyers, former officials, and retired congressmen who are adept at helping individual businesses get what they want from the government. These services are provided for a fee: a market has developed. The language is a shibboleth off the fact that in this sphere of politics collective goods are not involved, and that an informal, sometimes shadowy, price system exists: consider the "influence peddler."

43 Schattschneider, Semi-Sovereign People, p. 32.

44 *Ibid.,* P. 35.

45 Key, p. 96.

other organizations have to provide a noncollective good to attract members. Many trade associations distribute trade statistics, provide credit references on customers, help collect bills, provide technical research and advisory services, and so on. Merle Fainsod and Lincoln Gordon list seventeen different functions which trade associations perform *in addition* to their political or lobbying duties.[46] By performing these additional functions the trade associations offer a further incentive to membership.

The disproportionate political power of the "special interests" or particular business interests should not, however, lead one to suppose that the whole business community necessarily has disproportionate power in relation to organized labor, the professions, or agriculture. Although particular industries normally have disproportionate power on questions of particular importance to themselves, it does not follow that the business community has disproportionate power when dealing with broad questions of national concern. For the business community as a whole is not well organized in the sense that particular industries are. The business community *as a whole* is not a small privileged or intermediate group—it is definitely a large, latent group. As a result it has the same problems of organization as the other segments of society. .

The two major organizations purporting to speak for business as a whole—the National Association of Manufacturers and the Chamber of Commerce of the United States—illustrate this point rather well. Neither of them has disproportionate power in relation to the AFL-CIO, the AMA, or the American Farm Bureau Federation.

The Chamber of Commerce of the United States is only a "federation of federations."[47] Its principal members are the many local chambers of commerce and similar organizations around the country. These local chambers of commerce are normally small groups, and on that ground can normally organize with relative ease. They are made the more attractive to members by the fact that they are good places for businessmen to make "contacts" and exchange information. The Chamber of Commerce of the United States is built up from these local chambers of commerce on the principle-of federation; but in the process of federation much of the strength is lost. The national organization provides various informational and organizational services to the local organizations, but nonetheless the individual member and even the individual local chamber of commerce are essentially only individual units in a latent group. They can make no decisive contribution to the success of the national organization, and will get the benefit of any achievements of the national organization whether they have participated or not. A number of very large businesses will gain or lose so much from changes in national policy that they will find it expedient to make significant contributions—and the Chamber has found it

---

46 Merle Fainsod and Lincoln Gordon, *Government and the American Economy,* rev. ed. (New York: W. W. Norton, 1948), Pp. 529–530. E. Pendleton Herring, in *Group Representation before Congress,* p. 98, describes the diverse functions of the trade associations thus: "The trade association has succeeded upon its merits. It fulfills a definite need in industry. There are so many matters in which cooperation is necessary and economic that a clearing house such as a trade association is considered desirable."

47 Burns and Peltason, p. 293.

necessary to sell special individual memberships to such large businesses.[48] The money derived from big business, and a vague federal connection with the local chambers of commerce, can give the Chamber of Commerce of the United States a certain amount of power, but certainly not disproportionate power.

The National Association of Manufacturers is also based on the small group. It is in fact based on a *single* small group of very large businesses. Though nominally the NAM has a few thousand members, it is in practice supported and controlled by a handful of really big businesses. As Dayton McKean describes it: "The president of the Association is usually a small manufacturer of very conservative views, who serves for one or two years. The presidents of the giant corporations, which by general agreement dominate the Association because their concerns provide the funds by which it operates, do not serve as its president. About 5 per cent of the membership contribute about half the money."[49] About eight tenths of one per cent of the members of the NAM have held 63 per cent of all directorships.[50] Although these few big businesses have made it possible for the NAM to spend as much as 5.5 million dollars per year for political purposes,[51] they are still a small group, and are by no means more powerful than the major organizations representing labor, the professions, or the farmers. The NAM has not been successful in preventing the passage of measures it opposes, and its support of a cause is sometimes regarded as the "kiss of death."[52]

The business community as a whole, which is certainly a large, latent group, is therefore not fully organized. It has two organizations that attempt to represent it, but these two organizations draw much of their support from a small group of giant businesses: they do not attract the direct support of the whole business community. A small group is powerful in matters relating to a particular industry, because then it is normally the only organized force, but it is less formidable when questions which divide the entire nation are involved, for then it must take on organized labor and other large organized groups. The business community in the aggregate is for this reason not uniquely effective as a pressure group.

The judgment that the "special interests"—the individual industry groups—have disproportionate power, though the business community as a whole does not, is apparently consistent with the general trend of current affairs. For it seems that particular interests do win tax loopholes, favorable tariffs, special tax rulings, generous regulatory policies, and the like, but that .the business community as a whole has been unsuccessful in its attempts to stop the trend toward social-welfare legislation and progressive taxation.

---

48 McKean, p. 486.

49 *Ibid.,* p. 489; Robert A. Brady, *Business as a System of Power* (New York: Columbia University Press, 1943), Pp. 211–212.

50 Alfred S. Cleveland, "NAM: Spokesman for Industry?" *Harvard Business Review,* XXVI (May 1948), 353–371.

51 Key, p. 100.

52 R. W. Gable, "NAM: Influential Lobby or Kiss of Death?" *Journal of Politics,* XV (1953), 253–273.

E. Government Promotion of Political Pressure

The most striking fact about the political organization of farmers in the United States is that there has been so little. Farmers have not on the whole been well organized, except perhaps in recent years. And what organization the farmers have had has tended to be unstable. Many farm organizations have come and gone, but only a few have come and stayed.

There was no lasting, significant farm organization or lobby in this country until after the Civil War,[53] though farmers were the largest group in the population throughout the early history of the country. The first farm organization worth mentioning was the Grange—the Patrons of Husbandry. The Grange was started in 1867, and in the first few years of its life it spread like a prairie fire across the plains of the country.[54] It had very soon acquired an impressive membership and a considerable amount of power. But the Grange soon collapsed as fast as it had grown. By the 1880's it was already insignificant.[55] The Grange has survived with a small membership to the present day, but has never regained the power and glory of its youthful years. Indeed, the precipitous decline it suffered apparently affected the spirit as well as the body of the Grange, for since then it has generally avoided controversial economic or political issuer It has become to a great degree a social organization, and is no longer an aggressive pressure or lobbying organization, though it does some low-keyed lobbying.[56]

The remarkable achievement of the Grange is that it has managed to survive at all, when so many other farm organizations formed since it began have passed away. The Farmers' Alliances, the Greenback movement, the Free Silver movement, the Agricultural Wheel, the Gleaners, Populism, the Equity, the Brothers of Freedom, and other such organizations died within a few years of their birth.[57] This indeed has been the general pattern.

The Farmers Union and the Farm Bureau are the two distinct exceptions to that pattern. But these two organizations also have had their difficulties. The Farmers Union, the older of the two, was started in Texas in 1902.[58] During its early years it acquired a significant member-ship in the South. This membership was lost after the First World War and the organization nearly succumbed to this tragedy.[59] The organization began a new life in the Great Plains states during the interwar years, but its membership in this period was very small. In the late 1930's

---

53 Fred A. Shannon, *American Farmers' Movements* (Princeton, N.J.: D. Van Nostrand, 1957), Pp. -8–48.

54 *Ibid.,* Pp. 54–57; Charles M. Gardner, *The Grange—Friend of the Farmer* (Washington, D.C.: National Grange, 1949), Pp. 3–12.

55 Solon J. Buck, *The Agrarian Crusade* (New Haven, Conn.: Yale University Press, 1920), Pp. 60–76.

56 Gardner, *passim;* David Lindstrom, *American Farmers' and Rural Organizations* (Champaign, 111.: Garrard Press, 1948), p. 177.

57 Carl C. Taylor, *The Farmers' Movement, 1620–1920* (New York: American Book Co., 1953), *passim.*

58 Theodore Saloutos, *Farmer Movements in the South, 1865–1933* (Berkeley and Los Angeles: University of California Press, 1960), Pp. 184–212.

59 Lindstrom, p. 208; Taylor, Pp. 335–364.

and in the 1940's the Farmers Union built a firmer base of support in the states of the Missouri Valley, however, and it is from this region that it presently draws most of its strength.[60]

The Farm Bureau, which is now the largest of the farm organizations, and the only one with a nationwide membership, was from the very beginning completely different from other farm organizations. For the Farm Bureau was created by the government. The Smith-Lever Act of 1914 provided that the general government would share, with the states, the cost of programs for providing what have come to be called "county agents," who furnish farmers information on improved methods of husbandry developed by the agricultural colleges and agricultural experiment stations.[61] Many of the state governments decided that no county could receive any government money for a county agent unless it organized an association of farmers that would be evidence of an interest in getting more information on modern agricultural methods. These county organizations came to be called "Farm Bureaus."[62] They were the beginning of the Farm Bureau movement that exists today. There were, it is true, a handful of these county Farm Bureaus a year or two before the government started providing money for county agents,[63] but these were so few in number that they, were totally insignificant, and they were in any case like the county Farm Bureaus started by the government in that their purpose was simply to obtain better information on agricultural methods.[64]

The expenditure of government funds for "extension work," that is for the county agents, increased greatly during World War I, so the number of county Farm Bureaus naturally increased *pari passu*. These county Farm Bureaus, normally under the guidance of the county agent (who often had to maintain the Farm Bureau in his county or else lose his job), soon combined to form statewide Farm Bureaus. These state organizations in turn formed a national organization, the American Farm Bureau Federation, in 1919.[65]

Up to this time the Farm Bureau was, first, a quasi-official organization, set up in response to financial incentives provided by government, and second, an organization that provided individualized or *noncollective* benefits to its members. The second point is especially important. The farmer who joined his county Farm Bureau got technical assistance and education in return. The farmer who joined was normally put on the mailing list for technical publications: the farmer who did not join was not. The farmer who joined had first call on the county agent's services: the farmer who did not, normally had last call, or no call at all. A farmer thus had a specific incentive to join the Farm Bureau. The dues he had to pay were an investment (and probably a good investment) in agricultural education and improvement.

---

60 Key, p. 43; Theodore Saloutos and John D. Hicks, *Agricultural Discontent in the Middle West, 1900–39* (Madison: University of Wisconsin Press, 1951), Pp. 219–254.

61 Gladys L, Baker, *The County Agent* (Chicago: University of Chicago Press, 1939), Pp. 36–40.

62 *Ibid.,* p. 16.

63 Orville Merton Kile, *The Farm Bureau Movement* (New York: Macmillan, 1921), Pp. 94–112.

64 *Ibid., Pp.* 94–112.

65 *Ibid,,* Pp. 113–123; Grant McConnell, *The. Decline of Agrarian Democracy* (Berkeley and Los Angeles: University of California Press, 1953), Pp. 44-54.

Under the stimulus furnished by the increasing government expenditures on agricultural extension work, the membership of the county and state Farm Bureaus, and therefore of the American Farm Bureau Federation, increased very rapidly. By 1921, the Federation had a membership of 466,000.[66] In the next year, however, the membership was considerably less, and it continued to fall more or less steadily until 1933, by which time it was only 163,000.[67]

At the very time that its membership was falling, there was every reason to suppose that the value of the services the Farm Bureau was providing to farmers was increasing.[68] The Farm Bureau was taking on new functions. It had helped create the powerful "farm bloc" and was bringing the passage of much legislation that was popular among (and helpful to) the farmers. At the same time, with the help of the county agents, it was promoting a number of cooperatives designed to bring savings to farmers. Why then did the membership of the Farm Bureau continue to fall? The answer, almost certainly, is that, as the Farm Bureau took on these new functions, it naturally increased the competition of the political and business organizations already in the field. The result was that the nation began to notice that the Farm Bureau was at once a pressure group, and a (cooperative) business organization, subsidized by public funds. The situation was so anomalous that it naturally stimulated a negative reaction. The criticism led to the "True-Howard" agreement, which restricted the extent to which the county agent could work for the Farm Bureau organization or for Farm Bureau members alone.[69] The county agent was no longer supposed to "organize farm bureaus or similar organizations, conduct membership campaigns, solicit memberships, receive dues, handle farm bureau funds, edit and manage the farm bureau publications," and so on.[70] Though the extent to which the government could subsidize the Farm Bureau was then limited, these subsidies were not stopped altogether. The county agents continued to assist the farm bureaus, but they did so less regularly and less conspicuously as time went on.[71]

It was presumably this limitation on the amount of help that the county agent could give the farm bureaus that accounted for the decline in membership at the very time the organization was expanding its programs. As it became more convenient for farmers who were not members of the Farm Bureau to get the technical help of the county agent, and as it became harder for the farm-bureau organization to obtain the governmentally subsidized labor of the county agent, the incentive to join the Farm Bureau decreased.

This decline in the membership of the Farm Bureau Federation

---

66 McConnell, p. 185.

67 *Ibid.*, p. 185.

68 Kile, *Farm Bureau Movement, passim.*

69 Orville Merton Kile, *The Farm Bureau Through Three Decades* (Baltimore: Waverly Press, 1948), Pp. 110–111.

70 *Ibid., p.* 110.

71 William J. Block, *The Separation of the Farm Bureau and the Extension Service* (Urbana; Ill.: University off Illinois Press, 1960).

★ The Semi-Sovereign People
By E.E. Schattschneider

The line of thought developed in the preceding chapters of this book ought to shed some light on the meaning of democracy. The role of the people in the political system is determined largely by the conflict system, for it is conflict that involves the people in politics and the nature of conflict determines the nature of the public involvement.

The idea that the people are involved in politics by the contagion of conflict does not resemble the classical definition of democracy as "government by the people." The difference between the idea of popular "involvement" in conflict and the idea that people actually "govern" is great enough to invite a re-examination of the classical theory of democracy. Does the consideration of the place of conflict in a free political system open up the way for a redefinition of democracy in modern terms?

Whether we know it or not all speculation about American politics rests on some image of democracy. The literature on the subject has been so permeated by democratic and pseudodemocratic ideas that it is impossible to understand what we are talking about unless we isolate and identify these ideas and try to distinguish between the democratic and antidemocratic elements in them.

The devotion of the American public to the democraticideal is so overwhelming that we test everything by it. It is surprising to find, therefore, that political philosophers have had remarkable difficulty in defining the word *democracy*. As a matter of fact, the failure to produce a good working definition of democracy is responsible for a great part of the confusion in the literature of politics. An examination of the problem might be worth while, therefore.

The classical definition of democracy as government by the people is predemocratic in its origins, based on notions about democracy developed by philosophers who never had an opportunity to see an operating democratic system. Predemocratic theorists assumed that the people would take over the conduct of public affairs in a democracy and administer the government to their own advantage as simply as landowners administer their property for their own profit. Under the historical circumstances this oversimplification is easy to understand.

There is less excuse for the failure of modern scholars to re-examine the traditional definition critically in the light of modern experience.[1]

One consequence of our reliance on old definitions is that the modern American does not look at democracy before he defines it; he defines it first and then is confused by what he sees. In spite of the fact that the ancients made some astonishing miscalculations about democracy as an operating system, their authority is so great that the traditional definition is perpetuated in the textbooks and governs our thinking in the entire area.

The confusion of ideas about democracy looks like a job for the political scientists. What we need is a modern definition of democracy explaining the facts of life of the operating political system, a definition that distinguishes between the democratic and antidemocratic elements in the developing contemporary political situation. The great deficiency of American democracy is intellectual, the lack of a good, usable definition. A good definition might shed a flood of light on modern politics; it might clarify a thousand muddy concepts and might help us to understand where we are going and what we want. It might even help us get rid of the impossible imperatives that haunt the literature of the subject and give everyone a sense of guilt. We need to reexamine the chasm between theory and practice because it is at least as likely that the ideal is wrong as it is that the reality is bad. Certainly our chances of getting democracy and keeping it would be better if we made up our minds about what it is.[2]

Perhaps as good a point as any at which to test our ideas about democracy is in the general area of public opinion research. This research is based on the assumption that public opinion plays a great role in a democracy. Lurking in the background is the notion that the people actually do govern.

What image of democracy leads us to assign a central place in political theory to public opinion? The question is: Can we define the role of public opinion in a democracy before we make up our minds about what democracy is? Before we invest the energies of a generation of political scientists in public opinion research, would it not be wise to make an attempt to *test* the validity of the underlying propositions about the relations of public opinion to what is happening in the world about us?[3]

---

1 What the Greek philosophers had to say about Athens, a city-state having a population of thirty thousand, three-fourths of whom were slaves, has very little to do with democracy in a nation of 175 million.

2 There have been many attempts to define democracy. This is not the place to make a compilation of these definitions. The attack here is on the most pervasive and widely accepted common definition of democracy as "government by the people." At the same time that we have defined democracy as something unattainable, we have made democracy one of the most emotion-charged words in our civilization. This is the impossible imperative which threatens *to* entrap all of us.

3 See Bernard Berelson, "Democratic Theory and Public Opinion," Pp. 107 ff., in Eulau, Eldersveld and Janowitz, *Political Behavior,* Free Press, Glencoe, Illinois, 1956, for a good statement of what seems to be the concept of democracy prevailing among students of public opinion; it illustrates very well how much students of public opinion have been influenced by the common definition of democracy.

It requires no research to demonstrate that it is difficult to relate the copybook maxims about democracy to the operating political system. If we start with the common definition of democracy (as government by the people), it is hard to avoid some extremely pessimistic conclusions about the feasibility of democracy in the modern world, for it is impossible to reconcile traditional concepts of what ought to happen in a democracy with the fact that an amazingly large number of people do not seem to know very much about what is going on. The significance of this kind of popular ignorance depends on what we think democracy is.

Research might have enlightened us much more than it has if the researchers had taken the time to formulate an operating democratic theory. It is hard to see how anyone can formulate a satisfactory theory of public opinion without meeting this problem head on. What is the function of the public in a modern democracy? What does the public have to know? The failure to understand how the public intervenes in the political process, what the public can be expected to do, what it cannot do, how questions get referred to the public has led to quantities of remarkably pointless speculation. How do we find out what we are looking for?

The reader can make a test of the basic proposition for himself by spending some time examining the massive compilation of polls in Public *Opinion, 1935–1946* made by Hadley Cantril and Mildred Strunk.[4] While this compilation, twelve hundred pages of it, is no longer fully representative of the work done by scholars today, it has one incomparable advantage to students of politics—*the polls were taken at least thirteen years ago.* After a lapse of several years we are in a position to ask: How nearly do the data turned up in these polls correspond with what actually happened? For some reason when one now looks at this body of data, it seems to lack reality. If the assumption is that public opinion is important because it determines public policy, a comparison of the polls and the history of the decade raises a flood of doubts. How much difference did the opinions measured in these polls actually make?

It is necessary only to look at the polls on birth control, the budget, capital punishment, divorce, employee representation schemes, the excess profits tax, free speech, income limitation, industrial and labor relations, small business, socialized medicine, race relations, government ownership of public utilities, neutrality and the territorial expansion of the United States to realize that public opinion about specific issues does not necessarily govern the course of public policy.

The point of this discussion is that political research is never better than the theory of politics on which it is based. The theory of the polls is essentially simplistic, based on a tremendously exaggerated notion of the immediacy and urgency of the connection of public opinion and events. The result is that sometimes we seem to be interviewing the fish in the sea to find out what the birds in the heavens are doing.

See also Burdick's criticism of Berelson's ideas in Burdick and Brodbeck, *American Voting Behavior,* Free Press, 1959, Pp. 136 ff.

4 Princeton University Press, 1951.

What would it be worth to students of politics if by some miracle they could know precisely what everybody in the country was thinking at twelve noon last Friday? Probably very little. We are in trouble because we are confused about what is supposed to happen in a democracy.

The image implicit in the schoolbook definition of democracy is that of a mass of people who think about politics the way a United States senator might think about it. In this image public opinion has great consequences; what the people think has a compulsive impact on what the government does. It follows that the scholar ought to begin his studies at the grass roots.

The great difficulty here is theoretical, not technical; it concerns the assumptions made about the role of the people in a democracy. The unstated premise in a multitude of polls is that the people really do decide what the government does on something like a day-to-day basis. This assumption implies a definition of democracy. How can we get hold of the subject if we do not deal with this definition?

A hundred million voters have a staggering number of opinions about an incredible number of subjects. Under what circumstances do these opinions become important?

The problem is one of definition. What is the role of the public in a democracy? What have we a right to expect of the public? Is it possible to reformulate the question in terms of democratic concepts other than the primitive notions derived from the ancients?

Apparently the attitude of the public is far more permissive than the hortatory, high-pressure, special-interest school of theorists thinks it ought to be. The tendency of the literature of politics is to place a tremendous premium on the role of the interested and to treat indifference as a mortal sin, but the reluctance of the public to press its opinions on the government concerning a great multitude of issues is really not as bad a thing as we may have been led to think; it is a mark of reasonableness and common sense. The public is far too sensible to attempt to play the preposterous role assigned to it by the theorists. We have tended to undervalue this attitude because we have labored under an illusion about democracy.

We become cynical about democracy because the public does not act the way the simplistic definition of democracy says that it should act, or we try to whip the public into doing things it does not want to do, is unable to do and has too much sense to do. The crisis here is not a crisis in democracy but a crisis in theory.

The importance of democratic theory is demonstrated by the way in which students of public opinion have neglected what is perhaps their most important discovery, the discovery of the "don't knows," the very large category of people who are willing to confess that they do not seem to know very much about what is going on in the government.

The tendency has been to ignore this discovery because it does not fit very conveniently into our preconceptions about democracy and the democratic process. The "don't knows" are treated as unfortunate exceptions to the democratic proposition about whom we prefer not to think. This is remarkable because ignorance is an ancient condition of the human race. The significance of this widespread ignorance about public affairs depends largely on what we think democracy is.

One implication of public opinion studies ought to be resisted by all friends of freedom and democracy; the implication that democracy is a failure because the people are too ignorant to answer intelligently all the questions asked by the pollsters. This is a professorial invention for imposing professorial standards on the political system and deserves to be treated with extreme suspicion. Only a pedagogue would suppose that the people must pass some kind of examination to qualify for participation in a democracy. Who, after all, are these self-appointed censors who assume that they are in a position to flunk the whole human race? Their attitude would be less presumptuous if they could come up with a list of things that people must know. Who can say what the man on the street must know about public affairs? The whole theory of knowledge underlying these assumptions is pedantic. Democracy was made for the people, not the people for democracy. Democracy is something for ordinary people, a political system designed to be sensitive to the needs of ordinary people regardless of whether or not the pedants approve of them.

It is an outrage to attribute the failures of American democracy to the ignorance and stupidity of the masses. The most disastrous shortcomings of the system have been those of the intellectuals whose concepts of democracy have been amazingly rigid and uninventive. The failure of the intellectuals is dangerous because it creates confusion in high places. Unless the intellectuals can produce a better theory of politics than they have, it is possible that we shall abolish democracy before we have found out what it is!

The intellectuals have done very little to get us out of the theoretical trap created by the disparity between the demands made on the public by the common definition of democracy and the capacity of the public to meet these demands.[5] The embarrassment results from the reluctance of intellectuals to develop a definition that describes what really happens in a democracy.

The whole mass of illusions discussed in the foregoing paragraph arises from a confusion of ideas about what people need to know, what the role of the public in a democracy is, how the public functions in a democracy.

If we assume that the people "govern," it follows that the governing majority ought to know more than any majority has ever known or ever could know. This is the *reductio ad absurdum* of democratic theory. We cannot get out of the dilemma by (1) making a great effort to educate everyone to the point where they know enough to make these decisions nor (2) by restricting participation to the people who do know all about these matters. The first is impossible. The second is absurd because *no one* knows enough to govern by this standard. The trouble is that we have defined democracy in such a way that we are in danger of putting ourselves out of business.

---

5 So highly respected a modern theorist as Francis W. Coker deals with this subject in one short paragraph and disposes of the matter by quoting Bryce's definition of democracy as "majority rule." *Recent Political Thought,* New York, 1934, p. 291.

Among the textbook writers Carr, Morrison, Bernstein and Snyder, *American Democracy in Theory and Practice,* New York, 1951, p. 24, say, "As a political system it is the mechanism through which the people govern themselves." Examples could be multiplied indefinitely. The trouble with these definitions is that they leave us deep in a bottomless pit.

There is no escape from the problem of ignorance, because *nobody knows enough to run the government*. Presidents, senators, governors, judges, professors, doctors of philosophy, editors and the like are only a little less ignorant than the rest of us. Even an expert is a person who chooses to be ignorant about many things so that he may know all about one.

The whole theory of knowledge underlying these concepts of democracy is false—it proves too much. It proves not only that democracy is impossible; it proves equally that life itself is impossible. Everybody has to accommodate himself to the fact that he deals daily with an incredible number of matters about which he knows very little. This is true of all aspects of life, not merely of politics.

The compulsion to know everything is the road to insanity.

People are able to survive in the modern world by learning to distinguish between what they must know and what they do not need to know. We get a clue to the solution of the problem when we begin to realize that it is not necessary to be an automotive engineer to buy an automobile or to be an obstetrician in order to have a baby. Our survival depends on our ability to judge things by their results and our ability to establish relations of confidence and responsibility so that we can take advantage of what other people know. We could not live in modern society if we did not place confidence daily in a thousand ways in pharmacists, surgeons, pilots, bank clerks, engineers, plumbers, technicians, lawyers, civil servants, accountants, courts, telephone operators, craftsmen and a host of others. We pass judgment on the most complex mechanisms on the basis of the *results* they produce. Economists, trying to explain the operation of the economy, use a political expression when they speak of the "sovereignty of the consumer," precisely because they realize that it is not necessary to know how to *make* a television set in order to buy one intelligently. Democracy is like nearly everything else we do; it is a form of collaboration of ignorant people and experts.

Primitive democratic theorists never tire of telling us that democracy was designed to work in New England town meetings, not in a modern national state. The analysis is fatuous. We might as well attempt to return to a handicraft economy. The crisis is a purely theoretical one because operating democratic political systems have in fact already accomplished what is theoretically impossible and are doing it every day. It is only the theory that has broken down. The problem of modern democracy is the problem of learning to live in the modern world.

We can find our way through the maze if we learn to distinguish between different kinds of knowledge, between what amateurs know and what professionals know, between what generalists know and what specialists know. The problem is not how 180 million Aristotles can run a democracy, but how we can organize a political community of 180 million ordinary people so that it remains sensitive to their needs. This is a problem of *leadership, organization, alternatives and systems of responsibility and confidence*. The emphasis is on the role of leadership and organization in a democracy, not on the spontaneous generation of something at the grass roots. If we approach the problem from this side, it does not look impossible. The achievements of the American regime are tremendous, but they have been brought about in spite of the theoretical illusions under which we have labored.

The people are involved in public affairs by the conflict system. Conflicts open up questions for public intervention. Out of conflict the alternatives of public policy arise. Conflict is the occasion for political organization and leadership. In a free political system it is difficult to avoid public involvement in conflict; the ordinary, regular operations of the government give rise to controversy, and controversy is catching.

The beginning of wisdom in democratic theory is to distinguish between the things the people can do and the things the people cannot do. The worst possible disservice that can be done to the democratic cause is to attribute to the people a mystical, magical omnipotence which takes no cognizance of what very large numbers of people cannot do by the sheer weight of numbers. At this point the common definition of democracy has invited us to make fools of ourselves.

What 180 million people can do spontaneously, on their own initiative, is not much more than a locomotive can do without rails. The public is like a very rich man who is unable to supervise closely all of his enterprise. His problem is to learn how to compel his agents to define his options.

What we are saying is that conflict, competition, leadership, and organization are the essence of democratic politics. Inherent in the operations of a democracy are special conditions which permit large numbers of people to function.

The problem is how to organize the political system so as to make the best possible use of the power of the public in view of its limitations. A popular decision bringing into focus the force of public support requires a tremendous effort to define the alternatives, to organize the discussion and mobilize opinion. The government and the political organizations are in the business of manufacturing this kind of alternatives.

What has been said here has not been said to belittle the power of the people but to shed some light on what it is. The power of the people is not made less by the fact that it cannot be used for trivial matters. The whole world can be run on the basis of a remarkably small number of decisions. The power of the people in a democracy depends on the *importance* of the decisions made by the electorate, not on the *number* of decisions they make. Since the adoption of the Constitution the party in power has been turned out by the opposition party fourteen times, and in about six of these instances the consequences have been so great that we could not understand American history without taking account of them.

The most important thing about any democratic regime is the *way* in which it *uses* and exploits popular sovereignty, what questions it refers to the public for decision or guidance, how it refers them to the public, how the alternatives are defined and how it respects the limitations of the public. A good democratic system protects the public against the demand that it do impossible things. The unforgivable sin of democratic politics is to dissipate the power of the public by putting it to trivial uses. What we need is a movement for the conservation of the political resources of the American people.

Above everything, *the people are powerless if the political enterprise is not competitive.* It is the competition of political organizations that provides the people with the opportunity to make a choice. Without this opportunity popular sovereignty amounts to nothing.

The common definition of democracy may be harmless if it is properly understood, but the fact is that it is very commonly misunderstood. It would be more imaginative to say that some things we now are actually doing are democratic even though they do not fit the traditional definition. Definitions of democracy since the time of Aristotle have been made on the assumption that the "many" in a democracy do the same things that the "one" does in a monarchy and the "few" do in an aristocracy. But obviously the shift from the "one" to the "many" is more than a change in the number of people participating in power but *a change in the way the power is exercised.* The 180 million cannot do what a single ruler can do. This is not because the 180 million are stupid or ignorant but because it is physically impossible for 180 million to act the way one acts. In the interests of clarity and the survival of the political system we need a definition of democracy that recognizes the limitations that nature imposes on large numbers.

A working definition must capitalize on the limitations of the people as well as their powers. We do this when we say that liberty and leadership are the greatest of democratic concepts. *Democracy is a competitive political system in which competing leaders and organizations define the alternatives of public policy in such a way that the public can participate in the decision-making process.* The initiative in this political system is to be found largely in the government or in the opposition. The people profit by this system, but they cannot, by themselves, do the work of the system. We have already had a great deal of experience with this kind of system. Is it not about time that we begin to recognize its democratic implications?

Conflict, competition, organization, leadership and responsibility are the ingredients of a working definition of democracy. Democracy is a political system in which the people have a choice among the alternatives created by competing political organizations and leaders. The advantage of this definition over the traditional definition is that it is *operational,* it describes something that actually happens. It describes something feasible. It does not make impossible demands on the public. Moreover, it describes a going democratic concern whose achievements are tremendous.

The involvement of the public in politics is a natural out-growth of the kind of conflict that almost inevitably arises in a free society. The exploitation of this situation by responsible political leaders and organizations is the essence of democracy; the socialization of conflict is the essential democratic process.

Act V

The Periphery of Phantoms—The Indirect Influencers of Power—Inner Periphery: The Political Media

★ News Coverage of Political
★ Campaigns

By Girish J. Gulati, Marion R. Just, and Ann N. Crigler

To review research on news coverage of political campaigns, we start with a basic premise: All news is a construction of reality. News about political campaigns represents an on-going negotiation among key actors in the campaign process: on the media side—journalists, editors, and owners; on the campaign side—candidates, campaign staffers, and party activists. To a lesser extent the public, government institutions and their incumbents, interest groups, pundits, and experts also play a role in the news-making process.

Each actor endeavors to control how the news story is told (Bennett, 2001; Cook, 1996; Crigler, 1996; Edelman, 1988; Gans, 1979; Graber, 2002; Hollihan, 2001; Just et al., 1996; Neuman, Just, & Crigler, 1992; Tuchman, 1978). The outcome of negotiations over the news depends on the power of the source as well as on the relative social, political, or economic consequences of the news itself. In the past 20 years, presidential candidates have become savvy about how to stay "on message" and how to get journalists to cover what they want the public to hear (Miller & Gronbeck, 1994). Journalists, for their part, are dogged in the search for inconsistency, hypocrisy, or scandal and can require candidates to speak to issues that the press deems newsworthy. In presidential election campaigns, both journalists and the candidates bring a great deal of leverage to the negotiation of news. As a result, there is often a hotly contested struggle between reporters and officials or candidates for control of the news message.

Given the political stakes in campaigns, the idea that the news media might use their influence to promote the advantage of one side or the other has preoccupied scholars and worried citizens. To the great relief of most observers, partisan bias is not widespread in modern campaign news. Many researchers have shown, however, that although partisan bias is modest, structural bias, rooted in journalistic norms, infuses political coverage. (See Ansolabehere, Behr & Iyengar, 1993, for "episodic" bias; Bennett, 2001, for "normalization"; Gans, 1979, for "celebrity" bias; Hallin,1992, for "sound bite" news; Hofstetter, 1976, for "horse-race" bias;

Lippmann, 1922, for an "events" bias; Mann & Orren, 1992, for "horse-race/strategy" bias; and Patterson, 1980, for "the game" bias).

In addition to structural biases in the way news is reported, social scientists have found that the construction of news has many other subtle influences. These include, for example, agenda setting—that is, signaling the important issues of the campaign (Cohen,1963; Iyengar, 1991; McCombs & Shaw, 1972; Mutz, 1989; Weaver, 1981); priming—leading news audiences to particular interpretations of events that then shape their evaluations of political officials and candidates (Iyengar & Kinder,1987; Krosnick & Kinder, 1990); and candidate image building—both positive and negative (Bennett, 2001; Hacker, 1995; Hollihan, 2001; Nimmo, 1976; Sniderman, Glaser, & Griffin, 1990).

News media impact has also been observed in what people learn from the news and in their attitudes toward the democratic process (Graber, 1984, 1998, 2001; Neuman et al., 1992; Patterson, 1980; Popkin, 1991). On the whole, researchers have been disappointed in the amount of political learning that takes place during a campaign. Election studies in the 1940s (Berelson, Lazarsfeld, & McPhee, 1954) hoped to find that the new electronic medium of radio would make it easier for voters to become informed on the issues. Later on, television also raised hopes for a better-informed electorate (Campbell, Converse, Miller, & Stokes, 1960). Yet citizens' level of knowledge about candidates and issues appears to have remained constant in the face of new media of communication. Researchers have questioned whether the nature of news is the problem. In particular, they wonder whether or not journalists are providing the kind of campaign news that will help the electorate make voting decisions in line with their policy preferences and their assessments of candidates (Cappella & Jamieson, 1997; Graber, 1998).

The past 60 years of research into how journalists cover presidential election campaigns has given us a clear picture of what gets reported in newspapers and on television and how that coverage has evolved over time. Numerous studies have shown that campaign news is overly focused on strategies, tactics, poll results, and candidates' prospects for winning rather than on the substantive issues of the campaign. The news places campaigns within a competitive framework, or "gameframe" (Patterson, 1980), that characterizes elections in terms that would be more appropriate for a horse race or some other sports event.

This [article] begins with the study of journalism and American presidential election campaigns. The topics we consider include political bias, structural bias, group construction of news, and the rise of interpretive journalism. We examine how campaign coverage has changed in the face of television and the growth of local, cable, and Internet news sources. We evaluate news coverage of non-presidential campaigns in the United States, recognizing that the analysis of election news and its effects must necessarily take into account different levels of office (for congressional elections, see Clarke & Evans, 1983; Cook, 1989; Goldenberg & Traugott, 1984; Hess, 1986; Vermeer, 1987; for state and local elections, see Jeffries, 2000; Kanniss, 1995; Zisk, 1987). The [article] then explores how campaign news treats minority political candidates. We conclude by suggesting promising avenues for future research including comparative election studies.

Presidential Campaign Coverage

The Search for a Political Bias

Constructing campaign news takes place in an evolving media environment. In the early 19th century, news media in the United States were openly partisan. As wire services became prominent in the delivery of news, a more "objective" standard of reporting became the professional norm (Schudson, 1978). When scholars began evaluating the content and quality of the news media's coverage of elections, one of their primary questions was whether news reflected a partisan or ideological bias (West, 2001). Their concern was based on the assumption that the slant of the news would influence voters to make decisions not necessarily in their own or the public interest (Campbell et al., 1954; Campbell, Gurin, & Miller, 1960).

Experience with government propaganda during the world wars heightened concern about press bias. Two of the earliest empirical studies of campaign media were extensive content analyses of the 1940 and 1948 presidential election news coverage. Researchers examined local newspapers, popular national magazines, and radio broadcasts. The studies initially found substantial partisan bias in both the print and the broadcast media, which intensified as election day neared. A closer look revealed, however, that partisanship was found among the columnists and editorial writers, with almost no bias in the stories filed by individual reporters (Berelson et al., 1954; Lazarsfeld, Berelson, & Gaudet, 1948). These studies reassured observers that the wall between factual reporting and opinion, vaunted by the American press, was indeed in place and that citizens could depend on the objectivity of the news.

Repeated analyses of news coverage of recent presidential elections continue to find no evidence of partisan bias in news reporting (D'Alessio & Allen, 2000; Hofstetter, 1976, Just et al., 1996; Patterson, 1980; Patterson & McClure, 1976). This does not mean, however, that the coverage has been neutral. Some candidates receive more favorable coverage than others. For example, Lichter (2001), Lowry and Shidler (1995), and Zaller (1996) have found that Democrats have received slightly more favorable coverage than Republicans in the past 50 years, yet it has not been unusual in particular elections for Republican candidates to receive more favorable coverage than Democrats. A recent study found that in newspapers, the wall between editorial opinion and the news is not as impervious as previous research suggests, and some news slant in favor of editorially endorsed candidates may influence voters in Senate elections (Kahn & Kenney, 2002).

The diverse findings about which candidates are advantaged in news are widely acknowledged to reflect some kind of "structural bias" in reporting, i.e., that norms of journalism or reporter behavior favor news about some topics over others and that this news emphasis advantages some candidates and disadvantages others. For example, if reporters regard a candidate's loss of support in opinion polls as highly newsworthy, losing candidates will receive negative coverage regardless of party. The news is "biased" against losing candidates, not because of their policy positions, but because of reporters' decisions about what is "news" (Hofstetter, 1976). Some researchers find that candidates of both parties receive negative coverage when they are not doing well in the polls (Bennett, 1996; Stevenson, Eisinger, Feinberg, & Kotok, 1973) or that bad news about candidates is more likely to be covered than is positive news (Niven, 1991). Others maintain that it is the front-runner, or the candidate who is perceived as having some unfair advantage, who receives more negative coverage, whereas dark horse candidates benefit from a more positive tone (Robinson & Sheehan, 1983). One area of consensus among scholars is that third-party candidates and lesser-known candidates in the primaries get the least amount of coverage and, also, get very few opportunities to have their own words appear in print or heard over the air (Lichter & Smith, 1996).

Structural Bias and the Horse Race

As Walter Lippmann (1922) noted more than 80 years ago, reporters are drawn to covering factual stories that lend themselves to simple description and to concrete analysis. From the studies of news reporting of campaigns during the 1940s to the most recent election of 2000, researchers have shown that the most common themes of campaign stories are those that are simply about what is happening in the campaign itself (Hess, 2000). Many stories discuss the progress and dynamics of the campaign, the candidates' strategies, and even their itineraries. Campaign coverage focuses on which candidate seems to be winning and how campaign events might influence the remainder of the race. The incumbent administration's record and the candidates' policy positions, personal qualities, and leadership skills form a lesser but not insignificant part of typical campaign coverage (Arterton, 1984; Berelson et al., 1954; Brewer & Sigelman, 2002; Buchanan,1996; Graber, 2001, 2002; Just et al., 1996; Lazarsfeld et al., 1948; Patterson 1980; Patterson & McClure, 1976).

The framing of the election in terms of a sports event derives in part from political reporting norms. Journalists give high news values to events that have significant impact but whose outcomes are in doubt. Elections fall into this category, along with war, weather and sporting events. Because elections are contests, it is not surprising that reporters employ a game script in telling the story. Candidates contribute to the same script. Although candidates are eager to discuss the issues (Just, Crigler, & Buhr, 1999), they contribute to the media's emphasis on the horse race by using their speeches and events to construct an aura of victory around their candidacies (Berelson et al., 1954; Lazarsfeld et al., 1948).

The "game" focus also derives from a desire by newspaper columnists and broadcast commentators to demonstrate their skills as political analysts and to be recognized for their success in predicting the election outcomes (Berelson et al., 1954; Lazarsfeld et al., 1948; Patterson, 1993). Being the first to predict the election winner is tantamount to scooping the competition, an archetypal news norm (Mason, Frankovic, & Jamieson, 2001). Reporters believe that success in predicting the outcome will provide opportunities for advancement (Arterton, 1984). Furthermore, reporters find it safer and easier to write a story about process and strategy than to report on issues. Issue coverage involves more time for research and technical explanations (Kanniss, 1995). Even more onerous to reporters, however, is that a comparison of candidates' policy positions is likely to draw criticism of partisan bias, whereas examination of poll standings will not. As Lippmann (1922) observed, the "facts" are easier to report than the causes and consequences.

The ubiquity of polls has further increased the focus on strategy and tactics. Recently journalists have relied on daily tracking polls, often generated by their own news organizations. Tracking polls provide journalists with an objective measure of each campaign's recent progress and the ability to link recent campaign decisions to changes in the candidates' poll standings. Moreover, because tracking polls consist of 3-day, rolling samples, there is substantial volatility in the numbers, providing journalists with an ongoing story that includes mixes of objectivity, balance, and drama (Mann & Orren, 1992; Rhee, 1996).

The emphasis on the progress of the campaign rather than differences in candidate policy positions is even more pronounced in U.S. presidential primaries than in general elections. Because the nomination contests take place within parties, the area of policy agreement is naturally very wide and the voters are asked to decide among slight variations on a policy theme or on the personal qualifications of the candidates. The greater number and openness of primaries since 1972 have attracted correspondingly greater media attention to nominating contests than in the preprimary era, but the coverage is thin on substance. With the compression of the primary period and the emergence of "Super Tuesday," in which multiple primaries are held on the same day, national news reporters have little time for writing in-depth issue stories. Time pressures are compounded as the issues emphasized in the campaigns differ across states and among the major parties (Lichter & Smith, 1996). National news reporters find that they can construct a simpler narrative about the candidates' prospects and tactics than about issues in the primary campaigns.

Television and Print

In the 20th century, radio and television broadcasting brought citizens into intimate, if synthetic, contact with the candidates and the campaign. Radio and television provided live coverage of political party conventions and allowed citizens to see and hear the candidates' speeches in real time. Not long after television became established in American homes the televised presidential debate presented a new campaign phenomenon. Citizens could watch the candidates talk about the issues and compare them side-by-side for an extended period of time.

Although television brought profound changes in the ways that candidates waged their campaigns, it also seemed to enhance the discrepancy between "hoopla" and substance observed in print and on radio coverage 20 years earlier. In their study of the 1972 presidential campaign, Patterson and McClure (1976) found that television journalists devoted less time to the candidates' qualifications and positions on the issues than had been printed in the newspapers a generation before.

One explanation for the increasing gap between process-and substance-oriented coverage was that television was gaining dominance at the same time that parties were losing control over campaigns. Strategy seemed to become more central to the new candidate-centered presidential campaigns as political parties were losing their influence in selecting the nominees and mobilizing voters (Wattenberg, 1991). Television had a greater tendency than print to dramatize politics and to cover events that provided interesting and exciting pictures (Bennett, 2001; Graber, 2001). Television reporters were more willing than newspaper journalists to offer analysis and interpretation in their stories. Often when television news engaged in discussion of the issues, reporters drifted into behind-the-scenes political maneuvering and assessing how a candidate's policy position would affect the contest (Arterton, 1984; Patterson, 1993, Patterson & McClure, 1976; Robinson & Sheehan, 1983). Several observers found that television coverage was more negative in tone and featured journalists more prominently than print news (Hofstetter, 1976; Patterson & McClure, 1976).

As TV journalists have increasingly taken center stage, the opportunity for candidates to present their messages in their own words has decreased on television (Hallin, 1992). For example, from 1968 to 1988, candidate "sound bites" on television decreased from an average of 45 to 9 sec (Adatto, 1990). Subsequent studies (Lichter, 2001) saw the sound bite shrink to 7 sec (Hess, 2000). Some recent evidence suggests, however, that newspapers today present a more cynical tone to their stories and provide even less opportunity to hear the candidate's own words than television now does (Just et al., 1999; Plissner, 1989).

At the same time that television was transforming campaigns and campaign coverage, the print world was changing as well. Beginning in the mid-1960s, many family-owned newspapers were sold to larger newspapers or corporations, many of which had their own reporters working in Washington or assigned to the campaign trail. Smaller subsidiaries found it more cost-effective to publish information that was provided to them by the parent organization than to collect it themselves. Like their television counterparts, national newspaper journalists traveled with the candidates and focused heavily on campaign mechanics, organizational efforts and strategies, polling data, and prognostication (Arterton, 1984). Print reporters have told the "fly on the wall" story of the campaign trail, beginning with Theodore White's *Making of the President* series in 1960 and followed by observers such as Timothy Crouse (1990), Hunter Thompson (1985), and David Broder (1990).

Group Construction of the News

The groups of print and television reporters that follow candidates on the campaign trail—"the boys on the bus"—tend to rely on each other for the validation of their stories, discouraging innovation and increasing the ubiquitousness of their characterizations of the candidates and the campaign (Crouse, 1990; Swerdlow, 1988). Not only does professional socialization dominate the campaign trail, but it characterizes the main form of training in journalism. Over time new journalists learn common scripts for campaign events, such as a candidate's "misstatement," a whistle-stop tour, or an October Surprise. The 2000 election demonstrated what happens when a new phenomenon enters this scripted professional culture.

Until 2000, election night reporting was all about predicting the winner. Networks vied with each other to be first to declare a winner even though all of the networks relied on the same exit polling data for making projections of the outcomes. Networks rehearsed their staging for either a Democratic or a Republican victory. What none of the networks seemed to be prepared for was a tie. It was not until the early hours of the next morning that television reporters conceded that the 2000 election was still too close to call. The 2000 election provided a new phase of the election to be covered—the recounts in Florida and several other states, as well as the judicial proceedings in the U.S. Supreme Court and the Florida state courts. Although reporting about the unfolding postcampaign phase rebounded vigorously from election night, journalists tended to adhere to a common story line of "The System Works," consistent with the idea that journalists function to "normalize" the news (Bennett, 2001).

New Journalism Norms and Forms in the Construction of Campaign News

In the negotiation of campaign news, candidates have been constrained by the rise of interpretive reporting. With various electronic media superseding both print and scheduled news broadcasts for disseminating breaking news, older media have had to develop a new *raison d'être*. The result has been the emergence of "news analysis" in newspapers and on TV. By the 1980s, it became acceptable for both the television and the print media to include an interpretive, and therefore inherently subjective, component to their campaign coverage.

Today's political reporters not only predict the outcome of the race but also attempt to put campaign events into a broader context. Many journalists now consider it irresponsible simply to describe the campaign without delving into the candidate's motivation or without exploring why particular campaign decisions were made. Professional journalists perceive it as part of their duty to educate the public about the broader currents of politics, the underlying issues relevant for understanding a story, and the larger significance of particular campaign activities. By traveling with the candidates and observing what goes on behind the scenes, reporters assigned to the campaign trail feel that they are uniquely qualified to offer insights into the realities of presidential elections (West, 2001).

Interpretive reporting is supported by news media-sponsored polls, ad watches, and political punditry. The new style of interpretive reporting raises new questions about fairness in campaign news. The most common form of interpretive reporting has been found in news analysis pieces. These interpretive stories usually are paired with campaign reports and are placed immediately following evening news broadcasts or adjacent to more traditional coverage on the front pages of the newspapers—although the label "news analysis" has pretty much disappeared in print. For the television audience, an alternative way to put the news into a broader context is to bring in "political pundits" to offer analysis and commentary on recent campaign events. A long-term study by Page and Shapiro (1982) shows that pundits, along with popular presidents, are the most important forces influencing changes in public opinion. (See Beck, Dalton, Greene, and Huckfeldt, 2002, for additional perspectives on the relationship of media to public opinion and voter choice.)

Today, all the 24-hr cable news networks have entire programs devoted to pundits talking to other pundits. To construct an impression of objectivity on these programs, journalists and academics are frequently invited to appear or prominent liberals and conservatives are paired, to demonstrate a concern for ideological balance. Political punditry increasingly found its way onto news interview programs during the 1990s. Long a component of the networks' election coverage, these programs not only provided journalists with opportunities to act as commentators, but also provided the political operatives with opportunities to act as journalists.

As some former journalists have become full-time commentators and some former political operatives have become journalists, the line between reporter and "expert" has become considerably blurred. Often interviews today are simply opportunities for candidates and their surrogates to repeat the central messages of their campaigns or to provide their own "spin" on recent events (Baker, 2000). Although these programs may be less than useful sources for substantive information about campaigns, they have become an additional venue for the press to offer analysis and commentary, gain exposure, interact with the candidates, and become television celebrities in their own right. For the candidates, news interview programs also have become much more useful, giving them a forum to communicate more directly with the voters as the length of their sound bites on the nightly news has continued to decrease (Just et al., 1996).

Political commentary also has become a prominent feature of television networks' coverage of the national political conventions. At the same time that their total convention coverage has decreased dramatically during the past 25 years (from 50 hr in 1976 to only 12 hr in 2000), the networks have placed a greater reliance on "spin doctors" to interpret the events of the conventions (Waltzer, 1999). The contraction of television coverage has left the candidates' acceptance speeches as the primary substantive area for analysis. Newspaper reporters have tended to be much more active analysts than television reporters, writing stories about the candidates' political careers and background, analyzing public opinion data, and investigating campaign finance (Frankel, 2000).

A new form of interpretive journalism that uses some of the techniques of investigative reporting is the "ad watch" (Broder, 1990). During the 1988 presidential campaign, campaign ads were frequently broadcast on the news, followed by journalists' commentary on the ad's effectiveness or the impact it might have on the electorate. In response to a postelection plea by David Broder, a *Washington Post* columnist, for more rigorous testing of advertising claims, "watch dog" ad reports became prominent in the 1992 election campaigns. The main theme of the ad watch was to indicate points of misinformation in the ad. The ad watches in 1992 tended to follow a "grammar" proposed by Kathleen Hall Jamieson, airing only selected portions of the ads and placing the reporter's commentary in a more prominent role (see also Cappella & Jamieson, 1994). Ad watches focused on uncovering the symbolic meaning of the ad, underlying insinuations, and subtle distortions.

By the 1996 campaign, some observers found that ad watches put too much emphasis on evaluating the merit and factual accuracy of isolated claims within the ads, while ignoring the broad patterns of behavior and overall record of the candidates (Richardson, 1998). At least one study argued that no matter how the ad watches were presented, they tended to amplify the resonant candidates' messages, providing them with additional free exposure (West, 2001).

More generally, Just et al. (1996) have criticized the negative tone of ad watches, which seem to imply that all candidates are deceptive in their presentations. Ad watches have also contributed to the negative tone of campaigns by providing material to opposing candidates that they can use to counter their opponents' claims or even to produce their own attack ad. Moreover, it is not uncommon for candidates to encourage journalists to analyze opponents' ads, with the sole purpose of generating an apparently objective and credible source to support their claims. The use of ad watches has expanded to include congressional and state races. In addition, local media began using these reports as part of their election coverage.

Construction of the Campaign in the News Media

As network evening news viewership has declined, the audience for cable news and local TV news has increased. The 24-hr news cycle on cable stations means that stories can be updated continuously. Some cable stations present regular hour-long news broadcasts, twice the length of network evening news (Kerbel, 1994). The greater size of the news hole on cable television means that its reporters can tell a complicated story live, in real time, from many places at once, as they did during the controversy following the 2000 presidential election. On that occasion, cable news took the audience inside the courtroom and into the deliberations of a local canvassing board, not only live, but also for an extended period of time. Unfortunately, that round-the-clock reporting prevented the reporters from doing more in-depth stories, as they had to be near the of-ficial sources in case there was any breaking news. It was left to the print journalists to undertake analysis and interpretation (Hall, 2001). Some journalists and scholars are concerned that the overall impact of 24-hr cable news is to shorten deadlines and make it difficult for journalists to fact-check their stories before airing (Kalb, 2001; Kovach & Rosenstiel, 1999).

At the other end of the cable spectrum from the hectic pace of 24-hr headline news is C-SPAN. This nonprofit cable providers' network offers news junkies gavel-to-gavel cover-age of congressional proceedings. During political campaigns, C-SPAN also offers unedited cablecasts of candidate speeches, party conventions, candidate debates, and political advertise-ments. Government-supported public television has also partnered with commercial stations to take up the coverage of lengthy campaign events such as political party conventions. Similar partnerships have also emerged between commercial networks and their cable affiliates.

In addition to cable news, audiences have also begun to turn to local media for information about national politics. Local newspapers and television stations, particularly in the larger media markets, have increased their coverage of national and international news, including news about presidential campaigns. Moreover, the increasingly tight budgets faced by local stations (Just, Levine, & Belt, 2001) have forced them to depend on national wire services for content. This has allowed penetration of national news sources and values into local news outlets (Carroll, 1992) and has made the gap between horse race coverage and substantive discussion more pronounced on the local level. When local media do cover the issues and candidate qualities, their stories tend to be more positive and less cynical than the ones written and broadcast by their national counterparts (Just et al., 1996).

In general, local television stations have focused on news that can entertain viewers with dramatic video. In light of budget constraints, local TV favors topics that can be covered with low effort or cost, such as crime, consumer issues, and health. Thus, any local political campaign that is not competitive or does not have a scandal associated with it gets almost no attention (Kannis 1991, 1995; McManus 1994). The situation is not much better in print. Although metropolitan newspapers have traditionally covered national and international news, competition with suburban newspapers and cable television has resulted in an overall decrease in these topics in print. Larger newspapers have shifted resources to the suburbs, expanded their regional business sections, and added other specialty areas such as health and science, leaving less room for local politics. Front pages feature more "reader-friendly" stories. If a local campaign story is to gain a spot on the front page, or at least the front page of the local section, it must relate to something dramatic, such as a major shift in the horse race, analysis of a backroom deal, a shakeup in the candidate's organization, or an inside scoop. Issues, on the other hand, are pushed farther down on the news agenda. In the interest of their own careers, even the most conscientious and experienced print journalists have incentives to concentrate on stories that not only take less effort, but also will find a larger audience (Kannis, 1991, 1995).

Some other sources of campaign coverage that have become popular during the past 10 years include talk radio (Brokaw, Fallows, Jamiesons, Metalin, & Russert, 1997), tabloid newspapers, and news magazine programs. To date, however, there have not been many studies analyzing campaign coverage in any of these new venues. Talk radio is highly cynical and is predominantly conservative, although both tendencies have declined with the Republican ascendancy in the Congress and the White House. Candidates are also appearing on a number of entertainment talk shows such as late-night comedy programs and soft interview programs, including morning news. These venues have become more useful to campaigns, as they provide candidates with direct outlets for communicating with citizens.

A new media competitor that emerged full force in the 2000 election was the Internet. Most of the coverage on the Internet, however, was virtually identical to that provided on television newscasts and in print. Both local and national print and television outlets used their Internet connections to supplement their regular political coverage. About 55 Internet outlets reported the presidential race, but hardly any of the information was original. Candidate Web sites, however, did provide new material such as live feeds from the campaign and links to candidate profiles and policy stands. The attraction of the Internet in the 2000 election was generally lost, however, on users who did not have broadband connections and who had to wait interminably for candidate Web pages to load (Hershey, 2000). In general, Internet use went down when television covered the same events live, as it did during the political party conventions (Cornfield, 2000).

Although the Internet has the potential to provide an endless supply of detailed and individually tailored information to citizens, it is a medium that requires motivation and some sophistication to utilize. There are a number of nonpartisan Internet sites that can provide citizens with specific information, such as where to register to vote, which interest groups are supporting the ballot questions in their state, and how much money their neighbors gave to presidential candidates. Most nonprofit civic information Web sites, such as the Center for Responsive Politics, Cal Voter, Project Vote Smart, the League of Women Voters, and Web, White, & Blue are supported by charitable foundations. But attempts to make Web sites such as D-Net and Voter.org commercially viable have so far failed.

The Internet, however, offers an exciting opportunity for third-party and non-mainstream candidates to recruit supporters and broaden their electoral appeal. The entry cost for candidate participation on the Internet is far less than for any other campaign medium. A talented friend or relative can help a candidate establish a Web site. The problem faced by both civic and minority candidate Web sites is how to publicize their existence. Possibly the emergence of broadband access and the increasing familiarity of younger generations of voters with Internet navigation will make the World Wide Web a more significant player in future campaigns.

At present, the Internet's most important campaign role has been in helping candidates mobilize the supporters they already have. Candidates and political parties have used e-mail lists to customize their appeals for funds and organize participation in live campaign events. Jesse Ventura, the third-party candidate for governor of Minnesota, based his successful campaign on a lively use of e-mail and Web contact with potential supporters, especially young people.

Coverage of Campaigns for Other Offices

Although there have been numerous studies of the news media's coverage of presidential campaigns, relatively few studies have focused on campaigns for other offices. This imbalance is unfortunate in that presidential campaigns provide researchers with only a single case for analysis in any given year, making it difficult to construct a general theory of election coverage or to explore how coverage varies under certain conditions. Congressional elections and other lower-profile races offer researchers a potentially larger sample of cases to analyze, permitting them to study how coverage varies for incumbents, challengers, and candidates vying for open seats. Studying congressional races provides an opportunity to evaluate whether coverage is different for male and female candidates, Whites and minorities, competitive and noncompetitive races, geographic regions, and different-size media markets (Abramowitz & Segal, 1992; Kahn, 1991, 1996; Kahn & Kenney, 2002; Manheim, 1974; Smith, 1997).

The research that exists indicates that the news media have committed fewer resources to congressional races than to presidential races. Moreover, most of this coverage has been of Senate elections, whereas elections to the House of Representatives have generally been neglected. Only when one of the candidates is a national celebrity or when there is a scandal associated with the incumbent do the television networks report on a House race (Cook, 1989; Robinson & Sheehan, 1983). The metropolitan newspapers have not been much better than broadcast media, limiting their coverage to House districts engaged in competitive races or whose boundaries overlap with their circulation area (Tidmarch & Karp, 1983).

Most information about congressional races is found in smaller papers. Reporters working the congressional beat tend to be young and new to the profession. Most have limited experience in analyzing politics and campaigns and do not regard their assignments desirable. Congressional coverage is considered the "dog beat" of the newsrooms, because reporters are required to spend long grueling hours working during the election cycle and are left with few stories to write once the campaign is over (Clarke & Evans, 1983; Cook, 1989; Glaser, 1996; Goldenberg & Traugott, 1984; Herrnson, 2001).

As is the case with the coverage of presidential races, the most covered aspects of congressional campaigns are candidate qualities and the process of the campaign. Given the emphasis on horse race, elections that are not competitive are not considered newsworthy and receive little coverage. Since the vast majority of House contests falls into this category,[1] it is no surprise that the news media devote so little attention to elections for this powerful branch of government.

Journalists covering congressional campaigns rely even more on routines than their counterparts covering presidential campaigns. In general, coverage is more habitual than innovative, as reporters seek out the most accessible news gathering techniques while avoiding complex information that might slow them down. Consequently, local reporters rely on the streams of campaign press releases that are issued by the campaigns to construct their stories. In addition, congressional reporters tend to cover the big events, while ignoring the day-today activities of the candidates (Clarke & Evans, 1983; Glaser, 1996; Herrnson, 2001).

Another significant difference between the coverage of congressional and that of presidential campaigns is that congressional coverage is marked by even more attention to the candidates' personal characteristics than presidential coverage (Clarke & Evans, 1983). When reporters do cover issues in congressional campaigns, their stories tend to be simple summaries of the candidates' standard message, with almost no analysis or any attempt to put the substance of their stories into a larger context (Hale, 1987). One bright spot is that issues are covered more often when challengers run issue-oriented campaigns (Simmons, 1987). Almost all the issue coverage in congressional campaigns is devoted to domestic policies. When international affairs make news in congressional campaigns, the emphasis is on the contentious aspects of foreign policy, such as partisan differences over defense spending and the foreign aid budget (Wells & King, 1994).

The primary beneficiaries of typical congressional campaign coverage are incumbents seeking reelection whose name recognition is already high and who have substantial financial resources. Challengers who are well funded and have campaigned for office before also benefit, as they have campaigned under media scrutiny in the past and can afford large professional campaign staffs. Incumbents also have a structural advantage over their challengers because their work (e.g., speaking in favor of or in opposition to a bill, voting on a bill, holding a town meeting) is considered news. The promises and proposals of their challengers tend not to be

---

1 Charlie Cook (2002) reports that the number of House races in 2002 that were rated as competitive in the spring was only 39. In 1992, the last election cycle affected by redistricting, the number of races considered to be competitive was 121, representing only 27% of the seats.

considered newsworthy (Clarke & Evans, 1983). For challengers, the main factor in generating news coverage seems to be the number of personal appearances they can make in the district (Vermeer, 1987).

A seasoned congressional campaign manager, who understands the news norms that guide reporters, knows how to make the candidate accessible to the press and to generate favorable coverage (Herrnson, 2001). Good managers also know when to shy away from news coverage. White Democratic candidates in the South, for example, have been known to withhold their schedules from the press on days that include events meant to mobilize Black voters, in hopes of leaving White voters uninformed of these activities (Glaser, 1996).

Although Congressional campaigns are short-changed in the press, by far the least covered campaigns are those for judicial office. Even in the best of worlds, reporting judicial campaigns would be challenging for a variety of structural reasons. In 20 states, judges simply stand for retention in unopposed elections, removing any doubt about the outcome. Also, judicial ethics constraints in several states restrict what candidates for judgeships can say during the campaign. Judicial candidates are often not allowed to describe what they will do if elected. Despite these limitations, reporters could cover judicial races by relying on public records. For example, campaign contributions are easy to track, as all states require reports of contributions and expenditures. Judicial candidates' personal financial disclosures are on the public record, as are caseload statistics, legal decisions, disciplinary complaints, and court dockets. Furthermore, the press can interview judicial candidates in order to give citizens a better sense of their qualifications (Foley, 1996). The lack of coverage of judicial races casts a spotlight on the norms of journalism and the patterns of professional behavior that govern coverage of other kinds of election campaigns.

Race, Media, and Elections

To the extent that research has expanded beyond the presidency, opportunities have increased to examine media coverage of female and minority candidates. Much of this research is motivated by questions of fairness regarding the quantity and quality of coverage of women and African Americans. Although these studies do not indicate that coverage has a direct impact on the outcome of elections, there is considerable evidence that journalists have used a different set of norms to guide their reporting in elections that include either a female or a minority candidate than they have used when only White men are running.

Although a number of studies have explored the issue of race in election campaigns (Bullock & Johnson, 1992; Glaser, 1996; Key, 1984; Kinder & Sanders, 1996; Mendelberg, 2001; Pleasants & Burns, 1990; Snider, 1985) and the news media's portrayal of African Americans in general (Entman, 1992; Gilens, 1997; Gilliam and Iyengar, 2000; Van Dijk, 1991), only a few studies have addressed the media's coverage of elections that included Black candidates (Jeffries, 2000; Reeves, 1997). Jesse Jackson's campaign for the Democratic presidential nomination in 1984 helped open the door to questions about how the media covered a black candidate and whether Jackson's coverage differed significantly from that of his White counterparts.

Jesse Jackson was not the first African American to run for president, but prior candidacies (e.g., Shirley Chisolm in 1972) were largely symbolic, with no real potential for affecting either the outcome or the process. The historic nature of Jackson's candidacy helped to generate considerable media attention to his campaign. Jackson's bid for the Democratic nomination also presented journalists with a story that did not fit neatly into their conventional framework and might require them to adjust their routines without any precedent to guide them. In shaping their coverage, journalists were concerned that the public and the candidates would think that they were holding Jackson to a different standard than his White counterparts. They worried particularly about being perceived as too critical of Jackson by some, while being perceived as too soft on him by others (Cavanagh & Foster, 1984; Dates & Gandym 1985).

Interestingly, much of the coverage of Jackson relied on objective sources, such as campaign speeches and printed materials (Cavanagh & Foster, 1984). Journalists generally refrained from offering the interpretation and analysis that had come to characterize their coverage of presidential elections in recent years (Broh, 1987). This same pattern has been observed in other elections involving Black candidates and in elections that have an underlying racial dimension. Rarely do reporters explore the interplay between race and politics or press candidates on race-related issues (Gissler, 1996). In the Jackson campaign, the only form of analysis that journalists were willing to provide for their audience was the improbability that he would win the nomination (Broh, 1987).

Because Jackson was unlikely to win the presidential nomination, the media devoted little attention to the tactics and strategies or behind-the-scene accounts of his campaign. Rather, the emphasis in the coverage was on Jackson's leadership qualities and personal characteristics (Broh, 1987; Merrett, 1986). He was shown as a forceful critic of the administration, an articulate spokesman for the left, and a leader who was capable of mobilizing a large bloc of voters. Still, much of the coverage portrayed him in an unfavorable light in terms of the horse race.

Like the 1984 Jackson campaign, L. Douglas Wilder's historic campaign for the Virginia statehouse in 1989 generated considerable attention from the media and, subsequently, from scholars (Rozell, 1991; Wilson, 1991). The Wilder campaign was also seen as a potential history-making event. If victorious, Wilder would be the first African American to be elected governor. Adding to the drama was that this breakthrough could occur in the capital state of the Old Confederacy. Unlike Jackson's presidential candidacies in 1984 and 1988, however, Wilder had a real chance of winning. In fact, he led his opponent in the polls throughout the fall campaign.

In contrast to the usual election coverage, but similar to their approach to Jackson, journalists emphasized issues in the Wilder race and gave less attention to the contest (in which Wilder had a considerable lead). On the surface, neither racial issues nor Wilder's race received much media coverage. There was also very little discussion of the "Black vote" or Wilder's representation of Black interests, a significant difference from the coverage of Jackson's 1984 campaign. Both Wilder and his opponent, perhaps for different reasons, tried their best to downplay the issue of race, including its historical significance (Rozell, 1991; Wilson, 1991).

Wilder attempted to portray himself as a nonracial candidate, and his opponent did not wish to be labeled a racist.

Although few news stories in the Wilder campaign were explicitly about race, reporters made numerous indirect references to the issue, and race frequently served as an underlying theme for news reports. Many stories about Wilder referred to the campaign as "making history" and signaling a "new era" of racial progress (Jeffries, 2000). In a similar way, the media have helped bring race to the forefront in contests that have included a Black and a White candidate in congressional elections (Terkildsen & Damore, 1999). It is possible that the media's subtle references to Black candidates' race or about voting blocs in racial terms help to mobilize racially conservative Whites (Reeves, 1997). For example, the media's coverage of the 1988 Republican ads about the Massachusetts prison furlough program and an escaped Black convict, Willie Horton, provides some insight into how this might unfold. When these ads were first aired, the media described the spots in nonracial terms, even though the image of Horton was included in the stories. By emphasizing the criminal justice issues in the ad, news coverage helped George Bush's campaign appeal to racial conservatives while, at the same time, providing an ostensibly nonracial justification for supporting Bush, or for opposing Dukakis (Mendelberg, 2001). The analyses of the Jackson, Wilder, and other campaigns featuring contests between Black and White candidates show that the news media can adapt to new campaign situations and that they are capable of covering sensitive topics.

Conclusion and Avenues for Future Research

This [article] has focused on news coverage of political campaigns in the United States. Research on this topic has been conducted steadily from the 1940s and has examined the struggles among candidates, journalists, other political actors, and the public to construct meaningful campaign messages. These efforts are often thwarted by the competing needs of the participants. Candidates seek to persuade citizens to vote for them and, consequently, seek to gain favorable news coverage for themselves and less favorable coverage for their opponents. Journalists strive to break the big story and reveal the latest missteps of the candidates. An ongoing struggle to control the content of the news ensues.

As reviewed in this [article], researchers who have analyzed news about election campaigns have focused on questions of bias, the relative attention to the contest versus the issues, and the opportunity for candidates to break through the interpretive journalistic haze to present their views to the public. The evolving news environment and different kinds of elections have broadened the scope of research on campaign news. Case studies have focused on how particular candidates have tried to put their messages across (White, 1989) and how journalists have constructed the realities of particular campaigns (Correspondents of *The New York Times*, 2001; Crouse, 1990; Greenfield, 2001; Robinson & Sheehan, 1983; Rosenstiel, 1993; Thompson, 1985, Witcover & Germond, 1989).

Although many topics have been examined, much work remains to be done. For example, although there are many studies of news coverage of political campaigns within particular countries, there are relatively few comparative studies of media coverage of elections across nations. The expense, noncomparability of media and electoral systems, language differences, and mismatched timing of elections in different countries have contrived to limit research in this area. A few major comparative studies have been conducted. Some scholars focus on comparing American and European election coverage (Kaid & Holtz-Bacha, 2000; Schulz & Schoenbach, 1983; Semetko, 1995; Semetko, Blumler, Gurevitch, & Weaver, 1991). Other comparative analyses of news coverage have been conducted across European elections (Esser, Reinemann, & Fan, 2000; Kevin, 2001; Kleinnijenhuis, 2001; Schoenbach, Ridder, & Lauf, 2001) and more globally (Gross et al., 2001; Swanson & Mancini, 1996).

Not only are more truly comparative studies needed, but also these studies should take into account the relative impact of gender, race, and partisanship or ideology on the coverage of candidates in different political systems. Another line of potential study is to compare campaign coverage in the increasingly diverse media outlets both in the United States and abroad. In the United States, for example, studies of language and ethnic media could provide a counterpart to the study of the mainstream press; in Europe, the increasing availability of international channels may also challenge traditional approaches to news coverage. Scholars should consider the impact of globalization and supranational identities on campaign journalism. The media systems in newly democratized nations that are still developing journalistic norms for election coverage also offer new avenues for research.

On a more theoretical level, efforts should be made to explain divergent constructions of campaign realities. What factors govern the negotiations between candidates and journalists in the process of constructing election news? In the past, journalists and scholars have played catch-up in dealing with and analyzing communication strategies and tactics developed by candidates. More observational research is needed on the role of media consultants in the heat of the campaign. What kinds of assumptions do consultants make about journalists and citizens in designing campaign messages, attacks, and counterattacks? Future research should also consider how news norms develop and journalists adapt to changing conditions of ownership, professional recruitment and training, competition and convergence of media, political institutions, and the size and composition of the audience. Scholars will also have to take into account the specific historical, economic, and social contexts of elections on the construction of campaign news. Integrating the perspectives of journalists and candidates across time and space will help us to understand better the impact of campaign news on citizens.

Acknowledgment

We would like to offer our thanks to Anne Gulati and Kathy Regan for all their help in preparing this manuscript.

References

Abramowitz, A. I., & Segal, J. A. (1992). *Senate elections*. Ann Arbor: University of Michigan Press.

Adatto, K. (1990). *Sound bite democracy*. Cambridge, MA: John F. Kennedy School of Government, Joan Shorenstein Center on Press, Politics and Public Policy, Harvard University.

Ansolabehere, S., Behr, R., & Iyengar, S. (1993). *The media game: American politics in the television age*. New York: Macmillan.

Arterton, C. (1984). *Media politics: The news strategies of presidential campaigns*. Lexington, MA: Lexington Books.

Baker, R. (2000, November/December). Inner circles. *Columbia Journalism Review, 36*.

Beck, P. A., Dalton, R. J., Greene, S., & Huckfeldt, R. (2002). The social calculus of voting: Interpersonal, media, and organizational influences on presidential choices. *American Political Science Review, 96*(1) 57–73.

Bennett, W. L. (2001). *News: The politics of illusion* (4th ed.). New York: Longman.

Berelson, B. R., Lazarsfeld, P. F., & McPhee, W. N. (1954). *Voting*. Chicago: University of Chicago Press.

Brewer, P. R., & Sigelman, L. (2002). Political scientists as color commentators: Framing and expert commentary in media campaign coverage. *Harvard International Journal of Press/Politics, 7*(1), 23–35.

Broder, D. (1990, January 14). Putting sanity back in elections. *The Washington Post*, p. D1.

Broh, C. A. (1987). *A horse of a different color: Television's treatment of Jesse Jackson's 1984 presidential campaign*. Washington, DC: Joint Center for Political Studies.

Brokaw, T., Fallows, J., Jamieson, K. H., Matalin, M., & Russert, T. (with Kalb, M). (1997). Talk show democracy '96. *Harvard International Journal of Press/Politics, 2*(1), 4–12.

Buchanan, B. (1996). *Renewing presidential politics*. Lanham, MD: Rowman & Littlefield.

Bullock, C., III, & Johnson, L. K. (1992). *Runoff elections in the United States*. Chapel Hill: University of North Carolina Press.

Campbell, A., Converse, P. E., Miller, W. E., & Stokes, D. E. (1960). *The American voter*. New York: Wiley.

Campbell, A., Gurin, G., & Miller, W. E. (1954). *The voter decides*. Evanston, IL: Row, Peterson.

Cappella, J. N., & Jamieson, K. H. (1994). Broadcast adwatch effects. *Communication Research, 21*(3), 342–365.

Cappella, J. N., & Jamieson, K. H. (1997). *Spiral of cynicism: The press and the public good*. New York: Oxford University Press.

Carroll, R. L. (1992). Blurring distinctions: Network and local news. In P. S. Cook, D. Gomery, & L.W. Lichty (Eds.), *The future of news*. Washington, DC: Woodrow Wilson Center Press.

Cavanaugh, T., & Foster, L. S. (1984). *Jesse Jackson's campaign: The primaries and caucuses*. Washington, DC: Joint Center for Political Studies.

Clarke, P., & Evans, S. H. (1983). *Covering campaigns: Journalism in congressional elections*. Stanford: Stanford University Press.

Cohen, B. (1963). *The press and foreign policy*. Princeton, NJ: Princeton University Press.

Cook, C. (2002). Has GOP hit a bump or something more serious? *The Cook Election Preview: A Supplement to National Journal*, July 7, 2002, p. 3.

Cook, T. E. (1989). *Making laws and making news: Media strategies in the U.S. House of Representatives*. Washington, DC: Brookings Institution.

Cook, T. E. (1996). The negotiation of newsworthiness. In A. N. Crigler (Ed.), *The psychology of political communication* (pp. 11–36). Ann Arbor: University of Michigan Press.

Cornfield, M. (2000). *The Internet and the 2000 Republican Convention: An appraisal*. Shorenstein Center Internet Reports. Cambridge, MA: John F. Kennedy School of Government, Joan Shorenstein Center on Press, Politics and Public Policy, Harvard University.

Correspondents of *The New York Times*. (2001). *36 days*. New York: Times Books.

Crigler, A. N. (Ed.). (1996). *The psychology of political communication*. Ann Arbor: University of Michigan Press.

Crouse, T. (1990). *The boys on the bus* (Reissue ed.). New York: Ballantine Books.

D'Alessio, D., & Allen, M. (2000). Media bias in presidential elections: A meta-analysis. *Journal of Communication, 50*(4), 133–57.

Dates, J. L., & Gandy, O. H., Jr. (1985). How ideological constraints affected coverage of the Jesse Jackson campaign. *Journalism Quarterly, 62*, 595–600.

Edelman, M. (1988). *Constructing the political spectacle*. Chicago: University of Chicago Press.

Entman, R. M. (1992). Super Tuesday and the future of local news. In P. S. Cook, D. Gomery, & L. W. Lichty (Eds.), *The future of news*. Washington, DC: Woodrow Wilson Center Press.

Esser, F., Reinemann, C., & Fan, D. (2000). Spin doctoring in British and German election campaigns: How the press is being confronted with a new quality of political PR. *European Journal of Communication, 15*(2), 209–239.

Foley, D. J. (1996). Covering those forgotten judicial races. *Columbia Journalism Review, 35*(1), 61.

Frankel, M. (2000). 15,000 journalists in search of ... parties? *Columbia Journalism Review. 39*(5), 16.

Frankovic, forthcoming.

Gans, H. (1979). *Deciding what's news*. New York: Pantheon Books.

Gilens, M. (1997). Race and poverty in America: Public misperceptions and the American news media. *Public Opinion Quarterly, 60*(4), 515–541.

Gilliam, F., & Iyengar, S. (1995, April). *Race, crime and broadcast news: An experimental approach*. Paper presented at Annual Meeting of the Midwest Political Science Association, Chicago, IL.

Gissler, S. (1996). Who was burning the black churches? *Columbia Journalism Review, 35*(3), 34.

Glaser, J. M. (1996). *Race, campaign politics & the realignment in the south*. New Haven, CT: Yale University Press.

Goldenberg, E., & Traugott, M. (1984). *Campaigning for congress*. Washington, DC: Congressional Quarterly Press.

Graber, D. A. (1984). *Processing the news: Taming the information tide*. New York: Longman.

Graber, D. A. (1998). Whither televised election news? Lessons from the 1996 campaign. *Harvard International Journal of Press/Politics, 3*(2), 112–120.

Graber, D. A. (2001). *Processing politics: Learning from television in the internet age.* Chicago: University of Chicago Press.

Graber, D. A. (2002). *Mass media and American politics* (6th ed.). Washington, DC: Congressional Quarterly Press.

Greenfield, J. (2001). *Oh, waiter! One order of crow! Inside the strangest presidential election finish in American history.* New York: Putnam.

Gross, A. L., Gallo, T., Payne, J. G., et al. (2001). Issues, images, and strategies in 2000 international elections—Spain, Taiwan, and the Russian Federation. *American Behavioral Scientist, 44*(12), 2410–2434.

Hacker, K. (Ed.). (1995). *Candidate images in presidential elections.* Westport, CT: Praeger.

Hale, J. F. (1987). The scribes of Texas: Newspaper coverage of the 1984 U.S. Senate campaign. In J. P. Vermeer (Ed.), *Campaigns in the news: Mass media and congressional elections.* New York: Greenwood Press.

Hall, J. (2001). Flying high. *Columbia Journalism Review, 40*(1), 40.

Hallin, D. C. (1992). Sound bite news: Television coverage of elections, 1968–1988. *Journal of Communication, 42*(5), 5–24.

Hanson, C. (2001). All the news that fits the myth. *Columbia Journalism Review, 40*(1), 50.

Herrnson, P. S. (2001). *Congressional elections: Campaigning at home and in Washington* (3rd ed.). Washington, DC: Congressional Quarterly Inc.

Hershey, M. R., & Hollihan, D. (2000). Constructing explanations for U.S. state governors' races: The abortion issue and the 1990 gubernatorial elections. *Political Communication, 17*(3), 239–262.

Hess, S. (1986). *The ultimate insiders: U.S. Senators in the national media.* Washington, DC: Brookings Institution.

Hess S. (2000). Dwindling TV coverage fell to new low. *The Hess Report.* Retrieved May 8, 2003, from http://www.brookings.org/dybdocroot/GS/Projects/HessReport/week9.htm

Hofstetter, C. R. (1976). *Bias in the news: Network television coverage of the 1972 election campaign.* Columbus: Ohio State University Press.

Hollihan, T. (2001). *Uncivil wars: Political campaigns in a media age.* Boston: Bedford/St. Martin's.

Iyengar, S. (1991). *Is anyone responsible? How television frames political issues.* Chicago: University of Chicago Press.

Iyengar, S., & Kinder, D. R. (1987). *News That matters: Television and American public opinion.* Chicago: University of Chicago Press.

Jeffries, J. L. (2000). *Virginia's native son: The election and administration of Governor L. Douglas Wilder.* Bloomington, IN: Purdue University Press.

Just, M., Crigler, A. N., Alger, D. E., Cook, T. E., Kern, M., & West, D. M. (1996). *Crosstalk: Citizens, candidates, and the media in a presidential campaign.* Chicago: University of Chicago Press.

Just, M., Crigler, A. N., & Buhr, T. (1999). Voice, substance, and cynicism in presidential campaign media. *Political Communication, 16*(1), 25–43.

Just, M., Levine, R., & Belt, T. (2001). Thinner, cheaper, longer. *Columbia Journalism Review: Special Report: Local TV News, 40*(6), 12–13.

Kahn, K. F. (1991). Senate elections in the news: An examination of the characteristics and determinants of campaign coverage. *Legislative Studies Quarterly. 16*, 349–374.

Kahn, K. F. (1996). *The political consequences of being a woman: How stereotypes influence the content and impact of statewide campaigns.* New York: Columbia University Press.

Kahn, K. F., & Kenney, P. J. (2002). The slant of the news: How editorial endorsements influence campaign coverage and citizens' views of candidates. *American Political Science Review, 96*(2), 381–394.

Kaid, L. L., & Holtz-Bacha, C. (2000). Gender reactions to TV political broadcasts: A multi-country comparison. *Harvard International Journal of Press/Politics, 5*(2), 17–29.

Kalb, M. (2001). *One scandalous story: Clinton, Lewinsky, and thirteen days that tarnished American journalism.* New York: Free Press.

Kanniss, P. (1991). *Making local news.* Chicago: University of Chicago Press.

Kanniss, P. (1995). *The media and the mayor's race: The failure of urban political reporting.* Indianapolis: Indiana University Press.

Kerbel, M. R. (1994). *Edited for television: CNN, ABC, and the 1992 presidential campaign.* Boulder, CO: Westview Press.

Kevin, D. (2001). Coverage of the European parliament elections of 1999: National public spheres and European debates. *Javnost—The Public, I*(1), 21–38.

Key, V. O. (1984). *Southern politics in state and nation* (Rev. ed.). Knoxville: University of Tennessee Press.

Kinder, D. R., & Sanders, L. M. (1996). *Divided by color: Racial politics and democratic ideals.* Chicago: University of Chicago Press.

Kleinnijenhuis, J., Maurer, M., Kepplinger, H. M., & Oegema, D. (2001). Issues and personalities in German and Dutch television news: Patterns and effects. *European Journal of Communication, 16*(3), 337–359.

Kovach, W., & Rosenstiel, T. (1999). *Warp speed: America in the age of mixed media culture.* New York: Century Foundation Press.

Krosnick, J., & Kinder, D. (1990). Altering the foundations of support for the president through priming. *American Political Science Review, 84*, 497–572.

Lazarsfeld, P. F., Berelson, B. R., & Gaudet, H. (1948). *The people's choice.* New York: Duell, Sloan, and Pierce.

Lichter, R. S. (2001). A plague on both parties: Substance and fairness in TV election news. *Harvard International Journal of Press/Politics, 6*(3), 8–30.

Lichter, R, & Smith, T. (1996). Why elections are bad news: Media and candidate discourse in the 1996 presidential primaries. *Harvard International Journal of Press/Politics, 1*(4), 15–35.

Lippmann, W. (1922). *Public opinion.* New York: Harcourt, Brace.

Lowry, D. T., & Shidler, J. A. (1998). The sound bites, the biters, and the bitten: A two-campaign test of the anti-incumbent bias hypothesis in network TV news. *Journalism & Mass Communication Quarterly, 75*(4), 719–730.

Manheim, J. B. (1974). Urbanization and differential press coverage of the congressional campaign. *Journalism Quarterly, 51*, 649–653.

Mann, T. E., & Orren, G. R. (Eds.). (1992). *Media polls in American politics.* Washington DC: Brookings Institution.

Mason, H., Frankovic, K., & Jamieson, K. H. (2001). *CBS News Coverage of Election Night 2000.* University of Pennsylvania.

McCombs, M. E., & Shaw, D. L. (1972). The agenda setting function of the mass media. *Public Opinion Quarterly, 36*, 176–187.

McManus, J. (1994). *Market-driven journalism: Let the citizen beware?* Thousand Oaks, CA: Sage.

Mendelberg, T. (2001). *The race card.* Princeton, NJ: Princeton University Press.

Merrett, B. (1986). Jesse Jackson and television: Black images presentation and affect in the 1984 Democratic campaign debates. *Journal of Black Studies, 16*, 347.

Miller, A., & Gronbeck, B. (Eds.). (1994). *Presidential campaigns and American self-images.* Boulder, CO: Westview Press.

Mutz, D. C. (1989). The influence of perceptions of media influence: Third-person effects and the public expressions of opinions. *International Journal of Public Opinion Research, 1*, 3–23.

Neuman, W. R., Just, M., & Crigler, A. N. (1992). *Common knowledge: News and the construction of political meaning.* Chicago: University of Chicago Press.

Nimmo, D. D., & Savage R. L. (1976). *Candidates and their images: Concepts, methods, and findings.* Pacific Palisades, CA: Goodyear.

Niven, D. (2001). Bias in the news: Partisanship and negativity in media coverage of presidents George Bush and Bill Clinton. *Harvard International Journal of Press/Politics, 6*(3), 31–46.

Page, B. I., & Shapiro, R. Y. (1982). Changes in Americans' policy preferences, 1935–1979. *Public Opinion Quarterly, 46*, 24–42.

Patterson, T. E. (1980). *The mass media election: How Americans choose their president.* New York: Praeger.

Patterson, T. E. (1993). *Out of order.* New York: Knopf.

Patterson, T. E., & McClure, R. D. (1976). *The unseeing eye: The myth of television power in national elections.* New York: Putnam.

Pleasants, J. M., & Burns, A. M., III. (1990). *Frank Porter Graham and the 1950 Senate race in North Carolina.* Chapel Hill: University of North Carolina Press.

Plissner, M. (1989, March 10). Inkbites. *The Washington Post*, p. A11.

Popkin, S. L. (1991). *The reasoning voter: Communication and persuasion in presidential campaigns.* Chicago: University of Chicago Press.

Reeves, K. (1997). *Voting hopes or fears?* New York: Oxford University Press.

Rhee, J. W. (1996). How polls drive campaign coverage: The Gallup/CNN/USA Today Tracking Poll and *USA Today*'s coverage of the 1992 presidential campaign. *Political Communication, 13*(2), 213–229.

Richardson, G. W., Jr. (1998). Building a better ad watch. *Harvard International Journal of Press/Politics, 3*(3), 76–95.

Robinson, M. J., & Sheehan, M. A. (1983). *Over the wire and on TV: CBS and UPI in campaign '80.* New York: Russell Sage Foundation.

Rosenstiel, T. (1993). *Strange bedfellows: How television and the presidential candidates changed American politics.* New York: Hyperion.

Rozell, M. J. (1991). Local v. national press assessments of Virginia's 1989 gubernatorial campaign. *Polity, 24*(1), 69–89.

Schoenbach, K., DeRidder, J., & Lauf, E. (2001). Politicians on TV news: Getting attention in Dutch and German election campaigns. *European Journal of Political Research, 39*(4), 519–531.

Schudson, M. (1978). *Discovering the news: A social history of American newspapers.* New York: Basic Books.

Schulz, W., & Schoenbach, K. (Eds.). (1983). *Mass media and elections: International research perspectives.* Munich, Germany: Olschlager.

Semetko, H. A. (1995). Political balance on television campaigns in the U.S., Britain and Germany. *Harvard International Journal of Press/Politics, 1*(1), 51–72.

Semetko, H. A., Blumler, J. G., Gurevitch, M., & Weaver, D. H. (1991). *The formation of campaign agendas: A comparative analysis of party and media roles in recent American and British elections.* Hillsdale, NJ: Lawrence Erlbaum Associates.

Simmons, R. O. (1987). Why some constituencies are better informed than most about the positions of house incumbents. In J. P. Vermeer (Ed.), *Campaigns in the news: Mass media and congressional elections.* New York: Greenwood Press.

Smith, K. B. (1997). When all's fair: Signs of parity in media coverage of female candidates. *Political Communication, 14*(1), 71–82.

Snider, W. D. (1985). *Helms & Hunt: The North Carolina Senate race, 1984.* Chapel Hill: University of North Carolina Press.

Sniderman, P. J., Glaser, R., & Griffin, R. (1990). Information and electoral choice. In J. Ferejohn & J. Kuklinski (Eds.), *Information in democratic processes.* Urbana: University of Illinois Press.

Stevenson, R. L., Eisinger, R. A., Feinberg, B. M., & Kotok, A. B. (1973). Untwisting the news twisters: A replication of Efron's study. *Journalism Quarterly, 50,* 211–219.

Swanson, D. L., & Mancini, P. (Eds.). (1996). *Politics, media, and modern democracy.* Westport, CT: Praeger.

Swerdlow, J. (1988). The decline of the boys on the bus. In R. E. Hiebert and W. C. Renss (Eds.), *Impact of mass media.* New York: Longman.

Terkildsen, N., & Damore, D. F. (1999). The dynamics of racialized media coverage. *Journal of Politics, 61*(3), 680–699.

Thompson, H. S. (1985). *Fear and loathing on the campaign trail '72.* New York: Warner Books.

Tidmarch, C. M., & Karp, B. S. (1983). The missing beat: Press coverage of congressional elections in eight metropolitan areas. *Congress and the Presidency, 10*(1), 47–61.

Tuchman, G. (1978). *Making news: A study in the construction of reality.* New York: Free Press.

Van Dijk, T. A. (1991). *Racism and the press*. London: Routledge.

Vermeer, J. P. (Ed.). (1987). *Campaigns in the news: Mass media and congressional elections*. New York: Greenwood Press.

Waltzer, H. (1999). TV coverage of U.S. party conventions. *Harvard International Journal of Press/Politics, 4*(4), 119–121.

Wattenberg, M. (1991). *The rise of candidate-centered politics*. Cambridge, MA: Harvard University Press.

Weaver, D. H., Graber, D., McCombs, M. E., & Eyal, C. H. (1981). *Media agenda-setting in a presidential election: Issues, images and interest*. New York: Praeger.

Wells, R. A., & King, E. G. (1994). Prestige newspaper coverage of foreign affairs in the 1990 congressional campaigns. *Journalism Quarterly, 71*(3), 652–664.

West, D. M. (2001). *The rise and fall of the media establishment*. Boston: Bedford/St. Martin's.

White, T. H. (1961). *The making of the president 1960*. New York: Atheneum Publishers.

Witcover, J., & Germond, J. (1989). *Whose broad stripes and bright stars?: The trivial pursuit of the presidency 1988*. New York: Warner Books.

Wilson, H. L. (1991). Media treatment of black candidates: The 1989 Virginia gubernatorial campaign. *Virginia Social Science Journal, 26*, 82–90.

Zaller, J. (1996, August–September). *Negativity and bias in media coverage of presidential elections, 1948–1992*. Paper presented to the annual meeting of the American Political Science Association.

Zisk, B. (1987). *Money, media and the grassroots: State ballot issues and the electoral process*. Thousand Oaks, CA: Sage.

★ The Concept of a Normal Vote

By Philip E. Converse

In interpreting mass voting patterns, great importance is given to any signs of change that current balloting may betray. Patterns established in the past, even though they may nearly determine the outcome of the election, tend to be taken for granted, while results are eagerly scanned for departures from these patterns. These departures are then taken to represent the unique "meaning" of the electoral message or the beginnings of significant secular trends in partisanship for some segment of the population. Thus, for example, a minority party may lose an .election but show "strong gains" in the popular vote. In many contexts, such gains are taken to define the flavor of the election more clearly than the identity of the winning party. Although it remains historically important that the majority party did carry the election, the primary message of the voting may reasonably be construed as a rebuke to the party in power, if not indeed a trend indicating the future rejuvenation of the minority party.

Although such fascination with change is entirely to be commended, it is more difficult to specify, in any particular situation, the actual character of the change. Such a specification presumes some sort of baseline against which the change is registered, and conclusions about the change vary according to the choice of baselines. This ambiguity is a constant source of comfort to official party spokesmen after an election, for a "moral victory" can be claimed on the basis of a rather wide variety of results.

When aggregate statistics are analyzed on some geographic basis, it is customary to choose as a measuring stick for change the most recent prior election which is at all comparable to the current voting in turnout, level of office contested, and the like. This criterion of recency has both virtues and shortcomings. Most notable among its shortcomings, perhaps, is its insensitivity to the possibility that the most recent prior election was itself rather unusual. In that event, any observed change between the two elections may represent not so much a vital new reaction to the partisan scene as an absence of the peculiar forces which had characterized the benchmark election.

The obvious remedy for this shortcoming of a recency criterion in ecological studies is to establish baselines with a more extended time series of election results, through some averaging process. However, when the population is defined geographically, such extended series encounter severe problems because of population movement. Although geographical redistribution of partisans can be of extreme interest from the point of view of local politics, it is a confounding factor when the focus is on the changing reaction of individuals over time in a broader setting. If certain constituencies in Florida have shown dramatic secular trends toward the Republicans in recent years, it is important to determine whether this progression means some fundamental drift in sentiment on the part of native Floridians, or simply the influx of elderly and well-to-do Republicans from the North. In the latter case, the observed change in partisanship would not be an indication of any genuine re-evaluation of the parties; it would, in fact, indicate the stability of the evaluations of both groups over time.[1]

It has been documented that partisan preferences of individuals do tend to survive changes in residence very admirably, even when the voter migrates into strongholds of the opposition.[2] This fact, coupled with high American rates of residential mobility (particularly of the "short-hop" variety),[3] poses a severe dilemma for ecological analysis. On one hand, there is pressure to work with the smallest geographical units possible, in order to isolate populations that are sufficiently homogeneous to be unlikely to mask real partisan change by compensating internal shifts in preference. On the other hand, the prevalence of short-distance residential changes means that the finer the geographical subdivisions, the greater the personnel turnover of a district between elections. For example, we feel it is necessary to distinguish between central cities and expanding suburbs in aggregate analyses, but such distinctions run afoul of the movement problem in the most distressing fashion. If we are interested in individual change arid wish to extract baselines from long time series, we would be on much more solid ground to treat the metropolitan area as a whole, thereby keeping a very large part of the residential movement within the unit of analysis.

Complementary shortcomings are suffered by sample survey techniques. Here the problem of locating homogeneous groupings at differing points in time is relatively minor. If the universe is the nation as a whole, we can locate the set of people of white-collar occupations born in the 1920's in a succession of national samples, regardless of how they may have been

---

1 Many observers have noted that the partisan vote division in most constituencies most of the time tends to shift back and forth between the parties in phase with national shifts in partisanship. This was the thesis developed by Louis H. Bean in *How to Predict Elections* (New York: Alfred A. Knopf, 1948). See also V. O. Key, Jr., *Politics, parties, and Pressure Groups,* Fourth Edition (New York: Thomas Y. Crowell, 1958, Pp. 215–217). When a constituency departs dramatically from such a pattern over a substantial period of time, it is very often found to be a constituency undergoing unusual rates of emigration or immigration.

2 A. Campbell, P. E. Converse, W. E. Miller, and D. E. Stokes, *The American Voter,* New York: John Wiley and Sons, 1960, Chap. 16, Pp. 441 ff.

3 The Census Bureau estimates that some 20 per cent of the current American population moves from one address to another in the course of a year. However, relatively few of these moves carry out of the area, state or region completely.

geographically redistributed in the interim. On the other hand, sample surveys of the single cross-section variety provide much less reliable historical depth than district voting records, simply because of the unreliability of individual recall of past behavior.

Nonetheless, certain properties observable in data from the lengthening sequence of election studies conducted by the Survey Research Center lend themselves to the development of an operational construct of a "normal" vote, which may be estimated for any segment of the population on the basis of single-wave, cross-section survey data. Such a construct is, of course, primarily an analytic tool rather than a theory or a set of substantive findings. It suggests a means of splitting the actual vote cast by any part of the electorate into two components: (1) the normal or "baseline" vote division to be expected from a group, other things being equal; and (2) the current deviation from that norm, which occurs as a function of the immediate circumstances of the specific election. At the same time, the construct is an integral part of the theoretical view of the electoral process which we have been developing, and it makes possible a number of interesting deductions about the operating characteristics of the process in the current American period. In the following pages we shall first consider the conceptual underpinnings of the construct, and then discuss in nontechnical terms the characteristics of the data which encourage this type of treatment.[4] Finally, we shall illustrate the empirical use of the construct.

Theoretical and Empirical Backgrounds

The voting record of the American public in the last decade has shown unusual partisan fluctuation. If we examine the national division of the two-party vote as measured biennially (the presidential vote and alternately, in off-year elections, the accumulated votes for Congress), we find oscillation which is as strong as any in the past century. Indeed, the movement in a single two-year span from a 42 per cent Democratic vote for President (1956) to a vote for congressional candidates approaching 57 per cent Democratic (1958) almost defines the limits of the range of variation in the national two-party vote division observable in two-party races over the entire last century.

This picture of dramatic short-term variation becomes even more interesting as we discover, in sequences of sample surveys across precisely the same period, a serene stability in the distribution of party loyalties expressed by the same public (Table 2-1). Furthermore, this is not the sort of net stability which conceals gross turnover of individual partisanship over time. "Panel" studies, which involve the re-interview of a national cross-section sample after intervals of two and four years, confirm a remarkable individual stability in party identification, even in this

---

4 For those interested in details, an extended technical note is presented in the Methodological Note at the end of this chapter.

TABLE 2-1 The Distribution of Party Identification in the United States, 1952-1964

	Oct. 1952	Sept. 1953	Oct. 1954	April 1956	Oct. 1956	Nov. 1957	Oct. 1958	Oct. 1960	Oct. 1961	May 1962	Aug. 1962	May 1964
Strong Democrat	22%	22%	22%	19%	21%	21%	23%	21%	26%	25%	23%	24%
Weak Democrat	25	23	25	24	23	26	24	25	21	24	24	22
Independent Democrat	10	8	9	6	7	7	7	8	9	7	7	7
Independent	5	4	7	3	9	8	8	8	10	9	11	10
Independent Republican	7	6	6	6	8	6	4	7	5	4	5	5
Weak Republican	14	15	14	18	14	16	16	13	13	15	16	17
Strong Republican	13	15	13	14	15	10	13	14	11	11	11	11
Apolitical (do not know)	4	7	4	10	3	6	5	4	5	5	3	4
Total	100%	100%	100%	100%	100%	100%	100%	100%	100%	100%	100%	100%
Number of Cases	1,614	1,023	1,139	1,731	1,772	1,488	1,269	3,021	1,474	1,299	1,317	1,465

period of extravagant vote change.[5] It is clear that the electoral outcomes of the 1950's were shaped not simply by Americans who shifted their partisanship, but also by large numbers who indulged in what was, from their own point of view, "crossing party lines."

Indeed, the proportion of conscious defectors in our samples since 1952 supplies the numbers necessary in each election to account for partisan swings of the vote. That is, in 1952 and 1956, masses of Democrats expressed themselves as voting "this time" for Eisenhower; in 1956 in particular, the majority showed their continuing Democratic allegiance by returning to the Democratic column after they had made their choice for President. Similarly, Republican defections in 1958 outweighed Democratic defections in the same year, thereby creating the vast shift in the two-party vote division between 1956 and 1958. Once again, what is important to the current argument is not the shifting of the vote itself, but the fact that large-scale, and essentially unidirectional, defections occur while the participants continue to think of themselves as adherents to the original party.

Such facts make it useful to consider any particular vote cast by any particular group—the nation as a whole or some subpopulation—as consisting of a long-term and a short-term component. The long-term component is a simple reflection of the distribution of underlying party loyalties, a distribution that is stable over substantial periods of time. In any specific election the population may be influenced by short-term forces associated with peculiarities of that election (for example, a candidate of extreme attractiveness or a recent failure of party representatives in government) to shift its vote now toward the Republicans, now toward the Democrats. Therefore, although we start with a single variable (the vote itself) to be explained in any situation, we now commission two variables: the "normal" partisan division of the vote for the group over a long period of time, and the deviation of the group's vote from that norm in a specific election.

It is easy to see this stable central tendency to group voting patterns, as well as the short-term oscillation of actual votes around this central tendency, in many empirical situations. That is, if we erect time series of votes cast at a national level by politically interesting groups, such as organized labor, Negroes, the aged, and the like, we tend to find with monotonous regularity that sequences of the Democratic portion of the two-party vote behave as follows:

	Election				
	1	2	3	4	5
Group A	78%	70%	72%	82%	74%
Group B	48%	40%	42%	52%	44%
Group C	58%	50%	52%	62%	54%

5 A panel study conducted by the Survey Research Center which involved interviews in 1956, 1958, and 1960 was supported by grants from the Rockefeller Foundation. Materials from this extended study will be treated in a forthcoming book.

This is, to be sure, an idealized pattern. Yet the degree to which large masses of empirical data on the votes of social groups approximate this idealized pattern is striking.[6] And such a pattern underscores the importance of distinguishing between long-term and short-term components, for it is clear in such cases that two radically different explanatory chores are involved. The first has to do with how the partisanship of Group A came to be established in the 70 per cent range rather than in the 40 per cent range of Group B. The second has to do with the dynamics of short-term variations shared across all three groups. The roots of the first phenomenon lie so deep in the past that it is doubtful if the data gathered can help to explain them. The second phenomenon is notable primarily because it lacks continuity with the past; the explanations lie clearly in the present. Other differences between Groups A, B, and C in an earlier day are likely to have some bearing on the first phenomenon, but they are likely to be entirely irrelevant in understanding the second.

The election outcome in the population or subpopulations, then, may be construed as the result of short-term forces acting upon a certain distribution of party loyalties which have characterized the population. For the moment we shall not try to paint in any specific content for these forces, save to observe a general distinction between *forces of stimulation* (which act to increase turnout) and *partisan forces* (which are pro-Democratic or pro-Republican in varying degrees of strength).[7] The hallmark of the short-term partisan force is, of course, that it induces defections across party lines, yet defections which are unaccompanied by any underlying revision of party loyalty. The model does not preclude the possibility that the distribution of underlying loyalties itself may change over time for a population, and the initial phases of such a change might well be marked by defections not yet accompanied by partisan conversion.[8] However, it is empirically clear that in the lengthening period of our observation, vote shifts have not been accompanied by conversion but rather have been followed routinely by actual return to the party of original choice.

Let us imagine that we have subdivided a population on the basis of a continuum of party identification, running from strong Democrats through Independents to strong Republicans. A subdivision of this sort has been common practice in all of our recent election studies.[9] If the

---

6 Most departures from such a pattern which can be observed for groups traditionally studied are too slight to be distinguished reliably from sampling error. The most dramatic exception came in 1960 when the Protestant and Catholic votes, after a decade of motion in tandem, diverged sharply. Such an exception, however, poses no theoretical problems; it is encompassed easily in the model which is compelled by the total series of our observations.

7 For a fuller discussion of such forces see chapter 3.

8 For an expanded discussion of these points see chapter 4.

9 The primary party identification question is "Generally speaking, do you think of yourself as a Republican, a Democrat, an Independent, or what?" classify themselves as Republican or Democrat are then asked, "would you call yourself a strong (republican, Democrat) or a not very strong (Republican, Democrat)"Those who classified themselves as independent were asked this additional question."Do you think of yourself as closer to the republican or democratic party" Thus a maximum of seven classes are

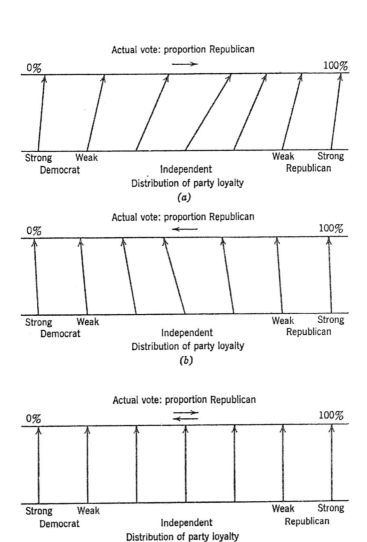

Figure 2.1 Varying strains induced on party loyalties by short-term net partisan forces. (a) Strong pro-Republican forces. (b) Mild pro-Democratic forces. (c) No forces; balance of forces.

distribution of the population in these classes remains stable over time, large-scale shifts in the vote from election to election must arise from shifting proportions of votes cast within each class of party identifier. Actually, such motion could occur in a number of patterns to produce any given vote. Most of these, however, are rather fanciful. Empirical data over a series of elections suggest that this motion takes a very straightforward form. This key pattern is shown, in a form only slightly idealized from empirical data, in Figure 2-1.

distinguished. These are often collapsed, as in this article, to five or three classes, in response to needs for greater case numbers per class, or under certain circumstances to assure monotanicity.

Several broad observations can be made. First, the strains introduced in the behaviors of identifiers of differing party and strength (Figures *2-1a* and 2-1 *b)* fairly plead to be quantified in terms of direction and strength, according to the slope of the arrows. This leads immediately to the concept of net short-term partisan forces. As in other realms, the net force cannot be directly measured; rather, it is posited and measured in terms of its observed effects. In this case, the observable effects have to do with the defection rates of classes of party identifiers.

Second, to the degree that empirical data collected over time and under a variety of net forces (pro-Republican and pro-Democratic as well as differing degrees of strength) conform to such regular patterns, it is more a mechanical than an intuitive matter to estimate the characteristics of a "normal" vote, conceived as one in which the behaviors of Republicans and Democrats of differing strengths show no distortion toward either party. The regularity of the patterns means that they may be readily formalized in a limited set of rules. If, for example, we are told that strong Democrats in a particular election turned out to vote in certain proportions and defected at certain rates, we can deduce from this limited information the properties of the two basic sets of forces operating in the election, and thence we can predict with quite gratifying reliability the turnout and defection rates characterizing each of the other classes of identifiers. By interpolation a normal vote can be located within this pattern as one in which the net balance of partisan forces is zero (either because of an absence of short-term forces or because existing partisan forces are in perfect equilibrium), even though within a limited range of time an actual "normal vote" is never cast.[10] With some oversimplification, this is essentially the situation illustrated by Figure 2-1 *c.*[11]

Finally, our stress on short-term forces should not obscure the fact that the normal vote associated with any population depends entirely on the underlying distribution of party loyalties, and that the actual vote in any election, although influenced by short-term forces, still is largely determined by that distribution. For example, a very Democratic grouping which casts a normal vote of 75 per cent Democratic may, under extreme pro-Republican forces, cast an actual vote only 60 per cent Democratic. Yet such a vote would remain much more Democratic

---

10 In the simplest of all possible worlds, the vote at this zero-point might be generated by all self-confessed Republicans voting Republican, whatever the strength of their loyalty, and all self-confessed Democrats voting Democratic, with the limited handful of pure Independents split evenly between the parties. However, it is clear empirically that voters undergo a tremendous range of idiosyncratic influences on their votes, many of which (such as a husband requiring his wife to vote with him and not against him) lead to persistent pressures toward defection. The probability that any individual will succumb to such pressures is a simple function of the strength of felt loyalty. Thus, as Figure *2-1c* suggests, even in a normal vote strong identifiers will vote in a more solid bloc than weak identifiers.

11 The simplifications in the figure are several. Quite notably, classes of identifiers are arrayed in even spaces along the party identification continuum. We have no assurance that our measure discriminates such equal intervals. In fact, there is reason to believe that it does not. Without such a property, however, there is a severe problem in judging when, in the terms of Figure 2-1c, the arrows are indeed vertical. However, the figure is presented to convey the intuitive notion intended by the "normal vote."

than an actual vote generated by a grouping of predominantly Republican identifiers, even if the latter grouping were responding to extreme pro-Democratic forces.[12]

Operationalizing the Normal Vote Concept

We have now discussed at a rather general level a number of the conceptual and empirical considerations that encourage us to operationalize the construct of a normal vote for a population. In so doing, we have suggested that the behavior of classes of party identifiers varies systematically as a function of the level of stimulation accompanying a given election, and as a function of the short-term net partisan forces created by the election. We have suggested further that the normal vote represents nothing more than an interpolation within this patterned variation. To arrive at criteria for this interpolation we must first establish what the more general patterns are.

Short-term stimulation and turnout It can be shown that in some instances strong partisan forces affect the turnout of different classes of identifiers, increasing the turnout of the advantaged party and depressing the turnout among its opponents. However, these instances are rarer than is commonly assumed, and it is a convenience to treat patterns of turnout as a function of short-term stimulation independently of partisan variation.

We cannot measure the level of stimulation directly. Nonetheless, the overall turnout figure for an election may be taken as a surrogate measure. Thus the relatively high turnout in presidential elections reflects high stimulation, whereas the sharp reduction in overall turnout in off-year congressional elections shows the greatly reduced stimulation. From this point of view, the most cursory inspection of turnout rates produced by different classes of identifiers over the range of elections that we have observed reveals a very clear pattern. When overall turnout is at a peak, as in 1960, Independents and weak identifiers are only moderately less likely to vote than are those who are strongly identified with a party. Thus a graph of the proportion turning out at each step across the party identification spectrum shows almost a straight line under conditions of very high stimulation (Figure 4-4). As we move to elections where turnout has been lower, however, we find that although strong identifiers are somewhat less likely to vote, Independents and weak identifiers are *much* less likely to vote. Hence as turnout declines, our graph shifts from a shallow slope to a V, and the V deepens as turnout declines still further (Figure 4-1). In other words:

---

12 The underlying distribution of party identifications has a strong bearing not only on the partisanship of the actual vote, but upon the amplitude of the deviation which a given short-term force can produce. A grouping such as a cohort of elderly people is likely to have a U-shaped distribution, since party identifications strengthen with age, and is likely to be pushed less far by short-term forces of a given magnitude than a cohort of the very young, which shows a much more bell-shaped distribution of identifications, with few strong identifiers and many weaker ones.

(1) *responsiveness of the turnout rate to the level of stimulation varies inversely with the mean strength of party identification.*

This "responsiveness" may be quantified quite congenially. Instead of erecting a graph election by election for all classes of identifiers, let us graph the variation in turnout for each class of identifier across five elections, as a function of the overall turnout in each election. Since this amounts to a part-whole correlation, it is of somewhat limited interest that these several graphs (five or seven, depending on the number of classes of identifiers we wish to distinguish) all strongly suggest linear relationships.[13] What is important is that the slope of the linear function varies systematically with the strength of identification, being steeper for the least partisan and shallower for the most partisan, as the V-phenomenon would necessitate. Thus the slope of the function estimated for each class of identifier (least squares method) can be seen as a representation of the "responsiveness" of the class to short-term stimulation. And in view of the systematic variation in slope as a function of identification strength, the degree of fit of the empirical observations for each class to its own characteristic linear function is quite remarkable.[14]

Figure 2-2 gathers up the estimated functions for the several classes of identifier in a single graph, illustrating the covariation of slope and strength of partisanship.[15] We note as well that

---

13 It is somewhat more interesting to note that if we set aside the South as a special case, the Southern observations for each class of identifier across elections extend beautifully, in a lower domain of turnout, the line of observations pertaining to the non-South. The degree of fit of all observations to a simple linear function is so excellent where underlying case numbers are at all numerous that isolation of the South and addition of its observations separately to give ten data points for five elections does little to change the optimal function. Indeed, the linear function for each class of identifier has been estimated on the basis of ten observations rather than five among Democrats and Independents.

14 The fit is poorest where case numbers are fewest (among Republicans), although it remains sufficiently good that one hardly hesitates to estimate an underlying linear function. Among both types of Democrats and Independents, where the South can be represented separately and the total range of variation in the independent variable is about 40 per cent, the observed turnout of the specific identification class departs from that predicted by its linear equation on the basis of overall turnout by less than 0.5 per cent in about one-quarter of the comparisons, and by less than 2.5 per cent in more than two-thirds of the comparisons. Given the known sampling error which must be attached to the observations despite the part-whole structure of the relationship, this degree of fit to the characteristic slope of each class of identifier leaves little to be desired.

15 The several functions converge quite well upon the point (100,100). The character of the functions toward the opposite extreme is less clear, and we have extended each function only as far as observed values warrant. While we can imagine that Independents might drop completely out of the electorate in elections of 10 to 20 per cent participation, the part-whole character of the relations represented requires as well that the functions for strong partisans "warp" to meet the point (0,0). Within the range of observed variation, however, such warping is not foreshadowed. For the moment, then, we must remain ignorant of patterns of variation when turnout is extremely low.

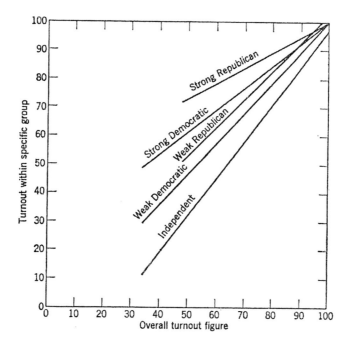

Figure 2-2. Turnout within classes of party identifiers as a function of overall turnout in five national elections.

at each level of partisan commitment, Republicans are less responsive than Democrats to the degree of immediate stimulation surrounding the election. Thus the V, which characterizes low-turnout elections, is not perfectly symmetrical across the party identification continuum: the arm of the V toward the Democratic pole tends to sag (lower Democratic turnout). This lack of symmetry is of both theoretical and practical importance. We shall consider it more systematically in a moment.

Short-term partisan forces and defection rates. Where partisanship and rates of defection are concerned, we have already constructed Figure 2-1 so that it reveals in advance that parallel patterns of variation occur. That is, under the influence of short-term partisan forces, movement toward the advantaged party tends to be slightly sharper (by a percentage metric) in the center of the party identification continuum than it is at the extremes. Thus it follows that:

(2) *responsiveness of the vote division to short-term partisan forces varies inversely with the mean strength of party identification.*

Because underlying party loyalties in the nation as a whole have remained essentially constant in the last decade, we can take the national division of the two-party vote as an indicator of net short-term partisan forces as they have varied from election to election and plot as we did in the turnout case the dependent variation in the vote division within each class of identifier.[16] Once again, the variation in slope across classes of identifiers commands our initial attention, and we find that these slopes correlate very highly with the set of slopes having to do with change in turnout (Figure 2-2). It is natural to reformulate propositions (1) and (2) more generally:

> (3) *responsiveness to short-term forces varies inversely with strength of party identification.*

As was the case with the turnout slopes, the partisan slopes are asymmetrical across the party continuum, with Republicans of a given strength of party identification showing less susceptibility to change than comparable Democrats. Now, susceptibility to change, or what we have called "responsiveness to short-term forces," has been classically associated with low political involvement (the floating voter hypothesis) ; furthermore we know that although there is some direct correlation between strength of party identification and political involvement, Democrats of a given level of party identification tend to show less political involvement than Republicans of the same partisan commitment, even if the South is excluded from consideration. If we take stock of these partisan differences in involvement, we find that they match almost perfectly the turnout and partisanship slopes for the different classes of identifiers (Table 2-2).[17] It is hard to imagine that these measures are not reflecting a certain unitary underlying property which affects voting behavior and which, incidentally, leads to some asymmetry between the parties in the current period. We may suggest, then, that:

> (4) *responsiveness to short-term forces varies inversely with the level of political involvement.*

The relationship between propositions (3) and (4) needs some further comment. We tend to view them as relatively independent propositions. That is, both political involvement and partisan identification can contribute independently to a reduced responsiveness to short-term forces. It is certainly true that political involvement and strong party commitment tend to occur in combination, and it is likely that the emergence of either in an individual facilitates the development of the other. However, the correlation is mild indeed, and it currently seems fruitful to assume two correlated entities rather than one underlying entity that we happen to be measuring by two rather imperfect means.

---

16 The data points in the partisanship case fit linear functions a little more loosely than in the turnout case, indicating both greater scatter and, as will become clear later, an incipient departure from linearity. Nonetheless, the fit remains sufficiently good that estimation of functions requires little apology,

17 Pearson correlation coefficients computed on the basis of five pairs of Observations are not very useful. However, it gives some crude indication of the mutual fit of this triad of measures to note that over the five observations the correlation of turnout and partisan slopes is .97; that of turnout slopes with involvement means is-.98; and that of partisanship slopes with involvement means is-.97.

TABLE 2-2 Some Basic Characteristics of Classes of Party Identifiers Bearing on Responsiveness to Short-Term Forces

	Turnout *	Partisanship†	Mean‡
	Slope	Slope	Involvement
Strong Democrats	0.76	0.57	0.81
Weak Democrats	1.05	1.09	-0.01
Independents	1.29	1.21	-0.23
Weak Republicans	0.98	0.75	0.16
Strong Republicans	0.52	0.29	1.18

*Let x be the overall turnout in a specified election, and let y be the turnout of the indicated class of identifier in that election. For five elections (10 observations including South and non-South) the linear function $y = mx\text{-}f\text{-}b$ is estimated. The slopes recorded are the m's. A slope exceeding 1.00 means that the change in turnout of the indicated class as a function of election stimulation exceeds that recorded by the population as a whole; a slope less than 1.00 means that change in turnout is less than that of the population as a whole.

†Let x be the national two-party division of the vote in a specified election, and let y be the two-party vote division of the indicated class of identifier in that election. The partisanship slope is the m computed for the least-squares solution of the equation $y = mx + b$.

‡The mean involvement is based on an index of two questions, in which positions are assigned and a simple integer scoring employed to extract means. The values themselves convey no ready intuitive meaning. While the general ordering of classes of identifiers in terms of mean involvement remains constant from election to election, the measure does show some responsiveness itself to party fortunes. Therefore the means presented are those summed across several elections.

Similarly, it seems useful to view the asymmetrical distribution of involvement between the two partisan camps as a mere coincidence of the current period, albeit one which demands empirical recognition. That is, we do not conceive Democrats as less politically involved because the Democratic Party is in any direct way a less stimulating object of affection. The stream of events which led the South to become a one-party Democratic region is of another order entirely. Yet this piece of history is partially responsible for the current asymmetry. Outside the South, the asymmetry stems from the fact that the Democratic Party tends to attract people of lower education on the grounds of the self-interest of "the common man," and since education is quite sharply correlated with political involvement for a totally different set of reasons, this biasing of the Democratic group toward the less-educated brings in its train a less politically involved group. To the degree that we can erect a model in which these involvement differences between the parties are taken into account (perhaps simply in the scale scores assigned to classes of identifiers), we can at the same time succeed in representing these empirical differences between the parties in the current period, at the same time providing a structure to encompass future situations in which these involvement differences favoring the Republicans may be ironed out or even become reversed.

In sum, then, we find that observations from five national elections reveal relatively simple patterns of variation in turnout and partisanship as a function of short-term forces.[18] The key operational question which remains is one of locating, within the pattern of partisan variation, the "zero-point" that represents the rates of defection of the varying classes of identifiers which would be expected under a perfect balance of short-term partisan forces.

Interpolation of the normal vote, Intuitively, we might suppose that a normal vote would be located where comparable classes of identifiers from the two partisan camps show equal defection rates. That is, when there are strong pro-Republican forces, strong Republicans are much less likely to defect than strong Democrats. Similarly, in the election of 1958, when there was reason to suppose that net forces were somewhat pro-Democratic, strong Democrats were less likely to defect than strong Republicans. Hence a perfectly natural point of interpolation for the normal vote is that point at which the defection rates of strong Republicans and strong Democrats (or weak Republicans and weak Democrats) are exactly equal.[19]

----

18 Since we have come to see responsiveness to short-term partisan forces and forces of stimulation as related to strength of party commitment in identical ways, the next logical step might be to unify our turnout and partisanship equations, thereby simplifying and generalizing the exposition. We shall not perform this step for several reasons, both conceptual and empirical. Our data indicate that it is useful to distinguish between nonvoting which occurs because the potential voter has failed to pass the various registration hurdles imposed by state law, or is sick or unexpectedly out of town on election day, and more "dynamic" sources of nonvoting, such as disgust with the alternatives proffered by the parties. If most nonvoting were of the dynamic variety, as is often thought, then it would be important to take joint account of turnout and partisanship. Instead, it seems that the frequency of "dynamic" nonvoting is negligible in high-turnout presidential elections, and becomes important if at all in low-stimulation off-year elections. In the same vein, there is evidence that the character of partisan forces "contaminates" turnout only among the weakest of partisans in elections of lowest stimulation, seen as more "optional" by the citizen. In short, we have ascertained with some care that we commit no violation on the current data by setting turnout aside as an independent problem.

19 There is less clarity as to what level of turnout should be presumed "underneath" the normal partisan division. Where the balance of short-term partisan forces truly represents an absence of forces, we should probably expect at best a low average turnout for the type of election being conducted. Indeed, we shall reserve the term "normal vote" for the situation in which turnout is to the low side of average for a presidential election in the current period. Fortunately, as we shall see below, this choice turns out to matter very little save in the instance of extremely Republican or Democratic subpopulations and extreme variation in turnout.

In effect, we do pursue this stratagem. The matter becomes somewhat complicated, since the asymmetry of involvement between comparable identifiers of the two partisan camps leaves Democrats slightly more susceptible to defection than Republicans, even when identification strength and strength of partisan forces are equated. However, we shall leave consideration of this complication to a methodological appendix, and shall treat only the idealized case here.

The linear partisanship equations were useful in indicating the fundamental regularity of some of these phenomena, pointing up at the same time the annoyance of partisan asymmetry in involvement. As we have already observed, however, the fit of the empirical partisanship observations to the linear functions was slightly poorer than in the turnout case. And despite the coherence of slope differentials, extrapolation of these functions to extreme values made no particular theoretical sense, as it had in the turnout case. Another mode of organizing the partisanship data provides functions which make sense at extreme values, which produce a better fit with the observations, and which, happily, leave little doubt about an objective location for the normal vote.

Since we have become interested in the relative balance of defection rates for Republicans and Democrats of comparable identification strength under varying short-term forces, let us simply plot this association for our sequence of elections. The new graph, once involvement complications are removed, lends itself to the simple formalization shown in Figure 2-3. The figure is less formidable than it may appear. Suppose we wish to know how different classes of identifiers would behave under moderately strong pro-Republican short-term forces. We need merely follow the appropriate ray from the origin (labeled simply "pro-Republican"), noting the points at which the ellipses for strong and weak identifiers are intercepted. Thus, under these partisan forces, we see that about 3 per cent of strong Republicans will defect as opposed to 6 per cent of strong Democrats, whereas about 12 per cent of weak Republicans as against 27 per cent of weak Democrats will defect. If we wish to reverse the partisanship of the forces, but maintain the same moderate strength, we find the same points mirrored above the natural midline of the figure (labeled $x = y$), for the figure is symmetrical around this midline.

The involvement problem disturbs the symmetry of the actual empirical functions which underlie Figure 2-3. However, this disturbance is slight, and it may be shown to reasonable satisfaction that correction for partisan differences in involvement restores the observations to symmetry (see Methodological Note at the end of this chapter). This disturbance aside, the "fit" of the empirical observations to the idealization in Figure 2-3 is exceptionally good. And, of course, to the degree that this presentation "accounts" for all of our data points under differing degrees and directions of short-term forces, there is no possible doubt about the location of the normal vote, which must of course lie along the midline $(x=y)$ of the figure.

From this point it is a simple mechanical matter to establish the actual norms which are used in computing a normal vote. Assuming a presidential election with a turnout somewhat below recent average, the data suggest the following:

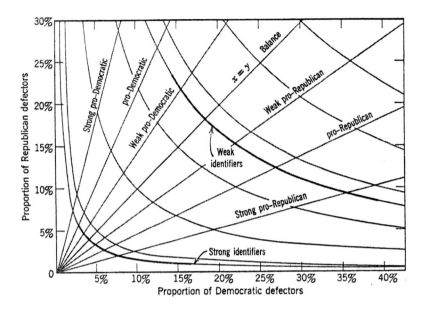

Figure 2.3 Defection rates as a function of short-term partisan forces.

	Expected Proportion Voting		Expected Proportion of Two-Party Vote Democratic
	Non-South	South	
Strong Democrats	0.79	0.59	0.957
Weak Democrats	0.71	0.43	0.818
Independents	0.62	0.28	0.492
Weak Republicans	0.76	0.50	0.162
Strong Republicans	0.86	0.72	0.037

The vote division to be expected in the normal case from any particular population group can be computed by applying these norms to the proportions of different classes of identifiers represented in the group. If we take the recent American electorate into consideration in these terms, for example, we find that the sample estimates of the normal vote characterizing the population from 1952 to 1960 have centered closely around 54 per cent Democratic. It is, of course, no coincidence that this figure is a little more than 1 per cent higher than the average national congressional vote for the five elections of this period and is almost identical with such an average if the two elections in which Eisenhower headed the ticket are excluded.

Some Illustrative Applications

Ultimately, of course, our interest lies less in the technical characteristics of the normal vote construct than in the new information which it permits us to extract from our data. We turn, therefore, to a brief illustration of the new types of substantive question which the construct encourages. We shall focus first upon the partisan implications of turnout variation when partisan forces are held constant at the zero or normal point, and second upon the information to be gained by dissecting the actual vote of a subpopulation into its long-term and short-term components.

Turnout variation. It has long been a matter of controversy as to whether the Republican or the Democratic Party tends to profit on balance from a general "non-partisan" campaign to stimulate turnout. If there has been a majority opinion, it has undoubtedly been that high turnout tends to favor the Democrats. Although this would seem on the surface to be a direct implication of our model as well, the matter turns out to be much more complex than appears at first glance. This is certainly true where changes in the strength or direction of short-term partisan forces are overlaid in systematic patterns on changes in the forces of stimulation, as is regularly the case in the alternation between presidential elections and off-year congressional elections. But it is true as well when we rule partisan forces out of the picture entirely.

Table 2-3 is constructed to represent this case. Rates of partisan defection established for the normal case have been applied to a range of levels of overall turnout, in accord with the equations underlying Figure 2-2. Hence the consequences of the differential turnout slopes may be examined for three subpopulations of varying partisan coloration.

It is obvious that two dynamic components of the model will come into play as the turnout level declines: (1) "Independent" voters move out of the electorate more readily; and (2) Democrats are more likely to drop out than comparable Republicans. Table 2-3 illustrates the fact that of these two components, the first is notably more powerful than the second. The

TABLE 2-3 Variation in Partisanship of Normal Vote as a Function of Changes in Turnout

	Overall Turnout *				
Hypothetical Population	25%	40%	55%	70%	85%
Preponderantly Democratic	74.7%	72.8%	71.7%	71.3%	71.1%
Relative Partisan Balance	52.5%	53.4%	53.9%	54.2%	54.4%
Preponderantly Republican	14.3%	20.3%	23.6%	25.2%	26.5%

*The turnout proportion entered has been roughly equated with the proportions usually cited for elections where the base is the "number of eligible adults over 21."
†The cell entry is the per cent Democratic of the expected two-party vote when partisan forces are balanced, for the specified subpopulation and turnout level.

first component has the effect of strengthening any majority as turnout declines, whether that majority be Republican or Democratic. A subpopulation with a strong Democratic coloration, for example, is made up typically of a large number of identifying Democrats, a lesser number of Independents, and a still smaller number of identifying Republicans. In a high-turnout election, therefore, a substantial proportion of the total Republican votes cast by such a population come not from hard-core Republicans but rather from Independents, even though as a class these Independents are splitting their votes approximately equally between the parties. As turnout declines and these Independents drop out, the Republicans in such a case would suffer *proportionally* heavier losses than the Democrats. Hence low turnout would increase the Democratic majority.

The other component—lesser Democratic involvement—has some effect as well, with Democrats losing strength more rapidly than Republicans as turnout declines. This second effect is, however, much weaker than the first. The Democratic losses with declining turnout become notable only where the Democrats are in a small minority (the Republican subpopulation), and much of this loss is due rather to the first component—the general penalizing effects of low turnout on the minority party. Where this penalty hurts the Republicans instead (the Democratic subpopulation), the effect of lesser Democratic involvement is quite eclipsed, and majority Democrats gain ground despite declining turnout. In the middle, where the majority factor is nearly ruled out, the Democrats do lose ground with declining turnout, but remarkably little.

Perhaps more striking than these differential shifts in partisanship is the general insensitivity of partisanship to large changes in turnout. Partisan change quickens in the ranges where turnout is relatively weak, and it is undoubtedly true that bizarre effects occur quite readily in certain municipal elections where turnout may be as low as 10 to 20 per cent. But where presidential elections involving two national parties in some rough numerical balance are concerned, we see that shifts of 20 to 30 per cent in turnout scarcely make a per cent difference in expected outcome, provided that short-term partisan forces remain in balance.[20] This latter clause is important, of course, since empirically it may well be that higher-turnout elections tend to be characterized by stronger partisan forces. However, it remains of some interest to see that turnout variation unaccompanied by shifts in partisan forces produces little partisan change, save at the most feeble levels of turnout. And although our data do suggest that Democrats are slightly penalized by low turnout *all other things equal,* it is not surprising that practical politicians in some areas swear that quite the opposite is true.

Long-term and short-term partisan components of the vote. As a second illustrative application, let us consider the increase in information which our data may yield if we employ the normal vote construct to break up any particular actual vote into its long-term and short-term components. We are particularly interested in those cases where some independent variable is thought to be correlated with only one of these two components. In any such instance,

---

20 Hence our note above that the choice of turnout level for the normal vote, within the rather large range of turnouts presidential elections have produced, was not particularly critical.

empirical correlations between the independent variable and the vote may be lacklustre due to the confounding influence of the other component, unless the vote itself has been broken into its components first.[21]

In some cases, of course, we may not know exactly what to expect of the relationship between the independent variable and the two components of the vote. When doubt arises, we may ultimately learn from the data what the contrasting correlations are, provided that we have gained some prior confidence in our analytic tools through work with situations in which theoretical expectations are quite clear. To create this confidence, we shall consider two instances in which our differential expectations are indeed so clear as to be almost trivial, at least from the point of view of the technician accustomed to data of this sort.

First, let us consider a case in which the religion of the voter is related in fair degree to the long-term component of the vote, but is not at all related to the short-term component. Such a situation might have been expected in 1952, when indignation at Democratic corruption, aggravation at the Korean War, and the attractiveness of the Eisenhower candidacy were primary among the short-term forces having strong pro-Republican impact. None of these elements has any obvious religious relevance in the strong sense that Kennedy's Catholicism had in 1960.[22] In short, then, although we know that there are abiding differences in partisanship between Protestants and Catholics, particularly if the South is excepted from consideration, there was little reason to expect that the short-term influences in 1952 would have much differential impact by religious category. And indeed, when the 1952 vote is divided into its components, we find that Catholic-Protestant differences did lie entirely in the long-term component:

Non-South	Long-Term	Short-Term
	Expected Proportion Democratic, Normal Vote	Demo-Deviation of 1952 Vote from Expected Vote
Protestants	44%	−13%*
Catholics	64%	−13%

* A negative deviation means a vote more Republican than normal.

---

21 Since the long-term component of the vote (prior party identification) is always the more powerful of the two terms, predicted relationships are less strongly confounded when the independent variable related to an actual vote has reason to be related only to the long-term component, than when the independent variable has reason to be related only to the short-term component.

22 To be sure analysts interested in predicting the voting trends among sociological groups in 1952 has surmised that Catholics, being more sharply anti-Communist, would evaluate the Korean War in a different light from that of Protestants, or that stevenson's divorce would cause more Catholic than Protestant indignation. But as usual where hypotheses get somewhat subtle and indirect, the evidence for differential perceptions of this sort by religious category in 1952 is poor indeed

In such situations, we may severely question the typical effort to "explain" the Protestant swing to the Republicans in one set of terms relevant to Protestantism, and then to search for another set of terms peculiar to Catholics to explain why the Catholic voters changed in a Republican direction as well. Obviously two groups can move in the same direction at the same time for different reasons, and this possibility must be kept open. Yet when evidence is strong that a certain configuration of forces produced the shift, and when these forces can only be given religious relevance, if at all, through somewhat subtle academic argument, it seems more reasonable to consider that religion was probably irrelevant to the dynamics of the particular vote. The long-term religious differences do indeed require explanation, but the fact that they turn up in the long-term component and not in the short is itself assurance that they have in no sense been caused by the specific features of the 1952 election.

It is equally easy to find illustrations of the opposite case, in which an independent variable is correlated with the effects of short-term forces, but is not correlated with the long-term component of the vote. We may continue with religious attitudes as independent variables, for we know that short-term forces in the 1960 election had unquestionable religious relevance. However, since Protestant-Catholic differences are "built into" the long-term component of the vote in the current period, we shall set aside Catholics entirely, restricting our attention to Protestants. Among Protestants, we argue, there is little theoretical expectation of correlation between attitudes toward Catholics and the long-term partisan component, but strong expectation of a marked correlation between such attitudes and the *short-term* component of the 1960 vote.

In 1956 we asked our respondents a battery of items having to do with their trust or distrust of political recommendations made by a variety of interest groupings in the population, including both "Protestant groups" and "Catholic groups." Responses to the two groupings can be ordered on an a priori basis to provide a scale of political anti-Catholicism, by placing individuals who distrusted Catholics and trusted Protestants at one extreme, and those who trusted Catholics and distrusted Protestants at the other extreme. For Protestants, of course, the latter extreme is vacant, although there is a fair range of variation from the anti-Catholic extreme through the neutral point to slightly pro-Catholic views (would distrust Protestants, but not Catholics, or would trust Catholics, would not distrust Protestants).

There is no systematic correlation between Protestants arrayed in this fashion and 1956 party preference. Furthermore, if we attempt to relate this 1956 measure to the vote cast by the same respondents in the 1960 election, we again find no regular differences in the predicted direction, despite the strong religious short-term forces in the latter year. The Democratic percentage of the 1960 presidential vote for these respondents reads:

Anti-Catholic			Slightly pro-Catholic	
25%	40%	34%	36%	25%

If, however, we compute a normal vote for each category and then a 1960 deviation from this vote, thereby isolating the short-term component, we find a perfectly mono tonic and rather close relationship:

Anti-Catholic			Slightly pro-Catholic	
-23%	-18%	-12%	-11%	+3%

where a negative deviation means a vote more Republican than normal, and a positive deviation means a more Democratic vote. Hence this rather obvious hypothesis shows no results until the dependent variable is broken into components. Then the influence of prior anti-Catholicism among Protestants becomes quite clear.

The important point for our current purposes, of course, is not so much the immediate substance of these data as the utility of the normal vote construct in sharpening our analyses of the meaning of voting change. If citizens approached each new election tabula rasa, then there would be no point in analyzing long-term components of the vote. The stability of party identifications, along with the apparent functional autonomy they gain for many individuals over time, however, has been amply documented. On the other hand, if all channels of political communication were to be shut off, so that citizens were obliged to go to the polls with no new political information to evaluate, there would be no short-term component to analyze.[23] In reality, voting decisions involve a blend of these components, and it is illuminating to be able to split them analytically. The normal vote construct enjoys a theoretical rationale and a sound operational base for this task. And, as is perhaps the true proof of the pudding, when put to use it leads to empirical findings of clear theoretical intelligibility.

Conclusion

For all of these reasons, then, the concept of a "normal vote" which may be expected of some subgroup in the American population, or of the American population as a whole, has increasingly become an integral part of our thinking about the flow of the vote registered across the history of American elections. Within the recent period for which sample survey measurements are available, the actual computation of normal votes under differing circumstances provides baselines which become crucial in assessing the meaning of electoral change, as we shall see most notably in Chapter 5. But even for the prehistory of survey research* where normal vote divisions can at best be crudely estimated from the general cast of election returns, the *concept* of an underlying normal vote remains crucial in finding new meaning in old statistics. It is to some of these insights that we now turn.

---

23 We will consider this contingency in Chapter 8.

Methodological Note

The problem of asymmetry of involvement The asymmetry of involvement between comparable identifiers of the two partisan camps means that the empirical "balance point" in defection rates does not represent too accurately what we conceive as the location of the normal vote. One further logical step beyond points made in the text is required to understand why this is so. The fact that turnout varies more sharply among the weakly involved as a function of level of stimulation than it does among voters of stronger political involvement does not of itself assure us that at an individual level involvement is positively correlated with turnout in any specific election, It is quite apparent, both on common-sense grounds and empirically, however, that this is the case. Although it is slightly less apparent on the face of the matter, there is also reason to believe that there is a parallel positive relationship between involvement and party fidelity. This observation, coupled with the partisan asymmetry in involvement, means that if strength of party identification and strength of short-term partisan forces are held constant, Democrats are slightly more likely to defect than are Republicans.

Hence the normal vote cannot be simply conceived as one in which defection rates of comparable identifiers "balance"; rather, this empirical balance point must be expected to be one in which there is already a sufficiently strong pro-Democratic net force to make up for some small involvement-based delinquency in the Democratic camp. Or, correlatively, the normal vote will be one in which, for example, weak Republican identifiers remain slightly more faithful to their party than do weak Democratic identifiers.

$$xy = 15.6$$

Where Figure 2-3 (see text) is concerned, this means geometrically that the hyperbolic tracks best fitting the empirical observations should be slightly displaced from their symmetrical position about the axis $(x = y)$. Actually, the displacement of the track for strong identifiers is imperceptible, and the symmetrical equation seems a perfectly adequate fit. The heavy segment of this track near the origin represents the range which our empirical observations cover.[24] The track suggested by the data for the pairing of weak partisan identifiers does indeed seem somewhat askew in the direction expected, however (fewer Republican defectors than

---

24 The character of the range covered by the elections we have studied has some implications for the partisanship slopes of Table 2-2. That is, for any of the symmetrical hyperbolas of Figure 2-3, $dy/dx = -c/x^2$. Therefore, where $x > y, > -1.dx$. Now if the symmetrical case pertained, and if we took a large enough sample of elections to arrive at a set of partisan forces averaging to zero, then dy\dx would equal $-1, dx$ meaning that the rates of change in partisanship with respect to changes in partisan forces would be equal between Democrats and Republicans. In this light, we can see that some of the discrepancy in slope between partisans of comparable identification strength in Table 2-2 is an artifact of our sampling of elections, in that we have oversampled cases in which $x > y$ and dy\dx > -1. It is our contention, however, dx that these partisan discrepancies are not entirely due to the biased set of elections we have observed.

the proportion of Democratic identifiers would lead us to predict if symmetry is assumed). It is possible to test the source of this asymmetry by controlling differences in involvement between the two sets of partisans, to see what defection rates would be were involvement levels equated. The data points corrected in this fashion do shift in the plane to a good fit with the symmetrical equation

$$xy = 336$$

and this track is represented by the heavy curve farther away from the origin.[25] All of these circumstances contribute to our confidence that involvement differences do account for much of any systematic asymmetry. They also suggest that quite in the spirit of some of our previous generalizations, the effects of involvement differences upon partisan defection are negligible where partisanship is strong, and become notable only among weaker partisans.

Nevertheless, the intrusion of the involvement problem undermines the most mechanical location of the normal vote suggested by Figure 2-3: along the axis $x = y$. The proper normal vote configuration must lie on a ray from the origin $y = mx$ where m is slightly less than unity. There is no very compelling mechanical method, given the paucity of data points, for determining just how much less than unity m should be. Hence an element of the arbitrary or indeterminate cannot be avoided. However, the range of indeterminacy involved is narrow by any lights. That is, if Figure 2-3 has any merit, the available data would make it appear entirely unreasonable to choose an m which lies outside the bounds

$$0.8 < m < 1.0$$

That is, while a more balanced sample of elections would reduce the partisan discrepancies materially, they would not erase them completely, due to the underlying differences in involvement.

25 A comparable correction of invlvement difference for strong partisans generates points which differ very little from the original points, and certainly suffests no systematic correction of the original equation. The correction does improve the fit of the observations to the function slighty, however. In general, we might note that the fit of the observed data to the equations is excellent in both cases. If the least distances (nonrectilinear) between the data points and the functions are computed, they average 0.7 per cent for the strong identifers without any involvement correction, for the weak identifies, where it is evident that the empirical observations require an asymmetrical function. A simple assumption as to the fashion in which involvement-based partisan asymmetry varies as a function of the strength of partisan forces produces an asymmetrical function which fits these skewed points very well. For our immediate purposes, however, it may be noted that the average deviation of weak identifers from the *symmetrical* function which is optimal when involvement is not corrected is 1.4 oer cent. This declines to an average deviation of 0.6 per cent relative to the new optical symmetrical funtion when the involvement correction is applied.

And while there are no clear criteria for locating *m* within this zone, a shift in *m* from one of these bounds to the other only produces a shift of 1.2 per cent in the estimation of an expected vote for a representative distribution of party identifiers with turnout level held constant. Such indeterminacy is hardly grave.

To establish the norms presented in the text, we have chosen an *m* in the middle of this zone. From these data we extrapolated to locate a cutting point which is comparable on the linear partisan equation for Independents.

Computation of a normal vote for a specific population. Once the turnout proportions are applied to the five classes of identifiers in the relative numbers characteristic of the specific population, then these five new proportions may be considered a row vector x, with the column headed "Expected Proportion of Two-Party Vote Democratic" (text) being taken as a five-component column vector *y*. The normal vote for the group is then simply the vector product *xy*. A somewhat less cumbersome method gives a very good approximation of the normal vote where the distribution of partisanship is not extremely skewed to one side or the other. Let *V* be the proportion Democratic of the expected vote; let M be a "mean party identification" for the distribution, where scale scores (+2, +1, 0,−1,−2) have been assigned to the five classes from Strong Democrats to Strong Republicans, respectively. Then

$$V = 0.268M + 0.483$$

the approximation being good to roughly ±1 per cent, where M < | 0.8 |.

Other sources of indeterminacy. Before concluding our technical observations, it is important to point out that our measurement of party identification is adequate to the model but is not perfect. That is, there is a tiny handful of people in any cross-section of the American population whose professions of general party loyalty largely reflect their current vote intention or most recent vote. While it may be an empirical reality that they have no "general" loyalty, their claims of loyalty, shifting with their actual votes, makes the trend of the division of underlying loyalties shift very faintly over time in periods of Republican or Democratic popularity. In other words it cannot be said that the division of party loyalties has been perfectly stable in the past decade, but only that it has been highly stable relative to the amplitude of variation shown by the actual vote.

Such respondents are so few in the population that the minor undulations which they produce in the division of party loyalties can never be reliably distinguished from sampling error. That is, if we compute an expected vote for each of our eight party identification readings between 1952 and 1960, we find that all of the readings lie within a band of about 4 per cent, although five of those eight readings lie in a narrow 1 1\2per cent range. Even the extremes of such variation could very reasonably be attributed to sampling error. The fact remains, however, that the most Republican of the eight readings was taken shortly before the Eisenhower landslide of 1956, while the most Democratic reading arose at the time of the 1958 Democratic sweep of Congress. This is probably more than accidental: the undulations do move slightly in phase with current partisan forces, as would occur if a handful of respondents in each year gave as a general loyalty a current vote intention. However, this undulation effect is slight at best, and its main influence in practice is to make for some little underestimation of the impact of short-term forces.

A second source of indeterminacy is of greater substantive interest. Far more often than not, it seems that cues from the world of politics which set up short-term partisan forces have a common valence, an "across-the-board impact" throughout the electorate. Thus, for example, there are not two sides to corruption as a political cue. Adherents of the erring party may defend against such a perception in a variety of ways, attempting to localize it in a wayward individual or maintaining some doubt that charges against the party are true. But the impact of the cue, individual partisanship aside, is unidirectional, favoring one party and disfavoring the other. Essentially the same may be said for a figure like Dwight Eisenhower, who failed to carry a positive valence only among the most extreme Democratic partisans resisting him on party grounds.

From time to time, however, there is an important political cue in an election which by its very nature has an opposite partisan impact for two different segments of the population. The Catholicism of Kennedy in 1960 provides a classic case: this basic cue set up strong pro-Republican forces for Protestants and strong pro-Democratic cues for Catholics at one and the same time. Now the basic model which we have laid out in order to locate a normal vote rests on data which reflect averaging processes at two levels: that of the individual weighing forces and deciding upon a vote, and the necessary averaging across individuals to arrive at aggregated data. Our question is whether, in the two-group conflict case, the cumulation of data across the two groups would stillyield a summary data point fitting the model, assuming of course that data from each of the two groups taken separately fit the model initially.

One can readily see that the cumulative estimate of forces operating in the case where two groups experience equal but opposite forces will depend very directly upon the relative size of the two groups. This is the sort of averaging across individuals which is a perfectly satisfactory implication of the model. At the same time, since the cumulation of results from two conflicting groups is a linear combination, one can see as well that if a point P on a hyperbolic track of Figure 2-3 represents the position of (e.g.) weak identifiers within Group A, while data from Group B produce a point Q on the opposite side of the axis $x = y$, the cumulation of the two sets of observations will give a data point which falls not at some intermediary point on the hyperbola, but rather on the chord PQ of the hyperbola. Thus the overall rate of defection summed over the two groups would be slightly higher than what one would have predicted if one had failed to recognize the conflict lines underlying the cumulation. And the possibility is open of somewhat slighter distortion in the estimate of the partisan balance of those forces.

Actually, the location of the data points fitting Figure 2-3 which would be cumulated in the conflict case are a complex function not only of the relative size of the groups, but of the degree of symmetry of the opposing forces around the zero point, the polarization of the forces, the correlation of the differential partisan forces with differences in prior partisanship between the two groups, and the like. Each of these factors, if given extreme values which are totally implausible from an empirical point of view, could introduce some distortion in the location of the cumulated data point; if all of these factors conspired at once in the proper extreme patterns, the distortion would be quite large indeed, representing an indeterminacy up to one part in four for the total likely range of variation in net partisan forces. Within the range of configurations which seem empirically plausible, however, the indeterminacy can be considered less than one part in fifty.

Discrepancies between the predicted and observed levels of defection in such combining problems are greater than are the shifts in the estimation of the net balance of forces on the cumulated groups. That is, factors which affect the location of the cumulated data point most strongly are factors which move the point toward or away from the origin more than "sideways" in a circle around the origin. The defection rate, for example, is most dramatically affected by the correlation of current partisan forces with prior partisan differences between the conflicting groups. That is, if a set of strong partisan forces had differential impact for groups A and B, where A is a Democratic group and B a Republican group, then other things equal the summed defection rates will be high if Group A is being pushed in a Republican direction while

Group B is being pushed in a Democratic direction; the rates will be lower than expected if the short-term forces coincide with prior partisan differences between the groups. But the estimate of the actual net partisan forces is not greatly affected unless other conditions are extreme.

The 1960 data provide a fine example of the good fit of the practical case despite mathematically possible indeterminacy. We have suggested that we would expect a cumulated data point for a given pairing of identifiers in Figure 2-3 based on results from two conflicting groups to fall on the appropriate chord of the hyperbola, and not on the hyperbola itself. However, this is true only if there is no correlation between the partisanship of the force to which the groups are subject and prior differences of party coloration between them. Other things constant, the cumulated data point shifts from the chord toward the hyperbola as some positive prior correlation of this sort is introduced. The point arrives at the hyperbola when the prior correlation is about .20. This is precisely the situation which pertained in 1960 between Catholics and Protestants, and it may not be too much to suggest that this is very likely to be the background situation in any case where cues have broad-scale, short-term "cleavage" impact. Thus the 1960 points, despite their clear base in the summation across conflicting groups, do indeed fit the model perfectly even when cumulated, in spite of the fact that the model had been largely formalized before the 1960 election had occurred.

Hence while there is mathematical room for indeterminacy in such combining problems, the practical effects we are likely to encounter are very limited indeed. This is particularly true if we restrict our use of the model, as in this paper, to a formalization which permits estimation of behaviors which would arise in a hypothetical normal case. For distortions in the estimates of net forces as a result of most of these sources of indeterminacy are at their minima when forces balance to the null case. If our use of the model does not extend to attempts at precise quantification of forces in particular extreme instances, then, the dangers of misleading distortions are slight indeed.

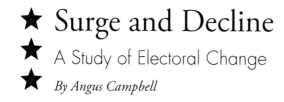

Surge and Decline
A Study of Electoral Change
By Angus Campbell

The study of election statistics has revealed certain impressive regularities in the voting behavior of the American electorate. It has been pointed out by Key[1] that in presidential elections since 1890 sharp upsurges in turnout have invariably been associated with a strong increase in the vote for one party, with little change in the vote for the other. Key also documents the well-known fact that since the development of the two-party system in 1860 the party which has won the Presidency has, with a single exception, always lost seats in the House of Representatives in the off-year election which followed.

The establishment of regularities of this kind through the use of aggregative data typically leaves unanswered the question as to why the regularity exists. We propose in this chapter to demonstrate the manner in which survey data can be used to illuminate the nature of aggregative regularities and to present a theory of political motivation and electoral change which will comprehend both of these seemingly unrelated characteristics of the national vote.

Fluctuations in the turnout and partisanship of the vote in the national elections are primarily determined by short-term political forces which become important for the voter at election time. These forces move the turnout by adding stimulation to the underlying level of political interest of the electorate, and they move the partisanship of the vote from a baseline of "standing commitments" to one or the other of the two parties. In the following pages we will first review a series of propositions which elaborate this general statement and then turn to certain national surveys conducted by the Survey Research Center for relevant empirical evidence.

Short-term political stimulation. Political stimulation in an election derives from several sources: the candidates, particularly those leading the ticket; the policy issues, foreign and domestic; and other circumstances of the moment. The intensity and character of this stimulation vary from one election to the next. There are occasions when none of these components

---

1 V. O. Key, Jr., *Politics, Parties, and Pressure Groups,* Fourth Edition, New York: Thomas Y. Crowell, 1958, p. 638.

of the world of politics seems important to the electorate, resulting in what we will refer to as a *low-stimulus* election. In other years dramatic issues or events may stir a great deal of interest; popular candidates may stimulate widespread enthusiasm. Such an election, in which the electorate feels the combined impact of these various pressures, we will speak of as a *high-stimulus* election.

The essential difference between a low-stimulus and a high-stimulus election lies in the importance the electorate attaches to the choice between the various party-candidate alternatives which it is offered. If the alternatives are generally seen as implying no important differences if one candidate or the other is elected, the stimulation to vote will be relatively weak. If the alternatives are seen as implying significantly different consequences, the stimulation to vote will be relatively high.[2] It may be assumed that in every election a certain air of excitement is created by the sheer noise level achieved by the mass media and the party apparatus. This type of direct stimulation undoubtedly has some impact that is independent of the particular alternatives which confront the voter and accounts for some of the variation in turnout from one election to another, but for the most part we may assume that the effectiveness of such stimulation varies in a dependent way with the significance the electorate attaches to the particular election decision at issue.

Underlying political interest. The individual members of the electorate differ substantially in their level of concern with political matters, in their responsiveness to political stimulation, and in the salience of politics in their psychological environment. This level of interest is an enduring personal characteristic. We assume that it typically develops during the process of early socialization and, having reached its ultimate level, persists as a relatively stable attribute of the adult interest pattern. It is not simply a function of social or economic background; people of high and low political interest are found at all levels of the electorate.

Party identification. Political partisanship in the United States derives in large part from a basic psychological attachment to one of the two major political parties. As we have seen in Table 2-1, a large majority of the electorate identify with greater or less intensity as Republicans or Democrats, and this identification is impressively resistant to change. To the extent that they so identify, their political perceptions, attitudes, and acts are influenced in a partisan direction and tend to remain consistently partisan over time. Those members of the electorate without party attachment are free of this influence and are consequently less stable in their partisan positions from year to year.

Turnout. Differences in turnout from election to election are brought about by one or both of two causes, either by changes in the other-than-political circumstances which face the electorate on election day, or by variations in the level of political stimulation to Which the electorate is subjected from one election to the next. The former factor can have only limited influence. We may assume that bad weather or an epidemic may affect the vote in restricted

---

2 Anthony Downs uses the term "expected party differential" to express the degree of importance the voter attaches to the difference between the various party-candidate alternatives offered. See his *Economic Theory of Democracy*, New York: Harper, 1957, Chap. 3.

areas or even nationally on occasion, but such external considerations cannot reasonably be associated with the kind of fluctuation which we know to exist. It is, for example, quite untenable to suppose that the weather or the health of the electorate is always worse in off-year elections than in presidential years. The explanation of these and other fluctuations must lie in the changing motivation of the electorate.

A large proportion of the turnout in any national election consists of people whose level of political interest is sufficiently high to take them to the polls in all national elections, even those in which the level of political stimulation is relatively weak. These "core voters" are joined in a high-stimulus election by additional "peripheral voters," whose level of political interest is lower but whose motivation to vote has been sufficiently increased by the stimulation of the election situation to carry them to the polls. There remains a sizable fraction of the electorate which does not vote even in a high-stimulus election; some of these people are prevented from voting by poor health, failure to meet eligibility requirements, or conflicts of one sort or another. Others do not vote because their level of political interest is so low that no amount of political stimulation will motivate them to vote.

The turnout in any specific election is largely a question of how many of the less interested, less responsive people are sufficiently stimulated by the political circumstances of the moment to make the effort to vote. An election in which a stirring issue or an attractive candidate makes the party-candidate choice seem unusually important may bring these peripheral voters to the polls in large numbers. In an election of lesser apparent importance and weaker total stimulation the participation of these peripheral voters declines, leaving the electoral decision largely to the high-interest core voters. A low-stimulus election is thus not simply a smaller version of a high-stimulus election; in the extent to which the peripheral voters differ from the core voters, the two elections may have quite different characteristics.

Partisanship. The partisan division of the vote in any particular election is the consequence of the summation of partisan forces on the voters. In every election there are superimposed on the underlying orientations the electorate has toward the two parties (party identifications) the contemporary elements of politics which tend to swing voters one way or the other. In a particular election these elements may be relatively weak and have little impact on the electorate. Despite the best efforts of the party publicists, the candidates may have little appeal, and the issues little apparent relevance to the basic interests of the electorate. In such a case the turnout would of course be low, and the division of the vote would approximate the underlying distribution of party identifications. In the absence of strong pressures associated with persons, issues, or circumstances prominent at the moment, party loyalty holds the adherents of the two parties to their respective tickets, and the independent voters divide their vote between the two. In other words, a low-stimulus election tends to follow party lines.

Contemporary events and personalities occasionally assume great importance for the public and exert a strong influence on the vote. The general increase in the motivation to vote in such an election will, as we have said, bring a surge of peripheral voters to the polls. It will also swing the partisan division of the vote toward the party which happens to be advantaged by the circumstances of the moment. It is very unlikely that a political situation which heightens the public's sense of the importance of choosing one party-candidate alternative or another will favor these alternatives equally. The circumstances which create a high-stimulus election may be expected to create simultaneously a strong differential in the attractiveness of the vote alternatives. Increases in turnout will consequently be accompanied by shifts in the partisanship of the vote.[3]

The partisan surge which characterizes a high-stimulus election consists of two components: (1) those peripheral voters for whom the stimulus of highly differentiated party-candidate alternatives provides the needed impetus to move them to the polls and who, depending on the strength of their party identification, are swung toward the ticket of the advantaged party, and (2) those core voters who are drawn from their normal position as Independents or identifiers with the disadvantaged party to the candidate of the party which is advantaged by the political circumstances of the moment. The number of voters who consistently turn out in presidential elections in support of their party's candidates is now sufficiently close to an equal balance between the two parties so that the movement of these two components of the partisan surge will almost certainly determine the outcome of any high-stimulus election.

If a high-stimulus election is followed by a low-stimulus election, the reduction in the general level of political stimulation will result in a decline in the total vote. There will also be a decline in the proportion of the vote received by the party advantaged by the political circumstances of the preceding high-stimulus year. This decline also consists of two components: (1) the dropout of those peripheral voters who had gone to the polls in the previous election, and who had given the advantaged party a majority of their votes, and (2) the return to their usual voting position of those core voters who had moved in the surge year from their normal position to support the advantaged party, the identifiers with the disadvantaged party moving back to the support of that party, and the Independents back to a position between the two parties. Those voters whose normal identification was with the advantaged party would, of course, support it in the high-stimulus election; of these, the less-involved peripheral voters would drop out in the subsequent low-stimulus election, and the core voters would continue to support their party.

The cycle of surge and decline. In the normal flow of events in American politics, fluctuations in turnout and partisanship follow the "natural" cycle which we have described. The long-run stability of the system depends on the underlying division of party loyalties. Short-term circumstances may swing large numbers of voters away from their usual partisanship or from a position of independence, but when the smoke has settled these people strongly tend to return to their former position, thus restoring the party balance to its former level. Only in the most extraordinary national crises has this cycle been broken, and a new balance of party strength created. Such elections, in which a basic realignment of party loyalties occurs, are rare

---

3 We omit from consideration in this chapter shifts in the partisanship of the vote which occur in periods of stable turnout. Substantial shifts of this kind can be found in the history of American elections, as for example in the presidential elections of 1928 and 1932, and they pose interesting questions as to how a shift in the absence of a surge in turnout differs from a shift which accompanies a voting surge. We will be concerned exclusively with the latter type of partisan change in the present discussion.

in American electoral history.[4] For the most part, fluctuations in the vote reflect the passing impact of contemporary events, and the subsequent decline toward the underlying division of partisanship after these events have lost their salience.

The Evidence

The study of individual change requires data from the same persons at different points in time. Such information can best be provided by a panel study covering the period in which the change took place. It can be obtained somewhat less satisfactorily by asking survey respondents to recall their attitudes or behavior at earlier points in time. Two surveys conducted by the Survey Research Center make available data regarding voting patterns which are relevant to our present concerns. The first of these was a study of the presidential election of 1952, in which a national sample of adults living in private households were asked to report their vote for President in 1952 and to recall their vote for President in 1948.[5] The second was a panel study of a similar national sample, interviewed first in 1956 and again in 1958, being asked on each occasion to report their vote in that year.

The presidential election of 1952 presents a unique opportunity for the study of electoral surge.,The election of 1948 had seen one of the lowest turnouts of presidential voters in recent history with only 48.4 million voters. The proportion of eligible voters who turned out lagged far behind the record of peacetime presidential elections prior to the Second World War. In 1952, 61.6 million voters went to the polls, an increase of more than 25 per cent above the total of the previous election. This great surge in turnout was associated, of course, with a tremendous increase in the vote received by the Republican presidential nominee, which far exceeded the increment in the Democratic vote.

The increase in turnout. The movement in the turnout of the vote from 1948 to 1952 was made up of four components. Of our sample interviewed in November 1952, 58 per cent said they had voted in both 1948 and 1952; 6 per cent said they had voted in 1948 but not in 1952; 15 per cent said they had voted in 1952 but not in 1948; and 21 per cent said they had not voted in either election.[6] When we examine the characteristics of these four segments of

---

4 A discussion of maintaining, deviating, and realigning elections is presented in Chapter 4.

5 A detailed report of this study appears in A. Campbell, G. Gurin, and W. E. Miller, *The Voter Decides,* Evanston, Ill.: Row, Peterson, 1954.

6 There is a clear discrepancy between these reports and the election statistics for 1948 and 1952. Survey reports of turnout are always higher than the proportion of total vote to the total adult population, partly because surveys do not cover the institutional, military, and "floating" populations and partly because some respondents report a vote they did not cast. In the present case, the report of the 1952 vote does not appear to be greatly overstated, but the recall of the 1948 vote is more seriously inflated. The proportions saying they voted in both elections or in 1948 but not 1952 are probably both somewhat high. This introduces some distortion in the relative size of the different components of the vote and some restraints on the uses we can make of the data.

the electorate we find that the core voters who had voted in both elections and the peripheral voters who had voted in one election but not the other differed very little in respect to those variables which are usually found to be associated with turnout. In education, income, occupation, and sex the two kinds of voter were very similar, although they differed significantly from the persistent nonvoters in all these respects. The characteristic which does discriminate sharply between the core voters and the peripheral voters is their level of political interest.

Several indicators of political interest are available to us from our interviews; the one which is freest from the impact of the specific election we are studying is the respondent's report on his previous voting history. In the 1952 interview our respondents were asked, "In the elections for President since you have been old enough to vote, would you say that you have voted in all of them, most of them, some of them, or none of them?" We assume that people who vote in all elections, regardless of the highs and lows of political stimulation, must be relatively responsive to political matters, and those who have never voted must be relatively lacking in political interest.

We can also use the respondent's direct statement about his degree of interest in the current campaign. In October 1952 we asked the question, "Some people don't pay much attention to the political campaigns. How about you, would you say that you have been very much interested, somewhat interested, or not much interested in following the political campaigns so far this year?" This question does not give us as clean a measure of long-term interest in political activities as we would like, since it related to the 1952 campaign specifically. The effect of this specific reference almost certainly reduces the range of response we would expect from a more general question, because the impact of current political activities might be expected to raise the interest level of those at the bottom of the range more than those near the top. In other words, the differences we find between the different types of voter would probably be larger if this question were more general in its reference.

When we now compare the levels of interest shown by the four components of the 1956 electorate, we find a very consistent pattern. That part of the electorate which reported voting in both the 1948 and 1952 elections was far more responsive to the stimuli of politics than any of the other groups. This is especially impressive in the report of previous voting: 90 per cent of those who voted in both elections said they had voted in all or most previous presidential elections, as compared to 66 per cent of those who voted in 1948 but not in 1952, 23 per cent of those who voted in 1952 but not 1948, and 6 per cent of those who did not vote in either election. The interest of the 1948–1952 voters in the campaign then current, as expressed by their subjective report, was also higher than that of any of the other groups: 48 per cent of those who voted in both elections said they were "very much interested in the campaign," as compared to 26 per cent of those who voted in 1948 but not 1952, 31 per cent of those who voted in 1952 but not 1948, and 14 per cent of those who did not vote in either election.

On both these measures those people who were responsible for the major part of the difference in turnout between the two elections (the 1952 voters who had not voted in 1948) gave substantially less evidence of high political interest. Although they appear to come from the same strata of society as the more persistent voters, they apparently are drawn from the less concerned and less attentive levels of the stratum to which they belong.

It is clear that the persistent nonvoters, those people whom even the high stimulation of the 1952 campaign could not move to the polls, are not prevented from voting by adventitious considerations of health or weather. For the most part, these people do not vote because their sensitivity to the world of politics is so low that political stimulation does not reach them. As one might expect, they come largely from the low-income and low-education groups. Two-thirds of them are women.

The swing in partisanship. The 1948 election may be taken as the prototype of a low-stimulus presidential election. In the absence of candidates, issues, or circumstances that might have aroused strong public interest in the choice of alternatives, the turnout was low, and the partisanship of the vote was determined largely by the established party loyalties of the voters. Of the total Democratic vote for President in 1948,[7] 74 per cent came from Democratic Party identifiers, 20 per cent from Independents, and 6 per cent from Republican Party identifiers Of the total Republican vote for President in 1948, 71 per cent came from Republican Party identifiers, 23 per cent from Independents, and 6 per cent from Democratic Party identifiers.

The high-stimulus election in 1952 brought to the polls millions of voters who had not voted in 1948 and shifted the partisanship of the vote of a sizable proportion of those who had. We see in Table 3-1 that the two parties received almost equal support among those people who voted for the same party in both years. Although these consistent core voters made up well over half the voters in 1952, the decisive margin for Mr. Eisenhower was provided by two other groups, those who switched from a 1948 vote for Mr. Truman and those who had failed to vote in 1948. The former group appears to have been considerably larger than the latter, although it is likely that the overstatement of the 1948 vote to which we have referred makes our estimate of the number of new voters in 1952 somewhat lower than it actually was. The Democratic Party also appears to have lost a little ground among the small proportion of 1948 voters who did not vote in 1952, but this figure is subject to the same overstatement, and we may assume that this component of the total shift of votes between 1948 and 1952 was not very significant.

We can illuminate the character of these movements considerably if we examine the degree and quality of the customary party identifications of the people in these groups of 1952 voters (Table 3-2). The greatest polarity of party attachment is found among those voters who supported the presidential candidates of the same party in both elections. The fact that the consistent Democratic vote is composed so heavily of Democratic Party identifiers conforms to our supposition regarding the high-stimulus surge. When the political tide is running against a party, it reduces that party to its loyal partisans; the party will lose most of the support it

---

7 All references to voting in 1948 are based on the respondent's recall of this event when interviewed in 1952. Those few individuals who reported having voted for Thurmond or Wallace in 1948 are included in the Democratic vote.

TABLE 3-1 Presidential Votes in 1948 and 1952 as Reported by Survey Research Center Sample in 1952 (N = 1614)

Vote for President in 1948	Vote for President in 1952	Per Cent
Democratic	Democratic	23
Republican	Republican	24
Democratic	Republican	11
Republican	Democratic	1
Democratic	Did not vote	4
Republican	Did not vote	2
Did not vote	Democratic	6
Did not vote	Republican	8
Did not vote	Did not vote	21
		100

may have received at other times from Independent voters or from defectors from the other party. The advantaged party benefits from this partisan movement, particularly among the Independents and weak adherents of the opposite party who are not strongly held by feelings of party loyalty. This gain is apparent in the Democratic-Republican column of Table 3-2.

The party affiliations of the two groups of 1952 voters who had failed to vote in 1948 provide additional evidence of the interaction of party identification and the partisan pressures of a surge year. Those previous nonvoters who came to the support of Stevenson in 1952 were largely Democratic Party identifiers. The high stimulation of the 1952 campaign brought them out of their nonvoting status, but their party loyalty was sufficiently strong to resist the pro-Republican drift of the times. In contrast, the nonvoters who were inspired to vote for Eisenhower came from all party groups. Some of them were indifferent Republicans who had sat out the Dewey campaign; a large number were Independents; there was a sizable number of Democrats, although few of them called themselves "strong" Democrats. None of these people had voted in 1948, but they contributed significantly to the increase in turnout and the Republican surge in 1952.

The fact that only 1 per cent of the electorate in 1952 moved against the Republican tide, from a Republican to a Democratic vote, provides an effective illustration of the nature of a partisan surge. Although the high level of stimulation in 1952 brought some peripheral Democrats to the defense of their party, there was no countervailing Democratic forte beyond that of party loyalty to offset the powerful impact of candidates and issues which advantaged the Republican Party. This we believe to be the basic characteristic of a surge election; the conditions which give rise to a sharp increase in turnout invariably greatly favor one party over the other. The political circumstances which create the surge in turnout also produce the shift in partisanship.

TABLE 3-2 Party Identification of Components of the 1948 and 1952 Vote for President (in per cent)

Party Identification	1948: 1952:	Democratic Democratic (N = 372)	Republican Republican (N-385)	Democratic Republican (N = 172)	Republican Democratic (N = 17)	Did Not Vote Democratic (N = 105)	Did Not Vote Republican (N = 130)
Strong Democrat		48	*	19	(4)	36	5
Weak Democrat		33	4	36	(2)	43	23
Independent		17	23	31	(7)	20	29
Weak Republican		2	28	11	(3)	1	26
Strong Republican		$	45	3	(1)	†	15
Apolitical, other		*	*	†	†	†	2
		100	100	100	100	100	100

* Less than one-half of 1 per cent.

† No cases.

Note. Figures in parentheses are number of persons rather than per cent; number of cases is too small to support reliable estimates.

1956–1958: A Case of Electoral Decline

One of the most dependable regularities of American politics is the vote decline in off-year congressional elections. The turnout in the off-year elections is invariably smaller than in the presidential elections which they follow, usually by a margin of over 25 per cent of the presidential vote. Almost as dependable is the loss which the party which has won the White House in the presidential year suffers in the midyear election that follows. As we have observed, in every off-year election since the Civil War, with the exception of 1934, the presidential party has lost seats in the House of Representatives.

The vote for President in 1956 totaled 62 million; the vote for congressional candidates in 1958 was 45.7 million, a decline of slightly less than 25 per cent from the vote cast two years earlier. President Eisenhower received nearly 58 per cent of the popular vote in 1956. The Republican candidates for Congress in 1958 received 44 per cent of the two-party vote, and the Republican Party lost 47 of the 200 seats it had held in the House of Representatives.

The decline in turnout. The off-year election of 1958 was a low-stimulus election. Within the framework of the American electoral system the off-year congressional contests must always present the electorate with a less intensely charged situation than the presidential elections which precede and follow. The election of a Congressman cannot have the importance to the average citizen that the election of a President has; the expected consequences of the election of one or the other congressional candidate cannot seem as great. Associated with this lesser significance is the fact that party activities are less intense, and the mass media somewhat quieter in off-year elections. The impact of the typical congressional election is considerably more muted than even the least exciting presidential election.

When we examine the components of the electorate in 1956 and 1958 we find the counterparts of the four segments of the electorate we identified in our 1952 survey. Of our panel interviewed in both 1956 and 1958, 56 per cent said they had voted in both elections, 19 per cent said they had voted in 1956 but not in 1958, 4 per cent said they had voted in 1958 but not in 1956, and 21 per cent said they had not voted in either election.[8]

Comparison of the core voters in 1956–1958 with those who voted only in 1956 reveals differences similar to those we observed in the core and peripheral components of the 1952 electorate. Those 1956 voters who dropped out in 1958 had somewhat more distinctive socioeconomic characteristics than the 1948 nonvoters who went to the polls in 1952. As compared to those who voted in both 1956 and 1958 they were of a somewhat lower status in occupation, income, and education. They were also younger. But these differences were small and very much less impressive than the differences in political interest which distinguished these groups: 92 per cent of those who voted in both elections said they had voted in all or most previous

---

8 We again have some problem of overreport of voting in the low-turnout election. This has the effect of understating the size and importance of the group of 1956 voters who dropped out in 1958. However, since the 19 per cent of our sample who place themselves in this category are very unlikely to include individuals who actually voted in 1958, we can regard this as a relatively pure group for analytical purposes, remembering that it is somewhat smaller in size than it should be.

presidential elections, as compared to 60 per cent of those who voted in 1956 but not in 1958, 59 per cent of those who voted in 1958 but not in 1956, and 17 per cent of those who did not vote in either election.[9]

Involvement in the 1956 campaign, as expressed in the interviews in that year, was also much lower among those parts of the electorate which did not vote in either or both elections: 40 per cent of those who voted in both elections said they were "very much interested" in the campaign, as compared to 21 per cent of those who voted in 1956 but not in 1958, 33 per cent of those who voted in 1958 but not in 1956, and 12 per cent of those who did not vote in either election.

Thus it appears that the people who accounted for the decline in the vote in 1958 were politically similar to the people who increased the vote in 1952. They were in-and-out voters, with a very irregular history of previous voting performance and a low level of sensitivity to political affairs. They appear to form a rather inert reservoir of voters, available for service under conditions of high stimulation but not highly motivated by an intrinsic interest in politics. Activated to vote by the highly charged circumstances of the 1956 campaign, they were not sufficiently moved to go to the polls by the lesser impact of the congressional election. Without them, the core voters who had made up 75 per cent of the vote in 1956 contributed virtually the entire vote (93 per cent) in 1958.

The swing in partisanship. Like the presidential election of 1948, the congressional election of 1958 attracted a relatively low turnout. Without strong national candidates, pressing issues or circumstances to move the electorate, the voting decision was determined largely by the standing party loyalties of those voters sufficiently concerned with politics to go to the polls. The sources of the vote which the two parties commanded in 1958 resemble those from which they drew their vote in 1948, although there was apparently more crossing of party lines in the latter election than there had been in the former.[10] Of the total vote for Democratic Congressmen in 1958, 69 per cent came from Democratic Party identifiers, 20 per cent came

---

9 The differences in these data from those obtained in 1952 derive in large part from the fact that in this case we are grouping voters according to their performance in a presidential and a congressional election, and in the previous case we were grouping voters according to their performance in two successive presidential elections. The 1952 data are further influenced by the fact that about one-fourth of those 1952 voters who had not voted in 1948 were too young to vote in that year. Since the 1956–1958 sample is a panel, there is no comparable group in the 1958 data.

10 A number of factors might be expected to contribute to party crossing in the congressional elections the personal impact of the Congressman in his district is not likely to equal that a highly publicized candidate, but it may be rather intense within a more limited range individual voters. Over time a congressman may establish suffcient personal contacts to have a visible effect on the vote. The repeated reelection of Congressmen in some districts tends to give them the character of nonpartisan fixtures: they attract cross-party votes which a less well-established candidate on the same ticket would not get. Of course, in those districts where a candidate runs without opposition, members of the minority party must cross party lines if they are to vote at all.

from Independents, and 11 per cent came from Republican Party identifiers. Of the total vote for Republican Congressmen in 1958, 65 per cent came from Republican Party identifiers, 26 per cent came from Independents, and 9 per cent came from Democratic Party identifiers.

The substantial shift from the comfortable majority which Mr. Eisenhower received in 1956 to the Republican congressional defeat in 1958 was almost wholly accounted for by two segments of the electorate, that is, those Eisenhower supporters in 1956 who switched to a Democratic vote in 1958 and the considerable number of people who voted for President in 1956 but failed to vote in 1958. The number of 1958 voters who had not voted in 1956 and of voters moving against the tide (Democratic to Republican) was much smaller than the two other groups (Table 3-3).

The similarities between Table 3-1 and Table 3-3 are striking, despite the fact that Table 3-1 compares succeeding presidential elections, and Table 3-3 compares a presidential election with a congressional election. We now find that when we distribute the party identifications of the people making up the major components of the 1956–1958 electorate, a table results which closely resembles Table 3-2 (see Table 3-4). We find again that those voters who support the same party through both low-turnout and high-turnout elections consist largely of people who identify themselves with that party. These are the core voters on whom each party relies. They were joined in 1956–1958 by a sizable number of Independent voters, but by very few people who identified with the opposite party.

Those people who fail to vote in a low-stimulus election after having been brought to the polls in a preceding high-stimulus election provide a counterpart to those peripheral voters in Table 3-2 who did not vote in 1948 but did turn out in 1952. We see that they have comparable partisan characteristics. The smaller group, people who had voted for Stevenson in 1956 but did not vote in 1958, had strong Democratic Party attachments and closely re-sembled the 1948 non-voters who went to the polls in 1952 to vote for Stevenson. Those 1956

TABLE 3-3 Partisanship of the Vote in 1956 and 1958 (N = 1,3Si4)

Vote for President in 1956	Vote for Congressman in 1958	Per Cent
Democratic	Democratic	22
Republican	Republican	22
Democratic	Republican	2
Republican	Democratic	11
Democratic	Did not vote	6
Republican	Did not vote	12
Did not vote	Democratic	3
Did not vote	Republican	1
Did not vote	Did not vote	21
		100

TABLE 3-4 Party Identification of Components of the Vote for President in 1956 and Vote for Congressman in 1958 (in per cent)

Party Identification	1956: 1958: Democratic Democratic (N = 303)	Republican Republican (N = 294)	Democratic Republican (N = 21)	Republican Democratic (N = 144)	Democratic Did Not Vote (N = 89)	Republican Did Not Vote (N = 159)
Strong Democrat	50	1	(4)	13	41	6
Weak Democrat	31	4	(9)	27	37	17
Independent	15	26	(6)	30	17	36
Weak Republican	3	25	(2)	20	5	27
Strong Republican		44	†	8	†	14
Apolitical, other	1	†	†	2	†	t
	100	100	—	100	100	100

* Less than one-half of 1 per cent,

† No cases.

Note. Figures in parentheses are number of persons rather than per cent; number of cases is too small to support reliable estimates.

Eisenhower voters who failed to vote in 1958, by contrast, were distinguished by having very few strong identifiers with either party. They include a high proportion of Independents and weak identifiers from each party, just as did the group of people who did not vote in 1948 but who turned out for Eisenhower in 1952. In all likelihood these two groups in 1958 consisted largely of people who had also failed to vote in the congressional election of 1954. They had been brought to the polls as peripheral voters by the stimulation of the 1956 election but dropped out again because of the weaker stimulus of the 1958 election. They contribute the major part of the surge and decline in turnout in these successive elections. Since these people tend to come to the polls more favorably disposed to one party than the other, they contribute to the partisan shift in a surge election, and their failure to vote in the succeeding election tends to reduce the proportion of the vote the previously advantaged party receives.

The other component of the shift in partisanship in both the 1952 and 1958 elections is the core voters who move from support of one party to the other. We saw in Table 3-2 that in 1952 the bulk of these people, moving then from a Democratic to a Republican vote, were Independents and weak partisans, and we see in Table 3-4 that the comparable group, moving in the opposite political direction, had the same characteristics. We assume that the large number of Democrats in the 1958 group were moving back to their "normal" party position after having supported Mr. Eisenhower in the 1956 election. The number of Republican identifiers in this group is larger than we would have anticipated and suggests that the partisan movement in 1958 cannot be entirely attributed to a normal decline toward standing party loyalties after the displacement of the vote in a surge year.[11]

Ticket Splitting and the Congressional Vote

A comparison of the vote for President and the vote for Congressman in the ensuing off-year election does not fully describe the movement of voters in this two-year election sequence. Because of the option which the American voter has of splitting his ticket, the relation of the presidential vote to the subsequent congressional vote may be very different from the relation of the vote for Congressman in a presidential year to the vote for Congressman in the subsequent off year. If we examine the consistency with which the 1956–1958 voting groups supported the ticket of the presidential candidate they preferred in 1956, we find convincing support for our earlier observations regarding the characteristics of these groups, and we discover a pattern of change in the congressional votes in the two elections quite different from what we found in the comparison of successive presidential and congressional votes.

Table 3-5 presents the 1956 voting patterns of the core and peripheral voters in the 1956 and 1958 elections. We see again that those voters who withstood the Republican surge in the 1956 election were strongly committed to the support of the Democratic Party, as indicated

---

11 Losses going beyond the normal decline have occurred in other off-year elections and may be taken to reflect the development of circumstances unfavorable to the presidential party in the first two years of its term.

TABLE 3-5 1956 Voting Patterns of Major Voting Groups in the Vote for President in 1956 and Vote for Congressman in 1958 (in per cent)

1956 Voting Pattern	1956: 1958:	Democratic Democratic (N = 289)	Republican Republican (N = 286)	Democratic Republican (N = 21)	Republican Democratic (N = 140)	Democratic Did Not Vote (N = 77)	Republican Did Not Vote (N = 143)
Voted straight ticket at national and local levels		68	60	(10)	26	66	46
Voted straight ticket at national level only		20	20	(5)	15	8	17
Split ticket at the national level		7	15	(6)	49	8	24
Did not vote complete ticket		3	1	*	3	13	8
Other		2	4	*	7	5	5
		100	100	*	100	100	100

* No cases.

Note. Figures in parentheses are number of persons rather than per cent; number of cases is too small to support reliable estimates.

by their high level of straight-ticket voting. Fewer than 1 in 10 of the voters in the two major Democratic groups, those who voted for Stevenson in 1956 and a Democratic Congressman in 1958 and those who voted for Stevenson in 1956 but did not vote in 1958, split their 1956 vote at the national level. The consistent Republican voters also had a high record of straight-ticket voting, although not quite as high as the consistent Democrats because of the large number of Independents included among them. The other Republican group, the Eisenhower voters who did not go to the polls in 1958, had a notably smaller proportion of straight-ticket voters and a much larger proportion who split their tickets at the national level. We have seen that this group of peripheral voters who came to the polls in 1956 to vote for Mr. Eisenhower was made up of people of heterogeneous party background, including many Independents and a considerable number of weakly identified Democrats. Many of these latter people obviously did not go all the way to the Republican position. Thirteen per cent of this group (not shown specifically in Table 3-5) voted for Mr. Eisenhower but otherwise supported a straight Democratic ticket.

The 1956 Eisenhower voters who voted for a Democratic Congressman in 1958 present an especially interesting picture of ballot splitting. As we have seen, these core voters consist very largely of Democrats and Independents. Only a quarter of this group voted a straight Republican ticket in 1956, although they all voted for Mr. Eisenhower. A fifth of them voted a straight Democratic ticket except for President, and an additional quarter or more failed to vote a consistent Republican ticket at the national level. They responded to the personal appeal of Mr. Eisenhower as the Republican candidate in 1956, but they did not accept his party. When Mr. Eisenhower was not on the ballot in 1958, these people moved back to their usual party positions.

It is significant that both groups of peripheral voters, those who voted for either Eisenhower or Stevenson in 1956 but did not vote in 1958, contain a number of people who reported that they failed to vote a complete ticket on their presidential ballot. These are the only groups in which such voters appear in any significant frequency. This evidence of limited involvement in the vote is consistent with our earlier picture of the peripheral voter. Having less intrinsic interest in political matters and coming to the polls only when there is strong stimulation to do so, their concern about voting is inherently weak, in contrast to those voters who go to the polls whatever the circumstances.

The decline from the Republican Party's proportion of the presidential vote in 1956 to its proportion of the congressional vote in 1958 was associated with a considerably smaller decline from its congressional vote in 1956 to its congressional vote in 1958. As our data on ticket splitting make clear, the Republican congressional candidates in 1956 received far fewer votes than their standard-bearer, Mr. Eisenhower; they did not in fact achieve a majority of the popular vote. The decline of their congressional vote in 1958 from their congressional vote in 1956 was much smaller than the decline from the high mark of Mr. Eisenhower's vote, and the components of this decline differ somewhat from those of the decline from the presidential vote (Table 3-6).

It is clear that the dropout of the peripheral voters in 1958 had very little effect on the distribution of congressional votes in that year, since, at the same time they were giving Mr.

TABLE 3-6 Partisanship in the Congressional Vote in 1956 and 1953 (N = 1301)

Vote for Congressman in 1956	Vote for Congressman in 1958	Per Cent
Democratic	Democratic	25
Republican	Republican	19
Democratic	Republican	3
Republican	Democratic	6
Democratic	Did not vote	9
Republican	Did not vote	8
Did not vote	Democratic	4
Did not vote	Republican	2
Did not vote	Did not vote	24
		100

Eisenhower a 2-to-l margin of their votes in 1956, they were dividing their votes for Congressman about equally between the two parties. We would ordinarily expect this component of the vote to have greater importance than it had in 1958. In most elections that the electorate is strongly motivated to vote, we would expect the congressional vote for the advantaged party to swing along with the presidential vote. It was precisely the failure of this joint movement to occur, however, which made the 1956 election remarkable and resulted, for the first time in over a hundred years, in the election of a President of one party and both houses of Congress of the other. The Republican surge in 1956 was largely an Eisenhower surge.

In the absence of any influence from the dropout of 1956 voters, the major contribution to the rather small decline in the vote received by Republican congressional candidates in the two elections was made by party switchers. There were movements in both directions from one election to the next, but there were twice as many changes from Republican to Democratic candidates as from Democratic to Republican. It is probable that part of the 3 percentage point Democratic advantage in this shift reflects the "coattail" effect which Mr. Eisenhower exerted on the 1956 election.[12] Some of these people were Democrats who had gone over to Mr. Eisenhower in 1956 and had voted his party ticket. But when Mr. Eisenhower was no longer on the ballot in 1958 they returned to their usual party choice.

The fact that the off-year elections typically reduce the congressional strength of the party which has won the Presidency two years earlier is readily understandable within the terms of our description of surge and decline. As long as there is no significant shift in the distribution of standing party attachments within the electorate, the decline in turnout in an off-year

---

12 Additional coattail influence was undoubtedly felt among those people who voted for Eisenhower and a Republican Congressman in 1956 but did not vote in 1958. For a discussion of the nature of coattail voting, see W. E. Miller, "Presidential Coattails," *Public Opinion Quarterly*, 19, 353–368 (1955).

election will almost certainly be associated with a decline in the proportion of the vote received by the presidential party. If the partisan pressures of the presidential election have induced any movement toward the winning candidate among the Independents and members of the opposing party, this movement will recede in the following congressional election, partly because of the dropout of voters who had supported the ticket of the winning presidential candidate and partly because of the return to their usual voting positions of those Independents and opposing partisans who had switched during the presidential year.

The one clear reversal of this pattern which has occurred in the last hundred years is instructive. The House of Representatives that was elected with Mr. Roosevelt in 1932 had 310 Democratic members; in the 1934 elections this majority was extended to 319 members, although the turnout in 1934 was approximately 18 per cent lower than it had been in 1932. According to our understanding of the nature of electoral decline, this could not have happened if the basic division of party loyalties was constant during this period. There is substantial reason to believe, however, that the distinguishing feature of American politics in the early 1930's was a realignment in the basic strength of the two parties. The economic collapse associated with the Hoover Administration brought millions of Independents and Republicans into the Democratic Party, not as temporary supporters but as long-term committed adherents. The Democratic gain in the 1934 election reflected a period of political conversion that gradually changed the Democratic Party from the minority party, which it had been since at least 1896, into the majority party of today. Such mass realignments of party identification, however, are very infrequent in American politics; more commonly the distribution of party loyalties remains stable despite the ups and downs of individual elections. Swings away from the basic division of party loyalties in high-turnout elections tend to swing back in the low-turnout elections which follow.

Conclusion

We have presented a theory of the nature of electoral change that is specifically intended to comprehend and explain two well-established regularities of American voting behavior, the highly partisan character of upsurges in turnout in presidential elections and the characteristic loss which the party winning the Presidency suffers in the ensuing off-year elections. We have proposed that fluctuations in turnout and partisanship result from a combination of short-term political forces, superimposed On the underlying level of political interest and on the long-standing psychological attachments of the electorate to the two parties. We have been able to present data from two election sequences, one illustrating electoral surge and the other decline. Additional evidence from other electoral situations would obviously be desirable, but the data in hand give convincing support to our understanding of the dynamics of voting change.

Our discussion has dealt entirely with electoral change within the American political system. We think it likely that the basic concepts which we have relied on in this analysis—political stimulation, political interest, party identification, core voters and peripheral voters, and high- and low-stimulus elections—are equally applicable to the understanding of political behavior in other democratic systems. But it is apparent that political behavior in other societies takes place within different institutional forms than those in the United States, and that they would have to be taken into account if we were to attempt an analysis in those societies comparable to the one presented here.

★ The Mainstream and Polarization
★ Effects

★ *By John Zaller*

With the national inflation rate approaching the then-startling level of 7 percent, President Nixon went on television in late summer 1971 to announce a surprise decision to impose wage and price controls on the economy. Although such controls were a major departure from administration policy, the decision was immediately hailed by commentators across the political spectrum as a necessary step in the battle against inflation.

By good luck, there exist excellent data on the effect of Nixon's speech on public attitudes. A Columbia University survey of political activists happened to be in the field at the time of Nixon's announcement, and Gallup surveys on price controls bracketed the speech. The Columbia study found, first of all, that the speech had little effect on Democratic activists, who tended to favor wage and price controls even before Nixon spoke. But the effect of the speech on Republican activists was dramatic. Virtually overnight, support for controls among Republican activists shot up from 37 percent to 82 percent, a rise of some 45 percentage points (Barton, 1974–5). The Gallup surveys, meanwhile, showed that the public as a Whole became about 10 percentage points more favorable toward price controls in the weeks following the Nixon speech.

This case suggests that a popular president backed by a unified Washington community can have a powerful effect on public opinion, especially that part of the public that is most attentive to politics.

This is the first of a series of chapters that aims at accounting for the effects of such elite communications on mass attitudes. In this chapter we examine two simple ideal typical situations, one type in which elites achieve a consensus or near consensus on a value or policy, so that virtually all communications take the same side of the given issue, and another type in which elites disagree along partisan or ideological lines, so that there is a roughly even flow of communications on both sides of the issue. The case of wage and price controls is an example of the first type of situation, and the nearly unified support of American elites for the war in Vietnam in 1964 is another. The sharply ideological division of elites over Vietnam in the late

1960s is an example of the second. The RAS model, as we shall see, leads us to expect that these two types of situations will have regular and predictable effects on public attitudes.

Later chapters will examine more complicated cases, ones in which the pattern of elite messages switches from mainly consensual to mainly conflictual, and others in which elites are divided, but in which the relative intensity of communications changes over time. Such changes in the flow of elite communications produce quite interesting and nonintuitive patterns of change in mass attitude reports, as will become apparent.

Mainstream Effect

What, we may now ask, would be the theoretically expected effect on public opinion if elites across the political spectrum were to achieve a consensus in support of a particular "mainstream" policy? Or, to ask the same question in the language of the model: What would be the expected effect on public opinion if virtually all the persuasive messages carried in political media on a particular policy were favorable to that policy, and if there were no cueing messages to alert people that the policy was inconsistent with their values?

Axiom A1 suggests, first of all, that the greater a citizen's level of political awareness, the greater the likelihood of reception of persuasive messages on this hypothetical mainstream issue. If all of the cueing messages on this policy were favorable, no one would have any basis via A2 for resisting it. From this we can deduce that the greater a person's level of political awareness, the greater the number of mainstream messages the person would internalize in the form of considerations and hence, all else equal, the greater the person's level of expressed support for the mainstream policy (D25).

Researchers working on a variety of substantive problems have reported support for this implication of the model. In fact, though using different vocabularies, several have made roughly the same argument as here. For example, in *Public Opinion and American Democracy* (1961), V. O. Key, Jr., wrote that a person's level of formal education may be an indicator of the extent to which the person has been influenced by society's traditional or "official" values. Key wrote:

> Probably a major consequence of education for opinion consists in the bearing of education on the kinds of influences to which a person is subjected throughout his life. The more extended the educational experience, the more probable it is that a person will be exposed to the discussions of issues as they arise. When, as so often occurs, the current discussion is heavily loaded on one side, it might be expected that this educationally conditioned exposure would have some bearing on the direction of opinion. (1961: p. 341)

Noting that education was associated with greater support for racial equality, private health insurance, and tolerance of nonconformists, Key explained that "formal education may serve to indoctrinate people into the more-or-less official political values of the culture" (p. 340).

Writing a few years later, Gamson and Modigliani (1966) noted a substantial correlation between political information and support for the government's foreign policies (see also Sigelman and Conover, 1981). Their explanation for this paralleled Key's argument. Information measured "one's attachment to the mainstream and the resultant exposure to influences such as the mass media" (1966: p. 189). McClosky and Brill's (1983) argument that education promotes the "social learning" of libertarian ideals, and Mueller's (1973) claim that better educated persons were more likely to support the Vietnam War because they were better "followers" of official policy likewise appeal to the notion that exposure to "mainstream" values tends to enhance support for them. More recently, the tendency of better educated persons to be more opposed to the quarantining of AIDS victims (Sniderman et al., 1991) appears to reflect the internalization of a medical consensus that such action is unnecessary to prevent the spread of the disease (Colby and Cook, 1991).[1]

In a comparative study of the United States and Britain, Cain, Ferejohn, and Fiorina (1987) turned up a finding that nicely illustrates the "indoctrinating effect" that exposure to a particular elite culture often produces. Citizens in both countries were asked whether elected representatives should "support the position their parties take when something comes up for a vote, or should they make up their own minds regardless of how their parties want them to vote." In Britain, where Parliament depends on a high degree of party discipline, college-educated persons were more likely than those with only high school education to say that representatives should hew the party line. But in the United States, with its antiparty and individualist political tradition, college-educated persons were more likely to say that representatives should vote their own opinions. Thus, the better educated in each country are the more faithful adherents of their country's respective national traditions.

If the mainstream argument is correct, correlations between awareness and support for a policy should be strongest when elite consensus is strongest and less strong when elite consensus is less strong or nonexistent *(D25)*. Much published evidence (to be supplemented later in this chapter) supports this expectation. For example, Mueller notes that the correlation between education and support for the Vietnam War was strong early in the war, when most elites supported it, and weak in the late phases of the war, when party and ideological elites became deeply divided. In a systematic test of this hypothesis in the domain of civil liberties, McClosky and Brill (1983: p. 421) classified more than 100 civil liberties items according to the degree of support for the libertarian option in relevant Supreme Court decisions and in the attitudes of some 2,000 elites they had surveyed. They found that for items on which the Court and other elites had strongly endorsed the civil liberties position, members of the general public who had attended college were, on average, 24 percentage points more libertarian than were those with less than a high school education. Yet education had a progressively weaker effect in inducing support for libertarian policies as elite support for them declined, until finally, education had a slightly negative association with support for civil liberties on those (few) items on which

---

1 This is my interpretation of the education effect reported by Spiderman, Brody, and Tetlock (1991, chap. 4). For a further discussion of this point, see Chapter 12.

the pre-Rehnquist Court and most elites took an antilibertarian position (for example, civil disobedience).[2]

It is widely supposed that political awareness-whether measured by knowledge, participation, or education-engenders resistance to elite influence rather than, as assumed in the mainstream model, susceptibility to it. As will become clear in Chapters 7–11, this supposition has some validity. Political awareness does appear to engender resistance to the political communications of governing authorities. But awareness does so less by engendering resistance per se than by increasing the person's sensitivity to the communications of countervailing elites, especially the ideological opponents of the regime. Thus, for example, it will turn out in Chapter 9 that a major source of opposition to the Vietnam War was the exposure of politically aware citizens to antiwar communications that were too faint to be picked up by the less aware. The notion that politically aware persons resist all forms of political persuasion is highly dubious.

One other comment. There are in every society ideas on which virtually everyone agrees. In such cases, the idea is unlikely to become the object of studies of public opinion, except perhaps in studies of culture. Such "motherhood issues" in the United States might include maintenance of free elections, tax-supported public schools, and state-organized attempts to repulse an invading enemy. The mainstream model is less useful for policies of this type than for policies on which there is popular reluctance to go along with an elite consensus, such as tolerance of disliked groups, or support for war when the nation is not immediately threatened.

The Polarization Effect

There are, of course, many cases in which political elites heatedly disagree, so that no "mainstream" exists. In cases of this type, the RAS model leads us to expect quite different patterns of mass attitudes.

To see why, let us assume a situation in which elites are roughly evenly divided on a partisan issue, with one partisan camp sponsoring persuasive messages favoring the liberal position and the other sponsoring messages in support of the conservative position. We further assume that each camp sponsors cueing messages indicating why the given policy is or is not consistent with liberal (or conservative) values. Finally, let us assume that all of these messages are equally intense in that a person at a given level of political awareness would be equally likely to encounter and take in any one of them.

Within the general public, increases in awareness will lead to increased reception of persuasive messages favoring both the liberal position and the conservative position (from Al) and also increased reception of dyeing messages concerning the issue. Let us focus first on how this affects liberals. Since politically aware liberals will be likely to possess cueing messages that enable them to see the ideological implications of the messages they receive, they will be likely to reject conservative arguments on this issue; these cueing messages will not, however,

---

2 See also Chong, McClosky, and Zaller, 1984.

impede their internalization of liberal messages. Less politically aware liberals, by contrast, will be Exposed to few persuasive messages, and, owing to their low reception of cueing messages and the lower accessibility of these cues in memory, will be less selective about the persuasive messages they internalize.

In consequence of this dynamic, the most aware liberals will fill their heads, so to speak, with a large number of considerations that are, on balance, favorable to the liberal side of the issue. Less aware liberals, for their part, will fill their heads with a smaller number of considerations, and these considerations will not consistently favor the liberal side of the issue.

The same argument, *mutatis mutandis,* applies to conservatives. Highly aware conservatives should fill their heads with mostly conservative considerations, while less aware conservatives should fill their heads with a smaller number of considerations that are less consistently conservative.

Our expectation, then, is that for cases in which there is a roughly even flow of opposing partisan messages, the ratio of ideologically consistent considerations to ideologically inconsistent ones should increase as political awareness increases.

Figure 4.1 has already confirmed this expectation. As shown there, the ratio of consistent considerations to total considerations increases from about .5 among the least informed persons to about .80 among the most informed. Two of the slopes in Figure 4.1 are statistically significant at the .01 level and the third is significant at the .10 level.[3]

One may expect that an increasing ratio of ideologically consistent to inconsistent considerations should translate into differences in people's attitude statements: More aware liberals will be more likely to call to mind considerations favorable to the liberal position and hence will be more likely to support it. Less aware liberals will be less likely to be able to recall considerations of any kind, which will lead to higher no-opinion rates, and less likely to endorse the liberal position when they do offer an opinion.[4]

The logic of this argument again applies equally to conservatives. That is, increases in awareness make mass conservatives increasingly likely to make conservative attitude statements when asked about the issue.

Thus, in the case of an evenly divided partisan elite and a balanced flow of partisan communications, the effect of political awareness is to promote the *polarization* of attitude reports as

---

3 The relationships depicted in Figure 4.1, however, apply to the sample as a whole; closer inspection of the data reveals that the expected relationships hold only for liberals, where they hold very strongly. For conservatives, there appears to be little change in the ratio of consistent-to-inconsistent considerations as awareness increases. The reason for this complication appears to be that the assumed conditions for the test have not been met, namely, a roughly even division of elite support for the opposing policy alternatives. For none of the three options is the division of mass opinion close to 50–50, as it ought to be in the case of an equal elite division. See Chapter 8 for further tests of the effect of awareness and ideology on the internalization of considerations.

4 See Krosnick and Milburn, 1990, for a review of the evidence on the effects of political awareness on no-opinion rates.

more aware liberals gravitate more reliably to the liberal position and more aware conservatives gravitate more reliably to the conservative position *(D26).*

Empirical support for the polarization effect

Much empirical evidence supports the expectation of an awareness-induced polarization of liberals and conservatives on partisan issues. The polarizing effect of political awareness on partisan (as against mainstream) issues was first noted by George Belknap and Angus Campbell (1951–2) and was incorporated into the Michigan school's classic, *The American Voter* (Campbell et al., 1960: Pp. 186, 207). Using different theoretical vocabularies, Gamson and Modigliani (1966) and Chong, McClosky, and Zaller (1984) have noted the same effect. They examine public attitudes toward numerous issues on which elites disagree, issues ranging from foreign policy to civil liberties to welfare to race to economic policy. In each case, increases in political awareness were associated with a sharper polarization of attitudes between liberals (or Democrats), on one side, and conservatives (or Republicans), on the other.[5]

The data in Figure 6.1 illustrate both the mainstream and polarization effects of political awareness. When, in 1964, American elites nearly all supported the Vietnam War, increases in awareness led nonelite liberals and conservatives to become more supportive of the "mainstream" war policy. Yet when, in 1970, American elites had become deeply divided about the war, increases in awareness are associated with greater polarization of the attitudes of mass liberals and conservatives.[6]

The Persian Gulf War affords another opportunity to observe both the mainstream and the polarization effect. From the Iraqi invasion of Kuwait in August 1990 through the fall 1990 congressional election, there was only light criticism of President Bush's handling of the crisis and, in particular, virtually no articulate opposition to the policy of sending U.S. forces to the region. Thus, as J. W. Apple wrote on the eve of the election,

> [A] midterm election campaign has taken place with war threatening in the Persian Gulf, and ... the major foreign policy issue confronting the nation has generated almost no debate among the candidates about what the U.S. should do.

---

5 In Gamson and Modigliani, these findings are the basis for a "cognitive consistency" model of opinion formation; in McClosky et al., they are the basis for a "contested norms" model of opinionating. Yet in both cases, the empirical regularity being explained, as well as the operational constructs in the models, are the same as in the Belknap and Campbell polarization model.

6 To validate these claims concerning elite consensus and division, I asked a research assistant to classify cover stories on Vietnam in *Newsweek* and *Time.* In 1964 prewar cover stories outnumbered antiwar ones by a margin of approximately 3 to 1; in 1970, the ratio was close 1 to 1. (See also Hallin, 1986.)

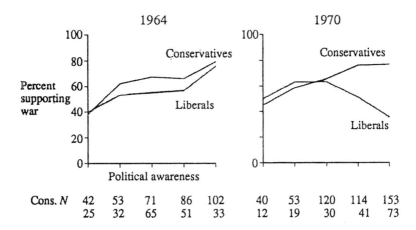

Figure 6.1. An illustration of the mainstream and polarization models. Liberals are defined as persons who rated liberals fifteen or more points higher than conservatives on separate 100-point feeling thermometers; conservatives are persons who exhibited the reverse pattern. Persons supporting the war are those who said either that the United States should "keep troops in Vietnam but try to end the fighting," which was the position of both the Johnson and Nixon administrations, or that the U.S. should take a stronger stand on the war. The awareness measure is described in the Measures Appendix. *Source:* 1964 and 1970 CPS surveys.

Instead, President Bush has traded insults with Saddam Hussein of Iraq, and the Democrats have barely mentioned the subject. *(New York Times,* 6 November 1991, p. A1)

Two days after the election, however, Bush announced a decision to send several hundred thousand additional troops to the gulf. This decision sparked strong congressional criticism, leading to congressional hearings in which administration policy was harshly criticized and later to a congressional vote on a war policy resolution. As in the Vietnam case, Democrats were the most salient critics of the administration's hawkish policies and Republicans were the most salient defenders.

In view of this, we should expect, in the period before Congress reacted critically to Bush's troop announcement, to find evidence of the mainstream effect; after criticism began, we should expect to observe the polarization pattern.

By good luck, the 1990 National Election Study went into the field on the day after the election and was able to complete more than 250 interviews before congressional criticism of Bush's military buildup began. It also carried a question asking whether "we did the right thing in sending U.S. military forces to the Persian Gulf, or should we have stayed out?"

Results, which are derived from a maximum likelihood logistic regression that controls for political awareness, party attachment, gender, race, and Jewish ethnicity are shown in Figure

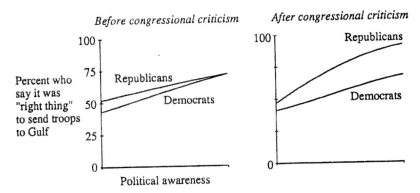

Figure 6.2. Partisans become more polarized over time on "right to send troops." Estimates are derived from coefficients in Table 6.3. *Source:* 1990 NES survey.

6.2.[7] (The coefficients on which the figure is based are in Table 6.3 of the appendix to this chapter.) As expected, the data betray little evidence of partisan polarization in the period prior to the congressional criticism of Bush's policies, but clear polarization afterward. Public division does not appear to be as sharp as in the Vietnam case, but this is probably because elite polarization on Persian Gulf policy did not approach that of the Vietnam period in terms of either duration or intensity.

Before continuing the analysis of opinion on Persian Gulf policy, I must discuss a methodological issue. In creating Figure 6.2 from the coefficients in a logistic regression model, I had to make certain coding decisions. For example, to show the effects of political awareness, I manipulated scores from roughly the 1st percentile on political awareness to the 98th percentile. Since I need to make many similar decisions about how to create graphs from coefficients in the next several chapters, I want to standardize my procedures in an intelligible set of conventions. A summary of these conventions, which will be used for the rest of the book, is given in the accompanying box.

The 1990 NES survey carried one other question which is useful for gauging public opinion on the gulf crisis. It reads:

Which of the following do you think we should do now in the Persian Gulf:

Pull out U.S. forces entirely.

Try harder to find a diplomatic solution.

Tighten the economic embargo.

---

7 Democrats and Republicans in the figure are constructed as persons with a score of ± 1.3 on the party variable, where party ranges from—2 (strong Republican) to +2 (strong Democrat). Awareness scores in the figure run from-1.8 SD to +2.57 SD.

Take tougher military action.

Conventions of graphical analysis

For graphs showing the relationship between political awareness, political predispositions, and a political attitude or attitude change, the following conventions will apply in the remainder of the book:

Basic design. In all cases, political awareness will be treated as the principal independent variable and plotted against the **jc**-axis. The dependent variable, usually the probability of a political attitude or attitude change, the will be plotted against the y-axis, as in Figure 6.2. The effect of differences in political dispositions (such as, being a Democrat rather than a Republican) will be shown by separate lines within the graphs, as in Figure 6.2.

Range of political awareness. Except as noted, graphs depict the simulated effect of moving from about the 1st percentile to about the 98th percentile on political awareness. This range leaves about 1 percent of the cases outside each endpoint, though, of course, lumpiness in the data makes it impossible to achieve this range in every case. Because different awareness scales have different skews, the range of political awareness scores will not always correspond to a particular z-score range, such as ±2 SD. The particular z-score ranges used in the simulations will be provided in footnotes.

Range of simulated attitude scores. With one clearly noted exception, graphs showing probabilities or proportions will use a scale of 0 to 1.0. When means are used, graphs will reflect the range of mean values in the data. Thus, in the case of means, the ranges can vary from figure to figure. However, unless explicitly noted, identical Scales will be used in figures that are being compared to one another.

Range of predispositional variables. Throughout the analysis, party attachment is coded from—2 (strong Republican) to—1 (weak or independent Republican) to +1 (weak or independent Democrat) to +2 strong Democrat, with all others assigned to the score of zero. In graphs that depict the effect of being a Republican or Democrat, partisans are simulated by scores of either—1.3 or + 1.3, as appropriate. The effects of other predispositional measures (such as equalitarianism, hawkishness) are simulated differently in different cases, depending on how many measures are available for use in a given model. For example, if only one measure is used in a model, the range may be ±2 SD for that variable; if three measures are used, their joint effect-that is, the effect of identical movements on all three variables-will be depicted over a smaller range. The exact values are provided in each case. The aim will be to approximate the raw data, insofar as the raw data can be directly observed.

All but the first of these options imply support for the basic United States policy of military involvement in the Persian Gulf. Since, with the possible exception of the congressional Black Caucus, virtually all of Bush's elite critics accepted this policy, we should expect to find that, among the public, political awareness I associated with greater support for keeping U.S. forces

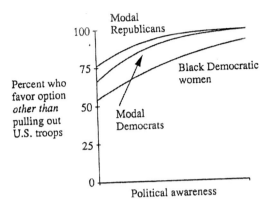

Figure 6.3. Support for keeping U.S. troops in the Persian Gulf. Estimates are derived from coefficients in Table 6.3. *Source:* **1990 NES survey.**

in the Gulf-which is to say, greater levels of rejection of the "pullout" option in favor of one of the other three response alternatives. This expectation is confirmed in Figure 6.3 (see Table 6.3, the chapter appendix, for coefficients). Even within the group most resistant to using military action against Iraq-black Democratic women-rejection of the pullout option rises from about 54 percent in the lowest awareness category to about 92 percent in the highest category.[8] The trends in Figure 6.3 were about the same throughout the period of the survey.[9]

It is difficult to be certain what to expect from the three response options-more diplomacy, a tighter embargo, and tougher military action-that I have counted as implying support for military involvement in the Gulf. Certainly, Democrats en masse would be expected to reject the choice of "tougher military action," since the Democratic party in Congress was clearly identified with opposition to this idea. The problem is that it is not clear that Republicans should be expected to embrace it. For Bush's public position, especially in the early months of the crisis, was that an embargo, in combination with skilled diplomacy, would make it possible to avoid the use of force. In mid-December, however, the Bush administration rejected a proposed January 12th meeting in Baghdad on the grounds that it was too near the United Nations deadline for Iraqi withdrawal from Kuwait to be useful for averting military action. By that point, therefore, it was clear at least that *willingness* to use force was a key feature of Bush policy. One might therefore expect that at about that time opposing partisan groups in the public became increasingly polarized over the question of military force.

---

8 In separate regressions for blacks and whites, political awareness is associated with rejection of the pull-out option at least as strongly among blacks as among whites. (In a simple linear regression of this question [scored 0–1] on political awareness, the intercept and slope for blacks are .55 and .047, respectively; for whites, the intercept and slope are .78 and .022, with all terms highly statistically significant; the range of political awareness is 0 through 13.) See Chapter 9 for additional discussion of the effects of elite opinion leadership on Afro-Americans.

9 Insofar as there was a time trend, it was toward less party polarization, but the trend did not significance.

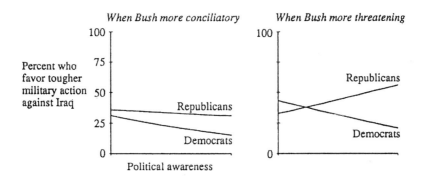

Figure 6.4. Partisans become more polarized over time on use of military force. Estimates are derived from coefficients in Table 6.3. *Source:* **1990 NES survey.**

Figure 6.4 appears to support this expectation. Highly aware Democrats and Republicans were apparently more polarized over the use of force after December 15 than they had been before. Despite this, however, the increase in polarization does not achieve statistical significance and must therefore be taken as equivocal support for my expectation (coefficients shown in Table 6.3).

The key point here is that exposure to public affairs, as measured by tests of political awareness, has important effects on mass attitudes, but that these effects differ across policies and across time, depending on the positions taken by political elites and reflected in the mass media. Awareness is associated with support for those aspects of government policy that have the consensual support of political and media elites, but is associated with higher levels of polarization over policies on which elites are divided.[10]

To demonstrate this point more rigorously, I selected items from the 1972-74–76 NES survey that seemed on their face to exemplify mainstream policies and partisan policies of the early 1970s.[11] Table 6.1 contains a list of these items. Selection of the items was based on my judgment of the positions of liberal and conservative elites, political party elites, and the mass media at the time of the NES study. To confirm these judgments, I asked a research assistant to read the platforms of the Democratic and Republican parties in 1972, and to rate each party on each issue. The research assistant was unaware of my expectations and did the

10 In showing that the public became more polarized in its attitudes toward Vietnam and Persian Gulf policy, I have been, in effect, examining mass opinion change. The actual patterns of change occurring in these cases are, however, considerably more complicated than I have been able to demonstrate in this initial treatment. For further examination of opinion change on Vietnam, see Chapter 9; for a treatment of opinion change on Gulf war policy along the lines sketched in Chapter 7, see Zaller (1992).

11 I used the panel data because this test was part of a study to test the comparative ability of political knowledge, education, political interest, media exposure, and political participation to specify relationships that a good measure of political awareness should specify. It turned out that political knowledge outperformed all of the alternative measures (see Zaller, 1990).

Table 6.1. *Question stems for opinions on mainstream and partisan issues*

Mainstream issues

This country would be better off if we just stayed home and did not concern ourselves with problems in other parts of the world.

Do you think that mainland China should be a member of the United Nations, or do you think it should not?

Should farmers and businessmen be allowed to do business with Communist countries or should they be forbidden to do business with Communist countries?

Should the government support the right of black people to go to any hotel or restaurant they can afford, or should it stay out of this matter?

Recently there has been a lot of talk about women's rights. Some people feel that women should have an equal role with men in running business, industry, and government. Others feel that women's place is in the home.

Partisan issues

There is much discussion of the best way to deal with racial problems. Some people think achieving racial integration of schools is so important that it justifies busing children to schools out of their neighborhoods. Others think letting children go to their neighborhood schools is so important that they oppose busing.

Some people feel the government in Washington should see to it that every person has a job and a good standard of living. Others think the government should just let each person get ahead on their own.

Do you think we did the right thing in getting into the fighting in Vietnam or should we have stayed out?

Source: 1972 NES survey.

ratings on the basis of instructions that were conveyed in writing.[12] I expected that both parties would explicitly endorse the policies I had identified as mainstream policies, and would take sharply opposing positions on policies I had identified as partisan policies. These expectations were largely confirmed. The one exception involved an item about whether the federal government should guarantee blacks the right to equal treatment in hotels and restaurants. A provision on equal accommodations was a key part of 1964 Civil Rights Act, which, Senator Barry Goldwater notwithstanding, passed the Congress with majority support from both the Democratic and Republican parties. The Democratic platform, as I had expected, explicitly endorsed this policy, but the Republican Party, although professing general support for equal rights, made no direct reference to it. I continue, in light of the bipartisan history of the Civil Rights Act and the fact that even Southern opposition to it had collapsed by 1972, to consider equal accommodations in hotels and restaurants a mainstream government policy.[13]

---

12 The written instructions are available from the author upon request.

13 In addition to the items in Table 6.1, I asked my research assistant to rate an item on whether the government should act against inflation. There was strong endorsement of this principle by both parties,

The model used to estimate the effect of awareness on each of these policy items was as follows:

Prob(Lib. Response) = Prob(Opinionation) x Prob(Lib. | Opinionation)

That is, the probability of a liberal response is the probability of offering any opinion at all, times the probability of making a liberal response, given that an opinion has been offered. The two parts of the model have been estimated separately.

The probability of a liberal opinion, given that an opinion statement has been made, has been modeled as a log it function of awareness, ideological self-designation,[14] party identification, and standard demographic variables (race, age, income, and residence in a Southern state). In addition to these variables, the initial specification of each equation contained an interaction term for Awareness x Ideology and Awareness x Party. This equation was estimated separately for each of the five mainstream and three partisan issues. To maximize comparability of results across different item formats, each item was coded to a three-point scale running from 0 to 0.5 to 1.0.[15]

The expectation from the model is that for partisan policies, the two Awareness x Values interaction terms will be strong, but that for mainstream policies these interactions will be anemic. The second expectation is that awareness will have an important positive impact on support for mainstream policies.

---

but a ceiling effect on mass support for the policy prevented a test on the effect of *political awareness on* support for this idea.

14 The question asked respondents to place themselves on a seven-point scale that ran from "extremely liberal" to "liberal" to "slightly liberal" to "moderate, middle of the road" to "extremely conservative." The question was asked in all three waves of the survey, and in the test reported below, responses over all three waves were averaged. People who gave no opinion in one year were assigned their average for the other two years; people who gave a response in only one year were assigned their response from that year. People who gave a no-opinion response all three times were assigned to the sample average. This way of including respondents with missing data would be expected to produce differences in item reliabilities across different respondents, but since this difference is constant across all dependent variables, and since the key hypothesis involves differences in the effect of ideology across different items, it would not be expected to produce biased results. Omitting respondents with any missing data would, on the other hand, undermine ability to detect the effect of awareness on support for mainstream policies, since the people omitted would be mainly less-informed persons.

15 When the original item was an agree/disagree item, "in between" responses were coded to .5 and other responses were coded zero or one. The jobs and women's rights items were originally seven-point scales; 4 was coded to .5 and the other points were coded to zero or one. Busing was also originally a seven-point scale, but it was so skewed in the antibusing direction that it was necessary to transform it; the far conservative position, which contained 68 percent of all respondents, was coded to zero, the next most conservative position was coded to .5, and the remaining five scale points were coded to one.

The first of these expectations is largely confirmed. The Ideology x Awareness term gets coefficients that are large for the three partisan issues and trivial for the five mainstream issues, exactly as expected. The Party x Awareness term behaves erratically, but its coefficients are either statistically insignificant or too small to have much impact, thus leaving the ideology interaction term to dominate the results. Let us look first at results for the three partisan issues.

The coefficients for the three partisan issues are shown in the left-hand side of Table 6.2, and a graphical analysis of these coefficients is shown in the top half of Figure 6.5. The results in the top half of Figure 6.5 are consistent with expectations: Increases in political awareness are associated with more polarized scale scores (see note 15) on all three issues.

The second expectation, concerning the effect of awareness on support for mainstream policies, was difficult to confirm because of the presence of severe multicollinearity. For all five of the mainstream policies-equal accommodations, women's equality, trade with communist nations, admission of China to the U.N., and antiisolationism-the estimated coefficient for awareness was correlated with the coefficient for Awareness X Ideology at the level of .96 or higher. Because of this, neither awareness, ideology, nor their interaction achieved statistical significance in some of the equations.

However, multicollinearity can greatly reduce the precision of estimates even when the true effect of one of the collinear variables is zero.[16] To test whether the Awareness x Value interaction terms had any real effect on the mainstream policies, I reestimated each equation without the interaction terms and did an F-test to see if the omissions had a significant effect on the residual sum of squares. For antiisolationism, women's rights, trade with communist nations, and admission of China to the United Nations, the F-test indicated that the interaction terms did not contribute significantly to the fit of the model. Moreover, with the interactions omitted, awareness took on a statistically significant positive coefficient in all four cases, as expected. In the fifth case, equal accommodations, the Party x Awareness coefficient remained significant, but with the nonsignificant Ideology x Awareness term omitted, awareness had the expected positive effect on support for this mainstream race policy.[17]

The right-hand side of Table 6.2 and the bottom half of Figure 6.5 present the results for the mainstream issues. Two mainstream issues-antiisolationism and trade with communist nations-are not shown in Figure 6.5 but closely resemble the pattern for the item on admission of China to the United Nations, which is shown in the figure.

Of the five mainstream issues, only the women's role item raises any doubts about the performance of the model. Though awareness does, as expected, have a positive effect on support for gender equality, the effect on liberals in this interactive model is modest. Moreover, the effect of ideology is quite large, especially if, as I maintain, elite messages consensually favored an equal role for women.

---

16 See Hanushek and Jackson, 1977: Pp. 231–3; Rao and Miller, 1971: ch. 3.

17 It is not permissible to do a parallel test omitting the direct awareness term, since awareness must be in the equation if awareness x ideology is included.

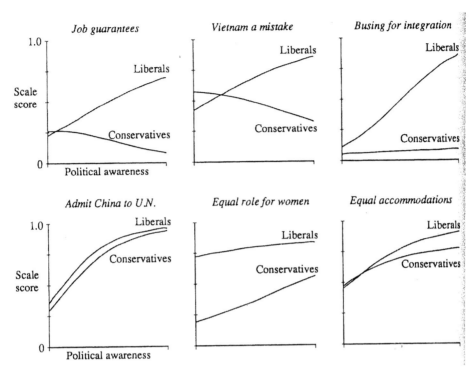

Figure 6.5. Effect of awareness on support for mainstream and partisan issues. Estimates are derived from coefficients in Table 6.2. "Liberals" in this figure have been constructed as persons who score +6 on a seven-point ideology variable and +1.3 on the party attachment scale; "conservatives"[1] have been constructed from scotes of +2 and-1.3 on these variables. Political awareness in this figure runs ±2 SD. See footnote 14 for additional information. Adapted from figure 2 of Zaller (1990). Original variables have been recoded to have roughly equal variance on a 0—.5—1 scale, with the liberal or mainstream pole coded high. See footnote 15 for additional information. *Source:* 1972 wave of NES panel survey.

One explanation for these results is that, despite the endorsement of the two parties in 1972, women's rights was not really a mainstream issue at that time; if so, it is no problem for the model, which takes elite consensus as an initial condition. Other explanations, however, appear more plausible. The modest slope for liberals, first of all, is the result of a ceiling effect among liberals. It would be hard to get very much positive slope in view of the fact that support among low-awareness liberals starts out at 71 percent. With respect to the large effect of ideology, recall that 1972 was near the highwater mark for radical feminism, a viewpoint that had little mass support and may have had deleterious spillover effects on support for equal rights for women (Mansbridge, 1986). Recall also that the Republican Party, although endorsing equal rights for women in 1972, was shortly to withdraw its support for the Equal Rights Amendment. All this makes the women's role issue a particularly tough test of the mainstream

Table 6.2. Coefficient estimates for partisan and mainstream issues

	Partisan issues			Mainstream issues				
	Job guarantee	Vietnam war	School busing	Equal accom.	Women's rights	China in UN	Comm. trade	Anti-isolation
Direction of response function[a]								
Intercept	-1.99	-0.57	-3.52	0.62	-0.74	1.33	0.40	2.28
Awareness (standardized)	-0.84*	-0.71*	-0.71*	0.26*	0.50*	0.65*	0.73*	1.12*
Ideology (7-point scale)	0.37*	0.27*	0.60*	0.18*	0.33*	0.13	0.14	-0.11
Awareness X ideology	0.18*	0.19*	0.30*	b	-.07**	b	b	-0.07
Party (range +2 to-2))	0.01	-.07	0.07	-0.09**	0.31*	0.01	0.01	0.01
Awareness X party	0.06	0.01	-0.13**	0.13*	0.02	b	b	-0.06
Opinionation function								
Intercept	1.98	2.70	2.48	2.64	2.83	2.68	1.35	5.01
Awareness	0.89*	0.62*	0.80*	0.99*	0.51*	1.32*	0.73*	1.58*

[a] Coefficients are from logistic equation described in text. Estimation was by nonlinear least squares. Equations also included controls for race, age, South, and income; these coefficients are the same as those used, but not reported for reasons of space, in Zaller (1990).

[b] Term omitted after F-test showed that coefficient had no statistical effect on equation; nonsignificant terms were omitted only when they caused severe multicollinearity; see text for further discussion. * Significant at .01 level. ** Significant at .05 level.

Source: 1972-74-76 NES panel survey.

hypothesis. And yet the hypothesis is, in the end, upheld in the sense that there is an important positive effect for awareness.

Altogether, then, the mainstream results, along with those for the three partisan issues, support the two basic deductions of the model: In cases of elite consensus, political awareness leads to increased support for the mainstream policy, and in cases of elite division, political awareness leads to increased polarization among groups having opposed value orientations.[18]

Attitude Constraint And Mass Belief Systems

An extensive research literature has documented that people who are liberal (or conservative) on one issue tend to be relatively liberal (or conservative) on a range of other issues. This tendency is most commonly explained by means of the concept of "attitude constraint," which implies that one sort of attitude (ideological orientation) constrains other attitudes (policy preferences), thereby linking a range of attitudes into a cohesive "belief system." The classic statement of this argument is Philip Converse's famous paper, "The nature of belief systems in mass publics" (1964).[19]

As it happens, the logic of the polarization argument is isomorphic with the logic of Converse's account of attitude constraint in his 1964 paper. Thus in explaining mass attitude polarization on partisan issues, the RAS model has also explained attitude constraint.

This point is easily demonstrated. According to Converse, ideologies originate among a "minuscule" number of "creative elites" and subsequently diffuse through the public. Elites, thus, are the source of mass ideologies. Converse argues, however, that the diffusion of elite-created belief systems is highly imperfect. Only the politically aware pay enough attention to elite discourse to find out the ideological implications of different policies-in Converse's terms, to learn "what goes with what." As a result, attitude constraint of the conventional liberal-conservative type develops mainly among the more politically aware strata.

Compare this argument to the representation of the polarization model in the upper half of Figure 6.5: Highly aware liberals and conservatives (or Democrats and Republicans) look to appropriate partisan elites to find out "what goes with what." Having acquired this

---

18 Mainstream norms are determined not by what all elites actually believe, but by what the elites who have regular access to the public say in their public utterances. If, for example, there were many Southern elected officials who continued to oppose equal accommodations for blacks in 1972 but who had no access to the media to express this view, and if, on the other hand, supporters of equal accommodations had good access to the mass media to publicize their side of the issue, then equal accommodations would be classified as a mainstream norm. The elites who count as shapers of public opinion in this model are those who have or control access to the mass media.

19 For the most recent work and bibliographies of the vast literature in this area, see Wyckoff (1987) and Jacoby (1991).

information, they are able to become consistently liberal or consistently conservative across a range of issues. The less aware, as shown in Figure 6.5, are less likely to acquire the attitude that is conventionally appropriate to their partisan orientation, and hence less likely to develop "attitude constraint" across issues. The well-established finding of belief systems studies-that average interterm correlations among issues are higher among more aware citizens-is just a generalization of this pattern to a cluster of ideologically charged issues (see, for example, Stimson, 1975; Jacoby, 1991).[20] Thus the existence of attitude consistency across issues, and the well-documented tendency for consistency to become stronger with increases in awareness, can both be explained by the RAS model *(D27, D28).*[21]

This account of attitude consistency does not, so far as I can tell, differ in any important way from Converse's. It is simply a somewhat more fully specified statement of his general argument.

I shall have more to say about attitude constraint in Chapter 9, where I show how it develops and changes in situations in which the flow of communications is not, as I have assumed it to be in this chapter, either stable over time or evenly balanced between liberal and conservative messages.

Alternative Explanations

There are alternative explanations for the empirical regularities noted in this chapter, and it is instructive to review them, for they illustrate the fragmented state of the public opinion field of which I complained in the opening chapter. For example, Cantril (1944) found that persons scoring high on a measure of political knowledge were more likely to support American involvement in World War II, including numerous particular policies of the Roosevelt administration, such as the foundation of a United Nations organization upon the defeat of the Axis powers. Cantril's explanation for this pattern is that better informed Americans are likely to have a correct understanding of their true interests. Stouffer (1954) argues that better educated persons are more supportive of civil liberties because they are more likely to give a "sober second thought" to freedom issues; Allport (1954: p. 405) cites the greater personal

---

20 Lane (1973) and Marcus, Tabb, and Sullivan (1974), among many others, criticize Converse's belief-systems argument on the grounds that it overlooks idiosyncratic ways in which individuals may structure their attitudes, and that it arbitrarily equates ideological consistency with sophistication. My account accepts the first point, claiming, in effect, that political awareness drives a socialization process that overrides idiosyncratic attitude structures. My account does not, however, equate consistency with sophistication except in the possibly perverse sense that an ideologically "consistent" individual has managed to absorb a particular set of conventions.

21 Even critics of Converse's position find evidence that constraint varies by political awareness (see Wyckoff, 1987). Wyckoff concludes with an excellent analysis of the conditions under which attitude constraint is most likely to appear.

security of better educated persons as a possible explanation for their greater racial liberalism; Bobo and Licari (1989) contend that education promotes political tolerance because it is associated with "more sophisticated modes of reasoning"[22]; and Hamilton(1968) and Hahn (1970) suggest that higher levels of support for the Vietnam War among educated persons may be due, as Hamilton puts it, to "upper-middle class authoritarianism" (p. 446). Each of these arguments is perhaps plausible on its face, but none generalizes easily to other issues. The more parsimonious explanation of the RAS model would be that better educated and otherwise more politically aware persons have been in each case more heavily exposed to mainstream elite values. (Although the work necessary to establish the existence of mainstream norms in some of these cases has not been done, I believe it could be.)

In a careful piece of work, Jackman (1978) notes that education is associated with liberalism on some race items (such as "strict segregation" of the races) but not on others (such as busing). She concludes from this that, contrary to much past research, education promotes only "superficial" learning of democratic values rather than genuine commitment to them. The alternative argument of the RAS model, of course, would be that the first type of item taps a mainstream policy and the second a partisan policy.[23]

---

22 In their study of *Political Tolerance and American Democracy,* Sullivan, Pierson, and Marcus (1981) maintain that better educated persons are *not* more tolerant, once dislike for the target group is controlled for. Two comments are in order here. The first is that the mainstream model would expect better educated people to be more tolerant only when a traditionally protected civil liberty is at stake-as in the case of freedom of political speech, which has been well protected by the Supreme Court in recent years. But the mainstream model would not predict education to be associated with support for civil liberties that have not achieved mainstream status, such as the right of members of a self-proclaimed terrorist group, like the Symbioses Liberation Army, to teach in the public schools. In looking for a global effect of education, Sullivan et al. fail to distinguish between cases in which the mainstream model would expect to find educationally induced tolerance and cases in which it would not. (From table 5.2 of Sullivan et al., it appears that the effect of education on tolerance is large in the case of free speech for one's most disliked group, but that the effect of education is nonexistent when it comes to being "pleased" at having one's child date a member of one's least liked group; it may be that citizens in a democracy ought, in some sense, to be tolerant of having their children date members of their least liked political group, but nothing in the mainstream model would predict that better educated people would be more likely to be so pleased than less well-educated ones.) Second, even if the better educated people are more tolerant in part because they are less frightened of certain groups, which appears to be the case, the support they give to mainstream civil liberties remains politically significant. It is, moreover, quite possible that learning to discount one's fears of radical groups is simply another element of mainstream civil liberties norms that is better learned by better educated persons. For example, learning to discount one's irrational fears of domestic communism seems to have been a principal "mainstream" lesson of the so-called Mc-Carthyism period.

23 For a critique of Jackman that uses different conceptual machinery to reach essentially the same conclusion, see chapter 4 of Sniderman, Brody, and Tetlock, 1991.

The explanation of the RAS model, which follows from Key's observation on the "indoctrinating effect" of exposure to elite discourse, is preferable in each of these cases because it is embedded in a theory having a wider range of applications. In particular, it can explain why awareness has a polarizing effect in some cases and a mainstream effect in others, even when the substantive issue domain is the same.[24]

There also exist alternative explanations for attitude constraint. Most stress the internal sources of constraint-that is, schematic associations that develop within the mind as a result of thought about the particular issues. These explanations also stress that more politically aware persons (often described as political "experts") are more ideologically consistent than are less aware persons (novices) because they think more about politics (Fiske and Kinder, 1981; Judd and Krosnick, 1989). Though approaching the problem quite differently, Luskin's (1987) treatment of the relationship between attitude constraint and political sophistication likewise stresses connections between idea-elements within a person's mind.

Though not denying the importance of intrapsychic connections and the individual's own thought in developing them, the RAS model manages to explain attitude consistency without referring to such mental organization. It instead stresses the extrapsychic or external sources of constraint, namely the pattern of elite division or nondivision on the given issue. In maintaining this external focus, the RAS model is able to explain the quite different effects that awareness has in different contexts, as in Figures 6.1 and 6.5. Also, the RAS model can better explain phenomena, including random response variation and response effects, that affect novices and experts alike. Finally, the present model, as shown in the next four chapters, adds a dynamic element to our understanding of how awareness (or expertise) affects attitude statements, namely an account of attitude change.

Appendix

Table 6.3. *Coefficients for Gulf War opinion*

	Right to send troops	Reject pullout of troops	Tougher military action
Intercept	-0.02	-2.19	1.33
Awareness	-0.24	-0.73	0.13
(standardized)	(.17)	(.09)	(.07)
Party	0.09	0.28	0.19
(range-2 to +2)	(.14)	(.07)	(.06)

24 The fact that, as Duch and Gibson (n.d.) point out, the effect of education on tolerance varies substantially from one nation to another is further reason to believe that it measures differences in socialization rather than differences in cognitive capacity or psychological adjustment.

Party x awareness	-0.03	0.12	0.06
	(.14)	(.07)	(.06)
Time	-0.18	—	-0.42
	(.19)		(.19)
Gender	-.60	-0.35	-0.81
(female = 1, else 0)	(.13)	(.16)	(.14)
Race	1.04	0.69	0.84
(black =1, else 0)	(.20)	(.17)	(.25)
Ethnicity	0.19	-0.15	-0.27
(Jewish = 1, else 0)	(49)	(.63)	(.49)
Time **X** party **X** awareness	0.15b		-0.12
	(.15)		(.17)
Time **X** party	0.23b	—	-0.05
	(.15)		(.15)
Time **X** awareness	-0.18b	-	-0.12
	(.19)		(.21)
N	1976	1987	1987

Notes to Table 6.3

Note: Cell entries are coefficients from ML estimation of logistic regression model, with standard errors shown in parentheses. First dependent variable is whether the U.S. did the right thing in sending troops to the Persian Gulf (0–1); the second is whether U.S. should pursue some policy *other than* a pullout of troops from the gulf region; the third is whether the United States should take tougher military action against Iraq. For the "right thing" question, time is coded 0 in the period through November 9, when congressional criticism of American involvement began, and 1 afterward. For the "tougher military action" question, time is coded 0 in the period through December 15, at which time President Bush rejected an Iraqi meeting proposal, thereby signaling clear intent to enforce a January 15 pullout deadline, and 1 afterward. [b] Block of three coefficients is statistically significant on F-test at p < .01.
Source: 1990 NES survey.

★ The Nature of Belief Systems in
★ Mass Publics
★
By Philip E. Converse

Belief systems have never surrendered easily to empirical study or quantification. Indeed, they have often served as primary exhibits for the doctrine that what is important to study cannot be measured and that what can be measured is not important to study. In an earlier period, the behaviorist decree that subjective states lie beyond the realm of proper measurement gave Mannheim a justification for turning his back on measurement, for he had an unqualified interest in discussing belief systems.[1] Even as Mannheim was Writing, however, behaviorism was undergoing stiff challenges, and early studies of attitudes were attaining a degree of measurement reliability that had been deemed impossible. This fragment of history, along with many others, serves to remind us that no intellectual position is likely to become obsolete quite so rapidly as one that takes current empirical capability as the limit of the possible in a more absolute sense. Nevertheless, while rapid strides in the measurement of "subjective states" have been achieved in recent decades, few would claim that the millennium has arrived or that Mannheim could now find all of the tools that were lacking to him forty years ago.

This article makes no pretense of surpassing such limitations. At the same time, our substantive concern forces upon us an unusual concern with measurement strategies, not simply because we propose to deal with belief systems or ideologies, but also because of the specific questions that we shall raise about them. Our focus in this article is upon differences in the nature of belief systems held on the one hand by elite political actors and, on the other, by the masses that appear to be. "numbered" within the spheres of influence of these belief systems. It is our thesis that there are important and predictable differences in ideational worlds as we progress downward through such "belief strata" and that these differences, while obvious at one level, are easily overlooked and not infrequently miscalculated. The fact that these ideational worlds differ in character poses problems of adequate representation and measurement.

The vertical ordering of actors and beliefs that we wish to plumb bears some loose resemblance to the vertical line that might be pursued downward through an organization or political movement from the narrow cone to top leadership, through increasing numbers of subordinate officials, and on through untitled activists to the large base formally represented in membership rolls. It is this large base that Michels noted, from observations of political gatherings; was rarely "there", and analogues to its physical absence do not arise accidentally in dealing with belief systems. On the other hand, there is no perfect or necessary "fit" between the two orderings, and this fact in itself has some interest.

That we intend to consider the total mass of people "numbered" within the spheres of influence of belief systems suggests both a democratic bias and a possible confusion between numbers and power or between numbers and the outcomes of events that power determines. We are aware that attention to numbers, more or less customary in democratic thought, is very nearly irrelevant in many political settings. Generally, the logic of numbers collides head on with the logic of power, as the traditional power pyramid, expressing an inverse relation between power and numbers, communicates so well. "Power" and "numbers" intersect at only one notable point, and that point is represented by the familiar axiom that numbers are one resource of power. The weight of this resource varies in a systematic and obvious way according to the political context. In a frankly designed and stable oligarchy, it is assumed to have no weight at all. In such a setting, the numbers of people associated with particular belief systems, if known at all, becomes important only in periods of crisis or challenge to the existing power structure. Democratic theory greatly increases the weight accorded to numbers in the daily power calculus. This increase still does not mean that numbers are of overriding importance; in the normal course of events it is the *perception* of numbers by democratic elites, so far as they differ from "actual" numbers, that is the more important factor. However this may be, claims to numbers are of some modest continuing importance in democratic systems for the legitimacy they confer upon demands; and, much more sporadically, claims to numbers become important in nondemocratic systems as threats of potential coercion.

I. Some Clarification of Terms

A term like "ideology" has been thoroughly muddied by diverse uses.[2] We shall depend instead upon the term "belief system," although there is an obvious overlap between the two. We define a *belief system* as a configuration of ideas and attitudes in which the elements are bound together by some form of constraint or functional interdependence.[3] In the static case, "constraint" may be taken to mean the success we would have in predicting, given initial knowledge that an individual holds a specified attitude, that he holds certain further ideas and attitudes. We depend implicitly upon such notions of constraint in judging, for example, that, if a person is opposed to the expansion of social security, he is probably a conservative and is probably opposed as well to any nationalization of private industries, federal aid to education, sharply progressive income taxation, and so forth. Most discussions of ideologies make relatively elaborate assumptions about such constraints. Constraint must be treated, of course, as a matter of degree, and this degree can be measured quite readily, at least as an average among individuals.[4]

In the dynamic case, "constraint" or "interdependence" refers to the probability that a change in the perceived status (truth, desirability, and so forth) of one idea-element would *psychologically* require, from the point of view of the actor, some, compensating change(s) in the status of idea-elements else where in the configuration. The most obvious form of such constraint (although in some ways the most trivial) is exemplified by a structure of propositions in logic, in which a change in the truth-value of one proposition necessitates changes in truth-value elsewhere within the set of related propositions. Psychologically, of course, there may be equally strong constraint among idea-elements that would not be apparent to logical analysis at all, as we shall see.

We might characterize either the idea-elements themselves or entire belief systems in terms of many other dimensions. Only two will interest us here. First, the idea-elements within a belief system vary in a property we shall call *centrality*, according to the role that they play in the belief system as a whole. That is, when new information changes the status of one idea-element in a belief system, by postulate some other change must occur as well. There are usually, however, several possible changes in status elsewhere in the system, any one of which would compensate for the initial change. Let us imagine, for example, that a person strongly favors a particular policy; is very favorably inclined toward a given political party; and recognizes with gratification that the party's stand and his own are congruent. (If he were unaware of the party's stand on the issue, these elements could not in any direct sense be constrained within' the same belief system.) Let us further imagine that the party then changes its position to the opposing side of the issue. Once the information about the change reaching the actor has become so unequivocal that he can no longer deny that the change has occurred, he has several further choices. Two of the more important ones involve either a change in attitude toward the party or a change in position on the issue. In such an instance, the element more likely to change is defined as less central to the belief system than the element that, so to speak, has its stability ensured by the change in the first element.[5]

In informal discussions of belief systems, frequent assumptions are made about the relative centrality of various idea-elements. For example, idea-elements that are logically "ends" are supposed to be more central to the system than are "means." It is important to remain aware, however, that idea-elements can change their relative centrality in an individual's belief-system over time. Perhaps the most hackneyed illustration of this point is that of the miser, to whom money has become an end rather than a means.

Whole belief systems may also be compared in a rough way with respect to the *range* of objects that are referents for the ideas and attitudes in the system. Some belief systems, while they may be internally quite complex and may involve large numbers of cognitive elements, are rather narrow in range: Belief systems concerning "proper" baptism rituals or the effects of changes in weather on health may serve as cases in point. Such other belief systems as, for example, one that links control of the means of production with the social functions of religion and a doctrine of aesthetics all in one more or less neat package have extreme ranges.

By and large, our attention will be focused upon belief systems that have relatively wide ranges, and that allow some centrality to political objects, for they can be presumed to have some relevance to political behavior. This focus brings us close to what are broadly called *ideologies,* and we shall use the term for aesthetic relief where it seems most appropriate. The term originated in a narrower context, however, and is still often reserved for subsets of belief systems or parts of such systems that the user suspects are insincere; that he wishes to claim have certain functions for social-groupings; or that have some special social source or some notable breadth of social-diffusion.[6] Since we are concerned here about only one of these limitations—the question of social diffusion—and since we wish to deal with it by hypothesis rather than by definition, a narrow construction of the term is never intended.

II. Sources of Constraint on Idea-Elements

It seems clear that, however logically coherent a belief system may seem to the holder, the sources of constraint are much less logical in the classical sense than they are psychological—and less psychological than social. This point is of sufficient importance to dwell upon.

Logical Sources of Constraint

Within very narrow portions of belief systems, certain constraints may be purely logical. For example, government revenues, .government expenditures, and budget balance are three idea-elements that suggest some purely logical constraints. One cannot believe that government expenditures should be increased, that government revenues should be decreased, and that a more favorable balance of the budget should be achieved all at the same time. Of course, the presence of such objectively logical constraints does not ensure that subjective constraints will be felt by the actor. They will be felt only if these idea-elements are brought together in the same belief system, and there is no guarantee that they need be. Indeed, it is true that, among adult American citizens, those who favor the expansion of government welfare services tend to be those who are more insistent upon reducing taxes "even if it means putting off some important things that need to be done."[7]

Where such purely logical constraint is concerned, McGuire has reported a fascinating experiment in which propositions from a few syllogisms of the Barbara type were scattered thinly across a long questionnaire applied to a student population. The fact that logical contingencies bound certain questions together was never brought to the attention of the students by the investigator. Yet one week later the questionnaire was applied again, and changes of response to the syllogistic propositions reduced significantly the measurable level of logical inconsistency. The conclusion was that merely "activating" these objectively related ideas in some rough temporal contiguity was sufficient to sensitize the holders to inconsistency and therefore to occasion readjustment of their beliefs.[8]

On a broader canvas, such findings suggest that simple "thinking about" a domain of idea-elements serves both to weld a broader range of such elements into a functioning belief system and to eliminate strictly logical inconsistencies defined from an objective point of view. Since there can be no doubt that educated elites in general, and political elites in particular, "think about" elements involved in political belief systems with a frequency far greater than that characteristic of mass publics, we could conservatively expect that strict logical inconsistencies (objectively definable) would be far more prevalent in a broad public.

Furthermore, if a legislator is noted for his insistence upon budget-balancing and tax-cutting, we can predict with a fair degree of success that he will also tend to oppose expansion of government welfare activities. If, however, a voter becomes numbered within his sphere of influence by virtue of having cast a vote for him directly out of enthusiasm for his tax-cutting policies, we cannot predict that the voter is opposed as well to expansion of government welfare services. Indeed, if an empirical prediction is possible, it may run in an opposing direction, although the level of constraint is so feeble that any comment is trivial. Yet we know that many historical observations rest directly upon the assumption that constraint among idea-elements visible at an elite level is mirrored by the same lines of constraint in the belief systems of their less visible "supporters." It is our argument that this assumption not only can be, but is very likely to be, fallacious.

Psychological Sources of Constraint

Whatever may be learned through the use of" strict logic as a type of constraint, it seems obvious that few belief systems of any range at all depend for their constraint upon logic in this classical sense. Perhaps, with a great deal of labor, parts of a relatively tight belief system like that fashioned by Karl Marx could be made to resemble a structure of logical propositions. It goes without saying, however, that many sophisticated people have been swept away by the "iron logic" of Marxism without any such recasting. There is a broad gulf between strict logic and the quasi-logic of cogent argument. And where the elements in the belief system of a population represent looser cultural accumulations, the question of logical consistency is even less appropriate. If one visits a Shaker community, for example, one finds a group of people with a clear-cut and distinctive belief system that requires among other things plain dress, centrality of religious concerns, celibacy for all members, communal assumptions about work and property, antagonism to political participation in the broader state, and a general aura of retirement from the secular world. The visitor whose sense of constraint has been drawn from belief configurations of such other retiring sects as the Amish is entirely surprised to discover that the Shakers have no abhorrence of technological progress but indeed greatly prize it. In their heyday, a remarkable amount of group energy appears to have been reserved for "research and development" of labor-saving devices, and among the inventions they produced was a prototype of the washing machine. Similar surprise has been registered at idea-elements brought together by such movements as Peronism and Italian Fascism by observers schooled to expect other combinations. Indeed, were one to survey a limited set of ideas on which many belief systems have registered opposite postures, it would be interesting to see how many permutations of positions have been held at one time or another by someone somewhere.

Such diversity is testimony to an absence of any strict logical constraints among such idea-elements, if any be needed. What is important is that the elites familiar with the total shapes of these belief systems have *experienced* them as logically constrained clusters of ideas, within which one part necessarily follows from another. Often such constraint is quasi-logically argued on the basis of an appeal to some superordinate value or posture toward man and society, involving premises about the nature of social justice, social change, "natural law," and the like. Thus a few crowning postures—like premises about survival of the fittest in the spirit of social Darwinism—serve as a sort of glue to bind together many more specific attitudes and beliefs, and these postures are of prime centrality in the belief system as a whole.

Social Sources of Constraint

The social sources of constraint are twofold and are familiar from an extensive literature in the past century. In the first place, were we to survey the combinations of idea-elements that have occurred historically (in the fashion suggested above), we should undoubtedly find that certain postures tend to co-occur and that this co-occurrence has obvious roots in the configuration of interests and information that characterize particular niches in the social structure. For example, if we were informed that dissension was rising within the Roman Catholic Church over innovations designed to bring the priest more intimately into the *milieu* of the modern worker, we could predict with a high degree of success that such a movement would have the bulk of its support among the *bas-clergé* and would encounter indifference or hostility at the higher status levels of the hierarchy.

Of course, such predictions are in no sense free from error, and surprises are numerous. The middle-class temperance movement in America, for example, which now seems "logically" allied with the small-town Republican right, had important alliances some eighty years ago with the urban social left, on grounds equally well argued from temperance doctrines.[9] Nonetheless, there are some highly reliable correlations of this sort, and these correlations can be linked with social structure in the most direct way. Developmentally, they have status similar to the classic example of the spurious correlation—two terms that are correlated because of a common link to some third and prior variable. In the case of the belief system, arguments are developed to lend some more positive rationale to the fact of constraint: The idea-elements go together not simply because both are in the interest of the person holding a particular status but for more abstract and quasi-logical reasons developed from a coherent world view as well. It is this type of constraint that is closest to the classic meaning of the term "ideology."

The second source of social constraint lies in two simple facts about the creation and diffusion of belief systems. First, the shaping of belief systems of any range into apparently logical wholes that are credible to large numbers of people is an act of creative synthesis characteristic of only a miniscule proportion of any population. Second, to the extent that *multiple* idea-elements of a belief system are socially diffused from such creative sources, they tend to be diffused in "packages," which consumers come to see as "natural" wholes, for they are presented in such terms ("If you believe this, then you will also believe that, for it follows in such-and-such ways"). Not that the more avid consumer never supplies personal innovations on the fringes—he is very likely to suppress an idea-element here, to elaborate one there, or even to demur at an occasional point. But any set of relatively intelligent consumers who are initially sympathetic to the crowning posture turns out to show more consensus on specific implications of the posture as a result of social diffusion of "what goes with what" than it would if each member were required to work out the implications individually without socially provided cues.

Such constraint through diffusion is important, for it implies a dependence upon the transmission of information. If information is not successfully transmitted, there will be little constraint save that arising from the first social source. Where transmission of information is at stake, it becomes important to distinguish between two classes of information. Simply put, these two levels are what goes with what and why. Such levels of information logically stand in a scalar relationship to one another, in the sense that one can hardly arrive at an understanding of why two ideas go together without being aware that they are supposed to go together. On the other hand, it is easy to know that two ideas go together without knowing why. For example, we can expect that a very large majority of the American public would somehow have absorbed the notion that "Communists are atheists." What is important is that this perceived correlation would for most people represent nothing more than a fact of existence, with the same status as the fact that oranges are orange and most apples are red. If we were to go and explore with these people their grasp of the "why" of the relationship, we would he surprised if more than a quarter of the population even attempted responses (setting aside such inevitable replies as "those Communists are for everything wicked"), and, among the responses received, we could be sure that the majority would be incoherent or irrelevant.

The first level of information, then, is simple and straightforward. The second involves much more complex and abstract information, very close to what Downs has called the "contextual knowledge" relevant to a body of information.[10] A well informed person who has received sufficient information about a system of beliefs to understand the "whys" involved in several of the constraints between idea-elements is in a better position to make good guesses about the nature of other constraints; he can deduce with fair success, for example, how a true believer will respond to certain situations. Our first interest in distinguishing between these types of information, however, flows from our interest in the relative success of information transmission. The general premise is that the first type of information will be diffused much more readily than the second because it is less complex.

It is well established that differences in information held in a cross-section population are simply staggering, running from vast treasuries of well organized information among elites interested in the particular subject to fragments that could virtually be measured as a few "bits" in the technical sense. These differences are a static tribute to the extreme imperfections in the transmission of information "downward" through the system: Very little information "trickles down" very far. Of course, the ordering of individuals on this vertical information scale is largely due to differences in education, but it is strongly modified as well by different special-ized interests and tastes that individuals have acquired over time (one for politics, another for religious activity, another for fishing, and so forth).

Consequences of Declining Information for Belief Systems

It is our primary thesis that, as one moves from elite sources of belief systems downwards on such an information scale, several important things occur. First, the contextual grasp of "standard" political belief systems fades out very rapidly, almost before one has passed beyond the 10% of the American population that in the 1950s had completed standard college training.[11] Increasingly, simpler forms of information about "what goes with what" (or even information about the simple identity of objects) turn up missing. The net result, as one moves downward, is that constraint declines across the universe of idea-elements, and that the range of relevant belief systems becomes narrower and narrower. Instead of a few wide-ranging belief systems that organize large amounts of specific information, one would expect to find a proliferation of clusters of ideas among which little constraint is felt even, quite often, in instances of sheer logical constraint.[12]

At the same time, moving from top to bottom of this information dimension, the character of the objects that are central in a belief system undergoes systematic change. These objects shift from the remote, generic, and abstract to the increasingly simple, concrete, or "close to home." Where potential political objects are concerned, this progression tends to be from abstract, "ideological" principles to the more obviously recognizable social groupings or charismatic leaders and finally to such objects of immediate experience as family, job, and immediate associates.

Most of these changes have been hinted at in one form or another in a variety of sources. For example, "limited horizons," "foreshortened time perspectives," and "concrete thinking" have been singled out as notable characteristics of the ideational world of the poorly educated. Such observations have impressed even those investigators who are dealing with subject matter rather close to the individual's immediate world: his family budgeting, what he thinks of people more wealthy than he, his attitudes toward leisure time, work regulations, and the like. But most of the stuff of politics—particularly that played on a national or international stage—is, in the nature of things, remote and abstract. Where politics is concerned, therefore, such ideational changes begin to occur rapidly below the extremely thin stratum of the electorate that ever has occasion to make public pronouncements on political affairs. In other words, the changes in belief systems of which we speak are not pathology limited to a thin and disoriented bottom layer of the *lumpenproletariat*, they are immediately relevant in understanding the bulk of mass political behavior.

It is this latter fact which seems to be consistently misunderstood by the sophisticated analysts who comment in one vein or another on the meaning of mass politics. There are some rather obvious "optical illusions" that are bound to operate here. A member of that tiny elite that comments publicly about political currents (probably some fraction of 1% of a population) spends most of his time in informal communication about politics with others in the same select group. He rarely encounters a conversation in which his assumptions of shared contextual grasp of political ideas are challenged. Intellectually, he has learned that the level of information in the mass public is low, but he may dismiss this knowledge as true of only 10 to 20% of the voters, who affect the course of mass political events in insignificant ways if at all.[13] It is largely from his informal communications that he learns how "public opinion" is changing and what the change signifies, and he generalizes facilely from these observations to the bulk of the broader public.[14]

III. Active Use of Ideological Dimensions of Judgment

Economy and constraint are companion concepts, for the more highly constrained a system of multiple elements, the more economically it may be described and understood. From the point of view of the actor, the idea organization that leads to constraint permits him to locate and make sense of a wider range of information from a particular domain than he would find possible without such organization. One judgmental dimension or "yardstick" that has been highly serviceable for simplifying and organizing events in most Western politics for the past century has been the liberal-conservative continuum, on which parties, political leaders, legislation, court decisions, and a number of other primary objects of politics could be more—or less—adequately located.[15]

The efficiency of such a yardstick in the evaluation of events is quite obvious. Under certain appropriate circumstances, the single word "conservative" used to describe a piece of proposed legislation can convey a tremendous amount of more specific information about the bill—who probably proposed it and toward what ends, who is likely to resist it, its chances of passage, its long-term social consequences, and, most important, how the actor himself should expect to evaluate it if he were to expend further energy to look into its details. The circumstances under which such tremendous amounts of information are conveyed by the single word are, however, twofold. First, the actor must bring a good deal of meaning to the term, which is to say that he must understand the constraints surrounding it. The more impoverished his understanding of the term, the less information it conveys. In the limiting case—if he does not know at all what the term means—it conveys no information at all. Second, the system of beliefs and actors referred to must in fact be relatively constrained: To the degree that constraint is lacking, uncertainty is less reduced by the label, and less information is conveyed.-

The psychological economies provided by such yardsticks for actors are paralleled by economies for analysts and theoreticians who wish to describe events in the system parsimoniously. Indeed, the search for adequate overarching dimensions on which large arrays of events may be simply understood is a critical part of synthetic description. Such syntheses are more or less satisfactory, once again, according to the degree of constraint operative among terms in the system being described.

The economies inherent in the liberal-conservative continuum were exploited in traditional fashion in the early 1950s to describe political changes in the United States as a swing toward conservatism or a "revolt of the moderates." At one level, this description was unquestionably apt. That is, a man whose belief system was relatively conservative (Dwight D. Eisenhower) had supplanted in the White House a man whose belief system was relatively liberal (Harry Truman). Furthermore, for a brief period at least, the composition of Congress was more heavily Republican as well, and this shift meant on balance a greater proportion of relatively conservative legislators. Since the administration and Congress were the elites responsible for the development and execution of policies, the flavor of governmental action did indeed take a turn in a conservative direction. These observations are proper description.

The causes underlying these changes in leadership, however, obviously lay with the mass public, which, had changed its voting patterns sufficiently to bring the Republican elites into power. And this change in mass voting was frequently interpreted as a shift in public mood from liberal to conservative, a mass desire for a period of respite and consolidation after the rapid liberal innovations of the 1930s and 1940s. Such an account presumes, once again, that constraints visible at an elite level are mirrored in the mass public and that a person choosing to vote Republican after a decade or two of Democratic voting saw himself *in some sense or other* as giving up a more liberal choice in favor of a more conservative one.

On the basis of some familiarity with attitudinal materials drawn from cross-section samples of the electorate,[16] this assumption seems thoroughly implausible. It suggests in the first instance a neatness of organization in perceived political worlds, which, while accurate enough for elites, is a poor fit for the perceptions of the common public. Second, the yardstick that such an account takes for granted—the liberal-conservative continuum—is a rather elegant high-order abstraction, and such abstractions are not typical conceptual tools for the "man in the street." Fortunately, our interview protocols collected from this period permitted us to examine this hypothesis more closely, for they include not only "structured" attitude materials (which merely require the respondent to choose between prefabricated alternatives) but also lengthy "open-ended" materials, which provided us with the respondent's current evaluations of the political scene in his own words. They therefore provide some indication of the evaluative dimensions that tend to be spontaneously applied to politics by such a national sample. We knew that respondents who were highly educated or strongly involved in politics would fall naturally into the verbal shorthand of "too conservative," "more radical," and the like in these evaluations. Our initial analytic question had to do with the prevalence of such usage.

It soon became apparent, however, that such respondents were in a very small minority, as their unusual education or involvement would suggest. At this point, we broadened the inquiry to an assessment of the evaluative dimensions of policy significance (relating to political issues, rather than to the way a candidate dresses, smiles, or behaves in his private life) that seemed to be employed *in lieu of* such efficient yardsticks as the liberal-conservative continuum. The interviews themselves suggested several strata of classification, which were hierarchically ordered as "levels of conceptualization" on the basis of *a priori* judgments about the breadth of contextual grasp of the political system that each seemed to represent.

In the first or top level were placed those respondents who did indeed rely in some active way on a relatively abstract and far-reaching conceptual dimension as a yardstick against which political objects and their shifting policy significance over time were evaluated. We did not require that this dimension be the liberal-conservative continuum itself, but it was almost the only dimension of the sort that occurred empirically. In a second stratum were placed those respondents who mentioned such a dimension in a peripheral way but did not appear to place much evaluative dependence upon it or who used such concepts in a fashion that raised doubt about the breadth of their understanding of the meaning of the term. The first stratum was loosely labeled "ideologue" and the second "near-ideologue."

In the third level were placed respondents who failed to rely upon any such over-arching dimensions yet evaluated parties and candidates in terms of their expected favorable or unfavorable treatment of different social groupings in the population. The Democratic Party might be disliked because "it's trying to help the Negroes too much," or the Republican Party might be endorsed because farm prices would be better with the Republicans in office. The more sophisticated of these group-interest responses reflected an awareness of conflict in interest between "big business" or "rich people," on the one hand, and "labor" or the "working man," on the other, and parties and candidates were located accordingly.

It is often asked why these latter respondents are not considered full "ideologues," for their perceptions run to the more tangible core of what has traditionally been viewed as ideological conflict. It is quite true that such a syndrome is closer to the upper levels of conceptualization than are any of the other types to be described. As we originally foresaw, however, there turn out to be rather marked differences, not only in social origin and flavor of judgmental processes but in overt political reactions as well, between people of this type and those in the upper levels. These people have a clear image of politics as an arena of group interests and, provided that they have been properly advised on where their own group interests lie, they are relatively likely to follow such advice. Unless an issue directly concerns their grouping in an obviously rewarding or punishing way, however, they lack the contextual grasp of the system to recognize how they should respond to it without being told by elites who hold their confidence. Furthermore, their interest in politics is not sufficiently strong that they pay much attention to such communications. If a communication gets through and they absorb it, they are most willing to behave "ideologically" in ways that will further the interests of their group. If they fail to receive such communication, which is most unusual, knowledge of their group memberships may be of little help in predicting their responses. This syndrome we came to call "ideology by proxy."

The difference between such narrow group interest and the broader perceptions of the ideologue may be clarified by an extreme case. One respondent whom we encountered classified himself as a strong Socialist. He was a Socialist because he knew that Socialists stood foursquare for the working man against the rich, and he was a working man. When asked, however, whether or not the federal government in Washington "should leave things like electric power and housing for private businessmen to handle," he felt strongly that private enterprise should have its way, and responses to other structured issue questions were simply uncorrelated with standard socialist doctrine. It seems quite clear that, if our question had pointed out explicitly to this man that "good Socialists" would demand government intervention over private enterprise or that such a posture had traditionally been viewed as benefiting the working man, his answer would have been different. But since he had something less than a college education and was not generally interested enough in politics to struggle through such niceties, he simply lacked the contextual grasp of the political system or of his chosen "ideology" to know what the appropriate response might be. This case illustrates well what we mean by constraint between idea-elements and how such constraint depends upon a store of relevant information. For this man, "Socialists," "the working man," "non-Socialists" and "the rich" with their appropriate valences formed a tightly constrained belief system. But, for lack of information, the belief system more or less began and ended there. It strikes us as valid to distinguish such a belief system from that of the doctrinaire socialist. We, as sophisticated observers, could only class this man as a full "ideologue" by assuming that he shares with us the complex undergirding of information that his concrete group perceptions call up in our own minds-. In this instance, a very little probing makes clear that this assumption of shared information is once again false.

The fourth level was, to some degree, a residual category, intended to include those respondents who invoked some policy considerations in their evaluations yet employed none of the references meriting location in any of the first three levels. Two main modes of policy evaluation were characteristic of this level. The first we came to think of as a "nature of the times" response, since parties or candidates were praised or blamed primarily because of their temporal association in the past with broad societal states of war or peace, prosperity or depression. There was no hint in these responses that any groupings in the society suffered differentially from disaster or profited excessively in more pleasant times: These fortunes or misfortunes were those that one party or the other had decided (in some cases, apparently, on whim) to visit upon the nation as a whole. The second type included those respondents whose only approach to an issue reference involved some single narrow policy for which they felt personal gratitude or indignation toward a party or candidate (like social security or a conservation program). In these responses, there was no indication that the speakers saw programs as representative of the broader policy postures of the parties.

The fifth level included those respondents whose evaluations of the political scene had no shred of policy significance whatever. Some of these responses were from people who felt loyal to one party or the other but confessed that they had no idea what the party stood for. Others devoted their attention to personal qualities of the candidates, indicating disinterest in parties more generally. Still others confessed that they paid too little attention to either the parties or the current candidates to be able to say anything about them.[17]

The ranking of the levels performed on *a priori* grounds was corroborated by further analyses, which demonstrated that independent measures of political information, education, and political involvement all showed sharp and monotonic declines as one passsed downward through the levels in the order suggested. Furthermore, these correlations were strong enough so that each maintained some residual life when the other two items were controlled, despite the strong underlying relationship between education, information, and involvement.

The distribution of the American electorate within these levels of conceptualization is summarized in Table I. The array is instructive as a portrait of a mass electorate, to be laid against the common elite assumption that all or a significant majority of the public conceptualizes the main lines of politics after the manner of the most highly educated. Where the specific hypothesis of the "revolt of the moderates" in the early 1950s is concerned, the distribution does not seem on the face of it to lend much support to the key assumption. This disconfirmation may be examined further, however.

Table I—Distribution of a Total Cross-Section Sample of the American Electorate and of 1956 Voters, by Levels of Conceptualization

	Proportion of total sample	*Proportion of voters*
I. Ideologues	2 1/2%	30 1/2%
II. Near-ideologues	9	12
III. Group interest	42	45
IV. Nature of the times	24	22
V. No issue content	22 1/2	17 1/2
	100%	100%

Since the resurgence of the Republicans in the Eisenhower period depended primarily upon crossing of party lines by people who normally considered themselves Democrats, we were able to isolate these people to see from what levels of conceptualization they had been recruited. We found that such key defections had occurred among Democrats in the two bottom levels at a rate very significantly greater than the comparable rate in the group-interest or more ideological levels. In other words, the stirrings in the mass electorate that had led to a change in administration and in "ruling ideology" were primarily the handiwork of the very people for whom assumptions of any liberal-conservative dimensions of judgment were most farfetched.

Furthermore, within those strata where the characteristics of conceptualization even permitted the hypothesis to be evaluated in its own terms, it was directly disproved. For example, the more sophisticated of the group-interest Democrats were quite aware that Eisenhower would be a more pro-business president than Stevenson. Those of this group who did defect to Eisenhower did not, however, do so because they were tired of a labor-oriented administration and wanted a business-oriented one for a change. Quite to the contrary, in the degree that they defected they did so *in spite of* rather than *because of* such quasi-ideological perceptions. That is, their attitudes toward the respective interests of these groups remained essentially constant, and they expressed misgivings about an Eisenhower vote on precisely these grounds. But any such worries were, under the circumstances, outweighed by admiration for Eisenhower's war record, his honesty, his good family life, and (in 1952) his potential for resolving the nagging problem of the Korean War. Among respondents at higher levels (ideologues and near-ideologues), there was comparable attraction to Eisenhower at a personal level, but these 'people seemed more careful to hew to ideological considerations, and rates of Democratic defection in these levels were lower still. In short, then, the supposition of changing ideological moods in the mass public as a means of understanding the exchange of partisan elites in 1952 seems to have had little relevance to what was actually going on at the mass level. And once again, the sources of the optical illusion are self-evident. While it may be taken for granted among well educated and politically involved people that a shift from a Democratic preference to a Republican one probably represents a change in option from liberal to conservative, the assumption cannot be extended very far into the electorate as a whole.

IV. Recognition of Ideological Dimensions of Judgment

Dimensions like the liberal-conservative continuum, as we have observed, are extremely efficient frames for the organization of many political observations. Furthermore, they are used a great deal in the more ambitious treatments of politics in the mass media, so that a person with a limited understanding of their meaning must find such discussions more obscure than enlightening. Aside from active cognitive use, therefore, the simple status of public comprehension of these terms is a matter of some interest.

It is a commonplace in psychology that recognition, recall, and habitual use of cognized objects or concepts are rather different. We are capable of *recognizing* many more objects (or concepts) if they are directly presented to us than we could readily *recall* on the basis of more indirect cues; and we are capable of recalling on the basis of such hints many more objects (or concepts) than might be *active* or *salient* for us in a given context without special prompting. In coding the levels of conceptualization from free-answer material, our interest had been entirely focused upon concepts with the last status (activation or salience). It had been our assumption that such activation would be apparent in the responses of any person with a belief system in which these organizing dimensions had high centrality. Nevertheless, we could be sure at the same time that if we presented the terms "liberal" and "conservative" directly to our respondents, a much larger number would recognize them and be able to attribute to them some kind of meaning. We are interested both in the proportions of a normal sample who would show some recognition and also in the meaning that might be supplied for the terms.

In a 1960 reentries of the original sample whose 1956 responses had been assigned to our levels of conceptualization, we therefore asked in the context of the differences in "what the parties stand for," "Would you say that either one of the parties is more *conservative* or more *liberal* than the other?" (It was the first time we had ever introduced these terms in our interviewing of this sample.) If the answer was affirmative, we asked which party seemed the more conservative and then, "What do you have in mind when you say that the Republicans (Democrats) are more conservative than the Democrats (Republicans)?" When the respondent said that he did not see differences of this kind between the two parties, we were anxious to distinguish between those who were actually cynical about meaningful party differences and those who took this route to avoid admitting that they did not know what the terms signified. We therefore went on to ask this group, "Do you think that people generally consider the Democrats or the Republicans more conservative, or wouldn't you want to guess about that?" At this point, we were willing to assume that if a person had no idea of the rather standard assumptions, he probably had no idea of what the terms meant; and indeed, those who did try to guess which party other people thought more conservative made a very poor showing when we went on to ask them (paralleling our "meaning" question for the first group), "What do people have in mind when they say that the Republicans (Democrats) are more conservative than the Democrats (Republicans)?" In responding to the "meaning" questions, both groups were urged to answer as fully and clearly as possible, and their comments were transcribed.

The responses were classified in a code inspired by the original work on levels of conceptualization, although it was considerably more detailed. Within this code, top priority was given to explanations that called upon broad philosophical differences. These explanations included mentions of such things as *posture toward change* (acceptance of or resistance to new ideas, speed or caution in responding to new problems, protection of or challenge to the *status quo,* aggressive posture towards problems *vs.* a *laissez-faire* approach, orientation toward the future or lack of it, and so forth); *posture toward the welfare state, socialism, free enterprise, or capitalism* (including mention of differential sensitivity to social problems, approaches to social-welfare programs, governmental interference with private enterprise, and so forth); *posture toward the expanding power of federal government* (issues of centralization, states' rights, local autonomy, and paternalism); and *relationship of the government to the individual* (questions of individual dignity, initiative, needs, rights, and so forth). While any mention of comparably broad philosophical differences associated with the liberal-conservative distinction was categorized in this top level, these four were the most frequent types of reference, as they had been for the full "ideologues" in the earlier open-ended materials.

Then, in turn, references to differences in attitude toward various interest groupings in the population; toward spending or saving and fiscal policy more generally, as well as to economic prosperity; toward various highly specific issues like unemployment compensation, highway-building, and tariffs; and toward postures in the sphere of foreign policy were arrayed in a descending order of priority, much as they had been for the classification into levels of conceptualization. Since respondents had been given the opportunity to mention as many conservative-liberal distinctions as they wished, coding priority was given to the more "elevated" responses, and all the data that we shall subsequently cite rests on the "best answer" given by each respondent.[18]

The simple distributional results were as follows. Roughly three respondents in eight (37%) could supply no meaning for the liberal-conservative distinction, including 8% who attempted to say which party was the more conservative but who gave up on the part of the sequence dealing with meaning. (The weakest 29% will, in later tables, form our bottom stratum "V," while the 8% compose stratum "IV.") Between those who could supply no meaning for the terms and those who clearly did, there was naturally an * intermediate group that answered all the questions but showed varying degrees of uncertainty or confusion. The situation required that one of two polar labels (conservative or liberal) be properly associated with one of two polar clusters of connotations and with one of two-parties. Once the respondent had decided to explain what "more conservative" or "more liberal" signified, there were four possible patterns by which the other two dichotomies might be associated with the first. Of course, all four were represented in at least some interviews. For example, a respondent might indicate that the Democrats were the more conservative because they stood up for the working man against big business. In such a case, there seemed to be a simple error consisting in reversal of the ideological labels. Or a respondent might say that the Republicans were more liberal because they were pushing new and progressive social legislation. Here the match between label and meaning seems proper, but the party perception is, by normal standards, erroneous.

The distribution of these error types within the portion of the sample that attempted to give "meaning" answers (slightly more than 60%) is shown in Table II. The 83% entered for the "proper" patterns is artificially increased to an unknown degree by the inclusion of all respondents whose connotations for liberalism-conservatism were sufficiently impoverished so that little judgment could be made about whether or not they were making proper associations (for example, those respondents whose best explanations of the distinction involved orientations toward defense spending). The error types thus represent only those that could be unequivocally considered "errors." While Table II does not in itself constitute proof that the error types resulted from pure guesswork, the configuration does resemble the probable results if 20-25% of the respondents had been making random guesses about how the two labels, the two polar meanings, and the two parties should be sorted out. People making these confused responses might or might not *feel* confused in making their assessments. Even if they knew that they were confused, it is unlikely that they would be less confused in encountering such terms in reading or listening to political communications, which is the important point where

Table II—Association of Ideological Label with Party and Meaning

Ideological label	Meaning	Party	Proportion of those giving some answer
Conservative	Conservative	Republican	83%
Liberal	Liberal	Democrat	
Conservative	Liberal	Republican	
Liberal	Conservative	Democrat	5
Conservative	Conservative	Democrat	
Liberal	Liberal	Republican	6
Conservative	Liberal	Democrat	
Liberal	Conservative	Republican	6
			100%

a. While this pattern may appear entirely legitimate for the southern respondent reacting to the southern wing of the Democratic Party rather than to the national party, it showed almost no tendency to occur with greater frequency in the South than elsewhere (and errors as well as lacunae occurred more frequently in general in the less well educated South). Data from a very different context indicate that southerners who discriminate between the southern wing and the national Democratic Party take the national party as the assumed object in our interviews, if the precise object is not specified.

transmission of information is concerned. If, on the other hand, they were wrong without realizing it, then they would be capable of hearing that Senator Goldwater, for example, was an extreme conservative and believing that it meant that he was for increased federal spending (or whatever other more specific meaning they might bring to the term). In either case, it seems reasonable to distinguish between the people who belong in this confused group at the border of understanding and those who demonstrate greater clarity about the terms. And after the confused group is set aside (stratum III in Tables III-VI), we are left with a proportion of the sample that is slightly more than 50%. This figure can be taken as a maximum estimate of reasonable recognition.

We say "maximum" because, once within this "sophisticated" half of the electorate, it is reasonable to consider the quality of the meanings put forth to explain the liberal-conservative distinction. These meanings varied greedy in adequacy, from those "best answers" that did indeed qualify for coding under the "broad philosophy" heading (the most accurate responses, as defined above) to those that explained the distinction in narrow or nearly irrelevant terms (like Prohibition or foreign-policy measures). In all, 17% of the total sample gave "best answers" that we considered to qualify as "broad philosophy."[19] This group was defined as stratum I, and the remainder, who gave narrower definitions, became stratum II.

Perhaps the most striking aspect of the liberal-conservative definitions supplied was the extreme frequency of those hinging on a simple "spend-save" dimension *vis-a-vis* government finances. Very close to a majority of all "best" responses (and two-thirds to three-quarters of all such responses in stratum II) indicated in essence that the Democratic Party was liberal because it spent public money freely and that the Republican Party was more conservative because it stood for economy in government or pinched pennies. In our earlier coding of the levels of conceptualization, we had already noted that this simple dimension seemed often to be what was at stake when "ideological" terms were used. Frequently there was reason to believe that the term "conservative" drew its primary meaning from the cognate "conservation" In one rather clear example, a respondent indicated that he considered the Republicans to be more conservative in the sense that they were "… more saving with money and our *natural resources.* Less apt to slap on a tax for some non-essential. More conservative in promises that can't be kept." (Italics ours.)

Of course, the question of the proportion of national wealth that is to be spent privately or channeled through government for public spending has been one of the key disputes between conservatives and liberal "ideologies" for several decades. From this point of view, the great multitude of "spend-save" references can be considered essentially as accurate matching of terms. On the other hand, it goes without saying that the conservative-liberal dialogue does not exhaust itself on this narrow question alone, and our view of these responses as an understanding of the differences depends in no small measure on whether the individual sees this point as a self-contained distinction or understands the link between it and a number of other broad questions. On rare occasions, one encounters a respondent for whom the "spend-save" dimension is intimately bound up with other problem areas. For example, one respondent feels that the Republicans are more conservative because … they are too interested in getting the budget balanced—they should spend more to get more jobs for our people." More frequently when further links are suggested, they are connected with policy but go no further:

> [Republicans more conservative because] "Well, they don't spend as much money." [What do you have in mind?] "Well, a lot of them holler when they try to establish a higher interest rate but that's to get back a little when they do loan out and make it so people are not so free with it."

Generally, however, the belief system involved when "liberal-conservative" is equated with "spend-save" seems to be an entirely narrow one. There follow a number of examples of comments, which taken with the preceding citations, form a random drawing from the large group of "spend-save" comments:

> [Democrats more conservative because] "they will do more for the people at home before they go out to help foreign countries. They are truthful and not liars."

> [Republicans more liberal judging] "by the money they have spent in this last administration. They spent more than ever before in a peace time. And got less for it as far as I can see."

> [Republicans more conservative because] "Well, they vote against the wild spending spree the Democrats get on."

> [Republicans more conservative because] "they pay as you go."

> [Democrats more conservative because] "I don't believe the Democrats will spend as much money as the Republicans."

> [Republicans more conservative because] "it seems as if the Republicans try to hold down the spending of government money." [Do you remember how?] "Yes," [by having] "no-wars."

From this representation of the "spend-save" references, the reader may see quite clearly why we consider them to be rather "narrow" readings of the liberal-conservative distinction as applied to the current partisan scene. In short, our portrait of the population, where recognition of a key ideological dimension is concerned, suggests that about 17% of the public (stratum I) have an understanding of the distinction that captures much of its breadth. About 37% (strata IV and V) are entirely vague as to its meaning. For the 46% between, there are two strata, one of which demonstrates considerable uncertainty and guesswork in assigning meaning to the terms (stratum III) and the other of which has the terms rather well under control but appears to have a fairly limited set of connotations for them (stratum II). The great majority of the latter groups equate liberalism-conservatism rather directly with a "spend-save" dimension. In such cases, when the sensed connotations are limited, it is not surprising that there is little active use of the continuum as an organizing dimension. Why should one bother to say that a party is conservative if one can convey the same information by saying that it is against spending?

Since the 1960 materials on liberal-conservative meanings were drawn from the same sample as the coding of the active use of such frames of reference in 1956, it is possible to consider how well the two codings match. For a variety of reasons, we would riot expect a perfect fit, even aside from coding error. The earlier coding had not been limited to the liberal-conservative dimension, and, although empirical instances were rare, a person could qualify as an "ideologue" if he assessed politics with the aid of some other highly abstract organizing dimension. Similarly, among those who did employ the liberal-conservative distinction, there were no requirements that the terms be defined. It was necessary therefore to depend upon appearances, and the classification was intentionally lenient. Furthermore, since a larger portion of the population would show recognition than showed active use, we could expect substantial numbers of people in the lower levels of conceptualization to show reasonable

Table III—Levels of Conceptualization (1956) by Recognition and Understanding of Terms "Conservatism" and "Liberalism" (1960)

| | Stratum | LEVELS OF CONCEPTUALIZATION | | | | |
		Ideologue	Near ideologue	Group interest	Nature of the times	No issue content
Recognition and understanding[a]	I	51%	29%	13%	16%	10%
	II	43	46	42	40	22
	III	2	10	14	7	7
	IV	2	5	6	7	12
	V	2	10	25	30	49
		100%	100%	100%	100%	100%
Number of cases		(45)	(122)	(580)	(288)	(290)

a. The definitions of the strata are: I. recognition and proper matching of label, meaning, and party and a broad understanding of the terms "conservative" and "liberal"; II. recognition and proper matching but a narrow definition of terms (like "spend-save"); III. recognition but some error in matching; IV. recognition and an attempt at matching but inability to give any meaning for terms; V. no apparent recognition of terms (does not know if parties differ in liberal-conservative terms and does not know if anybody else sees them as differing).

recognition of the terms. At any rate, we assumed that the two measures would show a high correlation, as they in fact did (Table III).

Of course, very strong differences in education underlie the data shown in Table III The 2% of the sample that occupy the upper left-hand cell have a mean education close to seven years greater than that of the 11 % that occupy the lower right-hand cell. Sixty-two per cent of this lower cell have had less formal education than the least educated person in the upper corner. The differences in education show a fairly regular progression across the intervening surface of the table (see Table IV). Although women have a higher mean education than men, there is some sex bias to the table, for women are disproportionately represented in the lower right-hand quadrant of the table. Furthermore, although age is negatively correlated with education, there is also rather clear evidence that the sort of political sophistication represented by the measures can accumulate with age. Undoubtedly even sporadic observation of politics over long enough periods of time serves to nurture some broader view of basic liberal-conservative differences, although of course the same sophistication is achieved much more rapidly and in a more striking way by those who progress greater distances through the educational system.

It is not surprising that political sophistication goes hand in hand with political activism at the "grass roots" (Table V). The relationship is certainly not perfect: About 20% of those in the most sophisticated cell engaged in none of the forms of participation beyond voting that were surveyed (see note a, Table V) in either the 1956 or 1960 election campaigns, and there is more "stray" participation than has sometimes been suspected among those who express little

Table IV—-Levels of Conceptualization (1956) and Term Recognition (1960) by Mean Years of Formal Education

| | Stratum | LEVELS OF CONCEPTUALIZATION | | | | |
		Ideologue	Near ideologue	Group interest	Nature of the times	No issue content
Recognition	I	14.9[a]	14.2	12.3	31.1	11.9
and	II	13.9	11.9	10.7	10.7	11.5
understanding	III	*	1U	10.6	9.8	9.6
	IV	*	*	10.4	9.9	10.3
	V	*	10.0	9.5	8.5	s.2

* Inadequate number of cases.

a. The cell entry is mean number of years of formal education. Partial college was arbitrarily assumed to represent an average of 14 years, and work toward an advanced degree an average of 18 years.

b. See Table HI for definitions of the five strata.

Table V—Amount of 1956–1960 Political Activity by Level of Conceptualization (1956) and Term Recognition (1960)

		LEVEL OF CONCEPTUALIZATION				
	Stratum	Ideologue	Near ideologue	Group interest	Nature of the times	No issue content
	I	3.8[a]	2.6	2.5	2.6	2.2
Recognition	II	3.4	3.0	1.7	1.8	1.3
and	III	*	2.5	2.2	1.5	1.1
understanding	IV	*	*	1.9	1.5	.8
	V	*	1.7	1.0	.8	.4

* Inadequate number of cases.

a. The cell entry represents a mean of the number of acts of political participation exclusive of voting reported for the two presidential campaigns of 1956 and 1960. For 1956, a point was awarded to each respondent for party membership, campaign contributions, attendance at political rallies, other party work, attempts to convince others through informal communication, and displaying campaign buttons or stickers. In 1960, essentially the same scoring applied, except that on two items more differentiated information was available. A point was awarded for attending one or two political rallies, two points for three to six rallies, and three points for seven or more. Similarly, a second point was awarded for people who reported having attempted in 1960 to convince others in more than one class (friends, family, or coworkers). A total score of 15 was possible, although empirically the highest score was 14. Only about 1 % of the sample had scores greater than 9.

b. See Table III for definitions of the five strata.

interest in politics or comprehension of party differences yet who may, for example, happen on a political rally. Furthermore, even the active hard core is not necessarily sophisticated in this sense: Two of the thirteen most active people fall in the lower right half of the table, and their activism is probably to be understood more in terms of mundane social gratifications than through any concern over the policy competition of politics.

Nonetheless, persistent and varied participation is most heavily concentrated among the most sophisticated people. This fact is important, for much of what is perceived as "public reaction" to political events depends upon public visibility, and visibility depends largely upon forms of political participation beyond the vote itself. Anyone familiar with practical politics has encountered the concern of the local politician that ideas communicated in political campaigns be kept simple and concrete. He knows his audience and is constantly fighting the battle against the overestimation of sophistication to which, the purveyor of political ideas inevitably falls prey. Yet, even the grass-roots audience that forms a reference point for the local politician is, we suspect, a highly self-selected one and quite sophisticated relative to the electorate as a whole.

Since we have 1960 information on the number of political rallies attended by each of our respondents, we may simulate the "sophistication composition" of the typical political gathering. "Typical" is loosely used here, for real gatherings are various in character; A dinner for the party faithful at $15 a plate obviously attracts a different audience from the one that comes to the parade and street rally. Nonetheless, the contrast between the electorate and an hypothetical average rally is instructive (Table VI). People located in the three upper left-hand corner cells of the matrix (6% of the electorate) form more than 15% of the composition of such rallies, and probably, in terms of further rally participation (vocal and otherwise), seem to form a still higher proportion. Yet on election day their vote (even with, a 100% turnout) is numerically outweighed by those votes mustered by people * in the single cell at the opposite corner of the table who do not attend at all.

One of the most intriguing findings on the surface of the matrix is that strength of party loyalty falls to one of its weakest points in the upper left-hand corner cell of the matrix. In other words, among the most highly sophisticated, those who consider themselves "independents" outnumber those who consider themselves "strong" partisans, despite the fact that the most vigorous political activity, much of it partisan, is carried on by people falling in this cell. If one moves diagonally toward the center of the matrix, this balance is immediately redressed and redressed very sharply, with strong partisans far outnumbering independents. In general, there is a slight tendency (the most sophisticated cell excepted) for strength of party loyalty to

Table VI—The Sophistication Composition of a "Typical" Political Rally, Compared to the Composition of the Total Electorate[a]

	A RALLY					*THE ELECTORATE*				
	High				*Low*	*High*				*Low*
High	5%	5%	11%	11%	2%	2%	3%	6%	3%	2%
	6	8	11	11	4	1	4	18	9	5
	0	5	9	0	*	*	1	6	1	2
	*	a	1	*	*	*	*	3	2	3
Low	*	2	7	1	0	*	1	11	7	11

* Less than half of 1 %.

a. Both five-by-five matrices are those employed in Tables III, IV, and V. Aside *from* rounding error, the proportions entered in each matrix total 100%. The table should be read by observing differences between proportions in the same regions of the two tables. For example, the three least sophisticated cells in the lower right-hand corner constitute *21* % of the electorate and 1 % of a typical rally audience.

decline as one moves diagonally across the table, and the most "independent" cell is that in the lower right-hand corner.[20]

This irregularity has two implications. First, we take it to be one small and special case of our earlier hypothesis that group-objects (here, the party as group) are likely to have less centrality in the belief system of the most sophisticated and that the centrality of groups as referents increases "lower down" in the sophistication ordering. We shall see more handsome evidence of the same phenomenon later. Second, we see in this reversal at least a partial explanation for the persistence of the old assumption that the "independent voter" is relatively informed and involved. The early cross-section studies by Lazarsfeld and his colleagues turned up evidence to reverse this equation, suggesting-that the "independent voter" tends instead to be relatively uninformed and uninvolved. Other studies have added massively to this evidence. Indeed, in many situations, the evidence seems so strong that it is hard to imagine how any opposing perceptions could have developed. The perception is somewhat easier to understand, however, if one can assume that the discernment of the informed observer takes in only 5, 10, or 15% of the most sophisticated people in the public as constituting "the public." This "visible" or "operative" public is largely made up of people from the upper left-hand corner of our preceding tables. The illusion that such people are the full public is one that the democratic sample survey, for better or for worse, has destroyed.

V. Constraints Among Idea-Elements

In our estimation, the use of such basic dimensions of judgment as the liberal-conservative continuum betokens a contextual grasp of politics that permits a wide range of more specific idea-elements to be organized into more tightly constrained wholes. We feel, furthermore, that there are many crucial consequences of such organization: With it, for example, new political events have more meaning, retention of political information from the past is far more adequate, and political behavior increasingly approximates that of sophisticated "rational" models, which assume relatively full information.

It is often argued, however, that abstract dimensions like the liberal-conservative continuum are superficial if not meaningless indicators: All that they show is that poorly educated people are inarticulate and have difficulty expressing verbally the more abstract lines along which their specific political beliefs are organized. To expect these people to be able to express what they know and feel, the critic goes on, is comparable to the fallacy of assuming that people can say in an accurate way why they behave as they do. When it comes down to specific attitudes and behaviors, the organization is there nonetheless, and it is this organization that matters, not the capacity for discourse in sophisticated language.

If it were true that such organization does exist for most people, apart from their capacities to be articulate about it, we would agree out of hand that the question of articulation is quite trivial. As a cold empirical matter, however, this claim does not seem to be valid. Indeed, it is for this reason that we have cast the argument in terms of constraint, for constraint and organization are very nearly the same thing. Therefore when we hypothesize that constraint among political idea-elements begins to lose its range very rapidly once we move from the most sophisticated few toward the "grass roots," we are contending that the organization of more specific attitudes into wide-ranging belief systems is absent as well.

Table VII gives us an opportunity to see the differences in levels of constraint among beliefs on a range of specific issues in an elite population and in a mass population. The elite population happens to be candidates for the United States Congress in the off-year elections of 1958, and the cross-section sample represents the national electorate in the same year. The assortment of issues represented is simply a purposive sampling of some of the more salient political controversies at the time of the study, covering both domestic and foreign policy. The questions posed to the two samples were quite comparable, apart from adjustments necessary in view of the backgrounds of the two populations involved.[21]

For our purposes, however, the specific elite sampled and the specific beliefs tested are rather beside the point. We would expect the same general contrast to appear if the elite had been a set of newspaper editors, political writers, or any other group that takes an interest in politics. Similarly, we would expect the same results from any other broad sampling of political issues or, for that matter, any sampling of beliefs from other domains: A set of questions on matters of religious controversy should show the same pattern between an elite population like the clergy and the church members who form their mass "public." What is generically important in comparing the two types of population is the difference in levels of constraint among belief-elements.

Where constraint is concerned, the absolute value of the coefficients in Table VII (rather than their algebraic value) is the significant datum. The first thing the table conveys is the fact that, for both populations, there is some falling off of constraint *between* the domains of domestic and foreign policy, relative to the high level of constraint *within* each domain. This result is to be expected: Such lowered values signify boundaries between belief systems that are relatively independent. If we take averages of appropriate sets of coefficients entered in Table VII however, we see that the strongest constraint *within* a domain for the mass public is less than that *between* domestic and foreign domains for the elite sample. Furthermore, for the public, in sharp contrast to the elite, party preference seems by and large to be set off in a belief system of its own, relatively unconnected to issue positions (Table VIII).[22]

It should be remembered throughout, of course, that the *mass* sample of Tables VII and VIII does not exclude college-educated people, ideologues, or the politically sophisticated. These people, with their higher levels of constraint, are represented in appropriate numbers, and certainly contribute to such vestige of organization as the mass matrix evinces. But they are grossly outnumbered, as they are in the active electorate. The general point is that the matrix of correlations for the elite sample is of the sort that would be appropriate for factor analysis, the statistical technique designed to reduce a number of correlated variables to a more limited set of organizing dimensions. The matrix representing the mass public, however, despite its

Table VII Constraint between Specific Issue Beliefs for an Elite Sample and Cross Sections Sample, 1958[a]

	DOMESTIC					FOREIGN		
Congressional candidates	Employment	Education	Housing	F.E.P.C.	Economic	Miltrary[b]	Isolationism	Party preference
Employment	—	.62	.59	.35	.26	.06	.17	.68
Aid to education		—	.61	.53	.50	.06	.35	.55
Federal housing			—	.47	.41	-.03	.30	.68
F.E.P.C.				—	—	.47	.23	.34
Economic aid					—	.19	.59	.25
Military aid						—	.32	-.18
Isolationism							—	.05
Party preference								—
Cross-Section Sample								
Employment	—	.45	.08	.34	-.04	.10	-.22	.20
Aid to education		—	.12	.29	.06	.14	-.17	.16
Federal housing			—	.08	-.06	.02	.07	.18
F.E.PC				—	.24	.13	.02	-.04
Economic aid					—	.16	.33	-.07
Soldiers abroad[b]						—	.21	.12
Isolationism							—	-.03
Party preference								—

a. Entries are taugarama coefficient, a statistic proposed by Leo A. Goodman and William H. Kruskal in "Measures of Association for Cross Classifications," *Journal of the American Statistical Association*, 49 (Dec., 1954), No. 268, 749. The coefficient was chosen because of its sensitivity to constraint of the scalar as well as the correlational type.

b. For this category, the cross-section sample was asked a question about keeping American soldiers abroad, rather than about military aid in general.

Table VIII—Summary of Differences in Level of Constraint within and between Domains, Public and Elite (based on Table VII)

	Average Coefficients Within domestic issues	Between domestic and foreign	Within foreign issues	Between issues and party
Elite	.53	.25	.37	.39
Mass	.23	.13	.23	.11

realistic complement of ideologues, is exactly the type that textbooks advise against using for factor analysis on the simple grounds that through inspection it is clear that there is virtually nothing in the way of organization to be discovered. Of course, it is the type of broad organizing dimension to be suggested by factor analysis of specific items that is usually presumed when observers discuss "ideological postures" of one sort or another.

Although the beliefs registered in Table VTE are related to topics of controversy or political cleavage, McClosky has described comparable differences in levels of constraint among beliefs for an elite sample (delegates to national party conventions) and a' cross-section sample when the items deal with propositions about democracy and freedom—topics on which fundamental consensus among Americans is presumed.[23] Similarly, Prothro and Grigg, among others, have shown that, while there is widespread support for statements of culturally familiar principles of freedom, democracy, and tolerance in a cross-section sample, this support becomes rapidly obscured when questions turn to specific cases that elites would see as the most direct applications of these principles.[24] In our estimation, such findings are less a demonstration of cynical lip service than of the fact that, while both of two inconsistent opinions are honestly held, the individual lacks the contextual grasp to understand that the specific case and the general principle belong in the same belief system: In the absence of such understanding, he maintains psychologically independent beliefs about both. This is another important instance of the decline in constraint among beliefs with declining information.

While an assessment of relative constraint between the matrices rests only on comparisons of absolute values, the comparative algebraic values have some interest as well. This interest arises from the sophisticated observer's almost automatic assumption that whatever beliefs "go together" in the visible political world (as judged from the attitudes of" elites and the more articulate spectators) must naturally go together in the same way among mass public. Table VII makes clear that this assumption is a very dangerous one, aside from the question of degree of constraint. For example, the politician who favors federal aid to education could be predicted to be more, rather than less, favorable to an internationalist posture in foreign affairs, for these two positions in the 1950s were generally associated wife "liberalism" in American politics. As we see from Table VII, we would be accurate in this judgment considerably more often than chance alone would permit. On the other hand, were we to apply the same assumption of constraint to the American public in the same era, not only would we have been wrong, but we would actually have come closer to reality by assuming no connection at all.

All the correlations in the elite sample except those that do not depart significantly from zero exhibit signs that anybody following politics in the 'newspapers during this period could have predicted without hesitation. That is, one need only have known that Democrats tended to favor expansion of government welfare activities and tended to be internationalists in foreign affairs, to have anticipated all the signs except one. This exception, the-.18 that links advocacy of military aid abroad with the Republican Party, would hold no surprises either, for the one kind of international involvement that Republicans came to accept in this period limited foreign aid to the military variety, a view that stood in opposition to "soft" liberal interests in international economic welfare. If these algebraic signs in the elite matrix are taken as the culturally defined "proper" signs—the sophisticated observer's assumption of what beliefs go with what other beliefs—then the algebraic differences between comparable entries in the two matrices provide an estimate of how inaccurate we would be in generalizing our elite-based assumptions about "natural" belief combinations to the mass public as a whole. A scanning of the two matrices with these differences in mind enhances our sense of high discrepancy between the two populations.

To recapitulate, then, we have argued that the unfamiliarity of broader and more abstract ideological frames of reference among the less sophisticated is more than a problem in mere articulation. Parallel to ignorance and confusion over these ideological dimensions among the less informed is a general decline in constraint among specific belief elements that such dimensions help to organize. It cannot therefore be claimed that the mass public shares ideological patterns of belief with relevant elites at a specific level any more than it shares the abstract conceptual frames of reference.

Constraints and Overt Behavior

There is still another counter-hypothesis that deserves examination. This view would grant that the political belief systems of the less well educated may be more fragmented and chaotic. It would maintain at the same time, however, that this fact is inconsequential in the determination of behavior. The presence, absence, or incoherence of these "intervening" psychological states is thus epiphenomenal: Social structure commits behavior to certain channels quite independent of specific cognitions and perceptions of the actors themselves.[25] In other versions, researchable intervening mechanisms are suggested. The "opinion leader" model is one of them. If it is true that the mass of less knowledgeable people rely upon informal communication from a few more informed people for cues about desirable or appropriate behavior, then the lines of behavior choices followed in politics might indeed show strong sociostructural patterns, even though many uninformed actors have little of the opinion leaders* coherent and organized understanding of why one behavior is more appropriate than another. What these points of view have in common is the insistence that strong constraints can be expected to operate

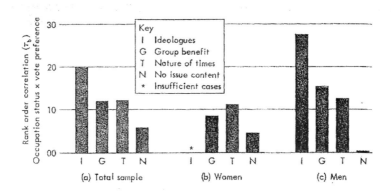

Figure 1. The Correlation of Occupation and Vote Preference within Levels of Conceptualization.

between sociostructural terms and conscious behavior choices quite apart from the presence or absence of appropriate intervening psychological "definitions of the situation."

Figure 1 is addressed to such arguments. The graphs indicate the varying degrees of association between objective class position and partisan preference in the 1956 presidential election, as a function of differences in the nature of political belief systems captured by our "levels of conceptualization." If objective locations in the social structure served to produce behavioral consequences regardless of the presence or absence of relevant intervening organizations of conscious beliefs, then we would not expect any particular slope to the progression of bars within each graph. As Figure 1(a) shows for a sample of the adult electorate as a whole, however, the differences in intervening belief organization produce very marked and orderly differences in the degree to which partisanship reflects social structural position. Of course, from one point of view, this observation seems only common sense, yet the doctrinaire position that the intervening psychological terms are unimportant or epiphenomenal continues to be argued with more vehemence than empirical evidence.

Since it can be seen that a perfectly functioning opinion-leader model would also produce something approaching a rectangular distribution of bars in Figure 1, the slope depicted in Figure 1(a) can also be taken as a commentary on the practical imperfections with which opinion leader processes operate in this domain. That is, the "ideologues" and "near-ideologues" represented by the first bar of each graph are opinion leaders *par excellence*. While they tend to be disproportionately well educated, they nevertheless include representatives from all broad social *milieux*. Empirically they differ sharply from the less sophisticated in their attention to new political events and in the size of their store of information about past events. They get news firsthand and, presumably, form opinions directly from it. By their own .report, they are much more likely than the less sophisticated to attempt to persuade others to their own political opinions in informal communications. Finally, much social data leads us to assume that the bulk of these informal communications is addressed to others within their own social *milieu*. Since social-class questions are important for these opinion leaders and since their own partisan preferences are rather clearly geared to their own class, we would suppose that "opinion leading" should serve to diffuse this connection between status and behavior through less knowledgeable members of their *milieu,* whether or not the more complicated rationales were diffused. In other words, most of what goes on in the heads of the less informed of our respondents would indeed be irrelevant for study if the respondents could at least be counted upon to follow the lead of more informed people of their own *milieu* in their ultimate partisanship. And to the extent that they can be counted on to behave in this way, we should expect Figure 1 to show a rectangular distribution of bars. The departure from such a pattern is very substantial.

Now there is one type of relationship in which there is overwhelming evidence for vigorous opinion-leading where politics is concerned in our society. It is the relationship within the family: The wife is very likely to follow her husband's opinions, however imperfectly she may have absorbed their justifications at a more complex level. We can do a fair job of splitting this relationship into its leader-follower components simply by subdividing our total sample by sex. As Figure 1(b) suggests, our expectation that the presence or absence of intervening belief systems is of reduced importance among sets of people who are predominantly opinion followers is well borne out by the relatively flat and disordered progression of bars among women. Correspondingly, of course, the same slope among men becomes steeper still in Figure 1(c).[26]

The fact that wives tend to double their husbands' votes is, from a broader "system" point of view, a relatively trivial one. If we are willing to consider the family as the basic voting unit, then Figure 1(c) suggests that diffusion of the sociostructurally "proper" behavior without diffusion of understanding of that behavior through simple opinion-leading processes is a very feeble mechanism indeed across, the society as a whole, at least where political decisions of this sort are concerned.[27] The organization of partisanship among those who give no evidence of intervening issue content shows no trace whatever of those residual effects that should be left by any systematic opinion-following (and that are visible among comparable women). Thus, while we are in no way questioning the existence of some opinion-leading, it seems doubtful that it represents the dominant, effective phenomenon sometimes supposed, a phenomenon that succeeds in lending shape to mass politics despite the absence of more detailed individual comprehension of the political context.[28]

Much more broadly, we have become convinced that this class of finding—the declining degree of constraint between a term representing social structure and one representing an important political choice as one moves from the more to the less politically sophisticated in the society—is a powerful and general one. It is powerful (for readers not accustomed to the statistics employed) in the simple sense that the variation in constraint as a function of sophistication or involvement is extremely large: There are no other discriminating variables that begin to separate populations so cleanly and sharply as these measures. It is a general finding in at least two senses. First, it replicates itself handsomely across time: In every instance within the span of time for which appropriate data are available, the finding is present where class and partisanship are concerned. Secondly, it has some incipient claim to generality where sociostructural terms other than "social class" are concerned: The same sharp finding emerges, for example, when the relationship between religion and partisanship (Protestant *vs.* Catholic) is examined. \

And, of course, if class or religious membership is considered to constitute one set of idea-elements and the predispositions that lead to particular partisan preferences and final choice to form another, then the whole phenomenon takes its place as another large class of special cases of the decline of constraints and the narrowing of belief systems to which this paper is devoted.

VI Social Groupings as Central Objects in Belief Systems

While for any unbiased sampling of controversial belief items we would predict that the relevant elite would show a higher level of internal constraint among elements than those shown by their publics, we would predict at the same time that it would be possible to bias a choice of issues in such a way that the level of constraint in the public could surpass that among the elites. This possibility exists because of the role that visible social groupings come to play as objects of high centrality in the belief systems of the less well informed,[29]

Such a reversal of the constraint prediction could be attained by choosing items that made it clear that a particular grouping, within the population and visible to most respondents, would be helped or hurt by the alternative in question. Consider, by way of illustration, the following set of items:

Negroes should be kept out of professional athletics.

The government should see to it that Negroes get fair treatment in jobs and housing.

The government should cut down on its payments (subsidies) on peanuts and cotton,

which are raised mainly by Negroes in the South.

The government should give federal aid only to schools that permit Negroes to attend.

Even though it may hurt the position of the Negro in the South, state governments

should be able to decide who can vote and who cannot.

If this country has to send money abroad, the government should send it to places like Africa that need it, and not to countries like Britain and France.

The strategy here is obvious. The questions are selected so that the same group is involved in each. In every case but one, this involvement is explicit. Some American adults would not know that Africa's population is largely Negro, for these people, the level of constraint between this item and the others would be relatively low. But the majority would know this fact, and the total set of items would show a substantial level of constraint, probably higher than the general level shown by the "mass" items in Table VII. Furthermore, the items are chosen to cut across some of those more abstract dimensions of dispute (states' rights, the strategy of economic development abroad, the role of the federal government in public education, and so forth) customary for elites, which means that constraint would be somewhat lowered for them.

The difference between the mass and elite responses would spring from differences in the nature of the objects taken to be central in the beliefs represented. For the bulk of the mass public, the object with highest centrality is the visible, familiar population grouping (Negroes), rather than questions of abstract relations among parts of government and the like. Since these latter questions take on meaning only with a good deal of political information and understanding, the attitude items given would tend to boil down for many respondents to the same single question: "Are you sympathetic to Negroes as a group, are you indifferent to them, or do you dislike them?" The responses would be affected accordingly.

While we have no direct empirical evidence supporting, this illustration, there are a few fragmentary findings that point in this direction. For example, following the same format as the issue items included in Table VII, we asked our cross-section sample an attitude question concerning the desirability of action on the part of the federal government in the desegregation of public schools. Since we had also asked the question concerning fair treatment for Negroes in jobs and housing, these two items form a natural pair, both of which involve Negroes. The correlation between the two (in terms comparable to Table VII) is .57, a figure very substantially greater than the highest of the twenty-eight Interco relations in the "mass" half of Table VII. It seems more than coincidence that the only pair of items involving the fortunes of a visible population grouping should at the same time be a very deviant pair in its high level of mutual constraint.

A parallel question was asked of the elite sample of Table VII, although the comparability was not *so* great as for those items presented in the table. This question was, "If Congress were to vote to give federal aid to public schools, do you think this should be given to schools which are segregated?" While the question was worded in such a manner as to avoid responses based on attitudes toward federal aid to education, a number of elite respondents insisted on answering in the negative, not because they were necessarily against desegregation, but rather because they were against any kind of federal aid to education. (The additional element of federal aid to schools was not present at all in the item for the cross-section sample). Setting aside those respondents who gave indications that they were deviating from the intention of the question (7% of the elite sample), the correlation between the desegregation item and the F.E.P.C. item was nevertheless only .31, or very much to the *low* side of the elite intercorrelations on domestic issues, instead of being uniquely to the *high* side as it was for the mass sample.

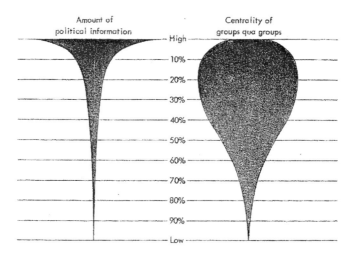

Figure 2. Political Information and the Centrality of Groups as Objects in Belief Systems.

We may summarize this situation in the following manner. Out of twenty-eight "trials" represented by the intercorrelations in Table VII, in only three cases did the mass sample show an intercorrelation between issues that was of the same sign and of greater absolute magnitude than its counterpart for the elite sample. Two of these "reversals" were completely trivial (.02 and .04), and the third was not large (.08). With respect to the only pair of items that explicitly, involved the fortunes of a well-known social grouping, however, there not only was a reversal, but the reversal was large: The constraint for the mass sample, by a simple difference of coefficients, is .26 greater. This isolated test certainly provides some striking initial support for our expectations.

Up to this point, we have discussed two broad classes of findings. The first, as exemplified by Table VII and our more recent elaborations on it, suggests that groups as attitude objects (groups *qua* groups) have higher centrality in the belief systems of the mass than of the elite. The second is exemplified by the many findings that the alignment of an individual's social-group membership (like class or religious membership) and his political behavior is sharpest among the most politically involved and sophisticated third of a mass sample and fades out progressively as involvement and sophistication decline.

In case these propositions do not seem to square perfectly with one another, Figure 2 provides a schematic view of the situation that may clarify the matter for the reader. Of course, the details of the figure (like the precise characters of the functions) are sheer fancy. But the gross contours seem empirically justified. The elite of Table VII would naturally be represented by a line along the top of Figure 2, which would be thin to the vanishing point. The "relative elite" of the mass sample, which defines "the public" as perceived by most impressionistic observers, might sweep in the top 2%, 5%, or 10% of the graph, as one chose. In the upper reaches of the group centrality graph, we have already seen glimmers of the inverse relationship between group centrality and sophistication in such diverse items as the falling-off of party loyalty at the very "top" of the mass sample or the lowered constraint for the Negro items in the elite sample.

On the other hand, why is it that when we work downward from the more sophisticated third of the population, the centrality of groups begins once again to diminish? We are already committed to the proposition that differences in information are crucial, but let us consider this point more fully. The findings that lead us to posit this decline come from a class of situations in which the actor *himself* must perceive some meaningful link between membership in a particular group and preference for a particular party or policy alternative. These situations are most typically those in which the link is not made explicit by the very nature of the situation (as we made it explicit in our battery of Negro questions above). In these cases, the individual must be endowed with some cognitions of the group as an entity and with some interstitial "linking" information indicating why a given party or 'policy is relevant to the group. Neither of these forms of information can be taken for granted, and our key proposition is that, as the general bulk of political information declines, the probability increases that some key pieces of information relevant to this group-politics equation will not show up.

The first item—the individual's cognition that a group exists—is a very simple one and may not even seem plausible to question. For certain groups at certain times and places, however, the possibility that such a cognition is absent must be recognized. AH groups, including those that become important politically, vary in their visibility. Groups delimited by physical characteristics "in the skin" (racial groups) are highly visible, if specimens are present for inspection or if the individual has been informed in some rather vivid way of their existence. Similarly, groups that have buildings, meetings, and officers (church, congregation, and clergy for example) are more visible than groups, like social classes, that do not, although the salience of any "official" group *qua* group may vary widely according to the individual's contact with its formal manifestations.

Some groups—even among those to which an individual can be said to "belong"—are much less visible. Two important examples are the social class and, the nation. Where social class is concerned, virtually all members of a population are likely to have absorbed the fact that some people have more means or status than others, and most presumably experience some satisfaction or envy on this score from time to time. Such perceptions may, however, remain at the same level as reactions to the simple fact of life that some people are born handsome and others homely; or, as Marx knew, they may proceed to cognitions of some more "real" and bounded groups. The difference is important.

Much the same kind of observation may be made of the nation as group object. On the basis of our analysis, it might be deduced that nationalist ideologies stand a much better chance of penetrating a mass population than would, for example, the single-tax ideology of the physiocrats and Henry George, for nationalist ideologies hinge upon a simple group object in a way that single-tax notions do not. This kind of deduction is perfectly warranted, particularly if one has in mind those Western nations with systems of primary education devoted to carving the shape of a nation in young minds as a "real" entity. But Znaniecki has observed, for example, that the vast majority of peasants in nineteenth-century Tsarist Russia was "utterly unconscious that they were supposed to belong to a Russian society united by a common culture." Again he reports that a 1934–1935 study in the Pripet marshes showed that nearly half of those inhabitants who were ethnically White Ruthenian had no idea that such a nationality existed and regarded themselves as belonging at most to local communities.[30] The nation as a bounded, integral group object is difficult to experience in any direct way, and its psychological existence for the individual depends upon the social transmission of certain kinds of information. What is deceptive here, as elsewhere, is that decades or even centuries after the *literati* have come to take a nation concept for granted, there may be substantial proportions of the member population who have never heard of such a thing.[31]

While cognitions of certain groups are not always present, the much more typical case is one in which the interstitial or contextual information giving the group a clear political relevance is lacking. For example, a substantial proportion of voters in the United States is unable to predict that any particular party preference will emerge in the votes of different class groupings, and this inability is particularly noticeable among the least involved citizens, whose partisan behavior is itself essentially random with respect to social class.[32]

One important *caveat* must be offered on the generalization represented in Figure 2. From a number of points we have made, it should be clear that the figure is intended to represent an actuarial proposition and nothing more. That is, it has merit for most situations, given the typical state of distribution of political information in societies as we find them "in nature." In certain situations, however, the cues presented to citizens concerning links between group and party or policy are so gross that they penetrate rapidly even to the less informed. In such cases, the form representing group centrality in Figure 2 would taper off much less rapidly with declining over-all information in the lower strata of the population.

For example, the linking information that made religion particularly relevant in the 1960 election was extremely simple, of the "what goes with what" variety. It was expressible in five words: "The Democratic candidate is Catholic." Studies have shown that, once Kennedy was nominated, this additional item of information was diffused through almost the entire population with a speed that is rare and that, we suspect, would be impossible for more complex contextual information. The linking information that made social class unusually relevant after World War II was, however, precisely this vague, contextual type.[33] It can be readily demonstrated with our data that the impact of the religious link in 1960 registered to some degree in the behavior of even the least sophisticated Protestants and Catholics, while the incremental impact of social-class cues in the earlier period had not registered at these lower levels.

The precise form of the centrality function in Figure 2 depends heavily therefore upon the character of the linking information at issue in the special case. Furthermore, if we wished to "tamper," it would not be difficult to supply a poorly informed person with a very tiny increment of linking information, too small to change his over-all amount of political information visibly yet large enough to increase considerably the centrality of a specific group in a specific situation. However this may be, Figure 2 is valid in an actuarial sense, for in "natural" populations the probability that any given individual possesses such linking information declines as over-all information becomes less.

VII. The Stability of Belief Elements over Time

All of our data up to this point have used correlations calculated on aggregates as evidence of greater or lesser constraint among elements in belief systems. While we believe these correlations to be informative indicators, they do depend for their form upon cumulations among individuals and there-, fore can never be seen as commenting incisively upon the belief structures of individuals.

It might then be argued that we are mistaken in saying that constraint among comparable "distant" belief elements declines generally as we move from the more to the less politically sophisticated. Instead, the configuration of political beliefs held by individuals simply becomes increasingly idiosyncratic as we move to less sophisticated people. While an equally broad range of belief elements might function as an interdependent whole for an unsophisticated person, we would find little aggregative patterning of belief combinations in populations of unsophisticated people, for they would be out of the stream of cultural information about "what goes with what" and would therefore put belief elements together in a great variety of ways.

For the types of belief that interest us here, this conclusion in itself would be significant. We believe however, that we have evidence that permits us to reject it rather categorically, in favor of our original formulation. A fair test of this counterhypothesis would seem to he in the measurement of the same belief elements for the same individuals over time. For if we are indeed involved here in idiosyncratic patterns of belief, each meaningful to the individual in his own way, then we could expect that individual responses to the same set of items at different points in time should show some fundamental stability. They do not.

A longitudinal study of the American electorate over a four-year period has permitted us to ask the same questions of the same people a number of times, usually separated by close to two-year intervals. Analysis of the stability of responses to the "basic" policy questions of the type presented in Table VII yields remarkable results. Faced with the typical item of this kind, only about thirteen people out of twenty manage to locate themselves even on the same *side* of the controversy in successive interrogations, when ten out of twenty could have done so by chance alone.

While we have no comparable longitudinal data for an elite sample, the degree of fit between answers to our issue items and congressional roll-calls is strong enough to suggest that time correlations for individual congressmen in roll-call choice on comparable bills would provide a fair estimate of the stability of an elite population in beliefs of this sort. It is probably no exaggeration to deduce that, in sharp contrast to a mass sample, eighteen out of twenty congressmen would be likely to take the same positions on the same attitude items after a two-year interval. In short, then, we feel very confident that elite-mass differences in levels of constraint among beliefs are mirrored in elite-mass differences in the temporal stability of belief elements for individuals.

We observed much earlier that the centrality of a specific belief in a larger belief system and the relative stability of that belief over time should be highly related. From our other propositions about the role of groups as central objects in the belief systems of the mass public, we can therefore arrive at two further predictions. The first is simply that pure affect toward visible population groupings should be highly stable over time, even in a mass public, much more so in fact than beliefs on policy matters that more or less explicitly bear on the fortunes of these groupings. Second, policy items that do bear more rather than less explicitly upon their fortunes.

CPSIA information can be obtained at www.ICGtesting.com
Printed in the USA
267521BV00004B/31-60/P